John
Paul
Jones

JOHN PAUL JONES
The Marble Bust by Houdon, Naval Academy Museum

John
Paul
Jones

A Sailor's Biography

by Samuel Eliot Morison

With a New Introduction
by Rear Admiral Daniel V. Gallery

RⓉP TIME Reading Program Special Edition

TIME INCORPORATED · NEW YORK

TIME-LIFE BOOKS
EDITOR *Norman P. Ross*
TEXT DIRECTOR *William Jay Gold*
ART DIRECTOR *Edward A. Hamilton*
CHIEF OF RESEARCH *Beatrice T. Dobie*
ASSISTANT TEXT DIRECTOR *Jerry Korn*

EDITOR, TIME READING PROGRAM *Max Gissen*
RESEARCHER *Ann S. Lang*
DESIGNER *Lore Levenberg*

PUBLISHER *Rhett Austell*
GENERAL MANAGER *John A. Watters*

TIME MAGAZINE
EDITOR *Roy Alexander*
MANAGING EDITOR *Otto Fuerbringer*
PUBLISHER *Bernhard M. Auer*

COVER DESIGN *David Klein*

Contents

List of Illustrations

List of Charts and Diagrams

Charts and Diagrams by Erwin Raisz

Thos. Hughes, 1781, "Paul Jones is arrived at Phila. in the brief of 20 guns, and it is reported he is already quarrelling with Congress [for a larger ship]. His character for cruelty is so universally detested that all the sailors of his ship have left him and no others will serve under him."

Editors' Preface

Few figures have entered the ranks of America's national heroes with a more mixed bag of credentials than the Scottish seaman variously known as John Paul, John Jones, Captain Paul, Captain John Paul Jones and Kontradmiral Pavel Ivanovich Jones. As the youthful master of a merchant ship in the West Indies, this short Scot with the towering temper was wanted for murder. As an officer in the Continental Navy, he became the new country's greatest naval hero. Yet he was a notorious complainer, impatient with superiors, haughty toward his peers and a tyrant among his crews (with considerable justification, it must be added). He described himself as "a free Citizen of the World" bent on defending "the violated rights of Mankind," but after the American Revolution he went on to battle Turks in the service of a Russian despot. Son of an unlettered gardener, he wrote letters which became a standard of style and deportment for generations of Annapolis middies. He was a man of powerful physical drives who, in the shrewd judgment of Abigail Adams, understood "all the etiquette of a lady's toilette as perfectly as he does the mast and sails and rigging of his ship." Yet he never married. He was, in brief, one of the most paradoxical and fascinating figures in all American history.

It is not surprising, therefore, that the life and legend of John Paul Jones have inspired novelists from Herman Melville to Alexandre Dumas and biographers from Benjamin Disraeli to Franklin D. Roosevelt, not to mention the composers of penny chapbooks, the writers of popular poems and innumerable folk balladeers. The result, for many decades, was to turn the story of Jones's life into an indiscriminate stew of fact and fiction that threatened to obscure completely the true personality of the subject.

It was while matters were at this stage that they were taken in hand by perhaps the only man who was capable of straightening them out. In 1959 Samuel Eliot Morison's *John Paul Jones: A Sailor's Biography* was published. For the first time it applied to the story of the legendary captain the painstaking research of a great scholar, combined with the judgment of a fine historian, the experience of a veteran sailor and, not least, the talent of an exceptional writer. The book became an immediate bestseller and won the 1960 Pulitzer Prize for Biography.

More to the point, it cleared away, once and for all, the confusion that had surrounded Jones's life for a century and a half. That was precisely what it was intended to do, as the author makes clear in his own preface—and in a delightfully indignant appendix in which he demolishes several of the hero's earlier biographers ("Any librarian who reads this Appendix will do a service to posterity by reclassifying [their books] as fiction").

In the researching of *John Paul Jones,* Samuel Eliot Morison followed a practice that had already made him unique among naval historians. He not only writes about the great men of the sea; wherever possible he retraces their voyages. Before beginning his famous biography of Columbus, *Admiral of the Ocean Sea,* Morison sailed some 10,000 miles in the Atlantic to authenticate the explorer's route. He collected material for his 15-volume history of U.S. naval operations in World War II not merely by interviewing survivors but while serving with the fleet; he rose to the rank of rear admiral and earned seven battle stars. Before writing *John Paul Jones,* Morison followed Jones's routes through the West Indies, along the U.S. east coast and off England's Flamborough Head, where in 1779 the doughty captain, in command of *Bonhomme Richard*, met Captain Richard Pearson of H.M.S. *Serapis* in the most spectacular naval battle of the Revolution.

When he writes of war at sea, Morison is without equal. In setting the scene for the historic confrontation between Jones and Pearson, he avoids needless rhetoric and, in his usual spare style, allows the simple facts to assert themselves, thus building up a tension which is relieved only when the first boom of broadsides signals the beginning of that terrible battle.

> Flamborough Head . . . is a broad headland of chalk cliffs rising 450 feet above the sea, cut by deep gullies with tiny beaches at the foot, and honeycombed by numerous caves which were favorite resorts of smugglers. The tide splits at the Head; half the flood, running from north to south, sweeps seaward off a sandbar called the Smithics; the other half, running between the Smithics and the shore, makes a great "boil" over a reef jutting out from the Head, known as the Flamborough Steel. . . . *Bonhomme Richard* in her long career had never looked so beautiful as she did that last full day of her life, when the westering sun gilded her towering pyramid of sail and touched up the high lights on her elaborate quarter galleries and carving. . . .
>
> Light airs were blowing from the southwest. *Serapis* cracked on sail to get between her convoy and the enemy. . . .
>
> At 4:00 studding sails were set on both sides and the gunners, seamen and officers quietly took their assigned stations aloft, on deck and below. At 5:00 the Marine drummers marched up and down beating the roll for General Quarters. At 6:00, just as the sun was setting, the Commodore made the agreed signal "Form Line of Battle."

Eighteenth Century warfare, Morison makes clear, was not all blood and thunder. It was occasionally comic, frequently disorganized and always ceremonious. In the spring of 1778, Jones, in command of the sloop of war *Ranger*, terrified the English coast with a series of audacious hit-and-run raids. But the raids tended to be monumentally anticlimactic—as when, following a daring attack on the seaport of Whitehaven, some of the landing party headed straight for the nearest pub and "made very free with liquor, etc." On another raid further up the coast, Jones's men plundered some silver from a local mansion. Jones felt that the whole venture had been lacking in a certain etiquette, even though Lady Selkirk, mistress of the house, reported that his men "behaved with great civility" and one of *Ranger's* lieutenants even started to leave a receipt. The commodore accordingly wrote a lugubrious letter of apology to the "Amiable Countess" and promised to return the silver—which he later did.

Jones never missed a chance to be the gentleman in his dealings with his foes. On the death of one enemy lieutenant, he offered his personal condolences. Later, Morison describes how the defeated captain of *Serapis* "hands his sword to Jones, who promptly returns it with a few gracious words about his gallant fight, and invites him below into his wrecked cabin to drink a glass of wine."

But elegant civilities are often the gifts which winners confer upon losers. The actual fighting at sea was no more polite then than it is today. And it was in battle that Jones affirmed the qualities which made him a great naval hero: tactical mastery, unfailing judgment, guile and, above all, boundless courage.

One of his most astonishing feats of bravery took place not against the English but against the Turks. On the night before a major engagement, Jones, accompanied by a single man, forayed into the middle of the Turkish fleet in an open rowboat. After reconnoitering the size and disposition of the force, he ordered his oarsman to head directly toward one of the biggest ships. Then he stood up and scribbled in chalk across the stern: TO BE BURNED. PAUL JONES. The following morning he saw to it that the marked vessel was destroyed as indicated.

In the course of his adventures the doughty commodore crossed the trails of many major figures in Revolutionary history, and Morison sketches them in with a swift, perceptive brush—often in their more intimate moments. Thus Ben Franklin in Paris is seen not only in his familiar role as minister to the court of Louis XVI but also while playing chess with a French lady seated demurely in her bathtub. Thomas Jefferson gets in touch with one of Jones's mistresses as a favor—and backs off hastily when she asks for a loan.

This is not merely a factual account of a hero's life and times; it is a brilliant evocation of an entire period. It is filled with real people —not least of whom is its central figure. Morison's biography is a modern masterpiece partly because Morison is a conscientious and painstaking scholar, partly because he loves the sea, but mostly because he understands the nature of a man who compelled others to see him as "sweet like a vine when he wished, but when necessary, like a rock."

In this book the central figure is indeed a genuine hero. But Morison, without straining the point, manages to convey the less obvious truth that Jones was also something more. He was a man who was in search of a personal destiny—and who was kept from finding the one that suited him by the frustrating complexities of his own character. In spite of much in his career that seems straight out of comic opera, the final impression is that of a man who lived out a personal tragedy. The friendship of the great, the mistresses, the halo of personal bravery and the fame that came so fast and diminished so quickly in his own lifetime all seem to underscore the sense of failure that shrouded even his most flamboyant moments.

Nothing ever seemed to go right for him long enough to build on. Battles won led only to delaying intrigues and jealousies that hindered his career. His sound suggestions for a U.S. Navy based on professional training and leadership were simply brushed aside. His Russian adventure, which at first seemed like the high road to greater fame, was doomed from the first by vendettas he was ill-equipped to cope with. And the end of his brief odyssey was so unseemly as to be almost squalid. He was a man without a country, a hero without a firm stage for his exploits, a superb adventurer forever stalled in his vocation. Perhaps, his turbulent career suggests, being a hero was not enough. Were the times out of joint for such a man? Or was it simply that John Paul Jones never learned how to survive beyond the moments of great seamanship and bravery? Like every good biography, this one both implicitly raises such questions, and creates a climate in which the reader can venture the answers.

—THE EDITORS OF TIME

Introduction

The U.S. Navy has good reason to be proud of and grateful to the hero whose body lies enshrined in the Academy chapel at Annapolis. Thanks to John Paul Jones, the Navy can claim the greatest hero of the Revolution next to George Washington. Aside from Jones the Navy didn't do much in the Revolution. Both the Navy's debt to Jones and its troubles in fighting its first war emerge sharply in Samuel Eliot Morison's *John Paul Jones*. Professor Morison does not go out of his way to make the Continental Navy look bad. He just couldn't tell Jones's story truthfully without doing so.

Sea power did play a vital role in the Revolution, but for the most part it was not official American sea power. Privateers—armed private vessels which fought for plunder—did most of the fighting in American waters. There were nearly 500 of them, freebooters who were little better than pirates by present-day standards. They harassed British commerce, captured much-needed supplies for the American armies—and made fortunes for themselves. But their overall effect on the war was small, except to infuriate the British Crown. It was French sea power, not American, which finally turned the tide with a battle fleet that bottled up Cornwallis at Yorktown.

Throughout the Revolution, the Continental Navy was steeped in politics and torn by internal jealousy and vicious intrigue. It accomplished little except to dissipate the new nation's meager resources on ships that never got to sea or that were destroyed or captured as soon as they did. The great exception was John Paul Jones. He got to sea, accomplished a great deal—and the British never laid hands on him, although he gave them plenty of opportunity.

The main reason why the United States couldn't have a proper navy in those days was something that also plagued the Royal Navy: prize money. The whole crew of a privateer shared in the loot taken at sea, and privateers took on only lightly armed merchant ships. Navy ships got prize money too, but a smaller share than the privateers. And their main job was to fight; prizes were supposed to be incidental. Few patriots were willing to go to sea in naval ships and fight for glory when they could ship in privateers, fight less and make much more money.

Although Jones was more than willing to fight, even he (quite rightly) insisted on his share of the prize money when he did happen to capture merchant ships. In fact, as Morison relates, he spent a large part of his time ashore trying to collect what was coming to him and his crew. Usually it took him a long time to get it. Histories of the Continental Navy are full of disputes over prize money, which was the main motivating force for seafaring men in those days.

But prize money was incidental to Jones. He thought in terms of high strategy and thoroughly understood how huge naval forces could be tied up by a lone, bold raider on the loose near the enemy homeland. Jones carried the war across the Atlantic and dumped it right on England's doorstep. In *Ranger* he cruised through the Irish Sea as if he owned it. In *Bonhomme Richard*, accompanied by a small, makeshift task force, he circled Ireland and Scotland and nearly got to the Thames, capturing merchant ships and men-of-war within sight of British shores. He sailed into the Bay of Belfast, the Firth of Clyde, Solway Firth and Firth of Forth, and twice he actually led armed parties ashore in Scotland. Then, in the famous battle off Flamborough Head, he boarded and captured the far-superior H.M.S. *Serapis*, only 150 miles from London.

The material damage which Jones did to the British Empire was insignificant. But the impact of his operations on morale was like an atom bomb. While he was in British waters, every coastal city in the British Isles howled for a squadron of naval ships as protection against the American "pirate." Their Lordships of the Admiralty had an unhappy time.

It seems incredible that the great Navy we have today sprang from the beginnings described in this book. The Continental Navy consisted for the most part of a ragtag, undisciplined bunch of scalawags. Mutiny was commonplace. When it occurred, it seems to have been customary for the captain to appease the mutineers as best he could and then sweep the whole thing into the lee scuppers and forget it. As Morison relates, Jones did this several times. But when the crew of his gig got drunk ashore and couldn't row him back to the ship, he triced them up in the rigging and flogged them. Several times during my naval career I have had occasion to think we were perhaps a bit premature in abolishing the old Navy custom of flogging. But never in my 44 years of active duty did I see anything in the U.S. Navy even remotely resembling a mutiny.

One interesting slant on life at sea in those days is given by Morison's list of the stores Jones put aboard the sloop *Providence*, which went with him on a raiding voyage. It includes 583 gallons of rum, intended to last a crew of some 70 for two months. This works out to be just about a pint of rum per man per day. Of course, a pint of rum isn't going to get a two-fisted seafaring man drunk. But I certainly wouldn't want to try to furl sail on a heaving yardarm with a gale of wind blowing and a pint of rum under my belt. Maybe it was the rum that gave the oldtimers the nerve to do it!

The utter lack of discipline in those days is shown by the conduct of Captain Pierre Landais, U.S.N., during the battle between *Bonhomme Richard* and *Serapis*. Theoretically, Jones had two other frigates under his command besides *Bonhomme Richard*. *Pallas*, a

French ship flying U.S. colors, behaved well enough in the battle and captured H.M.S. *Countess of Scarborough*. The other ship was *Alliance*, a fine American-built frigate better in every material way than the *Richard*. Landais, her commander, was an ex-French naval officer who had been commissioned captain in the U.S.N.

Serapis was a much more powerful ship than the *Bonhomme Richard*. But *Richard* and *Alliance* against *Serapis* would have had a pushover. As things turned out, it was *Richard* against both *Serapis* and *Alliance!*

Landais hated Jones and resented serving under him. Throughout the cruise leading up to the battle, he refused to obey Jones's orders and operated independently whenever he felt like it, doing his best meanwhile to discredit and undermine Jones. Early in the battle he fired one broadside which raked *Bonhomme Richard* and then hauled clear, making no move to help Jones fight his much bigger enemy. At the crucial point in the battle, after Jones lashed his battered ship alongside *Serapis*, Landais sailed up close aboard and deliberately let *Richard* have his full broadside. Then he came about and let her have another, inflicting more damage on Jones's ship than the British had done.

If I had been in Jones's shoes, I think that right after the battle I would have hanged this sneaking rat from his own yardarm, even though I might have swung for it myself later. As it was, Landais eventually was court-martialed and cashiered from the Navy, although not for his dastardly conduct in this battle. He later collected $4,000 as his share of the prize money taken during that cruise. Even a traitor's right to his prize money was sacred in those days.

Jones's feat in capturing *Serapis* was so remarkable that even the British gave him credit for it, in a sort of left-handed way: they made Richard Pearson, the defeated captain, a knight. (The old British custom of easing the sting of a defeat by honoring the beaten commander has persisted to modern times. After the inferior German High Seas Fleet gave the British Grand Fleet a sound tactical beating at Jutland, the British made their top commander at Jutland, Admiral John Jellicoe, a viscount, and his second-in-command, Admiral David Beatty, an earl.) Morison quotes a priceless comment from Jones upon hearing that Pearson had been knighted: "Let me fight him again . . . and I'll make him a Lord!"

Jones was a great captain by any standard. In single-ship actions he was superb. He was cut from the same canvas as Horatio Nelson, and he had the makings of a great admiral. But we will never know about that. The United States did not see fit to give him flag rank, and he never commanded a proper squadron. He *was* given flag rank when he fought for Catherine the Great (with U.S. permission). The result was a fiasco, but that proves nothing except that the Russians were just as hard to get along with then as they are now. Jones never really had a chance to show his naval genius in Russia. He stepped in near the top of a foreign navy riddled with court politics and international intrigue. He had no part in training the outfit which he commanded and didn't even speak their language. It's no wonder he didn't do much with the strange forces placed under him.

Morison tells Jones's story saltily and well, without trying to make a plaster saint out of him. In fact, he seems to have great fun doing the opposite. He devotes as much attention to Jones's conquests ashore as he does to those afloat—just as Jones himself did. Although the captain's favorite occupation was fighting against heavy odds at sea, he didn't get to do this often; between battles ashore he indulged in his next favorite pastime: courting the ladies, which is still popular among seafaring men. He was quite successful in that field too.

Morison has given us an authoritative account of our great naval hero to hand down to posterity. Such an account is especially useful in this era of change. The advent of radio has made it impossible for individual ship captains to operate on their own as Jones did. Current improvements in communications—coupled with the invasion of the Pentagon by mechanical brains and Whiz Kids—

may even end the era of more modern individualists like Admirals King, Nimitz and Halsey.

Meantime the stature of John Paul Jones as a naval commander grows, and this Pulitzer Prize book has helped the process. It is fascinating reading for anybody.

—DANIEL V. GALLERY
Rear Admiral, U.S. Navy (Ret.)

Author's Preface

In the words of a Scots ballad of over a hundred and fifty years ago:

> You have heard o' Paul Jones,
> Have you not, have you not?
> And you've heard o' Paul Jones,
> Have you not?

Of course you have! But have you read what a sailor has to say about him? That is the reason for this biography.

No character in naval history, with the exception of Lord Nelson, has been the subject of as much romance and controversy as has John Paul Jones. Eminent writers as far apart in their tastes as Alexandre Dumas (*Le Capitaine Paul*), Herman Melville (*Israel Potter*), J. Fenimore Cooper (*The Pilot*), the American Winston Churchill (*Richard Carvel*), Allan Cunningham (*Paul Jones, a Romance*), Rudyard Kipling ("The Rhyme of the Three Captains"), William Makepeace Thackeray (*Denis Duval*) and Sarah Orne Jewett (*The Tory Lover*) have made him the subject of novels, poems and plays. John Murray employed Benjamin Disraeli, when a young hack writer, to prepare a pirated edition of Sherburne's biography of Jones; and the authors of *Les Cloches de Corneville* wrote an *opéra comique* "Paul Jones," which was performed in Paris. Thomas Carlyle, fascinated by the character of Jones, brought him into *The French Revolution*. Franklin D. Roosevelt started a biography of him, but was called to higher things. Jones has been the subject of popular ballads and of at least forty chapbooks. He has been idolized and extravagantly praised, as well as unjustly censured and blackened. Although new and fabulous heights are to be expected in moving pictures and television about our hero, so far the top in prevarication has been the fictitious biography by Augustus C. Buell, to which I have paid my detailed disrespects in Appendix 6 to this volume.

It is much easier to write a novel about a complex character like Paul Jones than to write a biography; that is doubtless why some thirty different people have done so. "Happy novelists," wrote Daniel Halévy in his *Péguy*, "who know all about their heroes! Biographers know very little, and must never forget it." How true that is! After studying Paul Jones for years, I still feel that there are problems in his life that I can never clear up. It would have been so easy to set up an imaginary Jones whom I could "know all about." But I am an historian, not a novelist, and feel that I owe it to Paul Jones's memory to write a true biography, a sailor's biography, which will give a lucid description of his complex and fascinating character, as it develops, as well as a clear narrative of his war cruises and battles. No sailor has done that since 1841, when Lieutenant Alexander Slidell Mackenzie USN published a biography of Jones. During the last ten years I have had a delightful time reading letters to, by, and about Jones in the manuscript depositories of the United States, England and France, visiting his birthplace and the scene of his principal battles. If every statement I make were tagged by a footnote, the book would be twice its present length; so I have cut out all but explanatory footnotes and have added the briefest of bibliographies.

Since many of Jones's letters have been printed over and over again, each new transcriber making additional errors, I have gone to the original manuscript if it can be found and have transcribed it exactly as written, so far as the limitations of print permit. Like his contemporaries, Paul Jones was chary of punctuation, using a dash in place of a period, comma or semicolon; so I have taken the liberty to translate his dash into the appropriate punctuation and to start new sentences with capital letters. Otherwise I have scrupulously respected his erratic spelling, and that of his correspondents. With French letters, however, I have followed the usual French practice of revising spelling, which will make these letters easier for English readers to understand.

Toward stories and anecdotes which some consider beneath the dignity of history, I have adopted the principle announced by Sir Charles Firth in his *Oliver Cromwell* (1900), another historical character who was the target of much obloquy and many malicious tales. If a story conflicts with known facts about Jones, I reject it; if it fits in with or supplements ascertained facts, and is intrinsically probable, I tell it. But I have not taken up space and the reader's time to refute all the nonsense that has been written about Paul Jones.

My thanks are due, first to my wife Priscilla Barton Morison, who accompanied me on my tour of the "John Paul Jones country," helped me to understand the complex character of the hero, and by her challenging criticism has enabled me to make him clearer to the reader. Miss Helene and Miss Estelle Philibert, of Arlington, Virginia, generously placed their collection of photostats and typescripts at my disposal and have made many researches into Jones's movements during the mysterious period of his life. Professor Lawrence A. Harper of the University of California kindly lent me his microfilm of the British Naval Office lists. My daughter Catharine did valuable research in English archives and libraries; Mrs. Paul Hammond gathered material for me in New York and the Netherlands; Capitaine de Vaisseau Rostand and Médecin en Chef Hervé Cras of the French Navy helped me in the French archives, and Mademoiselle Armelin, historian of Passy, gave me details on the Chaumonts. I am also indebted to Captain Ward de Weese USN (Ret.), curator of the Naval Academy Museum; to Mrs. John Nicholas Brown, who trusted me with her rare copy of André and her collection of prints; to Preston Davie for the Wedgwood copy of the Paul Jones medal (before me as I write); to Ralph May and William Greenough Wendell, who provided me with information about Portsmouth in the Revolution; to Commander W. J. Morgan USNR of the Division of Naval History; to Commander Peter Kemp RN, Librarian of the Admiralty; to the authorities of the National Maritime Museum, Greenwich; to Mr. Graham of Kirkcudbright; to the late Sir Charles Hope-Dunbar, who showed me the original Jones-Selkirk correspondence; to his son Sir Basil and to their cousin the Earl of Selkirk, First Lord of the Admiralty, who placed H.M.S. *Wave* at my disposal to sail around Flamborough Head; to Major and Mrs. Blackett, who showed us over Arbigland; and to many correspondents in the United States and England, Scotland, France and the West Indies who have given me information. To my successive secretaries, Antha E. Card and Clare Silverman, I am grateful for having wrestled so successfully with my handwriting. And, of the recent biographers of Jones, I respect Mr. Lincoln Lorenz for his well-documented study of the great captain.

—S. E. MORISON

"Good Hope"
Northeast Harbor, Maine
September 1958

"WITHOUT
A RESPECTABLE
NAVY—ALAS
AMERICA"

—JONES TO ROBERT MORRIS
17 October 1776

I

The Barefoot Boy of Arbigland

1747-1760

"The life of John Paul Jones is an open book," wrote General Horace Porter after he had unearthed the Commodore's mortal remains in Paris. Like many writings about Paul Jones, even inscriptions on monuments, this statement is the reverse of the truth.

The boy born at Arbigland in Scotland on 6 July 1747 and christened John, who later added Jones to his surname Paul, and who was generally known as Paul Jones during the height of his naval career, had a complex character and far from a simple career. Born in obscurity and poverty, he rose through his own efforts to be a distinguished naval officer and a prominent figure at the Court of Versailles. He professed to have fallen in love with America at first sight, and declared undying allegiance to the new nation; but the last five years of his life were spent in Europe. On many occasions he wrote that he had drawn his sword from pure love of liberty as a "citizen of the world"; but he drew it for the last time in the service of the greatest despot of Europe, Imperial Catherine. He affected contempt for family and rank; but he longed to be accepted by the county families of Scotland, and his happiest years were spent in Paris under the shadow of royalty as *le Chevalier Paul Jones*. He professed to be indifferent to wealth; but no naval officer strove longer and more strenuously than he to exact the last penny due to him and his men for prize money. He could be tougher and rougher than the most apelike sailor on his ships; yet, when entertaining ladies on board or ashore, his manners were those of a very fastidious gentleman. He pretended total indifference to fame, but he took every possible means to place a far from modest estimate of himself before the public of two continents.

And well did he succeed in this effort. Today, for every one who has heard of his fellow captains of the young Continental Navy, such as Manley, Wickes, Barry and Biddle, thousands have heard of John Paul Jones. Benjamin Disraeli, an early biographer, remembered that "the nurses of Scotland hushed their crying charges by the whisper of his name," and called attention to the penny chapbooks in which Paul Jones was depicted "in all the plenitude of terrific glory, the rival of Blackbeard and the worthy successor of the Buccaneers." A ballad exalting him was struck off the press while the smoke of battle was still hovering off the English coast, and a Dutch song, "Here comes Paul Jones, that fine fellow," is still sung by schoolchildren in the Netherlands. With women he was a seagoing Casanova; and the untangling of his many love affairs is an exacting, if amusing, task for a biographer. His remains, buried in a forgotten cemetery outside Paris, were disinterred over a century after his death, transferred with due ceremony to the United States, and placed in a marble sarcophagus under the Naval Academy chapel in a setting comparable to Napoleon's at the Invalides.

Yet, first and always, Paul Jones was a fighting sailor. In the history of the United States Navy, whose rise to be the greatest navy in the world he desired and foretold, Paul Jones now occupies a place comparable only with that of Nelson in the Royal Navy of Great Britain. And, although he never had Nelson's opportunities for fame, I have no doubt that, given them, he would have proved himself to be a great naval tactician and strategist. In the board-to-board, hand-to-hand sea fights in which he did engage, he was without peer.

On the west coast of Britain the Solway Firth washes up between England and Scotland, all but cutting the island in two. It is a funnel-shaped gulf with a wide range of tides, twenty feet in neaps and twenty-five in springs. As Sir Walter Scott wrote in "Young Lochinvar," "Love swells like the Solway, and ebbs like its tide." The northern, Scottish, shore of the Solway fringes the ancient Lordship of Galloway, which maintained its independence from the breakup of the Roman Empire to the middle of the twelfth century, when it became part of Scotland. As such, Galloway shared all the vicissitudes of the Northern Kingdom—the incursions of the English Edwards and their successors, the Protestant Reformation, the civil wars that raged around the person of Queen Mary, and the Great Rebellion of 1745 when Prince Charlie made his unsuccessful drive for the throne. The tales of futile heroism and brutal repression in the "Forty-five" were current talk two years later, when John Paul was born.

He was born in the gardener's cottage of Arbigland, an estate belonging to William Craik, a landowner who did much to improve the husbandry of Galloway. John's grandfather, a yeoman farmer, had moved from Fifeshire to Leith where his father, John Paul, who showed an aptitude for gardening, was engaged by Mr. Craik in the 1730s and brought to Arbigland. There, on the edge of the Solway, he helped the owner to lay out a beautiful garden. The ten- to twelve-foot stone wall that surrounded it was built in 1745 while the Jacobite rebellion was hot; the masons must have been very glad that they were too busily employed to follow the Stuart banners.

Arbigland lies in Kirkbean, the easternmost parish of the Lordship of Galloway. Kirkbean is a broad peninsula pushing into the estuary of the River Nith, which flows past Dumfries into Solway Firth. The country is singularly fair, with a placid, tender beauty; this is no "Caledonia stern and wild," but a peaceful land of soft air, smelling of flowers and verdure, with added briskness from the sea. Owing perhaps to the influence of the dying Gulf Stream, Galloway and adjacent Ayrshire (the land of Robert Burns) are the gardens of Scotland. Flowers bloom the year round, the soil is rich; and in Arbigland the fields, divided by loose stone walls, are cultivated for wheat, oats and barley, or left in pasture for herds of cattle and flocks of merino sheep. The horizon line to the north is indented by heather-covered moors and mountains of soft, suave outlines, among which the Criffel, rising almost two thousand feet from the sea, is conspicuous. The opposite English shore is visible except in thick weather, and the ebb tide leaves long expanses of golden sands in the Firth. Salmon run up it and the adjacent rivers in season; the sea fishing, too, is excellent, and every beach and harbor had its fishing fleet. Dumfries used to import tobacco directly from America; and the town of Kirkcudbright (pronounced "Kirkoobry") was also an important seaport whence corn and cattle were exported to England and the Colonies.

The Galwegians are a mixed race of Gael, Briton and Saxon, with a dash of the Norse who came over from Ireland in the ninth and tenth centuries. Men had been living in fertile Galloway for at least three thousand years before Paul Jones was born, as the numerous prehistoric cairns, "stanes" and earthworks testify. In the Middle Ages it was famous for the number and beauty of its monastic foundations; so peaceful a land naturally attracted those who sought peace above all things. Particularly beautiful are the ruins of Dundrennan, where Mary Queen of Scots spent her last night ashore in her own kingdom; and of *Dulce Core* or Sweetheart Abbey. That foundation received its poetical name because the foundress, Devorgilla, always kept by her the embalmed heart of her husband in an ivory casket and had it buried with her there, as a token of her undying love. Paul Jones's mother, Jean MacDuff, was the daughter of a farmer in the village that had sprung up around the ruins of Sweetheart Abbey, only six miles north of Arbigland. Jean, a smart, clean little woman, was Mr. Craik's housekeeper when he engaged John Paul as gardener. She married John Paul the day before Mr. Craik married a neighboring lady—a coincidence which naturally suggested that Jean had been more than a housekeeper to Mr. Craik.

However that may be, Mr. Craik built for John and Jean a neat stone cottage of three or four rooms, not far from the shore and convenient to the garden. It was far from being a "poor and mean" dwelling, as a recent writer has described it; the present gardener of Arbigland and his family are happy there, and many a young couple planning a vacation by the sea would be glad to hire such a cottage nowadays. Lieutenant Alexander B. Pinkham USN, visiting Arbigland in 1831, found the cottage in ruins, and with the coöperation of Mr. Craik's son (who remembered being carried, as a child, on John Paul's back), had it restored. The position of the cottage, and its whitewashed walls, made it a landmark for sailors entering the Solway; when passing the spot they would doff their bonnets and say, "God bless the kind Lieutenant Pinkham!"

The cottage must have been crowded when several Paul children were living at home. William, the eldest, born about 1738, emigrated as a young man to Virginia, became a tailor at Fredericksburg and died there in 1774. Next came a daughter who did not marry, then Janet, who married a local shopkeeper named Taylor. John Paul, the subject of this biography, was the fourth child, born 6 July 1747. Junior to him were two children who died in infancy, and Mary Ann, who first married a sailor of Whitehaven, and, after his death, a local shopkeeper named Lowden or Louden who emigrated to Charleston, South Carolina, and became a merchant in a small way.

No credence need be given to the stories that John was an illegitimate son of Mr. Craik or of the Earl of Selkirk or of the Duke of Queensberry or of any other Scots laird. As Stevenson remarked in *The Master of Ballantrae*, a "trollop who had a child to the master" was no rarity in the Lowlands. Many years earlier, Mr. Craik had fathered a bastard, James Craik, who strangely enough became a friend and physician to George Washington. But Jean MacDuff was no trollop even if she did grant premarital favors to her employer. If John had been illegitimate, it is incredible that he would have provided the monument in Kirkbean churchyard to his father and inscribed it, "John Paul Senior who died at Arbigland the 24 October 1767 Universally Esteemed. Erected by John Paul Junior." Most of the stories of our John's illegitimacy are mere idle tattle. It seems to gratify snobs to imagine that every great man is of noble blood.*

Although his descendants tried to exalt the elder Paul's status to that of a "horticulturist," he was simply a good Scots gardener, which is enough distinction for any man. "Everyone goes to Scotland now for philosophers and gardeners," said Voltaire. To his employer, Paul was the indispensable servant at Arbigland. The following story indicates that, like most Scots gardeners, he was independent in his views and took no back wind from anyone.

Symmetry was an ideal of eighteenth-century architecture and horticulture to which Mr. Craik rigidly adhered. Robert Adam designed his new mansion house, which replaced the old one in 1755; and ten years earlier, after the great wall about the garden was erected, Mr. Craik insisted, against John Paul's objections, on building two round stone summerhouses, since one alone would have been unsymmetrical. The gardener, however, had his revenge. He caught a man stealing fruit, locked him up in one of the summerhouses; then clapped John Paul Jr. in the other and sent for Mr. Craik. The owner, astonished at seeing little John peering out of a window, inquired what he was doing there; to which John Paul Sr. replied, "I just put him in for the sake of symmetry!"

We know very little about John Paul's childhood. From his later portraits we may infer that he was a freckled, sandy-haired little boy,† below average height, with twinkling hazel eyes and a sharp,

---

* See Appendix I.

† The miniature of Paul Jones painted by the Comtesse de Lowendahl in 1780, now in the Naval Academy Museum, shows him with powdered hair; but in the back of the frame is preserved a lock of his own hair, which is chestnut with reddish tinges. A wax portrait in high relief, also in the Naval Academy Museum, has light brown hair. The Gombault miniature, now in the Masonic Library, Boston, shows him with blue eyes. The Charles Willson Peale portrait at Philadelphia, the only one in oils to have been

Silhouette of Lieutenant Jones
by Jean Millette, January 1776

Symmetry in the Garden

Caresthorne and the Criffel

Arbigland House, Kirkbean,
from an Early Painting

Cottage Where He Was Born

SCENES AT JOHN PAUL'S BIRTHPLACE

Model of Sloop *Providence,* by Robert I. Innes

inquisitive nose. He doubtless went barefoot most of the year like other boys of his class, and wore rough, warm, woolen clothes either handed down by his elder brothers or cast off by the boys in the Great House. No kilts, however; nobody then wore kilts in the Lowlands.

It would be strange if he ever went hungry in that fat land; Scots gardeners always had the right to all the milk and vegetables that their families could eat; fresh salmon was given away in season; and smoked salmon, along with dried codfish and finnan haddie, could be laid in cheap for winter food. Beef and mutton, too, were plenty. For breakfast the family had "the halesome parritch, chief of Scotia's food"—great bowls of porridge made of home-ground oatmeal, rich in vitamins, with plenty of milk and home-baked scones. For dinner there would be a stew, followed by pudding; and by the time he was six years old John could have his own "cue" of small beer; tea was still too expensive to give to children.

The Kirkbean parish church—Church of Scotland (Presbyterian) since the Reformation—situated a little over a mile from the cottage, was attended by John and his parents every Sabbath. The parson in his childhood, the Reverend James Hogg, an alumnus of King's College, Aberdeen, kept the parochial school, which John attended to the age of thirteen; and a good schoolmaster Mr. Hogg must have been, as Paul Jones always expressed himself well in writing.

John Paul grew up speaking the "braid Scots" dialect of Robbie Burns's poems, as everyone in Galloway did, and as most Galwegians still do. He probably never traveled twenty miles from his birthplace until he went to sea; boys of his class, in the age before bicycles and other cheap transportation, never had a chance to wander very far. Dumfries, only eleven miles distant, was the market town for Kirkbean and the nearest thing to the metropolis that the boy ever saw. Kirkcudbright, chief town of the Stewartry

---

painted from life, gives him light brown hair and hazel eyes. Hazel eyes can appear brown, blue, gray or green or hazel, according to the mood of the subject and the light; it is certain that he was sandy-haired as a boy and brown-haired as a man; and that his eyes were hazel. Statements to the effect that he was "swarthy" came from the penny chapbooks (since pirates were supposed to be swarthy) and were given wide currency by the charlatan Buell.

of that name, lies a good thirty-five miles distant by land, and twenty-five by sea.

The Pauls were a rising family. Two daughters of John Paul senior married into the middle class, but John was the most ambitious. He determined very young to better his station in society. He did not intend to be a gardener, farmer or fisherman. He had plenty of opportunity to observe the ways of Mr. Craik, an amiable gentleman and considerate employer, and of his friends who visited Arbigland. Every village in Galloway had its local squire or "laird"—the Maxwells, Cochrans, Douglases, Dunbars, McLellans, MacKenzies and Blacklocks, to mention only a few. They frequently dined at each other's houses, usually without their ladies so that they could sit late over their claret and drink deep. Young John would naturally be on hand to hold the visitors' horses, and could even hide in the pantry during dinner to hear the great ones converse.

It was not difficult for a young Scot to improve his station in life. Two Galwegians of humble origin, born within ten years of John Paul, were Thomas Telford, the great bridge builder, and John L. McAdam, who invented the macadam road. Every year a horde of youngsters flocked to London, where they did well because they were frugal, honest and industrious. Any good student among peasants' sons would be helped by his schoolmaster to obtain a scholarship at Glasgow, Edinburgh or Aberdeen, where, after a three-year course, he could take a master's degree and qualify as a physician, teacher, or minister of the Scots Kirk. And for a boy who was no scholar and whose family refused to let him seek his fortune in London, there was always the sea.

The sea! That was what young Paul wanted from the first, as his road to distinction. His waking eyes beheld it sparkling under the rising sun off the Arbigland shore. He missed no opportunity to go fishing in the Solway. Sloops, schooners and brigs passed before his eyes daily, inward bound to Dumfries or outward bound to the Isle of Man, Belfast, Liverpool, and even the Colonies overseas. If the tide did not serve sailing craft to mount the River Nith to Dumfries, they would call at the little port of Carsethorn, a mile and a half from Arbigland, and lie on the sand until floated by the flood. Mr. Craik's son recalled, after Paul Jones became famous, that the child would run to Carsethorn whenever his father would let him off, talk to the sailors and clamber over the ships; and that he taught his playmates to maneuver their little rowboats to mimic a naval battle, while he, taking his stand on the tiny cliff overlooking the roadstead, shouted shrill commands at his imaginary fleet. The great Seven Years' War was on; the year 1759, when John's formal schooling neared its end, was *annus mirabilis* of the century, when Britain won victories by sea and land in every quarter of the globe, and the newspapers told details of great naval victories. Already John Paul Jr. was an admiral in imagination.

With proper connections and a sum of money our John could have been entered as midshipman in the Royal Navy; but none of his friends had any influence that way, so he was constrained to join the merchant marine. His neighbors had connections with the English port of Whitehaven across Solway Firth, where a shipowner named John Younger had a berth for a stout lad on one of his trading vessels.

Early in 1761, at the age of thirteen, John packed a sea chest, received his parents' blessing and a handshake from Mr. Craik, and at Carsethorn went on board a packet sloop or fishing vessel which took him to Whitehaven—the very port later raided by the captain of U.S.S. *Ranger*. There, articles of apprenticeship were signed, binding John Paul Jr. to serve Mr. Younger for seven years, receiving next to no pay but learning the mariner's profession. And there he embarked as ship's boy in the brig *Friendship* of 179 tons, Robert Benson master, outward bound to Barbados and Virginia.*

* Jones's early biographers antedated his departure from Whitehaven in *Friendship* by one year, in the spring of 1760. That cannot be, as this brig, according to the British Naval Office lists, arrived at the Rappahannock *from* Whitehaven in January or February 1760, cleared thence *for* Whitehaven on 12 May, and arrived back in Virginia 7 May 1761 from Whitehaven via Barbados.

II

Apprentice
Seaman
to
Naval
Lieutenant

1760-1775

1. Years of Apprenticeship

Brig *Friendship* of Whitehaven carried a crew of 28 men and she was well armed with eighteen guns, as the war with France was still raging. Her first call was Barbados, where she picked up 270 hogsheads of rum and 189 barrels of sugar. These were entered in the customs office at Hampton, Virginia, on 7 May 1761. Thence she proceeded up Chesapeake Bay and the Rappahannock River, where, in the thriving town of Fredericksburg, John had the happiness of meeting his elder brother William, who had established himself as a gentleman's tailor.

The brig plied between Scotland and Fredericksburg for several years, making but one round trip annually, according to the leisurely fashion of the day. She cleared from the Rappahannock for Whitehaven on 7 August 1761, with 424 hogsheads of tobacco, 28 tons of pig iron and several thousand barrel staves. Probably she was back in Whitehaven by the end of September, and certainly John Paul was able to keep Christmas at home; for we next hear of *Friendship* entering the Rappahannock on 8 July 1762, with 163 hogsheads of rum and 138 barrels of muscovado sugar from Barbados. On this voyage, and probably on later ones too, the master, Captain Robert Benson, allowed John to stay with his brother in Fredericksburg while the brig was loading from plantation wharves. There is extant a receipt to a resident of Fredericksburg, signed "Jn° Paul," for "£23 3*d*" for "Sixteen Barrells Flour & cask," dated 22 September 1762. Probably Captain Benson found that he had contracted for more return cargo than the brig could hold, and sent fifteen-year-old John to sell the surplus and collect the money.

He spent almost the whole of that summer of 1762 in Virginia, for *Friendship* did not clear from the Rappahannock for Whitehaven until 5 October, when the brave westerlies promised a quick passage home. She was back in the Virginian river on 6 August 1763 with a cargo of 100 tons of salt (probably from Turks Islands—the entry is illegible), but carried no guns, since the war was over. This time she needed repairs, and did not sail for home until 30 November. Her master on this voyage was William Benson, a son to Robert, and her return cargo consisted of 406 hogsheads tobacco, 16 tons pig iron, 5000 barrel staves, 200 feet of plank and—of all things—"2 Caskes Snakeroot." Were temperance advocates in Scotland attempting to substitute *Aristolochia serpentaria* for whisky as "snakebite medicine"?

Upon arrival at Whitehaven, Captain Benson found that the owner, doubtless as a result of the postwar depression in merchant shipping, had gone broke and retired. He sold *Friendship* to A. Bacon & Co., and with the same master but a greatly reduced crew she made a voyage to Bordeaux in 1764. At the same time Mr. Younger released our John from his obligation to serve out the rest of his seven years as apprentice seaman.

Thus, John Paul at an early age became acquainted with the West Indies; and if he was a normal young chap and followed the example of the other sailors, he also became initiated into venery. Bridgetown, Barbados, was notorious for its "Cyprian hotel-keepers," large mulatto ladies who catered to the demands of seamen.

Far more important were his Virginian contacts of a different character. According to a letter that he wrote in 1779, John fell in love with America at first sight and determined to make his future home there. The fact of his brother's being a tailor in Fredericksburg gave him social contacts. Tailors enjoyed no better social status in the Old Dominion than in England, but the "best people" frequented William Paul's shop, and John, between voyages, had ample opportunity to meet gentlemen, listen to their conversation and imitate their manners and speech.

In any case, John Paul grasped every occasion to improve himself, socially and otherwise. He learned to avoid low company ashore and to associate, as far as he could, with gentlemen. He got rid of his Galloway brogue, taught himself English by good reading and practice in writing. In his earliest letter that has been preserved, written in 1773, he expresses himself clearly and well; and he continued to improve in that respect. It is said that a member of the British Ministry, upon reading the dispatches of Admiral Lord Collingwood, who had gone to sea at the age of twelve, used to exclaim, "Where did Collingwood get his style? He writes better than any of us!" A similar query about Paul Jones's style might even more relevantly have been put by the American politicians with whom he later had to deal. His spelling was always erratic; but gentlemen in the eighteenth century were not expected to spell correctly, and his letters during the War of Independence are markedly superior to those of brother officers like Dudley Saltonstall, Nicholas Biddle and Esek Hopkins, who had enjoyed a better formal education than John Paul could have obtained at the Kirkbean parochial school.

During these years afloat and ashore, John learned enough celestial navigation to conduct vessels anywhere he wished, and the octant that he acquired fairly early in life, judging from its construction, is now in the Naval Academy Museum at Annapolis.

What did John Paul do after his release by Mr. Younger in 1764?

There is no reason to doubt the statements of Jones's early biographers that he went directly from *Friendship* into the slave trade, and at the age of seventeen became third mate of *King George,* a blackbirder out of Whitehaven.* After about two years in her, he was engaged as chief mate of slaver *Two Friends* of Kingston, Jamaica; and of her we have record. The Naval Office lists at London note the arrival at Kingston on 18 April 1767 of the 30-ton brig *Two Friends,* James Woodhouse master, built at Philadelphia in 1763 and British owned. She had a crew of six officers and men and carried "77 Negros from Africa." One can imagine what a disgusting voyage that must have been, in a vessel not over 50 feet long; and one wonders how many Negroes died en route. *Two Friends* cleared from Kingston for "the windward coast of Africa" on 13 June of the same year, with a cargo of rum and naval stores and a bigger crew. We do not know the exact time when she returned to Kingston; but when she did, John Paul obtained his discharge. He would have no more of that "abominable trade," as he called it. The slave traffic not only outraged his sentiments of humanity; it was a nasty business in which the wretched Negroes, wallowing in their filth between decks, raised a foul stench that enabled other ships to detect a slaver many miles to windward.

On 30 July 1768 the 60-ton brig *John* of Liverpool, recently built in New York, entered Kingston from Cork, bringing pickled beef and Irish butter. We may suppose that on Harbour Street John Paul encountered her master and part owner, Samuel McAdam, a well-known native of Kirkcudbright. McAdam offered his young compatriot a free passage home, which he eagerly accepted.

Fortune now smiled upon our John for the first time. During this voyage both master and mate died of a fever; and since no one else knew how to navigate, Paul assumed command and brought the little vessel, with her crew of seven, safely to Kirkcudbright. The owners were so pleased with this performance that they appointed him

* In the Naval Academy Museum there is a cutting from the ledger of one Thomas Riche, merchant, for "£40 on account," signed 6 June 1764 by "Jnº Paul." This was probably for slaves delivered in some West Indian port.

master for *John's* next voyage to America, and in command of her he made at least two round voyages to the West Indies.

2. Merchant Skipper in the West Indies Trade

John Paul Jr., at the age of twenty-one, was master of a merchant vessel in the West Indies trade. He had done very well for himself. In New England it was not uncommon for a young man of eighteen to twenty-one, the son of a merchant shipowner, to be made master of one of his father's small trading vessels; but that was unusual in the British Isles, and John had no family influence to promote him. Throughout his life, whether in the merchant service or the United States Navy, our hero worked hard for every promotion, and accomplished what he did through sheer merit, persistence, and force of character.

He was a hard person to get along with. His career is studded with outbursts of temper and personal quarrels, which another man of less prickly character might have avoided. But it is equally significant that he impressed older men with his competence and integrity. First the owners of brig *John*, then those of ship *Betsy*, gave him a command at a very early age. In 1775, as we shall see, although a late arrival in America and in a sense a fugitive from justice, he was given a naval commission by a leading member of the Continental Congress. In his naval career, through all his troubles with subordinates, he retained the confidence of such men as Robert Morris, Benjamin Franklin, the Marquis de Lafayette, Thomas Jefferson and the French admirals D'Orvilliers and Vaudreuil. And he had a certain magnetism that captivated ladies such as Abigail Adams who were not easily impressed, as well as French ladies of quality who were only too ready to fall into the arms of a man whom one of his sailors described as one who could be "sweet like a vine when he wished, but when necessary, like a rock."

To be master of a merchant ship in overseas trade was a great responsibility for a man of twenty-one; and on a vessel as small as *John* the burden was greater. Captain Paul had complete charge of the rigging, the navigation (celestial and otherwise) and the internal discipline of his ship, which included preventing the sailors from getting at his alcoholic cargoes. He took one watch himself, since the only other officers were the two master's mates; and he had to try to sell his cargo to best advantage and decide what to load for the return passage. He had nobody to lean on, although he took the advice of friendly merchants in the Islands; nobody to give him orders, once his ship had cleared the Solway. It was a wonderful training in character. Horatio Nelson, eleven years younger than John Paul, made a voyage to the West Indies when he was fourteen years old, and always said it was a far better school of seamanship than the Royal Navy.

There was a great deal in common, besides small stature, between the future Commodore Paul Jones and the future Admiral Lord Nelson. Both possessed a vast ambition, great professional pride, and that quality for which we have no word, which the French call *panache* and the Italians, *brio*. They may have met in some West Indies harbor in 1772; for John Paul, after his early experiences at Barbados, avoided low company and cultivated officers and gentlemen when ashore. But there is no evidence that the famous two ever did meet.

The appearance of John Paul at the age of twenty-one can be inferred from the silhouette of him made in January 1776, and from the Houdon bust of 1780. He was slight and wiry in body, about five feet, five inches tall.* His characteristic features were a sharp, wedge-shaped nose, high cheekbones and a strong, cleft chin. His expression showed pride, eagerness and intellectual alertness. He was known as a "dandy skipper," having adopted the port and manners of a young gentleman; he always dressed neatly and well, more like a naval officer than a master mariner, and carried a sword, which was once the means of saving his life.

John was fond of good literature. He read the books that pleased

---

* The frequently repeated statement that Jones was five feet, seven inches tall is one of Buell's fabrications. Unfortunately this measurement was used to help identify Jones's body in 1905, and the people employed by General Porter were so eager to establish the identity that they made no correct measurement of the corpse. The height of five feet, five inches is my guess; Jones was called "little Jones" by John Hancock, who was far from a stalwart himself; and Abigail Adams too calls him a little man.

the average gentleman of his era—Shakespeare and Ossian, Addison's *Cato,* Thomson's *Seasons* and Young's *Night Thoughts.* He loved sentimental writing, and wrote sentimental verses himself. But one trait of this romantic era he did not share—an appreciation of natural scenery. During his career he visited some of the most beautiful parts of the world—Cape Breton, the Windward Islands, Jamaica, Galicia, Brittany, the Hebrides, the Baltic and the Black Sea; yet not once in his voluminous correspondence does he indicate any appreciation of them; and in only one letter, about the great gale of October 1780, does he mention the majesty of the sea. Nor, apparently, was he interested in religion. Presumably he read divine service on board ship, since that was regulation; but one searches his letters and memoirs in vain for evidence of religious feeling, or even those perfunctory references to "the Deity" that were common in his day. By exception, he was wont to express pious platitudes in letters to his mistresses, another trait that he had in common with Nelson.

Like scores of other small British and Colonial vessels, brig *John* carried salt provisions and miscellaneous consumers' goods to the West Indies and brought back local produce. Her first voyage under John Paul's command was to Kingston, Jamaica. The record of her entry is lost; but we know she was there on 12 April 1769 when John Paul gave bond to observe the Navigation Acts. On 23 June brig *John* of 60 tons, with a crew of seven, John Paul master, owned by Samuel McAdam (probably father of the deceased master), cleared Kingston for Kirkcudbright. Her cargo consisted of 49 hogsheads and 6 casks of sugar, 156 puncheons of rum, 44 bags of pimento, 6 bags of cotton, 75 mahogany planks, and 2½ tons of "Logwood & Fustick"—the dyewood that the Jamaicans cut at Campeche. John Paul made best speed in his little brig to leave Caribbean waters before the hurricane season. He may have sailed around the western cape of Cuba to catch the Gulf Stream, or he may have beat through the Windward Passage and then followed the Old Bahama Channel along the north coast of Cuba. In any case, he would have sailed through the Strait of Florida and as far north as Bermuda before catching the westerlies for a good summer crossing of the North

Atlantic. He probably made Kirkcudbright by the end of August 1769, and, as it was then too late to start another voyage to the West Indies, spent the winter ashore.

John's next voyage, to the Windward Islands, took somewhat longer. Not until nearly the end of 1770 did the master sign the customs declaration at Kirkcudbright, entering from Grenada a cargo of rum, sugar, "cotton wool" and ginger.

On this voyage John Paul's ungovernable temper led him into his first serious scrape. Mungo Maxwell, son of a prominent local character, was engaged by the owner of *John* as ship's carpenter in the fall of 1769. In the course of the outward passage, Mungo so got on the captain's nerves that he had the fellow triced up in the rigging and lashed with the cat-o'-nine-tails. When *John* arrived at Tobago in May 1770, Mungo lodged a complaint against the master in the vice-admiralty court and exhibited his scarred shoulders as evidence. Captain Paul declared that Mungo Maxwell had been not only incompetent but disobedient; and the judge of vice-admiralty, after examining Mungo's torso, declared that the stripes were "neither mortal nor dangerous," and dismissed the complaint as frivolous.

That was not the end of it. Mungo shipped home in *Barcelona Packet,* then in port. On board this vessel he was taken with a fever and died at sea. The packet arrived in London well before *John* reached Kirkcudbright; and the elder Maxwell, hearing of his son's punishment and subsequent death, decided that it had been caused by the flogging. He deposed that his son "was most unmercifully, by the said John Paul, with a great cudgel or batton, bled, bruised and wounded upon his back and other parts of his body, and of which wounds and bruizes he soon afterward died on board the *Barcelona Packet* of London." So, when Captain Paul warped his brig into the dock at Kirkcudbright, he was met by the sheriff with an order to clap him into the Tolbooth (the local prison), and to hold him there for trial.

Within a few days the Captain obtained bail, convinced the local judges that he would stand trial as soon as he could obtain evidence from the West Indies, and was released. After making a voyage to the West Indies to obtain it, he was able to show a declaration of James Simpson, surrogate or substitute judge of the court of vice-admiralty in Tobago, stating the facts of the case; and a declaration of James Eastment, master of the *Barcelona Packet,* to the effect that Mungo Maxwell acted and appeared to be "in perfect health" when he shipped on board that vessel, but was later "taken ill of a fever and lowness of spirits," of which he died at sea. These documents cleared John Paul of the charge of murder.

That few respectable people at Kirkcudbright took any stock in the murder charge is proved by the fact that a few days after his release from the Tolbooth, John Paul applied for admission to the Master, Wardens and Brethren of Free and Accepted Masons of the St. Bernard Lodge of Kirkcudbright; and, recommended by James Smith of that town, he was "initiated into the mysteries and privileges of Ancient Freemasonry" on 27 November 1770. This was a step upward for John Paul. Masonry enjoyed great repute in the United Kingdom, France and the British Colonies; members of the nobility and gentry, even royalty, belonged to it as well as professional men, merchants and shopkeepers. Any Freemason in good standing in his home lodge could attend meetings of any other lodge in the Empire and thereby meet prominent members of the community. John's membership in the Kirkcudbright lodge later helped him to establish himself at Fredericksburg, Boston, Portsmouth and Paris.

The owners of *John* sold her early in 1771 and gave Captain Paul an honorable discharge, dated 1 April, stating that on two round voyages to the West Indies, "he approved himself every way qualified both as a navigator and supercargo." A supercargo was an officer who took charge of buying and selling cargoes; in small vessels such as *John* the master handled that function in addition to being captain of the ship. This recommendation meant that Paul had been as good a trader as a seaman.

His next job, it was said after he became famous, was the command of a local packet that traded between Galloway and the Isle of Man. But no trace of him can now be found in the Manx records.

By some means, whether as an officer or a passenger we do not know, he made a voyage to Tobago in the spring of 1772, on which he obtained the affidavits to clear his name in the Mungo Maxwell affair. Back in London on 24 September, he forwarded the documents to his mother at Kirkbean. These satisfied the authorities, though not the elder Maxwell. John was released from bail and his record cleared, but the story that he had flogged a sailor to death continued to dog him his entire life.

Captain Paul must have made a name for himself in London during the years that he was master of *John*, because in October 1772 he obtained command of a large, square-rigged ship, the *Betsy* of London, which plied between England, Ireland, Madeira and Tobago. And it is probable that he became her part owner. Of his life in London between voyages, and his connections there, we have only a few meager and tantalizing hints in some letters of 1779, after he had become famous. Thomas Scott writes to him from London enclosing a bill of £162 3s 5d for supplies (probably ship chandlery), £6 5s 6d for insuring £300 of *Betsy's* cargo from London to Tobago, and £3 13s for insuring £270 worth of Madeira wine from that island to Tobago. Jones replies in friendly fashion to "Alex" Scott, evidently of the same house, assuring him that his draft for £225 5s 6d (the debt plus six years' interest) would be honored. (He did not have to do this, since the war was on and all such debts had been legally placed in escrow.) At the same time he received a letter and a bill, neither of which has been preserved, from Alexander Smith of London. In the draft of his reply he refers to their friendship before the war and adds that if he were not "an old Man" (he was then thirty-two!) he would ask "many Questions concerning the fair Ladies," among whom "Miss Drew is still held in Remembrance," as well as the "hospitality in P. Street." Now, since "Miss" was seldom used in England at that time except for very young girls or women of ill repute; and considering that Poland Street, Soho, was a favorite residence of the high-class prostitutes, then known as "Covent Garden Ladies," it is a fair assumption that "Miss Drew" was one of them, and that young Captain Paul enjoyed a gay time in London between voyages.*

Betsy was a successful ship and John Paul a clever trader. At Tobago he established a partnership with Archibald Stuart, a local merchant-planter, and was in a fair way to become a well-to-do man at the age of twenty-five, judging from the small fortune of twenty-five-hundred pounds that he made in less than two years. The nature of his business we may infer from the detailed list of the debts due to him in Tobago when the war broke out. Although the total population of that island was only 243 whites and 4716 Negro slaves, about 50 different men, mostly with Scots names, owed various sums of money, from a few shillings up to £60—the price of a pipe of Madeira wine—to Captain Paul. The debts were for claret at £4 10*s* a dozen, porter at £4 15*s* a barrel, butter at 1*s* 6*d* a pound, oats at £8 5*s* a hogshead, potatoes at £1 4*s* 9*d* a hundredweight, lime at £3 a hogshead, and "2 neat fouling pieces at £6 12*s*." All these, except the wine and possibly the shotguns, were products of Ireland. Since the American colonies produced very little butter, the Irish farmers did a big business packing salted butter for the colonial market in wooden firkins holding about sixty-five pounds each.

John Paul, at the age of twenty-six, had learned about all there was to learn about rigging, loading and handling a full-rigged ship. He could navigate across the ocean by dead reckoning and noon latitudes of the sun. He had got the hang of a lucrative branch of commerce. He was already half merchant-shipowner and in a position to pyramid his profits every voyage. But, like thousands of other professional sailors, he had not grown to love the sea and ships. For him, seafaring was only a means toward the end of settling down,

---

* An enterprising London printer got out an annual list of "Covent Garden Ladies," listing their names, ages, addresses and charges (about one to three guineas), with remarks such as: "Miss S——h has been in trade not above three years, good looking and of amiable disposition if she can be prevented from imbibing too many strong waters, whereupon her language becomes abusive and her temper unbearable." No list for Jones's years in London has been preserved, but in others Poland Street is prominent.

marrying and becoming a gentleman farmer, preferably in Virginia, where he had been fascinated by the life he observed in the intervals of his boyhood voyages.

By 1773 that end, for John Paul, was already in sight when a murderous shipboard brawl changed his entire future, and even his name.

3. The Unfortunate Affair at Tobago

John Paul's second and last voyage in *Betsy* was unfortunate from the start. After departing Plymouth in January 1773, the ship "proved so very Leakey that it was with the greatest Difficulty that we could keep her free with both Pumps," as he wrote to John Leacock, his consignee at Madeira, on 15 April. He had been forced to put in at Cork, discharge the cargo and have the ship surveyed. It was found that no fewer than thirty of her futtocks (the curved timbers that formed the ribs of her mid-section) were broken. And, while waiting word from the underwriters in London to go ahead with the repairs, John came down with a "severe fever" which confined him to "a bed of sickness" for sixteen days and left him very much "reduced." *Betsy* was detained at Cork for repairs until mid-June, possibly later; and in the summer season of light winds she could not have made Tobago until the autumn, after calling at Madeira. (One would think that the Irish butter might have become somewhat high.) At Scarborough, Tobago, probably in October of 1773 when Paul was engaged in selling his wine and provisions and procuring a return cargo, there occurred an incident that he later called "the greatest misfortune of my life," one that dashed all prospects for an early retirement. His own account of this affair, the only one that we have, is incorporated in a letter to Benjamin Franklin written over five years later.

The trouble started because Captain Paul refused to advance wages to his seamen at Tobago. He wished to save all cash on hand to invest in a return cargo, and pay the men off in the United Kingdom. That, as he should have known, was an incautious thing to do, especially as a number of his people were natives of the island and wanted money to spend with their friends ashore. One seaman, whom Jones refers to as "the Ringleader," who had behaved insolently on the outward passage, now stirred up the crew to demand payment at once. The master tried to appease them with a gift of clothing out of his slop chest, but the Ringleader insisted on lowering the ship's boat and attempting to go ashore without leave. When the master tried to prevent this the Ringleader, whom he describes as a prodigious brute of thrice his strength, forced him to take refuge in the master's cabin under the poop deck. Thence, picking up his sword from the cabin table, John Paul sallied forth, hoping to intimidate the fellow; but his appearance had the contrary effect. The Ringleader, who was just stepping into the boat with his cronies, leaped back on deck, picked up a bludgeon and rushed on the master, roaring threats and imprecations. John, retreating backward toward the door of his cabin, encountered with his heel the coaming of an open hatchway and there made a stand, since the only alternative was to fall into the hold. The Ringleader was in the very act of swinging the bludgeon to strike a lethal head blow when John ran him through the body with his sword, and he fell dead upon the deck.

John immediately went ashore, roused out a justice of the peace and offered to give himself up. The J. P. said that that was not necessary until he was about to stand trial; but Paul's friends, declaring that there was no authority in Tobago to try an admiralty case and that Paul's life would be in danger if he stood a jury trial in a civil court, persuaded him to flee at once. He rode horseback from Scarborough to a bay on the other side of the island where a vessel was ready to leave, and got away in her, leaving all his affairs and property, except fifty pounds which he took with him, in the hands of his partner Archibald Stuart and his agent Stuart Mawey.

It is regrettable that we have no other testimony on this affair except Jones's letter to Franklin, because several questions about it are now insoluble. In the first place, why could not the case have been tried at once? Paul's friend William Young, who had a vice-admiralty commission, was still Lieutenant Governor of Tobago. He was also

Governor of Grenada, the Grenadines and St. Vincent, and he may have been in one of those islands when the brawl occurred. But Jones says in his letter to Franklin that the Governor was one of those who advised him to flee. Why, then, should he have fled? In those days, mutinous seamen seldom got a break in any admiralty court; if the Ringleader met his death as John Paul asserted, there is no question but that the master would have been acquitted. And it seems strange for one who feared no man, and who not only faced but sought danger, to abandon a ship for which he was responsible, leaving the command to an insubordinate first mate, and (as he wrote to Franklin) to "retire Incog. to the continent of America and remain there until an Admiralty Commission should arrive in the Island, then return." One can only assume that the death of the Ringleader, a Tobago man, had so stirred up local sentiment that John Paul's friends could not be responsible for his safety and prevailed upon him to escape at once.

4. The Mysterious Twenty Months*

From the time that he fled from Tobago, to the month of October 1775 when he received a letter in Philadelphia that is still preserved, John Paul's movements are almost a complete mystery. To reconstruct them is like trying to solve a picture puzzle with 90 per cent of the pieces missing; and the problem is complicated by John's change of name, first to John Jones, then to John Paul Jones.

We are justified, moreover, in assuming that he made his first change of name in the West Indies. On demand of the Tobago government, Master John Paul might have been extradited from any of the islands. But there was no occasion for him to change his name

---

* In a letter of 4 May 1777 to Stuart Mawey of Tobago (*Memoirs*, Edinburgh 1830, 1 23), Jones stated that he had to live for twenty months on the fifty pounds he carried away from Tobago. He obtained his naval commission on 7 Dec. 1775 but may have drawn pay earlier for helping fit out *Alfred*. In his letter of 1779 to Franklin he says that he waited on the Continent 18 months before "Swords were drawn and the ports of the Continent were shut." Fighting began in April 1775, which was 18 months from October 1773; but Congress did not forbid exports until 10 Sept. 1775, which was 20 months from January 1774.

after reaching the Continent. Any of his friends could have told him that nobody had ever been extradited from Virginia to the West Indies.

He cannot have sailed straight from Tobago to any Continental colony because Tobago had no direct trade with the Continent, only with the United Kingdom; its Continental trade went largely through Barbados. Between 5 October 1773 and 17 January 1774 there were five arrivals of small sloops and schooners at Bridgetown, Barbados, from Tobago. Tobago was also a port of call for the official British Post Office packets that started at Falmouth in Cornwall, first touched at Barbados and then made the circuit of the islands before returning to England. As these small vessels, measuring only 45 tons each, called at Courland Bay across the island from Scarborough, and Captain Paul tells us that he had to borrow a horse to reach his departing ship, it seems likely that he embarked in one of these. If so, he may have gone ashore at any one of the packet's ports-of-call— Grenada, St. Vincent, Dominica, Antigua or Jamaica—and there picked up a vessel to the Continent.

There can be no question that Paul's motive for changing his name was to conceal his identity while this prosecution for murder at Tobago was hanging over him. In his letter to Franklin about that affair he quotes the advice of his Tobago friends, "that I should retire Incog. to the continent of America," and that until the troubles were over between Britain and the Thirteen Colonies, he should "remain Incog." That word, a common abbreviation for "incognito," meant of concealed identity, under an assumed name or other disguise. Undoubtedly John intended to return to Tobago and stand trial in due course, since he had money tied up in the island; but, having arrived in Virginia as "Mr. John Jones" (which is the way he is addressed in a letter of 13 October 1775), he decided to stick to it in case rumors about the mutineer's "murder" reached Virginia. He had had enough trouble already in the Mungo Maxwell affair.

But why Jones? Possibly, as his earliest biographer suggests, because Jones is a patronymic, meaning the son of John. Possibly there were other reasons, which are so detailed and conjectural that I have placed them in Appendix 4.

John Jones, as he now called himself, must have left Tobago at some time during the last three months of 1773. We next hear of him in Virginia in 1774. His brother William Paul, the tailor of Fredericksburg, died that year, leaving all his property to his sister Mary Ann and her children, in Scotland; none to his widow, who had long been separated from him, and none to brother John. The executors named in the will, probated 16 December 1774, declined to serve, possibly because they disapproved of cutting off the widow; and although brother John was not invited to act in their place, he as the nearest relative may have been allowed by the court to occupy William's house, pending the settlement of the estate.

But his first problem was to find a job. The fifty pounds he carried with him from Tobago were running out. At Edenton, North Carolina, he had a connection. Robert Smith, brother to that James Smith of Kirkcudbright who had promoted his election to the local Masonic lodge, was partner with Joseph Hewes, the leading shipowner, merchant and politician in that part of North Carolina. It is possible that Jones traveled overland to Edenton via Richmond in 1774 or early 1775, to seek a master's billet in one of Hewes & Smith's ships. If he did so, he was disappointed. In those troublous times Hewes & Smith had nothing to offer.

The only other person besides Joseph Hewes who is known to have befriended Jones during this mysterious period of his life was Dr. John K. Read. That interesting character, a nephew of Benjamin Franklin's wife "Debby," was educated as a physician in Philadelphia, removed first to Charleston, South Carolina, then to Hanover County, Virginia, and in 1774 to the adjoining Goochland County. He was a pleasant, easygoing chap who ran up bills that he was unable to pay until after marriage to a rich widow. And he was an important Freemason who later became instrumental in founding the Grand Lodge of that order in Virginia. Since both Fredericksburg and Richmond are on the main highway that leads from Baltimore through Virginia to the deep South, Dr. Read may have met our John Jones at the lodge in Fredericksburg when John was there in connection with his brother's last illness and death. But in sociable Virginia, where everyone who was "anybody" knew everybody else, it requires no particular explanation for two congenial souls coming together. Read was only a year older than John Paul; they became warm friends and remained so for life. Read wrote him an affectionate letter on 13 October 1775, addressed to "Mr. John Jones, to the Care of Mr. David Sproat, Merch[ant], Philadelphia." In it he sends greetings to his parents and refers to two earlier letters he had written to Jones, which were still unanswered.

This letter proves that John Jones went to Philadelphia not later than September 1775, probably several months earlier; and also that he made important friends there, through Dr. Read. He may there have first met Joseph Hewes, a delegate from North Carolina to the Second Continental Congress. He certainly met Thomas Jefferson, who was a friend of Dr. Read and the bearer of one of his letters to Jones.

The next letter from Dr. Read to John Jones that has been preserved, of 28 February 1778, gives a few more tantalizing hints as to what the future Commodore was doing in 1774-1775. The doctor observes that he was beginning to fear lest his friend had forgotten him; "but those fears were momentary & gave place to other feelings when I reflected on the many sentimental hours which (solitarily enough) passed between us at the Grove." And he goes on to refer to Dorothea Dandridge (of whom more presently) in terms which indicate that she was the subject of Jones's sentiments at that time.

Dr. Read in 1773-1775 was living on a farm owned by his second wife in Goochland County, and there practiced medicine. Was this "the Grove"? That name was almost as common then as "Bide-a-Wee" and "The Laurels" are today; but there is no record that Mrs. Read's farm had a name. There was, however, and still is, an estate called "The Grove" in Hanover County adjoining Goochland. This "Grove" is only three miles from Patrick Henry's home at Scotchtown, and five and a half miles from the plantation then owned by

Dorothea's father, Nathaniel West Dandridge. It would have given our John a three-mile start on Patrick in courting the young lady. Dorothea's elder sister Martha, named after her cousin Martha Washington, was married to Archer Payne, brother to Mrs. Read's first husband; and Archer Payne's place was near Dr. Read's in Goochland County. So, if Dorothea stayed with her sister, the Read place would have been very convenient for John, and too far for Patrick, to have made frequent calls.

It seems, therefore, reasonable to assume that John Jones (as we should call our hero during this period of his life) met Dr. Read through Masonic or other associations, and stayed with him both at his Goochland County home and at his Crenshaw neighbors' "Grove" in Hanover County; through him met Dorothea Dandridge, and used one or the other "Grove" as base for a courtship of the young lady. We may further assume that if John had won Dorothea's hand, and the times had been prosperous, he would have attempted to purchase a Virginia estate with the £2500 credit he had accumulated in Tobago and London, and have settled down, at the age of twenty-eight, to a life of "calm contemplation and poetic ease," his favorite quotation from Thomson's *Seasons*.

Dorothea may have been dark or fair, short or tall; we do not know. Absolutely nothing is known about this courtship, except what we learn from Dr. Read and from Jones's Edinburgh biographer of 1830—"their affection was mutual, but circumstances forbade their union." This statement, evidently inspired by Jones's sentimental niece Janette Taylor, is somewhat vitiated by what follows —"from this period he formed the resolution of never marrying." As we shall see, Jones was always talking about taking a wife. But, assuming that Dorothea did fall in love with John, the circumstance which "forbade their union" would naturally have been a parental prohibition. The Virginia gentry were more democratic than their English counterparts. They might invite an unemployed shipmaster, brother to the local tailor, to dine; but to allow a daughter to marry such a person—never!

In 1777 Dorothea Dandridge married Governor Patrick Henry of

Virginia, a widower forty-two years of age with six children by a former wife. From a worldly point of view, that was a proper match for her; but I think that Dorothea would have had more fun as Mrs. John Paul Jones than she did bearing nine children to Patrick Henry and listening to him rehearsing his orations.

As for Jones, he quickly erased Dorothea from his mind—she was no "love of his life," as the romancers would have us believe; nobody was, for that matter. Our John was determined to improve his social status by marriage, or remain single. And single he remained, although his fascination for women was such that after he became a famous naval officer he could have had almost anyone he chose.

Thus, the sea, from which he had hoped to retire before the age of thirty, became John's path to glory, which one side of his nature craved. And on that element he won a fame that could never have come to him as a simple planter of Virginia.

5. First Lieutenant, Continental Navy

While John Jones courted Dorothea Dandridge and lived in sentimental semisolitude with Dr. Read at "the Grove," the American Revolution was working up to a crisis. Boston Tea Party, Coercive Acts, Committees of Correspondence and First Continental Congress in 1774; Second Continental Congress, Virginia Resolves and outbreak of hostilities near Boston in April and May of 1775; prohibition of trade between the Thirteen Colonies and the West Indies in August. This last measure meant, among other things, that the moneys owed to John in London and Tobago were sequestered and that he could not, if he would, return to Tobago to stand trial and try to collect his debts. And he was at an end of the fifty pounds that he had carried away from Tobago. "Calm contemplation" no longer became possible for a man of his active spirit, and he did not wish to depend any longer on the hospitality of friends.

At this juncture a completely new prospect opened up. Congress had created a Continental Army with George Washington as commander in chief, and a Continental Navy with Esek Hopkins as commander in chief. Competent officers were wanted to man the new Navy. So to Philadelphia, probably in July or August of 1775, went "Mr. John Jones" to look for a job. There he found David Sproat, a fellow Scot from Kirkcudbright, well established as a merchant, and stayed with him. There, too, he began courting another girl of whom we know only that she was a friend of the wife of Captain John Young, whom he met in Philadelphia. Presumably it was in Philadelphia, where you could hardly throw a stone without hitting a John Jones, that our John decided to retain his original name, together with that by which he had lately become known. It would now be awkward to revert to John Paul.

Joseph Hewes, whose partner was brother to John Paul's Freemason sponsor at Kirkcudbright, not only represented North Carolina in the Second Continental Congress, but became member and chairman of the Marine Committee which established the Navy and selected the officers. Either at Philadelphia (where he attended Congress from 10 May into July, and from the last week of September on), or at Edenton, Hewes met Jones and was favorably impressed with him. I believe that they were fellow lodgers with David Sproat, since Jones later wrote to Hewes under cover to Sproat, who came from the same place as Hewes's partner. What went on between Jones and the Marine Committee is lost in the mists of history. The bare record shows that on 7 December 1775 "John Paul Jones Esq." was commissioned first lieutenant in the Continental Navy, and that four days earlier he raised the flag in the armed ship *Alfred.* So it is probable that the Marine Committee had employed John in fitting out that vessel for a month or more. But Jones always acknowledged that Joseph Hewes obtained him his naval commission.

Before taking up his naval career, we may consider the statement frequently made by Paul Jones in his later letters, that he drew his sword, not for riches, of which he claimed to have enough for his needs, but from pure love of liberty, "universal philanthropy" and the like; not even as an American but as a "Citizen of the World." These expressions were eighteenth-century stereotypes. The same or similar sentiments may be found in the writings of Thomas Jefferson, Samuel Adams and other American founding fathers, as well as in those of their English sympathizers. For instance, Edward Gibbon the historian wrote in 1785, "I never was a very warm Patriot and I grow every day as Citizen of the World." James Otis, known to contemporaries as "The Patriot," adopted as his motto UBI LIBERTAS, IBI PATRIA—"Where Liberty Is, There Is My Country"; and in patriotic American songs of the 1770s one encounters the simile of the Goddess of Liberty leaving her home in England in disgust and flying overseas to inspire the revolted Colonies.

Thus, when John Paul Jones accepted his commission on 7 December 1775—a date when only a few radicals wanted a complete separation from England—he well and truly believed that he was fighting not for American independence but for the principle of Liberty—the right of a free people to determine their destiny without coercion by a misguided king and a corrupt ministry. And the flag that he raised with his own hands on the jackstaff of his first temporary command, the *Alfred*, on 3 December 1775, was not the Stars and Stripes of an independent republic, but the "Grand Union Flag," the Union Jack and Stripes, which symbolized a united resistance to tyranny, but loyalty to the English King.

III

Earliest Service in the Continental Navy

December 1775-April 1776

1. The United Colonies Build a Navy

It was not much of a navy in which Paul Jones received his lieutenant's commission, only a haphazard collection of converted merchant ships. But it was the best that anyone could fairly expect. The Continental Congress, engaged in a desperate struggle to prevent the North ministry from working its will on the Thirteen Colonies, yet flinching from independence, could have done nothing more as a temporary expedient.

Fighting at sea between colonists and the British armed forces began only a few days after the Battles of Lexington and Concord. Natives of Martha's Vineyard recaptured two American sloops which had been seized by H.M.S. *Falcon* in Vineyard Sound. On 9 May 1775, the minutemen of Maine roughed up Captain Henry Mowatt RN when he came ashore at Falmouth (now Portland), took him prisoner and attacked his ship at anchor; for which, after his release, he took an excessive revenge by bombarding the town with red-hot cannon balls and incendiaries, and burning most of it. This created a violent resentment in the Colonies and, as much as any other event, prevented reconciliation.

During the autumn of 1775, Massachusetts and other Colonies began to issue letters of marque and reprisal to merchantmen, authorizing them to make prize of certain categories of vessels; this authority was gradually widened to include any British property at sea. These commerce-destroying privateers, which increased in numbers and audacity after Congress too authorized them in March 1776, became rivals rather than associates of the Navy. Service on board a privateer was more popular than in the Continental or State Navies. There was less discipline; it was safer, since a privateer was generally so heavily sparred that she could outsail a more powerful vessel; and it was far more lucrative. Undoubtedly the two thousand or more American privateers that were sent out during the war accomplished a great deal for the cause by preying on English commerce and obtaining supplies for the people of their country. But their popularity made it difficult for the regular armed forces to recruit men in seaport towns. Paul Jones and other captains in the Continental Navy had frequent reason to complain of privateers who enticed their men to desert.

Probably the greatest handicap the Navy had to overcome was in the matter of prize money. In the eighteenth century prize money was one of the advantages of naval over military service, since the Army was no longer supposed to loot private property. British admirals grew rich on prize money, purchased estates in England and even seats in Parliament; junior officers expected to gain far more from this source than from their pay; and common seamen, although their share was the least, could count on a few golden guineas to spend ashore. The British government recognized this inducement by granting the Royal Navy the full product of every prize taken; but Congress did not. The Marine Committee, which Commodore Hopkins was fond of calling "a pack of damned fools," and "ignorant lawyers' clerks," naïvely imagined that the Navy could help pay for the war. In the first prize regulations of 25 November 1775, Congress reserved for the public treasury half the value of a prize if it were a warship, and two thirds if it were a transport, supply ship or merchantman. This caused such discontent that in October 1776 Congress relinquished its right to any part of a captured warship, and thereafter took only one half the proceeds of merchant prizes made by the Navy. But privateers took all; and they had more opportunities for captures than a naval vessel, which had other missions, such as escorting merchant convoys and carrying dispatches and diplomats across the Atlantic.

If any one person should be called the "Father" or "Founder" of the United States Navy, he was George Washington, who, in addition to his other talents, had a keen appreciation of the value and capabilities of sea power. Appointed Commander in Chief of the Army of the United Colonies by Congress, the General assumed his command at Cambridge on 15 July 1775 over the provincial forces which were besieging the British in Boston. In order to harass the enemy's supply line, he chartered, armed, and manned with soldiers from the New England regiments several fishing schooners and small merchantmen. The first vessel of this "Army's Navy," as we would call it today, was schooner *Hannah* (Captain Nicholas Broughton), which sailed 5 September 1775. These vessels operated off the New England coast during the autumn and winter and captured many prizes, including the British ordnance storeship *Nancy*, laden with two thousand muskets, many tons of ammunition, and a 13-inch brass mortar. The Army's Navy continued to operate through the year 1776, after which it was disbanded. Three of the more successful captains, John Manley, Samuel Tucker and Hector McNeill, were taken into the Continental Navy.

Nor should we forget the freshwater Army's Navy on Lake Champlain, built by General Benedict Arnold, which in the Battle of Valcour Island held up the advance of British forces from Canada to the Hudson.

The movement for a Continental Navy started even before Washington organized his fleet. On 26 August 1775, the Colony of Rhode

Island and Providence Plantations resolved that an "American Fleet" should be built, and the Rhode Island delegation pushed it in Congress. Samuel Chase of Maryland said, "It is the maddest idea in the world to think of building an American fleet, . . . we should mortgage the whole Continent." To this George Wythe of Virginia retorted: "Why should not America have a navy? No maritime power near the sea-coast can be safe without it. . . . The Romans suddenly built one in their Carthaginian war. Why may we not lay a foundation for it?" He wished and hoped that it would be said "that America *inter nubila condit*"—that she built in time of tribulation; and that is what she did.

It seemed mad indeed to challenge the Royal Navy, or even that part of it already deployed in North American waters. On 30 June 1775 Vice Admiral Thomas Graves RN had three ships of the line and six smaller warships, with a total of over 300 guns and 2000 men, based on Boston and northern New England ports; two sloops of war with 36 guns and 230 men in Narragansett Bay; one ship of the line and two sloops (total 96 guns, 700 men) at New York; three sloops (total 56 guns, 360 men) in Chesapeake Bay or en route thither; a 16-gun sloop at Charleston, South Carolina, and ten small armed vessels of 6 to 8 guns and 30 to 60 men each, at various ports between Halifax and Florida. And these squadrons were constantly being relieved and reinforced by other ships coming from England, the West Indies and the Mediterranean.

On 30 October 1775 Congress appointed a Naval Committee of Seven for the management of its maritime affairs, and authorized the purchase and arming of a few ships "for the protection and defense of the United Colonies." This is regarded as the birthday of the Continental and United States Navies.

The Naval Committee consisted of four New Englanders (Stephen Hopkins, John Langdon, John Adams and Silas Deane), Richard Henry Lee of Virginia and Joseph Hewes and Christopher Gadsden of the Carolinas. Subsequently enlarged to the number of eleven, this committee became known as the Marine Committee until mid-1779, and, when reduced to three members, as the Board of Admiralty. It was our first Navy Department.

On 10 November 1775, Congress created the Marine Corps. On the 25th, the capture of British warships and auxiliaries—but not, as yet, of merchant vessels—was authorized; and on the 28th the "Rules for the Regulation of the Navy of the United Colonies of North America" were adopted. This first set of Navy Regulations, precursor of the manual known today as "Rocks and Shoals," was framed by John Adams, printed in a neat pamphlet and widely distributed. Each commanding officer was required to punish men "Heard to swear, curse, or blaspheme the name of God," by causing them to "wear a wooden collar, or some other shameful badge of distinction"; or, if an officer, to be fined a shilling. Punishment with the "cat of nine tails" was limited to one dozen lashes upon the bare back. A thrifty Yankee touch by Adams was the requirement that all ships were to be "furnished with fishing tackle," and that commanding officers "being in such places where fish is to be had," were "to employ some of the company in fishing"; the catch to be distributed to the crew in addition to their daily allowance.

At about the same time Congress adopted, and published as a broadside, a "Naval Pay List." A captain drew $32.00 per month, a lieutenant or master, $20.00; a surgeon, $21.33; petty officers from $9.00 to $15.00; able seamen, $8.00; "landsmen" or ordinary seamen, $6.66. A mess bill was also adopted. This required that every member of a ship's company be issued daily except Wednesday a pound of bread, a pound of beef or pork, a pound of potatoes or turnips or a half pint of peas, and half a pint of rum; "and discretionary allowance on extra duty, and in time of engagement." Butter once and cheese thrice a week, pudding Tuesdays and Fridays; and "canvas for pudding bags to be issued gratis; half a gill of vinegar per man per week." The old English custom of observing once a week a "banyan" or short commons day, when only butter, cheese and rice were issued, was taken over by the Continental Navy.

During the month of November 1775, the Naval Committee

purchased and began to fit out the first four vessels of the Continental Navy. Here they are, with whatever data I can find about their size, crews and armament:

	Tonnage or Length	Former Name	Guns	No. of Men*	First C.O.
Ship *Alfred*	about 350 t.	*Black Prince*	20 9-lb. 10 6-lb.	220	Saltonstall
Ship *Columbus*	about 300 t.	*Sally*	18 9-lb. 10 6-lb.	220	Whipple
Brig† *Cabot*	189 t., 75 ft.	?	14 6-lb.	120	Hopkins
Brig *Andrew Doria*	?	?	16 6-lb.	130	Biddle

Before these were ready for sea, four smaller vessels had been added to the fleet:

Sloop *Providence*	about 70 ft.	*Katy*	12 4-lb.	73	Hazard
Sloop *Hornet*	100 t.	*Falcon*	10 6-lb.	?	Stone
Schooner *Wasp*	?	*Scorpion*	8 6-lb.	48	Alexander
Schooner *Fly*	?	*Lizard*	6 9-lb.	30	Hacker

In addition, three more merchantmen were purchased and converted early in 1776. These were not ready in time to sail with the fleet, but their names are still preserved in the modern Navy:

Brig *Lexington*	86 ft.	*Wild Duck*	14 4-lb. 2 6-lb.	57 to 83	Barry
Ship *Reprisal*	100 ft.	*Molly*	18 6-lb.	130	Wickes
Sloop *Independence*	?	?	10 4-lb.	30	Young

2. Lieutenant Jones Goes on Board

On 5 November 1775 the Naval Committee of Congress appointed, as "Commander in Chief," Esek Hopkins of Rhode Island, an elderly merchant skipper who had followed the sea for forty years and

---

* Including Marines in the New Providence expedition.

† The brigs here mentioned are often referred to as "brigantines"; since there is little difference between the two rigs, I have let them go as brigs—two-masters, square-rigged.

commanded privateers in the French and Indian War. His appointment was not unconnected with the fact that his brother Stephen was chairman of the Naval Committee. John B. Hopkins, his son, was given command of brig *Cabot*. The command of *Alfred*, which should have gone to John Barry, her former master in the merchant service, went to Dudley Saltonstall of Connecticut because he was the brother-in-law of Silas Deane of the Committee. We shall find a great deal of nepotism during the war; almost all the leaders except Washington practised it, the Lees of Virginia most of all. But it must be remembered that in a revolutionary society nepotism is natural; one sees plenty of it in the new republics of today. It is not merely a question of getting your relative a job, but of having people you can trust in positions of responsibility during a social upheaval.

Paul Jones, as we have seen, had been in Philadelphia for several months in 1775. It is probable that he was employed in converting *Alfred*, and he acted as her commanding officer until Captain Saltonstall reported for duty on 23 December. It was Jones who, with his own hands and in the presence of Commodore Hopkins, raised the Grand Union Flag to the jackstaff of *Alfred*, lying at her dock in Philadelphia. He probably persuaded the Commodore to make a little ceremony of it, the crew standing at attention or manning the yards, and Marine Corps fifers and drummers playing a lively air such as "The British Grenadier," which the colonists had preëmpted under the title "War and Washington."

Four days later, on 27 December 1775, "John Paul Jones Esq." was commissioned First Lieutenant in the Continental Navy and formally assigned to *Alfred*. This was the earliest naval lieutenant's commission granted by Congress. Commodore Hopkins, who had sailed to Philadelphia from Providence in *Katy* of the Rhode Island State Navy, had that sloop taken over by Congress and converted to a twelve-gun warship, renamed *Providence*. Jones later said that Joseph Hewes offered him the command of this vessel with the rank of captain, and that he declined for two reasons, the first being that "he had never sailed in a sloop." *Providence* was a 70-footer with a whale of a gaff-headed mainsail, a long boom overhanging the stern and a bowsprit almost as long as the deck. Square-rigger sailors of that era regarded these big sloops as dangerous and difficult to handle, as indeed they were. Jones's other reason for declining was that in December 1775, having "no idea of the declaration of independence that took place the next year . . . and having then no prospect that the American Navy would soon become an established service," he believed that he could be immediately useful, and learn more seamanship, as first lieutenant under a flag captain. This admission is in line with Joseph Hewes's sentiments; he wrote to an English correspondent, "We do not want to be independent; we want no revolution. But every American to a man is determined to die or be free." A great majority of Americans then hoped that a stout resistance would force George III to give in or compromise; that within a few months all would be happy and peaceful between Mother England and her unruly daughter. Jones could then recover the moneys due to him in London and Tobago, renew his quest for a Virginia plantation and bride, and begin the desired life of "calm contemplation and poetic ease."

He later regretted that he had not then accepted the command of the sloop, which would have bettered his seniority in the Navy and given him a chance to distinguish himself. It went to John Hazard of Rhode Island, whom Captain Biddle, even before the fleet sailed, described as "A Stout Man very Vain and Ignorant—as much low cunning as capacity."

A weary and dreary time was had by all hands in this fleet for almost three months. It was a very cold winter; the Delaware River was blocked with ice; sails had to be bent and rigging rove in freezing weather. Lieutenant John Paul Jones, in temporary command of *Alfred* pending the arrival of her captain, had to use ingenuity to keep people busy and prevent them from deserting. What he mainly did, he tells us, was to "exercise the guns"—the best thing he could have done.

All naval ordnance at that time, except for a few brass pieces, was of cast iron, smooth-bore and muzzle-loading. Each gun was classed by the weight of the round shot that it fired. *Alfred's* nine-pounders, for instance, were so called because they threw a cannon ball weighing nine pounds; their caliber was 3.7 inches. An eighteen-pounder, biggest gun in the American Navy at this time, threw an eighteen-pound shot and had a caliber of 5.3 inches; smaller vessels carried six-pounders and four-pounders. These guns, mounted in broadside, were those that counted. Besides round cannon balls, they could fire grape and chain shot, useful for tearing the enemy's rigging and mowing down men on deck; and they could also shoot an incendiary shell for shore bombardment. Every man-of-war carried, in addition, small swivel guns and mortars mounted on her bulwarks and in her tops, which could be dismounted to arm the ship's boats if desired; and she always took to sea a small arsenal of muskets, blunderbusses, pistols, cutlasses, pikes and hatchets, for close fighting or boarding.

Alfred's cannon, like those of all contemporary men-of-war, were mounted on wooden-wheeled gun carriages, secured by rope tackles which were used both to run the guns in and out of the gunports and to take up the recoil. In the "exercise," the gun crews are first assembled by beat of drum. The chief gunner of each piece, or a midshipman, checks the rammer, sponge, tub of water, powderhorn, crow, spike, quoin (wedge) and bed that go with each cannon, and sees that a sufficient number of powder cartridges and balls are in the proper boxes. The ships' boys, commonly called "powder monkeys," replenish the boxes with cartridges made of black powder in cloth bags, from the magazine in the hold. At the order "Cast Loose Your Guns," the muzzle lashings are taken off and coiled, the breach lashings secured, and the spikes, sponges, etc., put in place. Next comes "Level Your Guns," to make them parallel to the deck. At "Take out Your Tompions," the stoppers in the muzzles are removed. At "Load with Cartridge," the bag of powder, with a wad behind it, is placed in the muzzle and rammed in; and at "Shot Your Guns," the cannon ball or other shot is rammed home. At "Run out Your Guns," the men bowse them outboard until the carriage hits the vessel's topsides and the muzzles are sticking out, and the tackle-falls that take up the recoil are neatly flaked on deck. At "Prime" the touch-hole is primed with gunpowder from a powderhorn. At "Point Your Guns" the cannoneer who attends the lighted slow-match brings it near the breech, kneels down, and blows gently on the match to keep it alight; while the others, by adjusting bed and quoin, "Elevate" their guns "to the Utmost Nicety" by means of the side sights, and draw a bead on the target from the top sight.

At "Fire," which in an engagement is given when the roll of the ship brings the top sights of a battery on the target, the gunner with the lighted match applies it to the touch-hole; and if everything has been done properly and the gunpowder is dry, the gun goes off. Next comes "Sponge Your Guns." The sponge, at the end of a stave or a thick, stiffened rope, after being dipped in the tub of water, is rammed down the muzzle and twisted, to extinguish any sparks or scraps of the cartridge bag still burning. Then the process of loading and firing is repeated. If the gun is not fired after being loaded, the shot and powder are extracted by a long-handled corkscrew-like implement known as a "worm."

At the end of the exercise, the tompions are replaced and the guns housed with muzzles flush against the bulwarks or topsides and lashings drawn taut so that the cannon will not work loose in a seaway. The most awkward situation for a sailor was to be chased around the deck by loose cannon.

Paul Jones was exceedingly proud of the shooting by his gun crews, and when he chose a coat of arms, he saw to it that naval cannon and a sponge and worm were included in the mantling.

Captain Dudley Saltonstall, who had just been offered the command of *Alfred* in a letter of 27 November, was unable to reach Philadelphia and take it over until 23 December. Lieutenant Jones disliked him at sight. Saltonstall, ten years older than his first lieutenant, had been a master mariner and served in privateers in the French and Indian War. A scion of the three first families of New England, he seems not to have resembled the Saltonstalls, who for generations have been noted for their genial and democratic manners, but rather his mother's family, the Winthrops, who were notorious for their condescending attitude toward social inferiors; his maternal grandfather, John Winthrop F.R.S., was the stuffiest of the family. Captain Biddle described Saltonstall as "a Sensible indefatigable Morose man." Jones complained of his "Rude Unhappy Temper," and he later proved to be incompetent. Saltonstall's opinion of his First Lieutenant is not known; but it is probable that he regarded Jones as an officious upstart, for Paul was one of those "eager beavers" who could not refrain from giving unwanted advice. Even today it is sometimes difficult for an executive officer who has put a new warship in commission to get on with a commanding officer placed over him at the eleventh hour. Jones all his life had been angered and humiliated by snobs—Scottish snobs, English snobs, and Virginian snobs; now he had to endure a New England snob.

Commodore Hopkins,* however, was no snob but an old-fashioned salt-horse sailor (an "antique character," said General Knox, like the pictures of old Van Tromp). He covered a fumbling approach to naval problems by a profanity that shocked even some of his tough young officers. His attitude toward the First Lieutenant of his flagship was friendly and benign; and Jones was loyal to him up to the point where he got the idea that the Commodore had done him out of a command.

3. The New Providence Expedition

The Commodore received his orders from the Naval Committee on 5 January 1776. He was instructed "with the utmost diligence to proceed with the said Fleet to Sea and if the Winds and Weather will possibly admit of it to proceed directly for Chesapeak Bay in Virginia and when nearly arrived you will send forward a small swift sailing

---

* Commodore, during the War of Independence, was not, as it later became, a rank between Captain and Rear Admiral, but the courtesy title of the senior captain or officer in tactical command of a squadron or task force.

Vessel to gain intelligence of the Enemie's Situation and Strength. If by such Intelligence you find they are not greatly superiour to your own you are immediately to Enter the said bay search and attack, take and destroy all the Naval force of our Enemies that you find there." And if that succeeds, he should destroy enemy ships off the Carolinas. But—and here was the clause that let the Commodore out:

> Notwithstanding these particular Orders, which 'tis hoped you will be able to execute, if bad Winds or Stormy Weather, or any other unforseen accident or disaster disable you so to do, You are then to follow such Courses as your best Judgement shall Suggest to you as most useful to the American Cause and to distress the Enemy by all means in your power.

Congress badly wanted naval action in the Chesapeake. The British Navy had stationed two or three warships there; and Lord Dunmore, Royal Governor of Virginia, having organized a Tory navy out of loyal merchant vessels, was constantly augmenting it by captures of American ships. The British had obtained almost complete control of waters inside the Capes, which meant that the American hold on Virginia and Maryland was insecure.

On 4 January 1776, *Alfred, Columbus, Cabot* and *Andrew Doria* cast off from their wharves or moorings at Philadelphia, and attempted to drop down Delaware Bay to blue water. Ice prevented them from reaching even Reedy Island until the 17th. There they remained icebound for another four weeks, and were joined by *Providence* and *Fly.* Jones and the other lieutenants had to stand anchor watch day and night to prevent the men from deserting. On 14 February the fleet proceeded to Whorekill Roadstead inside Cape Henlopen. *Hornet* and *Wasp,* which had been converted in Baltimore, there joined. As a captain was wanting for *Fly,* Hopkins offered her command to Paul Jones, who again declined, this time because he considered her to be nothing better than a dispatch boat, the proper command for a midshipman. That was another mistake. *Fly's* command was given to the First Lieutenant of *Cabot*, Hoystead Hacker of Rhode Island, who thereby obtained seniority over Jones.

Even before his departure from the Delaware, Commodore Hopkins had made up his mind not to enter the Chesapeake. On 14 February, three days before the fleet sailed, he ordered his captains to rendezvous, if the fleet became separated, at the Great Abaco. The Commodore had decided, on his own responsibility, to make a surprise attack on New Providence in the Bahamas to capture gunpowder and ordnance for Washington's army. Congress had voted that measures be taken to obtain powder from the Bahamas; but Hopkins, unless he had oral orders unknown to us, had not been told to go in search of it.

Paul Jones later stated that he acted as the Commodore's planning officer, strategist and master brain on this cruise. That, of course, is nonsense. Hopkins and Saltonstall not only knew the Bahamas well, through their former merchant voyages; they had fought ships in the French and Indian War. But, knowing Jones, we may be sure that he did give his Captain and his Commodore plenty of advice.

The fleet got off to a good start, and the ships must have made a brave sight as they bowled along past Hatteras in a smart north wind of winter. *Alfred* had yellow topsides, and a figurehead of a knight holding a sword—originally meant for the Black Prince, but it did well enough for King Alfred. *Cabot* had yellow topsides; *Columbus*, *Andrew Doria* and sloop *Providence* were all black, the usual color for small vessels. They made a fast run south and anchored near Hole-in-the-Wall off Great Abaco on 1 March 1776. Two local sloops were seized and their skippers impressed as pilots.

At that time, New Providence bore little resemblance to the resort island of today. Nassau was a tiny settlement on the harbor behind Hog Island, with a stone fort on either side to protect it; the rest of the island was mostly brush. A British regiment and H.M.S. *Savage*, formerly stationed there, had been withdrawn, leaving the island undefended except by civilians. It was easy to capture, but the operation very nearly became a fiasco.

On 2 March Hopkins stowed 200 Marines and 50 sailors below decks in the two captured sloops and sent them into Nassau harbor, hoping to take the town by surprise; but he made the mistake of displaying his fleet within sight of shore. The Governor, warned what to expect, caused civilians to fire cannon from the nearest fort; that scared the sloops off, and in the night the Governor sent away 150 barrels of gunpowder to St. Augustine in a sloop. So the main object of the expedition was frustrated.

Commodore Hopkins now held a council of war on board his flagship. Here (according to fiction) Paul Jones took the lead, suggested a new landing place out of cannon range, and led the landing party in *Alfred*, posting himself in the foretop alongside the two impressed pilots to see that they tried no monkey business. But it seems highly improbable that the views of Lieutenant Jones, who had never sailed in these waters, would have prevailed over those of the Commodore and several of his captains, who knew them well. All contemporary accounts of the actual landing, which took place at the east end of the island, state that it was made by the men in the captured sloops, covered by *Wasp* and *Providence*. No competent seaman would have sent his flagship, with the deepest draught of any vessel in the fleet, to spy out a channel through the shoals.

The landing party, commanded by Captain Samuel Nicholas USMC, was unopposed. It occupied the nearest stone fort, spent the night there, and next morning (4 March) marched on the town, demanded and received the keys of the other fort from the Governor, and signaled the fleet to enter the harbor.

The next two weeks were spent loading the loot, which comprised 88 cannon, ranging from nine-pounders to thirty-sixes, 15 brass mortars, 5458 shells, 11,077 cannon balls, sundry fusees, gun carriages and ordnance tools, but only 24 casks of powder. Also "part of a Cask of Spirits," the sailors and Marines having helped themselves to the rest. These lads overindulged themselves, with the result that many came down with "tropical fever" in the passage home and were of no further use to the Navy.

Carrying these valuable munitions for the Army, together with three important prisoners—the Lieutenant Governor, his secretary and a Tory councillor of South Carolina—Commodore Hopkins ordered anchors aweigh on 17 March 1776, with Block Island Channel off Rhode Island as destination. The ships had a rough passage, with a great deal of northerly wind and rain. By 3 April they were on soundings south of Montauk Point, Long Island.

4. The Fight with H.M.S. "Glasgow"

Since the spring of 1775, Admiral Graves had kept a detachment of his fleet in Narragansett Bay under Captain Wallace in H.M.S. *Rose*, hoping to check the privateers that were beginning to swarm out of Newport, Providence and Bristol. These British ships had a very unhappy time. Armed boats fired upon them at night; inhabitants were forbidden by the Assembly, under pain of death, to supply them with provisions; and if they selected a sheltered anchorage, the local patriots would roll up a cannon or two and render it untenable. As Commodore Hopkins's fleet approached Block Island on 4 April, it encountered two small vessels of this force, armed schooner *Hawk* and bomb brig *Bolton*, and captured both. "We had at sunset 12 sail," wrote Captain Nicholas; "a very pleasant evening."

The following day, too, was pleasant, but not the night. The fleet cruised south of Block Island in hope of picking up more prizes. At sunset it stood offshore before a light northwest wind. The Commodore, expecting to make more easy pickings, formed scouting disposition, two columns abreast. Brig *Cabot* took the lead in the larboard or easterly column, followed closely (about a hundred yards) by flagship *Alfred*. The starboard or westerly column, about a quarter of a mile distant, consisted of brig *Andrew Doria* and ship *Columbus*. Close behind these four sailed sloop *Providence;* and at a greater distance schooners *Fly* and *Wasp,* escorting the prizes taken the previous day.

At 1:00 A.M. April 6, when about twenty miles southeast of Block Island, with a nearly full moon riding high and wind from the north, *Andrew Doria* sighted a ship to leeward, crossing the formation's bows. It was a safe assumption that she was enemy, and she turned out to be H.M.S. *Glasgow,* 20 guns, Captain Tryingham Howe RN, carrying dispatches from Newport to Charleston. The word passed around the fleet and each ship went to general quarters; but Commodore Hopkins made no attempt to form line of battle, for which he had plenty of time before the enemy came within range. He issued not one order during the action, but left it to each captain to fight as he considered best—"helter-skelter," as Captain Biddle put it.

In that respect, the fight that followed reminds one in miniature of the Battle off Samar on 25 October 1944 when Admiral Kurita was so flabbergasted at encountering Admiral Sprague's escort carriers that he, too, committed his ships piecemeal and was defeated by a greatly inferior force. And, by a curious coincidence, Commodore Hopkins's battle, the earliest fleet action by the Continental Navy, took place only a few miles from the last fight of the United States Navy against Germany in World War II, the battle of 5-6 May 1945 off Block Island, in which U.S.S. *Atherton* and *Moberly* sank *U-853.*

H.M.S. *Glasgow* sighted the fleet "of seven or eight sail" on her weather (starboard) beam about the same time that Captain Biddle of *Andrew Doria* clapped his spyglass on her. Captain Howe at once brought his ship about on the port tack and stood toward the fleet, which he did not yet know to be hostile. Commodore Hopkins maintained course and formation. Within half an hour *Glasgow* was nearly alongside and within pistol shot of *Cabot,* a lightly-armed brig commanded by the Commodore's son, which led his larboard column. Upon being hailed from *Glasgow* and asked what ships were in her company, Captain John B. Hopkins answered, apparently in the hope of scaring the Englishman, "The *Columbus* and *Alfred,* a 22-gun frigate." At that moment a zealous Marine in *Cabot's* maintop punctuated the Captain's reply by hurling a hand grenade at

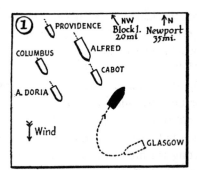

1:00 A.M. GLASGOW sights fleet, comes about on port tack and stands toward CABOT.

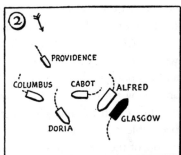

1:45 A.M. GLASGOW, having knocked out CABOT, is hotly engaged by ALFRED.

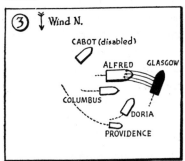

2:15 A.M. ALFRED falls broadside to fire and is raked. DORIA engages GLASGOW. PROVIDENCE comes about to cross her stern.

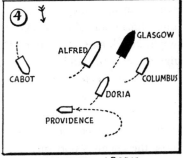

2:50 A.M. ALFRED and DORIA are engaging GLASGOW, COLUMBUS just getting into action.

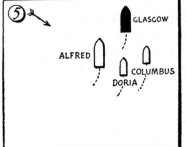

3:00 A.M. Wind shifts to NW. GLASGOW heads for Newport pursued by ALFRED, DORIA and COLUMBUS.

Action of Commodore Hopkins's Fleet with H.M.S. GLASGOW.

6 April, 1776.

Glasgow's deck, which touched off the battle. Immediately after, the brig's weak broadside of six-pounders was discharged at the enemy. *Glasgow* answered with two broadsides of nine-pounders, which wounded Captain Hopkins, killed the master and several men, and temporarily disabled *Cabot*. All she could do was to sheer off and allow flagship *Alfred* to come up broadside to the enemy.

Alfred, with 20 nine-pounders and 10 six-pounders, should have been able to take care of *Glasgow*; and Lieutenant Jones was in charge of the lower gundeck, directing the fire of the nine-pounder battery whose gunners he had trained. Presently the two vessels were hurling broadsides at each other. A lucky shot from *Glasgow* carried away *Alfred's* wheel-block and the lines that led to the tiller. She became unmanageable and fell off broadside to the wind, so that the Englishman was able to rake her fore and aft, holing her under water, knocking chunks out of the mainmast and cutting up her rigging. Several minutes passed before *Alfred's* crew could rig new steering gear and bring her under control.

In the meantime, Captain Biddle was doing his best to get *Andrew Doria* into the fight. First he had to tack to avoid a collision with drifting *Cabot*, then alter course to avoid *Alfred*; but he managed to close the enemy's port quarter and engage him briskly. *Columbus* was blanketed by the other ships so that her sails would not draw, and Captain Whipple was slow in working her into the fight. Sloop *Providence* never did engage.

The battle continued for three glasses—one hour and a half—according to the Commodore's and several other accounts; but Captain Biddle, when he read this in the newspapers, snorted, "They must mean half-minute glasses!" *Columbus* finally managed to work up within range, on *Glasgow's* starboard quarter, raking her as she crossed her stern; but her gunners aimed so wild that they did the Englishman no damage. Captain Howe, expecting that he was about to be boarded and overcome by sheer numbers, now disengaged and bore away for Newport "with the whole fleet" (actually only three sail) "within Musket shot on our Quarters and Stern." An American prisoner on board *Glasgow* stated that her hull was damaged, that she had ten shots through her mainmast, 110 holes in her mainsail, 88 in her foresail, 52 in her mizzen staysail, some spars carried away, "and her rigging cut to pieces"; yet she managed to make good her escape. Captain Howe brought stern-chaser guns to bear on the Americans, who occasionally yawed in order to bring their broadsides to bear on him, but to no avail. After a pursuit that lasted until well after daylight, Commodore Hopkins made signal to come about and steer SSW, in order to secure disabled *Cabot* and the prizes. That was his only wise order of the day. Had he carried the chase much farther he would have run into the jaws of several British warships standing out of Newport to cover *Glasgow's* retirement.

It seems odd that none of the three Continental ships could catch up with damaged *Glasgow*; but "a stern chase is a long chase," according to old naval lore, and Hopkins's ships were probably logy from the heavy cannon they had loaded at Nassau, and foul from their sojourn in southern waters.

Casualties were surprisingly light, considering how close the action was fought; the shooting on both sides must have been very, very bad. *Glasgow* lost only one man killed and three wounded—all by United States Marines' musketry, not by cannon shot. *Alfred* lost a lieutenant of Marines and five men killed and six wounded; *Cabot* had her master and three Marines killed and seven wounded; *Columbus*, one man wounded.

The Commodore at least accomplished his self-appointed mission. He got his entire fleet, including the prizes, safely into New London on 8 April; whilst H.M.S. *Glasgow* was so badly damaged as to be sent home for repairs.

He was congratulated by Congress on his success, and on "the Spirit and Bravery shown by the men." His expedition was hailed by the American press as a great victory. The Salem *Gazette* even got out a special broadside on the expedition, headed "Good News for America," and a local poet produced an ode about Hopkins ruling the waves and Neptune resigning his crown and trident to Congress!

But the men who had done the fighting were disgusted. Captain Biddle wrote to a friend that although the Commodore "could not help the action being brought on, . . . a more imprudent, ill conducted Affair never happened." Paul Jones, later, would have agreed; but on 14 April he wrote to Joseph Hewes:

> I have the pleasure in assuring you that the Commr. in Chief is respected thro' the Fleet and I verily believe that the Officers and men in general would go to any length to execute his orders. It is with pains that I confine this plaudit to an individual. I should be happy in extending it to any *Captain* and Officer in the service—praise is certainly due to some—but alas! there are Exceptions. It is certainly for the Intrest of the Service that a Cordial interchange of Civilities should subsist between Superiour and Inferiour Officers—and therefore it is bad policy in Superiours to behave toward their inferiours indiscriminately as tho' they were of a lower Species. This is a Conduct too much in Fashion in our Infant Fleet—the ill Consequence of this is Obvious. Men of liberal Minds, who have long been Accustomed to Command, can Ill brook being thus set at nought by others not Posted to Claim to the monopoly of sense. The Rude ungentle treatment which they experience creates such heartburnings as are no wise consonant with that Chearful ardour and spirit which ought ever to be the Characteristick of an Officer. And therefore whoever thinks himself hearty in the service is widely mistaken when he adopts such a line of conduct in order to prove it—for to be well obeyed it is necessary to be Esteemed.

He meant Captain Saltonstall, of course. Within two years, Paul Jones's officers in *Ranger* were making similar complaints about him.

Captains Saltonstall and Whipple and several junior officers, but not Jones, were summoned to Philadelphia for an informal investigation. The Marine Committee, after quizzing them, reported to Congress that the complaints against Saltonstall were not well founded, and "that the charge against Captain Whipple amounts to nothing more than a rough, indelicate mode of behaviour to his Marine officers." Whipple must have been a tough character indeed. He stood a court-martial at his own request to defend himself against the charge of cowardice in not getting *Columbus* earlier into the fight, and was acquitted. Captain Hazard of sloop *Providence*, who had accumulated a mass of misdemeanors, including the embezzlement of his vessel's stores, was found guilty on several counts and broken. John Paul Jones sat on both courts-martial; and it was to him, on 10 May 1776, Commodore Hopkins entrusted the command of sloop *Providence*, with the temporary rank of captain.

Paul Jones accepted this command with alacrity. The mental reservations as to independence with which he had enlisted in 1775 had vanished. It was now evident that independence would be declared shortly, that the war would last a long time, and that Congress was planning to create a respectable Navy.

IV

First
Independent
Commands

May-December 1776

1. Lieutenant Jones Tells How to Run the Navy

On 10 May 1776, when Paul Jones received from Commodore Hopkins the command of sloop *Providence*, the fleet was in Narragansett Bay. It had sailed thither from New London after landing the captured ordnance. About two hundred sailors, discharged at New London owing to overindulgence in the tropical delights of Nassau, had
been replaced by soldiers from Washington's army, then en route
from Boston to New York. The General now wanted his men back,
and the first independent mission of Captain Jones was to lift about a
hundred of them to New York.

While awaiting a fair wind in New York to return to Narragansett
Bay, Captain Jones wrote an important letter to his friend and patron Joseph Hewes. It contains his oft-quoted statement (which generations of midshipmen have been required to memorize) as to the

qualifications of a naval officer. It shows what may appear to be an undue concern for rank and seniority, and an unfortunate tendency to criticize his superior officers. But it must be remembered that, unlike other captains in the Navy, Paul Jones had no family, friends or neighbors to thrust him forward. He had hardly taken root in Virginia when the war broke out, and the Virginia members of Congress cared nothing for him. He rightly suspected that in the competition for naval and military appointments he would be sunk unless Joseph Hewes kept him in view. He was anxious for his future, since he had merely oral orders from Commodore Hopkins to command sloop *Providence* with temporary rank. And he knew that Congress was building a fine new fleet of frigates, one of which he naturally yearned to command. It is in the light of these conditions and circumstances that the letter should be read.

> On board the Sloop *Providence*
> N. York 19th May 1776

Sir

I had the honour of writing you the history of our Cruise in the Fleet from the Capes of Delaware 'till our Arrival at N. London the 14th Ult^a inclosing an inventory of all the stores taken at N. Providence &^{ca}

The letter contained a particular account of the action with the *Glascow* in an Extract from the *Alfred's* Log Book. It also contained some free thoughts on Certain Characters in the Fleet. It was inclosed to Mr Sproat, and by ill luck fell into hands not the most agreeable on its way to the Post Office, from which circumstance I much fear it hath miscarried—for, I have just now parted from Captn Lenox* and tho' he is late from Philadelphia he hath no account of any letters from me to his Uncle Mr Sproat.

I now inclose you the minutes of two Court Martials held on board the *Alfred*, the Evidences at large excepted. These minutes have not yet been seen in print. In Consequence of

---

* Robert Lenox, David Sproat's clerk and nephew, also a native of Kirkcudbright.

the last Trial I was ordered to take the Command of this Vessel the 10th Curr! I arrived here yesterday afternoon in 36 hours from Rhode Island with a return of upwards of 100 men besides Officers which Gen! Washington lent to the Fleet at N. London. I left the *A. Doria* & *Cabot* at Rhode Island ready to sail together on a four Weeks Cruize. What will become of the *Alfred* & *Columbus* heaven only knows—the Seamen have been so very Sickly since the Fleet returned to the Continent, that it will be Impossible to man them without others can be entered. I have landed Gen! Washington's Soldiers, and shall now apply to Shipping men, if any can be Obtained but it appears that the Seamen almost to a man had entered into the army before the Fleet was set on Foot, and I am well informed that there are four or five thousand Seamen now in the Land Service.

The Unfortunate Engagement with the *Glascow* seems to be a general reflection on the Officers of the Fleet. But a little reflection will set the matter in a true light—for no Officer who acts under the Eye of a Superiour and who doth not stand charged by that Superiour for Cowardice or misconduct can be blamed on any Occassion whatever. For my own part I wish a General Enquiry might be made respecting the Abilities of Officers in all Stations and then the Country would not be Cheated.

I may be wrong but in my opinion a Captain of the Navy ought to be a man of Strong and well connected Sense with a tolerable Education, a Gentleman as well as a Seaman both in Theory and Practice—for, want of learning and rude Ungentle Manners are by no means the Characteristick of an Officer. I have been led into this Subject on feeling myself hurt as an Individual by the Censures that have been indiscriminately thrown out—for altho' my station confined me to the *Alfred's* lower Gun Deck where I commanded during the Action—and tho' the Commodores letter which hath been published says "all the Officers in the *Alfred* behaved well"—Yet Still the Publick blames me among others for not taking the Enemy.

I declined the Command of this Sloop at Philadelphia—nor should I now have accepted it had it not been for the Rude

Unhappy Temper of my late Commander—I now reflect with Pleasure that I had Philosophy sufficient to avoid Quarreling with him—and that I even Obtained his blessing at Parting. May he soon become of an Affable even disposition, and may he find pleasure in Communicating Happiness around him.

There is little Confidence to be placed in reports Otherwise the Lieutenents of the Fleet might have reason to be Uneasier when they are told that the several Committees have orders to appoint all the Officers for the New Ships except only the Captains. I cannot think that they will be so far overlooked who have at first stept forth and Shewn at least a Willingness—nor can I suppose that my own Conduct will in the Esteem of the Congress subject me to be superseded in favour of a Younger Officer especially one who is said not to Understand Navigation—I mean the Lieutenant of the *Cabot* who was put in as Comm.ᵉ of the *Fly* at Reedy Island after I had declined it. I was then told that no new Commission would be given—and I considered her as a paltry message Boat fit to be Commanded by a Midshipman. But on my appointment to the *Providence* I was indeed Astonished to find my seniority Questioned— the Commodore told me he must refer to the Congress—I have rec.ᵈ no New Commission—I wish the matter in dispute may first be cleared up. I will Chearfully abide by whatever you may think is right—at the same time I am ready at any time to have my pretentions enquired into by men who are Judges.

When I applied for a Lieutenancy I hoped in that rank to gain much useful knowledge from men of more experience than myself—I was however mistaken for instead of gaining information I was obliged to inform others. I formed an Exercise and trained the men so well to the Great Guns in the *Alfred* that they went thro' the motions of Broadsides & Rounds as Exactly as Soldiers generally perform the Manual Exercise.

When I get what men are to be had here, I am ordered back to Providence for further Instructions. The Sloop must be hove down, and considerably repaired and refitted before she can proceed properly on any Cruise. I should esteem myself happy in being sent for to Philadelphia to act under the more immediate direction of Congress especially in one of the new Ships. I must rely on your interest herein.

The largest and I think by far the best of the Frigates was Launched the day after I left Providence—but from what I can learn neither of them will equal the Philadelphia ships. I left the *Columbus* heaving down and the *Alfred* hauling to the Wharf. I send this by the Commodores Steward who hath leave to visit his wife at Phil.ª and will call on you on his return in a day or two. I expect that he will overtake me here if I succeed in getting men—if not he will follow me to Rhode Island and Providence. May I hope for the honour of a letter from you by his hands—it will most singularly oblige me and greatly add to the favours already Conferred on

Sir
Your much obliged
and very humble Servant
Jnº P. Jones

If you have not recᵈ my last I will send a Copy if desired.

After returning to Providence, Captain Jones hove down his sloop on the banks of the river. This operation, which had to be done to wooden ships every few months in order to cleanse their bottoms of weed and barnacles, required expert handling. All ballast, cannon and heavy stores were removed, upper masts taken down, the vessel run onto a smooth sand beach or mud flat near high tide, and rolled over on her bilge by means of tackles attached to trees or bollards ashore, so that half her bottom was exposed at low water. When one side was cleansed and painted, the ship's position was reversed and the process repeated. Then the vessel was reballasted, rearmed, rerigged, and floated. If the heaving down was not done properly, she might get so bogged down in the mud as to be immovable until a spring tide, or she might be capsized by a squall and her hull badly damaged.

Between cruises in the sloop, Paul Jones managed to have a fairly good time ashore. To Captain Whipple of Providence, one of the friends he had made in the Hopkins fleet, he wrote later, "You have been very unkind in not telling me a Word about our agreeable Widow, or my little affair of the Heart at Providence." The names of these ladies do not appear, and they were soon forgotten.

Under the Commodore's orders, on 13 June, Captain Jones attempted to escort *Fly,* carrying New Providence cannon for Washington's army to Fishers Island at the entrance to Long Island Sound, where she would be relieved by an escort from New London. Two tries were thwarted by British cruisers which chased the two little vessels back into Narragansett Bay, but the third attempt succeeded. Jones then picked up merchant vessels at Stonington to escort to Newport. In so doing he went out of his way to rescue from the fangs of H.M.S. *Cerberus* a brigantine bringing military stores from Hispaniola, which that British frigate was chasing. The details are not recorded; probably *Providence* engaged the frigate until the brigantine could get into shoal water, and then escaped herself by one of the quick maneuvers that fore-and-afters can make in comparison with square-riggers.

Next, sloop *Providence* was sent to Boston to escort a convoy of colliers to Philadelphia, where she arrived 1 August, having successfully evaded the fleet of Admiral Lord Howe which was escorting General Billy Howe's army from Halifax to New York.

The call at Philadelphia gave Jones a much desired opportunity to mend his political fences. Congress was sitting, and Joseph Hewes saw to it that he met the Naval (now renamed the Marine) Committee. He was introduced to John Hancock the chairman, and to Robert Morris, who, in addition to his other capacities, had a firm grasp of maritime affairs. Jones evidently anticipated that his friend Hewes would not always be available, and during his next cruise began sending confidential letters to Morris, even asking Hewes to tell Morris about the "very great misfortune" (the Tobago mutiny) "which brought me into North America."

As a result of these personal contacts, Paul Jones obtained a regular captain's commission from Congress, dated 8 August 1776. And the Marine Committee gave him the choice of two vessels in which to sail on an independent mission, as he had requested. The first was the brigantine rescued from H.M.S. *Cerberus;* she had been taken into the Continental Navy and renamed *Hampden.* But Jones had observed that she was a slow sailer, and decided to stick to sloop *Providence.* He had got used to her fore-and-aft rig; she was fast, handy, and took the seas well; he liked her crew, and her armament of 12 four-pounders was sufficient for his purposes.

2. Independent Cruise in Sloop "Providence"

It was a proud day for Captain Jones when he received the following orders direct from the Marine Committee of the Continental Congress:

In Marine Committee
Philad:ᵃ August 6ᵗʰ 1776

Sir

We have ordered the Provisions & Stores you requested, to be sent on board the Sloop *Providence* which you Command under Authority of the United States of America, so that the said Sloop being now ready for Sea, you are to proceed immediately on a Cruize against our Enemies & we think in & about the Lattitude of Bermuda may prove the most favourable ground for your purpose.

Herewith we deliver you an extract from the Journals of Congress respecting the Navy Prizes &c by which you will know with precision what Vessells can be made Prizes and which not.* You have also herewith a list of the Continental Agents in each State & to some of them your Prizes must be addressed according to the Port they arrive in. Your Cruize may be for Six Weeks, two or three Months just as Provisions,

---

*The latest regulations of Congress were of 23 March 1776, to the effect that all ships and cargoes belonging to inhabitants of Great Britain or any ship carrying supplies to the "ministerial armies" shall be lawful prize.

Water & other Circumstances point out to be best. If you gain any material Intelligence you must put into the nearest port of the Continent & dispatch an Express to us with the same. You must by all opportunitys transmit us an Account of your proceedings & of such Occurances as you meet with. You are to be particularly attentive to protect, aid & assist all Vessells & property belonging to these States or the Subjects thereof. It is equally your duty to Seize, take, Sink, Burn or destroy that of our Enemys. Be carefull of the Sloop her Stores and Materials, use your People well thereby recommending the American Naval Service to all who engage in it, and we also recommend Humane kind Treatment of your Prisoners.

These things duely observed will recommend you to the attention & regard of this Committee

We are Sir
Your hble servants

JOHN HANCOCK	GEO: READ	FRAˢ LEWIS
ROBᵀ MORRIS	GEO WALTON	FRAˢ HOPKINSON
JOSEPH HEWES	ARTHUR MIDDLETON	Wᴹ WHIPPLE

To
JOHN PAUL JONES ESQᴿ
COMMANDER OF THE SLOOP *Providence*

This cruise was the happiest and most rewarding of Paul Jones's naval career. He had a crew of over seventy men, the best (he declared in later years) that he ever commanded. He was on his own, with nobody to give him orders once he had dropped down the Delaware. He had plenty of sport, made numerous prizes, and at last was ahead of the game financially.

He had a tight little vessel under him. The sloop, formerly owned by John Brown of Providence and flagship of the Rhode Island Navy in 1775, was deep, beamy and fast. The model of her, by Robert I. Innes, of which we show a photograph, was constructed not from her plans or pictures, since none exist, but from the model-maker's knowledge of contemporary vessels of that rig. In my opinion, it is substantially correct. Following this model, she would have been 70 feet long overall, not including a 39-foot bowsprit and flying jib boom, 20-foot beam, with 84-foot mast. She is rigged to carry a gaff-headed fore-and-aft mainsail, three headsails (fore staysail, jib and flying jib), a big square topsail and a small, square topgallant sail. Probably she could also drop a square course from the topsail yard when running free, and both yards were rigged to carry studding-sails. Eight of her four-pounder cannon were mounted on the open gun deck, and the other four on the quarterdeck; in addition she carried swivel guns on the bulwarks. The captain's and officers' cabins, together with the galley and wardroom, were under the quarterdeck; the enlisted men slept in hammocks slung on the berth deck below the gun deck, which had no ventilation except what came through the hatches in fair weather. When all hands were below decks, she was as crowded as the old *Mayflower*.

The officers of *Providence* under Captain Jones were two first lieutenants, William Grinnell and John Peck Rathbun, master William Hopkins, and surgeon Henry Tillinghast, all from Providence or the vicinity. The cruise began with only one midshipman, Joe Hardy, on board, but Jones picked up another, Barney Gallagher, from a prize. Her muster roll shows 7 petty officers, 10 seamen, 3 boys, 13 Marines under Captain Matthew Parke USMC, whom Jones had met in *Alfred,* and 17 soldiers of the Rhode Island Brigade, which appears to have been a local amphibious organization. Just before sailing her complement was made up by the transfer of 6 petty officers, 3 seamen and 7 "landsmen" or ordinary seamen from sloop *Hornet*. These, with a few odd ratings, made a total of 73 officers and men, ample to sail and fight the sloop, and to provide prize crews. A majority of them were veterans of a few months' standing who had already served in Commodore Hopkins's fleet. Jones was always successful in persuading British prisoners to enlist with him; he obtained 28 more men, including a lieutenant and a midshipman, from prizes taken on this cruise.

Providence departed the Delaware Capes on 21 August 1776. Within a week she had captured the whaling brigantine *Britannia,* placed a prize crew on board, and sent her to Philadelphia. Dropping down to the latitude of Bermuda, on 1 September she fell in with a convoy of five sail, bound from Jamaica to New York, escorted by H.M. frigate *Solebay*, Captain Symonds, of 28 guns. The frigate chased *Providence* from 7:00 A.M. to 5:30 P.M., at the end of which she had worked up to within musket shot of the sloop's lee quarter and fired two nine-pounders. Jones showed his colors. "Upon this, they also hoisted American Colors, and fired guns to the Leeward," which was the old signal for "I am friendly." The ruse did not succeed, since Jones knew that no such vessel was in the United States Navy, and he escaped by a bold bit of ship handling.

Taking advantage of the sloop's nimbleness in maneuver, he bore away northeasterly before the wind, right across the frigate's bows, promptly setting all his "kites" (as seamen called the light sails), so that before the square-rigger could trim her yards, set studding sails and gather headway, *Providence* was beyond cannon range. Captain Symonds was so astounded by Jones's audacity that he failed to fire when the sloop lay athwart his bows, although she was then within pistol shot; and the nine-pounder balls that he fired subsequently went wild. "Our 'Hairbreadth Scape' and the saucy manner of making it must have mortified him not a little," wrote Jones to the Commodore. Obviously it did, since *Solebay* chased *Providence* until nightfall, and Captain Symonds says nothing about her escape in his log except that she "bore away."

A century later, Commander Stephen B. Luce USN took down from the lips of an old boatswain a ballad recounting a fictitious adventure of Paul Jones during his cruise in *Ranger*. But one verse of it must relate to this brush with H.M.S. *Solebay:*

> "Out booms! Out Booms!" our skipper cried.
>   "Out booms and give her sheet!"
> And the swiftest keel that was ever launched
>   Shot ahead of the British fleet.
> And amidst a thundering shower of shot
>   With stunsails hoisting away,
> Down the North Channel Paul Jones did steer
>   Just at the break of day.

On 3 September *Providence* took the Bermudian brigantine *Sea Nymph* (Francis Trimingham, master) bound from Barbados to London with a cargo of rum, sugar, ginger, oil, and "Twelve Pipes best particular London market Madeira wine." "The Brig is new & Sails very fast so that this is a pretty good prize," wrote Jones when dispatching her to Philadelphia. By the same conveyance he sent a personal letter to Robert Morris which proves that he was still brooding over rank and seniority. His captain's commission of 8 August, he says, should properly have been dated 10 May when the Commodore gave him command of *Providence;* if that is not done, he will have to yield seniority to men who were his junior in 1775, and he would rather "be fairly broke and dismissed the Service" than suffer such humiliation. The gift of a turtle, entrusted to the prize master of *Sea Nymph*, enforced this request; but Morris did nothing about the commission.

On 6 September *Providence* made a third capture, brigantine *Favourite* bound from Antigua to Liverpool with a cargo of sugar. A prize crew was placed on board, but when trying to sail her to a Continental port they encountered H.M.S. *Galatea*, which recaptured *Favourite* and took her into Bermuda.

For a week from 7 September not a sail was sighted by *Providence*. Captain Jones, deciding that most of the homeward bound British West Indiamen were now beyond his reach, and wanting both wood and water, decided to run north for Nova Scotia. Also, as he wrote to Morris, he hoped to recruit his crew, depleted by manning the prizes, with Bluenose fishermen. On 16-17 September he encountered a heavy gale which forced him to dismount his guns "and stick everything I had into the hold." Two days later he raised Sable Island, the so-called graveyard of the Atlantic, a hundred miles off the Nova Scotia coast.

On 20 September when (following United States Navy Regulations) *Providence* hove-to in order to give the crew a chance to catch fish, she sighted to windward a British frigate escorting a merchantman. The frigate bore down immediately. Paul Jones waited until she was within cannon shot, then cracked on sail; and, finding *Providence* much the faster on a quartering wind, "shortened sail to give him a wild goose chase, and tempt him to throw away powder and shot." When the frigate finally rounded-to in order to give *Providence* a broadside at extreme range, Captain Jones ordered a Marine to reply with a contemptuous musket shot. This recalls the "blurr with a trumpet" with which Sir Walter Raleigh replied to the forts at Cadiz. "Night, with her sable curtains, put an end to this famous exploit of English knight-erranty," wrote Jones.

Next morning the frigate was seen hull-down, standing toward Halifax; *Providence* made for Canso. She anchored in the harbor 22 September, took on wood and water, recruited several willing fishermen to fill the billets of men placed in charge of the prizes, burned an English fishing schooner in the harbor, sank another and made prize of a third. Captain Jones loaded that schooner with dried fish from the other two, and placed Midshipman Gallagher in charge as prizemaster. And he also picked up a fast sailing shallop for a tender.

A tender did not then mean a towed boat as it generally does today, but any small, light sailing vessel which was attached to a larger ship to serve her. A proper tender should be fast enough to keep up with her mother ship, but small enough to be towed if necessary. Tenders were used for many purposes—to reconnoiter, send messages, transfer men and prisoners between a ship and her prizes, recover men who fell overboard, run out an extra anchor, tow pulling boats and act as lighter for stores and ordnance. No captain on an independent cruise felt properly equipped without a tender to his ship; Paul Jones, when subsequently captain of *Ranger*, felt the lack of one keenly.

Having received intelligence at Canso that there was a small fleet of Jerseymen in the harbors of nearby Île Madame, Captain Jones sent the new tender and his own boat, both full of seamen, to investigate. In the harbors which he calls "Narrow Shock" and "Peter the Great" (his phonetic spelling of Arichat and Petitdegrat), the boats took the Jerseymen by surprise, and the entire lot surrendered. As

Jones had not enough people to man all these vessels, he made a deal with his captives, by virtue of which they kept schooners *Betsy* and *Hope* to take the Jersey fishermen home, and in return helped him fit out and rig the others as prizes.

This "business," as Jones calls it, had just been completed when a violent equinoctial gale made up on the night of 25 September. *Providence* rode it out successfully at the entrance to Arichat Harbor with both anchors and all cables, as did one of her prizes, 250-ton ship *Alexander*. But another, schooner *Sea Flower*, drove ashore and had to be burned, and schooner *Ebenezer*, taken at Canso, dragged onto a reef and broke up.

On the afternoon of 26 September *Providence* put to sea in company with her recent prizes which survived the gale: *Alexander*, *Kingston Packet* and *Success*. A fourth, a brigantine named *Defence* or *Defiance*, was saved from dragging ashore by a boat's crew from *Providence* which cut her cable, made sail and put to sea. *Providence* was now so short-handed that the Captain decided he had better make for home; and that he did, after taking one more prize, whaling sloop *Portland*. He entered Narragansett Bay with four prizes on 8 October, after a cruise of forty-nine days. The three vessels he had taken earlier in the voyage also reached port and were duly condemned. And Paul Jones prided himself on having ruined the English fishing fleet at Canso and Île Madame.

The fate of Midshipman Gallagher and the fishing schooner of which he was prizemaster illustrates the vicissitudes of naval warfare in 1776. His vessel was captured by privateer schooner *General Gates* of Salem, whose skipper, finding that she had no papers, judged her to be British and took Gallagher and his crew prisoner. A British warship then chased *Gates* into Petitdegrat and ran her ashore, where her crew and the prisoners took to the woods. The British man-of-war crew, helped by "all the exasperated inhabitants," rounded them up and carried them to Halifax. There they were confined in a prison hulk until October, when they were sent to Marblehead in a cartel, a prisoners' exchange ship under flag of truce.

3. Prize Money, Pay and Uniforms

Commodore Hopkins was still commander in chief of the Navy, but he had lost much of his prestige and authority. Summoned to Philadelphia, and examined before the Marine Committee of Congress, he found the Southern members furious with him for having ignored orders to operate in the Chesapeake and southward. And he was unable to explain his inactivity since the New Providence expedition. Congress censured him publicly for his conduct, yet confirmed him in his command! Captain Jones, in a flattering opening paragraph to his report on the encounter with H.M.S. *Solebay*, remarked that the "Admiral" (as he addressed Hopkins) was now "Gold from the Fire," fully vindicated. But he must have guessed that the Hopkins sun was setting; at least, that is how he acted.

Before departing on his next cruise, Jones wrote an important letter to Robert Morris. It was almost impossible, he said, to engage seamen for the Fleet in Narragansett Bay, because privateers offered them the full value of prizes they took, while the Navy had to be content with one third. Unless this is corrected, and "the private Emoluments of individuals in our Navy is made superiour to that in Privateers it never can become respectable—it never will become formadable. And without a Respectable Navy—alas America! . . . If our Enemies, with the best established and most formadable Navy in the Universe, have found it expedient to assign all Prizes to the Captors—how much more is such policy essential to our infant Fleet."

Wise words indeed, to which Congress listened. On 30 October 1776, it increased the captors' share of the net product of prize merchantmen, transports and storeships from one third to one half, and granted captors the entire value of a prize if it were a privateer or man-of-war.

This helped, but it did not go far enough. Competition with privateers and squabbles over prize money continued to bedevil Congress and the Navy throughout the war, and for many years after the war was over. What proportion of the captors' 50 per cent, for instance, should each officer and man have? And how divide prize money among a fleet? Congress on 6 January 1776 resolved that the captors' share of a prize be divided into twentieths. One twentieth (5 per cent) was to go to the commander in chief for prizes taken by ships "under his orders and command," two twentieths (10 per cent) to the captain, if cruising alone, or divided among all the captains of a fleet; three twentieths to be divided among captains of Marines, masters and Navy lieutenants; two-and-a-half twentieths (12½ per cent) to be shared equally by Marine lieutenants, masters' mates, surgeons, chaplains, chief gunners and chief carpenters; three twentieths to midshipmen and other warrant and petty officers (such as stewards, cooks and coxswains) and sergeants of Marines; and the remaining eight-and-one-half twentieths (42½ per cent) among the rest of the ship's company or (in case of a fleet) ships' companies.

This did not compare favorably with the British system, especially when one reflects that the twentieths were really fortieths, since 50 per cent of the net proceeds of a merchantman went to Congress. In the Royal Navy the captors took all, and the proceeds were divided thus: three eighths (37½ per cent) to captains, except that if a flag officer were present he took one eighth (12½ per cent); one eighth divided among lieutenants, masters and captains of Marines; one eighth to chaplains, chief petty officers and lieutenants of Marines; one eighth to midshipmen, master sailmakers and certain other petty officers; and the remaining two eighths (25 per cent) to able and ordinary seamen, cooks, stewards, bakers, Marines and anyone else doing duty.

Thus, suppose two merchant prizes of equal value were taken, one by an American, the other by a British warship. The captain USN would have only one fifth to one seventh the take of the captain RN; the next class, the masters, lieutenants and Marine captains, would get 7½ per cent in the United States Navy as against 12½ per cent for their opposite British numbers; and the lowest class, the seamen, would get 21¼ per cent in the United States Navy, whilst the British tars, dividing their share with cooks, stewards, swabbers, and so on, would take 25 per cent.

Then, what about prizes taken by vessels belonging to a fleet? All officers and men under Commodore Hopkins, before sailing for New Providence, signed an agreement that they would share equally the product of all prizes taken on the cruise, even those taken by a ship that separated from the rest. It would obviously be unfair for a small schooner like *Wasp* or *Fly* to have the same share as a ship like *Alfred* or *Columbus* which did most of the shooting and had a far bigger crew; but that is what the captains agreed to, and what Congress prescribed on 6 January 1776. The system in the Royal Navy, which Jones applied when he wore his pennant in *Bonhomme Richard*, was to establish a factor for each ship by multiplying the number of her crew by the sum of the calibers of the cannon that she mounted, said factor establishing the proportion by which each ship's share is determined. Thus, a ship with 150 men armed with 20 nine-pounders would rate 150 x 180, or 27,000; whilst a ship in the same fleet with 200 men, 20 nine-pounders and 10 twelve-pounders would rate 200 x 300 (180 + 120), or 60,000. If the total for the fleet added up to 270,000, the first ship would get 10 per cent and the second 45 per cent of the prize money.

The master of a warship and the master's mates, who shared in this division, were the men who directed the handling and sailing of the ship, as distinct from the lieutenants, who directed the gunnery and fighting. A master in this first United States Navy ranked as an officer and drew the same pay as a first lieutenant. * By the same token, the chief carpenter ("Chips") and chief sailmaker ("Sails") were very important people in the sailing Navy; the first had charge of the pumps and of making emergency repairs under fire; the second was in a sense the engineer of a sailing vessel, since he had to repair or make over her only power plant, the sails. The Marines played an essential rôle in close fighting and so rightly shared the prize money,

*The rank of master lasted in the U.S. Navy until 1870, when it was replaced by that of lieutenant junior grade.

which the seamen did not like; and everyone objected to the Commodore taking 5 per cent of every prize taken by his fleet offshore, while he lived comfortably on board flagship *Warren* in Newport Harbor or Providence River. One of Jones's objects in cruising under direct orders of the Marine Committee was to save that 5 per cent for himself. He insisted on keeping three twentieths of prize money when captain of *Ranger,* and was furious with a Continental agent who questioned his right to it.

Thus, prize money was extremely important to the Navy of the Revolution, indeed to all navies in days of sail. The net amounts of prize money shared by the great fleets of England and France were astounding. For instance, D'Estaing's fleet, in its expedition to North America and the West Indies in 1778-1779, shared 2,423,535 livres tournois—484,707 dollars in gold—prize money; and the total take of De Grasse's fleet in 1781-1782 was over three million livres. Paul Jones wrote to Joseph Hewes on 7 August 1777 that up to date he had "received little more than" three thousand dollars as his "share of prize Money." That strikes one as not too bad for eighteen months' naval service; anyway, it was enough so that Jones could live on his prize money alone, and even make advances from it to his seamen, while allowing his pay to accumulate. That was good judgment, as he finally got paid off in hard money instead of paper.

In comparison with prize money, naval wages and salaries were unimportant. The pay scale of the Continental Navy, established by Congress before the end of 1775, ranged from $6.66 per month for a common seaman and $8.00 per month for an able seaman up to $15.00 for a chief petty officer, $20.00 for a lieutenant, $21.33 for a surgeon and $32.00 for a captain. Commanding officers were also allowed $5.66 a month for subsistence while in port, but all officers paid their own mess bills at sea. The smaller vessels, under 10 guns, were commanded by a lieutenant, but his pay was not increased with his responsibility.

This pay scale was commensurate with that of the Continental Army, and in 1776 it probably had a greater purchasing power than United States Navy pay has today. A comparison of pay scales in the British and American Navies at that time is revealing. Every rating was better paid in America than in Great Britain (the American able seaman, for instance, got 1*s* 2¼*d* as against the British tar's 10¾*d*); but the British officers were very much better paid than the American. A captain RN got 8*s* per diem, a captain USN 4*s* 9½*d*; a lieutenant RN got 4*s* 8*d*; his American opposite number, 3*s*.* Congress, however, was prevailed upon—Jones being one of the chief prevailers—to raise officers' pay in November 1776. Lieutenants and masters thenceforth got $24.00 per month in the smaller (10 to 20 gunned) and $30.00 in the larger ships; captains, $48.00 and $60.00. This meant that until inflation set in, as it did about April 1777, the captain of a ship like *Alfred* was paid a shilling more per diem than the captain of a 5th-rate (32-gun) ship in the Royal Navy.

One great advantage of American bluejackets over British tars was a short and definite term of enlistment—twelve months—which Paul Jones thought very unfortunate; but it is unlikely that the Continental Navy could have been manned on any other terms. In the Royal Navy, both volunteers and impressed seamen were in for the duration of the war. It became so difficult to obtain recruits, even by the press gang, that the city council of Liverpool around 1780 offered bounties of five guineas to landsmen and ten guineas to able seamen of that city if they would enlist in the Royal Navy.

Naval uniforms were prescribed by Congress on 5 September 1776. For captains, a blue coat with red lapels, "slash cuff," stand-up collar, flat yellow buttons with anchors on them, red waistcoat with narrow gold lace, and blue breeches. Paul Jones is shown in this uniform coat in his portrait by Charles Willson Peale, but he is wearing a buff waistcoat. There was no uniform hat; officers wore the usual gentleman's three-cornered hat with a cockade affixed. Lieutenants and masters wore the same uniform as captains, except that they were not allowed gold lace on waistcoats, or slashed cuffs. Midshipmen were distinguished by red facings on the cuffs and red stitching on

---

* The British figures are for a 32-gun ship; the U.S. for 20 guns up. Jones gives the sterling equivalents to the American dollars before depreciation set in, and I have reduced them to daily pay because the fiscal month in the R.N. was 28 days, that in the U.S.N. 30 days.

the buttonholes of the uniform coat. All officers were entitled to wear one gilt epaulet on dress occasions, and were supposed to carry a sword on every occasion. Marine officers were given a dashing green coat faced with white, white breeches edged with green, and black garters; "green shirts for the men if they can be procured."

The adoption of the epaulet is interesting because it was a French naval fashion which did not become regulation in the British Navy until 1795. Epaulets were favored by short men like Nelson and Jones as appearing to increase their height.

Paul Jones, always a stickler for neatness and proper *tenue* on board ship, convened a group of naval officers at Boston in March 1777 to discuss a change in the uniform. Their decision is described in a paper endorsed by him, "Uniform dress for the Navy agreed to at Boston by the Major Part of the Captains." The new captains' dress uniform is a dark blue coat with white linings and lapels and stand-up collar; white waistcoat, breeches and stockings. One gold epaulet inscribed with a rattlesnake device and DON'T TREAD ON ME, to be worn on the right shoulder; a black cockade in the hat, gold rattlesnake buttons and embroidered buttonholes, and gold lace edging the coat and waistcoat. Undress uniform the same, except that the coats have "Frock Backs and turn down white Collars." Lieutenants omit the gold lace, embroidery and epaulet, and wear a short "coatee" or jacket for undress uniform, and a plain anchor on their buttons. Masters and midshipmen the same as lieutenants, but with no lapels to their coats.

This was a much smarter uniform than the blue and red of 1776, and had the advantage of looking so much like the British naval uniform that an American ship could use deceptive tactics at close quarters, impossible if her officers wore red waistcoats and blue breeches. Congress never formally adopted this new uniform, but it was generally worn, especially by Jones. He evidently dressed the officers of *Bonhomme Richard* in the blue uniform, as an Englishman who had a close look wrote that "all the officers on the quarter deck were drest in Blew turn'd up in white the same as in the British Navy." Jones's epaulets, both in his portraits and in the Houdon

CAPTAIN JONES'S ACHIEVEMENT OF ARMS
PAINTED IN 1776 OR EARLY 1777

ARMS: Jones (gold stag, red field) quartering Paul (blue fess, ermine tails).
FLAGS: Upper left, Grand Union Flag, red, white and blue stripes; upper right,
British Red Ensign; lower left: blue command pendant; lower right: Pine Tree
Flag, thirteen red, white and blue stripes.

A FRENCH 40-GUN FRIGATE COMING ABOUT, BY OZANNE

In this maneuver the vessel F in the picture (D in plan) comes about from starboard to port tack and from ENE to SSW, following dotted line A-B-C. The direction of the wind, SE, is shown by the arrow, which flies with it. At position F (D in plan), she has just begun the maneuver and is headed E with headsails, forecourse and foretopsail shivering. At position G (E in plan), she has completed "Mainsail Haul" and is making sternway, with sails on foremast still aback. At position H (C in plan), she has completed "Let Go and Haul" and is making headway on port tack with all sails drawing, but not yet braced up sharp on her new course SSW.

Captain Jones, from Sketch by Unknown Artist
at Theater in Amsterdam, 9 October 1779

bust, show thirteen small stars; I have seen no evidence that the rattlesnake design was ever used.

No attempt was made at any time during the war to prescribe a uniform for enlisted men; but Paul Jones eventually did something about it. The same Englishman whom we have quoted on the officers' uniforms in *Bonhomme Richard,* reported that "the whole crew were clean drest." A clue to what their dress may have been appears in a description of ten deserters from *Ariel* in 1780. Each one wore a "brown jacket and round hat." And all common seamen of that day wore long baggy trousers; knee breeches were proper only for gentlemen and officers.

4. Handling the Square-riggers

Before we are further involved in Paul Jones's fights and stratagems, a few paragraphs on ship handling are in order. We must keep in mind that no sailing vessel can sail directly into the wind. The most modern and advanced racing cutter, such as the twelve-metre *Columbia* which defended the *America's* Cup in 1958, cannot profitably sail closer to the wind than 35 degrees—about 3⅛ points of the compass—and that in a moderate breeze and fairly smooth water. Even she must zigzag, that is, tack, to fetch a mark directly to windward. The average cruising yacht of today can seldom sail closer than four points (45 degrees). In Paul Jones's day, a sloop such as *Providence* could probably do almost as well as that, but a square-rigger could not expect to do better than six points. In other words, 67½ degrees was the nearest to the wind that *Ranger* and the new frigates could count on sailing.

Any modern yachtsman, with a little practice, could handle a sloop like *Providence*. He could slap her about from one tack to another by shoving the helm hard down and trimming the headsails. But in a smart breeze he could wear ship (change the sail from one side to the other *before* the wind, as distinct from coming about through the *eye* of the wind) only with great caution, lest the big main boom and mainsail "take charge" and smash things up.

A square-rigged ship is handled very differently. Bringing her about through the eye of the wind is a complicated maneuver which always runs the risk of the ship's being taken aback and getting "in irons." It is much easier to wear ship (or jibe, as it is now called), but in a strong wind and heavy sea that maneuver is dangerous, because the ship has to go through the trough of the sea twice and run the risk of being pooped when she is directly before the wind. Under ordinary circumstances, a prudent shipmaster who (for example) wished to tack from ENE to SSW in a SE wind, would come about from the starboard to the port tack, passing through the wind's eye in so doing.

We are fortunate to have Paul Jones's own station bill "for working ship" that he made out for *Alliance*. This proves that the maneuver was even more complicated in those days than for square-riggers in the latest days of sail. She not only had all their complicated gear —braces, sheets, tacks, clewlines, buntlines and halyards—but two backstays for each mast, and a crowfoot-shaped bowline on every leach (edge) of the larger square sails to keep them taut and flat.

Jones stationed one officer and the boatswain on the forecastle to handle the jib sheets, "to see the Brest Backstays let go & the others well set up as soon as the Headsails are Hauled." An officer stood on each side of the foremast, with hands ready to cast off and haul in tacks and sheets, to let go the lee staysail sheets, and to handle the fore bowlines. Two officers stationed on the lee side of the ship's waist are "to see the Main Tack and Lee Main Topsail Bowline well manned; and when the Head sails are haul'd to shift sides and see [that the] fore and staysail sheets [are] haul'd aft." Each brace of the mainsail and main topsail yards has a stout crew ready under an officer for "Mainsail haul!" The crojick (mizzen lower course) and mizzen topsail braces, hardly less important, will be hauled by other hands who also have the duty to let go the "Weather Brest Backstays" when she comes up into the wind, see that the lee ones are set up, and that the mizzen staysail sheets are shifted. The captains of fighting tops have to overhaul a good part of this gear so that it does not foul; especially to see "Backstays borne aft clear of the Top."

Here is how you brought the ship about, using for example a southeast wind, so that she has to be brought from ENE to SSW. First, the helmsman is instructed to give her a good "rap full" so as to afford maximum headway, while the seamen trim the yards as close as possible to the axis of the hull, and haul in taut the sheet of the fore-and-aft driver or spanker on the mizzenmast so as to kick her stern around. (Nowadays, with short crews, the mainsail and crojick would be clewed up to save strength, but Jones didn't have to do that.) The officer of the deck shouts "Ready, about!" and the boatswains pass the word by piping. The man at the wheel turns it hard—all the way—to starboard, which puts the helm that connects with the rudderhead to leeward, and when he has done so, he sings out, "Helm's hard a-lee, sir!" The jib and staysail sheets, which trim the headsails, are let go. As the rudder brings the ship up into the SE wind, the yards point directly into it, the sails shiver, and the lines, with tension released, dance about wildly. As soon as the ship's head has passed through the eye of the wind and is heading about SE by S, the port jib and staysail sheets are hauled taut; and their action, added to that of the foresail, fore topsail and fore-topgallant sail, which are now back-winded—that is, blown against the mast—act as levers to throw the ship's bow away from the wind onto the desired new course. As soon as the wind catches the starboard leach (edge) of the square mainsail or maintopsail, the officer of the deck cries, "Mainsail haul!" This is the great moment in coming about, and that is why John Masefield chose it as the title of one of his books. All hands not otherwise employed then lay ahold of the lee braces on the main and mizzen yards and haul them around an arc of about seventy degrees until the sails catch the wind from the port side. If done at just the right moment, the wind helps whip them around. By this time, unless the ship is very sharp and smart and the sea smooth, her headway has been lost and she begins to make sternway. It is therefore necessary to shift her helm so she will not get in irons.

The next important order is "Let Go and Haul!" This means to let go fore braces and sheets, and haul the foreyards, whose sails have been flat aback all this time, until the wind catches them on their after surfaces. The weather jib and staysail sheets are now let go and the lee ones hauled taut, and all other sails are trimmed so that she gathers headway and shoots ahead on her new course, SSW. In a warship such as *Alfred*, with a big crew, this process would take at least ten minutes, probably more. It was quicker to wear ship, as the vessel never lost headway during the process; but because her entire course had to be reversed she lost distance in wearing.

Paul Jones usually tried to get the "weather gauge"—a position to windward—of any ship he intended to fight. It enabled him, if he could forge ahead, as he might do by "blanketing" the enemy's sails, to cross her bows and rake her, or do the same thing in reverse by crossing her stern. But in a strong wind that made the ship heel over the lee gauge was preferable because lee gun ports were apt to be too close to the water for the lower guns on that side to be used.

A square-rigger was far more flexible than a fore-and-aft-rigged vessel. You could check her speed or bring her to a standstill by backing her fore topsail, and then leap ahead by swinging the fore yards so that all sails drew again. You could sail her sideways, or even stern-first, by a proper adjustment of the sails. In a narrow channel where there was little room to maneuver, you could even tack stern-first, which was called "box-hauling." I have heard of a United States frigate being box-hauled through the entrance of Narragansett Bay. Paul Jones was an expert at getting the most out of a ship, using the wind to best advantage, as we shall see when he maneuvered *Alfred*, and still more in his battles with H.M.S. *Drake* and *Serapis*.

5. "Alfred"'s Raid on Nova Scotia

In the same letter of 17 October 1776 to Robert Morris from which we have already quoted, Captain Jones suggested that a naval expedition be sent promptly to the West Coast of Africa to destroy

England's African trade. A part of his plan was to occupy the island of St. Helena, in order to capture the British East Indiamen which called there on their passage home.

Commodore Hopkins had other and less ambitious plans for Jones. Two months earlier the Marine Committee had ordered the Commodore to send *Alfred, Columbus, Cabot* and *Hampden* on a six months' cruise to destroy the British fishery at Newfoundland, capture storeships bound to Quebec, take the Hudson's Bay fleet returning to England, show the flag and flourish the Declaration of Independence in the French islands of St.-Pierre and Miquelon. Quite an order! Hopkins had as yet done nothing to comply, largely because he found it impossible to recruit sailors. The privateers, offering up to twelve and sixteen dollars a month against the Navy's eight dollars for able seamen, were getting all the men. Hopkins was so desperate that he tried to induce the Rhode Island General Assembly to lay an embargo on merchant ships and privateers until his own complements were filled; but the politicians turned him down. "I thought I had some Influence in the State I have lived so Long in," he wrote to the Marine Committee of Congress, "but now I find that Private Interest bears more sway."

The best that the Commodore could set on foot was the first part of the Marine Committee's plan. He ordered Captain Jones to take command of *Alfred* (Captain Saltonstall having been assigned to a new frigate) and, with *Hampden* in company, to raid Cape Breton. There, after releasing American prisoners who were being forced to work in the Sydney coal mines, he was to capture the British collier fleet upon which General Howe depended for fuel for his army at New York. Having done this, Jones might proceed to Newfoundland if it were not too late in the season.

Paul Jones embarked on this mission from Providence, Rhode Island, on 27 October 1776. He managed to increase *Alfred's* complement to 140 officers and men by taking everyone out of sloop *Providence* and her prizes. But before clearing Narragansett Bay he lost *Hampden*. Captain Hacker, who should have known those waters since (according to Jones) his only marine experience prior to 1775 was running a packet between Providence and Newport, managed to hit a "sunken rock" and damaged *Hampden* so badly that she could not proceed. Her officers and crew were then shifted to sloop *Providence,* which sailed in company with *Alfred* on 1 November. The discipline of the transferred crew was evidently none too good, since only a week earlier Captain Jones had presided over a court-martial to try *Hampden's* gunner, James Bryant, for having "collard and otherwise abused" Captain Hacker and challenged him to single combat. Bryant was dismissed from the Navy and deprived of his share of prize money.

Some idea of the food and drink supplied by the Navy in those days may be gained from Captain Jones's own list of the provisions that he sent on board sloop *Providence* from *Alfred* at the beginning of this cruise. The complement of *Providence* was 70 to 75 officers and men, and she was not supposed to be out for over two months. It is evident that Jones was treating his men far better than Navy regulations required.

> 13 tierces* and 42 barrels salt beef and pork
> 10 tierces and 53 barrels ship's bread [hardtack] and 500 pounds "Bread Baked out of Ship's Flour"; 10 barrels flour
> 1 tierce and 7 hogsheads pease
> 2 barrels "Sous'd Heads" [probably pickled pigs' heads]
> Two thirds of a cask of oatmeal [Jones probably wanted the other third for his own "parritch"]
> 453 gallons "Continental Rum"; 130 gallons W.I. rum
> 170 pounds coffee [a surprising luxury for those days]
> 118 gallons molasses; 4 barrels vinegar
> 14 bushels onions; 10 of turnips and 50 of potatoes
> 179 pounds cheese; 600 pounds butter
> 440 pounds brown sugar
> 219 pounds candles

---

* A tierce was a cask holding 42 gallons.

This second independent cruise afforded Captain Jones intense satisfaction, although the weather for the most part was tempestuous. He rejoiced at last to have command of a square-rigged warship with nobody to give him orders. Be it noted that he owed this command to Hopkins, and that, as evidence of their friendliness at that time, he took the Commodore's son Esek Hopkins Jr. on board as a volunteer.

Alfred first called at Tarpaulin Cove in the Elizabeth Islands, off Cape Cod. Anchored there was privateer *Eagle* of Rhode Island, which, as Jones knew, had enlisted deserters from the Navy. He boarded and searched her, discovering two deserters from the fleet and two from the Rhode Island Brigade skulking behind a false bulkhead. And, while he was about it, he impressed about twenty more men. This created a terrific hullabaloo in Rhode Island; *Eagle's* owners sued the Captain for damages. Unfortunately, when the cruise ended, Jones got it into his head that Hopkins had disavowed his action and refused to defend him on the ground that his orders to impress deserters were oral, not written. The contrary was true. Hopkins wrote to the Marine Committee of Congress about the affair on 8 November 1776, defending Jones; "I can't but believe that Captn. Jones did as he thought best for the good of the Publick," he wrote, and added that he hoped it met with the Marine Committee's approval. When Jones returned to port in December, Hopkins wrote to him that he had brought a countersuit action against the skipper of the privateer for enlisting Navy deserters; and, a month later, "I shall do whatever is in my power to excuse you in that matter." The action of the *Eagle's* owners against Jones was eventually nonsuited, and the affair was finally concluded by Hopkins advising Jones to let the impressed sailors share his prize money. But Paul Jones never revised his original impression that the Commodore had let him down, and his letters (as well as his biographers) breathe implacable hatred of the old salt.

Alfred's first prize, taken off Cape Breton on 11 November, was brigantine *Active* bound from Liverpool to Halifax with an assorted cargo. Placing Midshipman Spooner on board as prizemaster, Captain Jones dispatched her to the port of Edenton, North Carolina, consigned to Joseph Hewes's partner Robert Smith. The reason for this odd destination of a prize taken in a high latitude was to do a favor to his congressional patron and his fellow Scot from Kirkcudbright. "I have seen and do esteem yourself," he wrote to Robert Smith, "but I knew your Brother James well when I was myself a son of Fortune." Robert Smith, as Continental prize agent for the State of North Carolina, would take 10 per cent of the proceeds of the prize before the captors got anything, and Jones estimated the value of *Active's* cargo as six thousand pounds. But Midshipman Spooner, after a bout with bad weather, took *Active* into Rhode Island, and the Captain's friends at Edenton failed to profit.

On the morning of 12 November *Alfred* took an even more valuable prize, 350-ton armed transport *Mellish,* carrying a cargo of winter uniforms and other supplies to Quebec for the British Army. She surrendered after only a token resistance. "This will make Burgoyne 'shake a cloth in the wind' and check his progress on the Lakes," wrote Jones jubilantly; and he later had the satisfaction to learn that some of the clothing reached Washington's army before the Battle of Trenton. *Mellish* also carried sixty passengers, including British soldiers and their wives and the children of British officers. She was too valuable a prize to risk being recaptured on a voyage to North Carolina, so Jones put Lieutenant Philip Brown in command, with 25 of *Alfred's* crew and ten guns, and ordered her to stay within signaling distance.

On the 16th, *Alfred* and *Providence* captured snow *Kitty* of London, bound from Gaspé to Barbados with oil and fish. Lieutenant Joseph Allen was appointed prizemaster to take *Kitty* into Rhode Island.

Trouble now developed on board sloop *Providence,* Jones's former command. Her officers signed a respectful petition to Captain Hacker, declaring that she was leaking so badly after the foul weather she had encountered, and had lost so many men assigned to prizes, that it would be dangerous to sail farther north. Jones tried to inspire them to their duty "to relieve our Captive, ill treated Brethern from the Coal Mines," but to no avail; and the following night, under cover of a snow squall, *Providence* gave Jones the slip and sailed back to Rhode Island.

The "epidemicall discontent," as Jones called it, now extended to his own crew; they also "wanted home," but their indomitable captain insisted on carrying on to the northward. On 22 November, from off Canso, he sent in armed boats which burned a grounded British supply ship, destroyed an oil warehouse, and carried off a small, fast schooner to take the place of *Providence*. And a gentleman of Canso informed Jones that three British frigates were looking for him. Actually, Commodore Sir George Collier RN had dispatched two frigates *(Juno* and *Milford)* and two smaller warships *(Lizard* and *Hope)* to patrol the Gulf of Maine and the line between Cape Cod and Cape Sable.

Off Louisbourg, daybreak November 24 revealed to *Alfred's* lookouts three strange sail. Fortunately they were not Sir George Collier's ships but (by a curious coincidence), colliers from Sydney, bound for New York as part of a convoy under escort of H.M. frigate *Flora*, then out of sight in the fog. Jones captured all three colliers easily, and one of them was a fairly large ship named *Betty*. The captured crews informed Captain Jones that his "Brethern," the American seamen prisoners working in the coal mines, had solved their problem and his by enlisting in the Royal Navy! The Sydney mission was given up, and *Alfred* with her new tender, storeship *Mellish* and the three captured colliers turned southward.

Next day, 25 November, *Alfred* made another good prize, the ten-gun letter-of-marque ship *John*,* bound from England to Halifax. Captain Jones placed Midshipman Robert Sanders on board as prizemaster, formed his five prizes and the schooner tender into a squadron, and shaped a course for Boston, the nearest United States

---

* A letter-of-marque ship, as distinguished from a privateer, was an armed merchant vessel authorized to take prizes if she had opportunity, but whose main duty was to carry cargo.

port. More foul weather impeded their progress, and some of the prize ships became separated. When crossing the northern edge of Georges Bank east of Cape Cod, steering W by S with the wind northwest, they encountered a British frigate which proved to be H.M.S. *Milford* of 28 guns and 603 tons burthen, with a crew of 200 men. Much larger and stronger than *Alfred*, she was commanded by a Captain Burr RN.

Captain Burr's log shows that at noon 8 December, with a fresh gale blowing from the northwest and freezing weather, he was steering H.M.S. *Milford* W by S. At 3:00 P.M. she sighted "5 strange sail" ahead and to leeward, distant about twelve miles. These were *Alfred* and her tender, *John*, *Mellish*, and one or two of the captured colliers. Burr cleared for action and closed range. Jones recognized *Milford* as a British frigate and, anxious to save his prizes, made such deceptive signals that Burr took him for H.M.S. *Flora* escorting the collier convoy bound to New York. Darkness descended before he discovered his error.

Jones now pulled a Navy version of the old fox-hunting trick of dragging a red herring across the scent to draw off the hounds. He hoisted a brightly lighted lantern to his main truck and instructed his prizemasters, except Sanders in *John*, to hold their westerly course toward Boston when they saw by the lantern that he had tacked and was standing northeasterly. His purpose was to attract the British frigate by the light into following him, so that the prizes could escape. Actually this ruse was unnecessary since Captain Burr still believed them to be friendly; but it was good insurance.

Alfred and *John* came about at midnight (Diagram 1, p. 81), heading about NE by E on the port tack. *Milford* followed, because of Captain Burr's becoming suspicious of *Alfred's* change of course, which a ship escorting a convoy to New York would not have done. As a result, sunrise revealed *Alfred*, *John* and the tender on the weather bow of *Milford*, distant about nine miles (Diagram 2, p. 81).

Jones had a keen desire to try conclusions with a British frigate, but he did not care to risk losing his ship and his prizes. He had not

Encounter of ALFRED and JOHN with H.M.S. MILFORD, 8-9 Dec.1776.

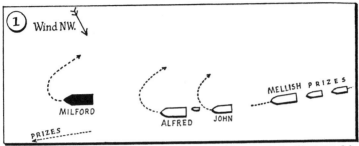

Midnight. ALFRED, tender and JOHN come about to port tack. MILFORD follows later. The prizes hold their course W by S.

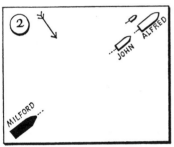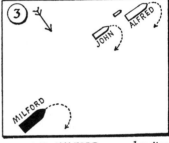

7:30 A.M. MILFORD nine miles astern of JOHN.

10:00 A.M. MILFORD wears, heading SW. Americans follow.

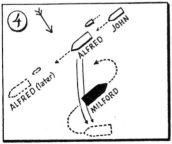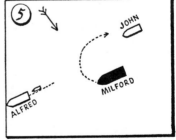

11:30 A.M. MILFORD tacks to meet ALFRED, which fires at her at noon. MILFORD tacks again in pursuit. JOHN falls astern of her.

3:00 A.M. MILFORD, outdistanced by ALFRED, tacks, bears down on JOHN and captures her. ALFRED holds her course.

got a good look at *Milford* the night before, and as he now viewed her bow-on he could not count her broadside. So he ordered Sanders in *John* to drop slowly astern "until he could discover by a view of the Enemies side whether she was of Superiour or Inferiour Force and to make a Signal accordingly." At last, Captain Burr began to feel sure that these vessels were not friendly. When all three ranged up abeam, he suddenly shook the reefs out of *Milford's* topsails, set topgallant sails and wore ship, standing southwest (Diagram 3, p. 81).

Alfred and *John* followed suit and gave chase. At 11:30 *Milford* tacked ship to meet them and by noon Jones was near enough to fire four cannon shot at the Englishman, who now for the first time definitely knew that he had to deal with Americans (Diagram 4, p. 81). *Alfred* and her tender were now on the weather bow of the Englishman, who cracked on all the sail he could carry in the fresh, squally gale, tacked, and gave chase. *Alfred* made best speed to escape her, and proved to be faster; but *John,* carrying out Jones's prior orders to count the Englishman's broadside, maneuvered astern of him and took station there.

At 3:00 P.M., when Captain Burr estimated that *Alfred* and her tender were about twelve miles ahead and increasing their lead, he gave up the chase, came about on the port tack and bore down on little *John* (Diagram 5). That 10-gun merchant vessel under a prize crew was no match for a 28-gun frigate; and in the "Fresh gales & Squals with Hard Showers of Hail" (as *Milford's* log informs us), *John* labored so that her speed was curtailed and she had no chance to flee. *Milford* forced her to heave-to by a few well-placed cannon shot, and sent over a boarding party which received Sanders's surrender and recaptured the prize. Captain Burr sent her into Halifax and turned *Milford's* bow northward.

By his strategy Paul Jones had saved his most important prizes, but the loss of *John* took some of the joy out of this cruise. Midshipman Sanders, from his prison in Halifax, managed to get word to Commodore Hopkins that he felt Jones had let him down by not coming to his assistance when he needed help. Jones, in his account of the affair written three years later, accused Sanders of having surrendered unnecessarily through cowardice or treachery. Neither was correct. As we have seen, Sanders was fairly caught and had to surrender or be blown to bits; and Jones, if twelve miles ahead of *Milford* as the British log states he was when she turned on *John,* could not possibly have got there in time to help. But why did not Jones signal Sanders to follow him instead of lagging astern, after he had fired at *Milford* and ascertained her strength? That is a question that nobody seems to have asked at the time, and which cannot now be answered.

Alfred and her tender, after shaking off the British frigate, shaped a course for Boston, and after much beating to windward entered Massachusetts Bay on 14 December. The wind, as often happens in the winter, blew so strong off shore that Jones's only alternatives were to haul off to the eastward, or squeeze into Plymouth on the starboard tack. That is a very difficult harbor to enter, as the Pilgrim Fathers had discovered some time earlier. *Alfred* had to beat in, and when tacking during a snow squall, got in irons making sternway. Any good sailor can get a ship out of that predicament if he has sea-room; but *Alfred* had a shoal close astern and drifted onto it. Many a master would then have given her up for lost, but Jones with the help of his tender got anchors out to windward, which saved her from going hard-and-fast aground; he floated her off on the flood tide next morning, and sailed into Boston with only superficial damage to report. Owing to his generosity in stocking sloop *Providence* from his own stores, he had no provisions left and only two days' fresh water on board.

Mellish, his principal prize, and *Active* were taken into Dartmouth (New Bedford); *Kitty* reached Boston safely, and sloop *Providence* made her home port. Only one of the three colliers was saved; *Milford* recaptured one, and another, *Betty* by name, was retaken by H.M.S. *Chatham* of Sir Peter Parker's squadron off Newport, which she was seeking to enter, not having learned that it had been occupied by the British. But the capture of *Mellish* alone made this short cruise of *Alfred* a great success, and the sale of her valuable çargo gave Jones and his crew a packet of prize money. Warned by what had passed at Tobago, Jones paid off out of his own pocket the crews of *Alfred* and *Providence* whose one-year terms of enlistment had expired. He was reimbursed by Congress at the end of the war.

Shortly after his arrival in Boston, Jones visited Providence and encountered the owners of privateer *Eagle* whose sailors he had impressed at Tarpaulin Cove. They employed an elderly lawyer named Joseph Lawrence to go with the sheriff to arrest Jones in the street. Captain Jones drew his sword and swore he would "clip" any man who touched him; and Lawrence, so excited as to use language no longer appropriate, exclaimed, "Oppose this man if you dare. He is a King's officer!" Jones, flourishing his sword, replied, "Is he? By God, I have a commission then to take his head off!" The sheriff retreated and cried, "He lies, he lies, I ain't no King's officer!" Lawrence, turning to the sheriff, said, "Why don't you take him?" to which Dogberry replied, "The devil—don't you see his poker?" So Jones was not arrested; and as we have seen, his skin was saved by a countersuit started by the Commodore.

Instead of reaping credit and promotion from these two cruises, Captain Jones now suffered two of the bitterest disappointments of his life—demotion to Number 18 in the Navy's list of captains, and loss of a chance to command a fleet.

December 1776-June 1777

1. The Seniority List

Captain Jones kept Christmas 1776 at a tavern in Boston, where he stayed through the winter and early spring, except for a trip to Philadelphia. He seems to have made friends with Thomas Russell, one of the "solid men of Boston," and formed a mess with several congenial characters, including Abraham Livingston, a son of Philip Livingston who was on the Marine Committee of Congress, a merchant named William Turnbull, and Major John Gizzard Frazer of Virginia. These he later referred to as "our Boston family." He was busy refitting *Alfred,* paying off the men, and defending himself against the owners of privateer *Eagle;* and as usual he had plenty of thoughts which he expressed in a series of letters to Joseph Hewes, Robert Morris and the Marine Committee of Congress.

To Hewes, on 12 January 1777, Paul Jones wrote that Hoystead

Hacker should be court-martialed for deserting him in sloop *Providence*. Two days later Commodore Hopkins (who flew his flag in frigate *Warren*, blockaded by the British in Providence River) wrote to Jones a rather cool letter informing him that by vote of Congress he was relieved of the command of *Alfred* by Captain Elisha Hinman, and that all Hopkins could do for Jones was to give him back the command of sloop *Providence*, or of "any other vessel that is in his power to give him."

This letter, reaching Jones at Boston on 19 or 20 January, infuriated him. On the 21st he wrote a strong letter to the Marine Committee, under cover of a personal letter to Robert Morris. In this he complains of his demotion, and inquires whether it is official; he remarks, unnecessarily, that Commodore Hopkins alone was responsible for the failure to take H.M.S. *Glasgow,* and declares that most of the existing officers of the Navy are incompetent. And he offers a few suggestions as to the proper qualifications of a naval officer that have received wide circulation by being prescribed reading for midshipmen at Annapolis:

> . . . It follows not that the Gentleman or Man of Merit should be Neglected, or overlooked on their [the unfit officers'] Account. None other than a Gentleman, as well as a Seaman both in Theory and in Practice is qualified to support the Character of a Commission Officer in the Navy, nor is any Man fit to Command a Ship of War, who is not also capable of communicating his Ideas on Paper in Language that becomes his Rank. . . .

He couldn't have been more right! And what he wrote goes for oral orders, too. Admiral Luce, in his classic work on seamanship, remarked, "Those officers who give their orders in accordance with the time-honored customs of the service, so familiar to all men-of-war's men, and in a tone and manner which command attention and inspire respect, will get more work out of a ship's company, and get it done with far greater spirit and alacrity, than those who coin expressions for the occasion, and assign their orders as if obedience were doubtful or indifferent to them."

Having delivered himself of generalities, Jones in the same letter repeats his former assertions about having entered the service "as a free Citizen of the World in defense of the Violated rights of Mankind." He would, however, be a degenerate were he not "in the highest degree Tenacious" of his "Rank and Seniority—as a Gentleman." He gives his side of the *Eagle* affair at Tarpaulin Cove and complains that the Commodore let him down. This, as we have seen, was neither fair nor accurate.

On 21 January 1777, when he wrote this letter, Paul Jones did not yet know the really bad news for him, although Hopkins had given him a hint of it. Congress, on recommendation of the Marine Committee, had, on 10 October, drawn up a list of captains in the Navy in order of seniority and assigned each to a ship; Jones was not only ranked Number 18 but put back in command of sloop *Providence*.

So we must pause to examine this list, which drove Jones to fury, and continued to anger him as long as he lived.

RANK OF CAPTAINS IN THE NAVY, AS ESTABLISHED BY CONGRESS 10 OCTOBER 1776 AND SHIPS TO WHOSE COMMAND THEY WERE ASSIGNED

1.	James Nicholson of Maryland	Frigate *Virginia*
2.	John Manley of Massachusetts	Frigate *Hancock*
3.	Hector McNeill of Massachusetts	Frigate *Boston*
4.	Dudley Saltonstall of Connecticut	Frigate *Trumbull*
5.	Nicholas Biddle of Pennsylvania	Frigate *Randolph*
6.	Thomas Thompson of New Hampshire	Frigate *Raleigh*
7.	John Barry of Pennsylvania	Frigate *Effingham*
8.	Thomas Read of Pennsylvania	Frigate *Washington*
9.	Thomas Grinnell of New York	Frigate *Congress*
10.	Charles Alexander of Pennsylvania	Frigate *Delaware*

11. Lambert Wickes of Pennsylvania	Sloop-of-War *Reprisal*
12. Abraham Whipple of Rhode Island	Frigate *Providence*
13. John B. Hopkins of Rhode Island	Frigate *Warren*
14. John Hodge of New York	Frigate *Montgomery*
15. William Hallock of Maryland	Brig *Lexington*
16. Hoystead Hacker of Rhode Island	Brig *Hampden*
17. Isaiah Robinson of Pennsylvania	Brig *Andrew Doria*
18. John Paul Jones of Virginia	Sloop *Providence*
19. James Josiah	(No ship assigned)
20. Elisha Hinman of Connecticut	Ship *Alfred*
21. Joseph Olney of Rhode Island	Brig *Cabot*
22. James Robinson	Sloop *Sachem*
23. John Young of Pennsylvania	Sloop *Independence*
24. Elisha Warner	Schooner *Fly*

Although this order of seniority at first glance seems completely irrational, there was a principle about it that one might call *localitis*. Appointments to command the new frigates, if checked against the places where they were built, show that almost every captain was a native of that place. The reason is clear. There was then no pool of naval recruits; nothing like a modern "boot camp." Nor could officers of ships already in commission be assigned to new construction. Seamen for every new ship had to be freshly recruited in the region where she was built; and, after the first flush of enthusiasm had faded, men would enlist only under a master mariner or other local character whom they knew. Thus, Manley, a star of the Army's Navy of 1775-1776, and McNeill, an experienced Boston master who had served in the French and Indian War, were given the two Massachusetts-built frigates; Thompson, the inspector of *Raleigh* when under construction at Portsmouth, New Hampshire, obtained her command; Barry and Biddle were given Philadelphia-built frigates. Even if Jones's exploits in *Providence* had been known to the Marine Committee at the time they made up this list (which probably they were not), the members could hardly have awarded him a new frigate in competition with so many "favorite sons." But they might and should have confirmed him in command of *Alfred,* the biggest ship of the 1775 Navy. There were no frigates constructed in the South which he might have been given. The command of the one Baltimore-built ship, frigate *Virginia,* went to James Nicholson, a gentleman of the Eastern Shore who had formerly served in the Royal Navy. Nicholson, moreover, was put at the head of this list, and so became the senior captain. Jones's best friend in Congress, Joseph Hewes, was absent when this list was drawn up, and the Virginia members, neither then nor at any other time, lifted a finger for Jones. He was the maverick of the Navy, with no shipbuilder, family or community to lean upon.

We who are wise after the event would have placed Jones among the first four captains, with Barry, Biddle and Wickes; but the capacity of a military or naval commander can be tested only by battle, and by that test Congress had a very small panel to choose from in October 1776. Paul Jones, we may say, met that test and every other; and he had something that Barry, Biddle and Wickes did not have, as far as the record shows—sound ideas on naval command, organization and administration, most of which were adopted long after his death. But the Marine Committee of Congress were not crystal-gazers. They had to do the best they could under the conditions that prevailed.

Jones suffered from lack of roots in the country, but was under no additional handicap of sectional prejudice. Some of his biographers, picking up an outburst of John Adams in 1813 against "emigrants" like Barry and Jones being called fathers and founders of the Navy, as compared with sailors like Broughton, Tucker and Manley, who had captained the Army's Navy months earlier, have rashly concluded that all Yankees were down on Jones. Actually, the four men who consistently tried to pull Jones down and keep him down were Sam (not John) Adams of Massachusetts, Arthur and Richard Henry Lee of Virginia, and Captain

James Nicholson of Maryland. Those who consistently helped and supported him were Joseph Hewes of North Carolina, Robert Morris and Benjamin Franklin of Pennsylvania. Three New Englanders, John Hancock, John Langdon and Esek Hopkins, opened opportunities to Jones from which he profited, although he quarreled with the last two. And his best friends in the Navy itself appear to have been Hector McNeill of Boston, John Young of Philadelphia, and Richard Dale of Virginia. The truth is that Paul Jones was a stranger in every part of the new nation that he served, and his friends and enemies were personal, not sectional.

So I shall not echo the soprano (and falsetto) shrieks of Jones's biographers about the injustice of Congress, sectional prejudice and the like. After all, the Marine Committee did Jones justice, after they had tested his capacity; he was the first officer without local backing to receive the command of a new ship, *Ranger*. Others, too, were badly treated. John Barry, who had been fifteen years in America and master of *Alfred* when she was a merchant ship, and who had supervised her conversion to a man-of-war, was passed over in favor of Saltonstall; but Barry did not complain. He accepted the command of brig *Lexington*, and that led to a better command later.

Jones never ceased to protest against his assigned seniority, in letters to Morris, Hewes, the Marine Committee and the President of Congress, occasionally lashing out at some of the officers placed ahead of him, especially Manley, Thompson and Hacker. And the habit of repeated complaint grew on him, unfortunately. Naval officers who assault the Navy Department (or the Admiralty) with cries of ill treatment in matters of promotion and seniority succeed only in getting themselves regarded as querulous bores. And admirers of Jones wish that he had left on record, in his many letters and memorials, a little more praise of brother officers. He could never have fought successfully without the help of brave and competent lieutenants, petty officers and seamen; but very seldom does he mention any by name. Of Lieutenant John P. Rathbun, for instance, his first lieutenant in the cruise of *Alfred*, we should never even have heard had not Commodore Hopkins written to John Hancock that most of Jones's success in that cruise was due to Rathbun's "Valour and Conduct"; and Rathbun's later career in the Navy indicates that this estimate of his ability was correct. Paul Jones was once rebuked for this trait by Franklin: "Hereafter, if you should observe an occasion to give your officers and friends a little more praise than is their due, and confess more fault than you can justly be charged with, you will only become the sooner for it, a great captain. Criticizing and censuring almost every one you have to do with, will diminish friends, increase enemies, and thereby hurt your affairs." Unfortunately this rebuke came too late, in 1780, to change Jones's ways. Like Christopher Columbus in this as in other respects, he was a colossal egotist, seldom generous enough to share credit with his subordinates.

2. The Captain and the Commodore

Paul Jones's expostulations to Morris and the Marine Committee and, still more, the news of his recent cruises, brought results. John Hancock wrote from Baltimore, whither Congress had adjourned, to Robert Morris, who had remained in Philadelphia to transact government business, "I admire the spirited conduct of little Jones; pray push him out again. I know he does not love to be idle, & I am as certain you wish him to be constantly active, he is a fine fellow & he shall meet with every notice of mine & I am confident you will join me." On 1 February 1777 the Marine Committee made an almost desperate effort to "push him out" from under the nose of Commodore Hopkins. Robert Morris, in the name of the Committee, ordered Jones to take command of *Alfred, Columbus, Cabot, Hampden* and sloop *Providence* on a long ambitious cruise. First they were to capture the British sugar island of St. Kitts, where "I fancy you will make a considerable booty," says Morris. Thence, to proceed to Pensacola on the Gulf of Mexico, to capture some British sloops-of-war which were becoming a nuisance, and pick up brass cannon. Next they were to cruise off the Passes of the Mississippi to capture British vessels coming down-river with cargoes reported to be worth at least one hundred thousand pounds, "give them an alarm at St. Augustine," show the flag in Georgia and the Carolinas; and finally make a choice between an incursion on the West African Coast or a cruise to windward of Barbados to capture British slavers bound for the West Indies. Quite an order, which Paul Jones would have dearly loved to execute. The main object of this expedition, as stated by Morris, indicates he had been thinking in terms of strategy:

> It has long been clear to me that our Infant fleet cannot protect our own Coasts; and the only effectual relief it can afford us is to attack the enemies' defenceless places and thereby oblige them to station more of their Ships in their own Countries, or to keep them employed in following ours, and either way we are relieved.

That is exactly the correct strategic principle upon which Paul Jones acted, when he had the opportunity. Commerce-destroying should have been left to privateers.

A serious misunderstanding now arose between the Captain and the Commodore, because Jones's orders from the Marine Committee, dated 1 February and received at Boston on the 19th, were not communicated to Hopkins until the 28th. In the meantime Jones had written twice to Hopkins that he wished to take his new command to sea immediately. He received no reply because the Commodore, very properly, was waiting for authorization from Philadelphia. On the 28th Jones lost patience and wrote an outrageous letter accusing the Commodore of leaving him "in the Lurch," telling him his duty, and even reminding the old gentleman that he, Captain Jones, had stood by him when he "needed friends" in the *Glasgow* affair!

The Commodore did not lose a day after receiving orders from Philadelphia that Jones was to take command of *Alfred, Columbus, Cabot, Hampden* and *Providence*. On the 28th, before receiving Jones's angry letter, he wrote to Robert Morris that he would do his best, but *Hampden* had already sailed, *Columbus* and sloop *Providence* were in upper Narrangansett Bay "with but a few men on board," and unlikely to fill their complements for some time; *Alfred* was being repaired in Boston and would not be ready for sea for six weeks or two months, and *Cabot* at Boston was already under sailing orders but had been ordered to return within six weeks to take part in the expedition under Jones. The concluding part of the Commodore's letter to Morris is significant:

> On the whole it is Impossible to mann and get these Vessels together Soon for any Expedition and from the number of Complaints I have had from the Officers and people Late under Capt.ⁿ Jones's Command in Respect to his Conduct during the Last Cruize, and Since he came home in Regard to both their wages and prize money, I am well Convinced that it will be more difficult to mann Vessels under his Command than to do it under any Officer of the Fleet that I am acquainted with and Necessity will Oblige me to wait for your further Orders Respecting the Expedition you have Order'd. And as Six Weeks' time will be soon enough for the *Alfred*, I have thought best to let Capt.ⁿ Olney [of *Cabot*] range for Six Weeks to prevent his men from deserting.

And to Jones, on 1 March, the Commodore sent this curt note in reply to his angry letter:

> Sir:
> I received yours per Express, and do absolutely think it is impracticable to get those vessels fitted and mann'd

for your propos'd Expedition and Shall acquaint the Hon. Marine Board with my Reasons.—

I am Sir

Your Humb¹ Servant

ESEK HOPKINS

P.S. If you have anything to Communicate or to apply to me for, I am always to be found on board the *Warren* where you will be safe.—

"Safe from what?" the reader may wonder. From the British, who now controlled all Narragansett Bay except Providence River.

This unpleasant dispute cannot be dismissed as evidence of jealousy or senility on the part of the Commodore. Hopkins had received an account of Jones's conduct in *Alfred's* cruise from his own son on board, and Jones had been unpardonably rude to him. The Commodore may have exaggerated Jones's unpopularity with Rhode Island seamen (who, of course, regarded him as a "furriner"), but he had received many complaints about his handling of prize money. And these need looking into.

Jones had refused to pay off members of *Alfred's* crew whose terms of enlistment had expired, unless they made him their agent to collect prize money and agreed to ship with him on the next cruise. He was within his moral rights, since he had to advance their pay out of his own pocket, but it was not legal. Jones acted thus for good reasons. First, he wished to help his people get what was coming to them. Continental agents were so lazy or dishonest that they made seamen wait for months for their prize money and pay—another reason why men preferred privateering to naval service. So notorious did this condition become at Boston and elsewhere that Captain Hector McNeill urged the Marine Committee of Congress, in a very plain-spoken letter, to have each ship's company appoint its own agents for sale of prizes. The other reason for Jones's action was to persuade his people to reënlist. He was disgusted with the Congressional system of signing seamen on for twelve months only. On board *Alfred* and *Providence* were trained men who had entered the service in December 1775, and he hated to lose them.

However, sailors being sailors, they suspected that Captain Jones was trying to do them out of their rights. In addition to this misunderstanding about prize money and enlistment, Jones was accused of deserting prize *John* during the last cruise. "Indeed," writes Hopkins in a letter to John Hancock, chairman of the Marine Committee, "I have had so many complaints against Capt.ⁿ Jones that I should be glad of your directions whether it will be best to call a Court Martial upon him or not, as I see no other way of Satisfying the Officers and People, and I am loth to take such a Step without your Orders for it."

No such order came, Paul Jones was never court-martialed, and he could afford to thumb his nose at the old Commodore whose naval career was tottering to a fall. Congress was sick and tired of Hopkins letting himself be blockaded in Providence River. And when H.M. frigate *Diamond* ran aground on Warwick Neck, Hopkins through vacillation and timidity lost a good opportunity to destroy her. The entire wardroom and chief petty officers' mess of the Commodore's flagship, frigate *Warren,* petitioned the Marine Committee to remove him as unfit for command, and sent Captain John Grannis USMC to Philadelphia to present their complaints.

Congress, on mere ex parte testimony of the disgruntled officers, voted on 26 March 1777 to suspend Hopkins from his command, and later formally dismissed him from the Navy. This action, one admits, was for the good of the service; as Jones remarked in one of his letters, "The Navy would be far better without a Head than with a Bad one." But it was a nasty way to turn out a loyal officer whose ability was unequal to his task.

In my opinion, nine tenths of the Commodore's troubles were caused by inability to man the ships under his command; and for that, the greed and selfishness of his fellow citizens of Rhode Island were responsible. In Howard Chapelle's apt phrase, Rhode Island set up a "political clambake" to construct frigates *Warren* and *Providence*. Leading merchants who were also privateer owners had a hand in the business, and when Hopkins caught them diverting materials and workers from new naval construction to their own vessels, they ganged up on him. Toward Paul Jones, the Commodore had been consistently friendly. He gave him his first command, defended him against the owners of the *Eagle,* and only reprimanded him after repeated complaints.

The old boy had a redeeming sense of humor. The Reverend Stephen Hopkins of Newport—not a relation, but founder of a branch of hellfire theology—became so exercised over the stories of horrible language among the Commodore's sailors, and their behavior on Thames Street, that he made a written remonstrance. In reply the Commodore wrote: "I did not enter into the Navy as a Divine. . . . The Congress whom I serve made provision for a Chaplain to perform that necessary duty, but to my Mortification I have not been able to get a single Man to act in that Character, although I have applied to many. If you know of any that has the good of Mankind at least Sufficient to expose himself to necessary Danger of that Service should be glad you would Send him, who you may depend shall be treated with due Respect. And if none can be procured I cannot but Condole with you on the depravity of the times."

The Marine Committee on 4 April 1777 ordered Captains J. B. Hopkins, Whipple and Saltonstall to make every effort to get frigates *Warren, Providence* and *Trumbull* to sea, but the British were too strong for them. The first two lay idle in Providence River for a year. *Warren* broke out of Narragansett Bay on a dark night in March 1778, and after a short cruise put in at Boston; the popular Captain Whipple, after obtaining a short crew of 160 men for *Providence* "with great difficulty," fought his way out of Rhode Island waters on 30 April 1778 and made France safely. *Trumbull* for two years stayed bottled up in Connecticut River, and spent another year at New London before she got into the fighting, which ended with her capture by the British.

3. The New Frigates

That, unfortunately, was symptomatic of the fate of the new frigates, one of which Captain Jones longed to command, but, fortunately for his fame, never obtained. A short account of this new Navy, which we may now call the United States Navy as distinct from Commodore Hopkins's converted Continental Navy, will elucidate.

Congress on 13 December 1775 passed an act for the construction of thirteen frigates, and hopefully announced that they would be ready for sea in three months' time. The construction was allotted to shipbuilders in various ports between Baltimore and Portsmouth, New Hampshire. Philadelphia got four and the others one or two each.

The classification of naval vessels to which the United States Navy conformed is as follows. The largest, known as a SHIP OF THE LINE (because a unit in the line of battle), or SEVENTY-FOUR (because that was the average number of her guns), corresponded to the battleship of yesterday or the aircraft carrier of today. She was 170 to 180 feet long, carried a crew of 450 to 1000 men, and mounted 60 to 120 guns, usually on three decks. The United States built only one of this class during the war—the *America*, which should have been Paul Jones's flagship. Next in order was the FRIGATE, corresponding roughly to the cruiser of today. She was 115 to 160 feet long, carried normally 220 to 350 men, and 24 to 50 guns. Most of the American warships built in 1776-1780 were of this class. Third came the SLOOP OF WAR* or CORVETTE, 80 to 120 feet long, carrying 100 to 200 men, and 16 to 20 guns. Paul Jones's *Ranger* was of this class. In addition there were converted merchantmen like *Alfred*, man-of-war brigs like *Cabot*, armed schooners like *Wasp*, and armed sloops like *Providence*.

The master plans of the new frigates, which have been preserved, prove that these vessels were designed to be as fast as possible con-

---

* Not to be confused with a single-masted sloop like *Providence;* all three of these classes were full-rigged, three-masted ships.

sistent with their armament. There was a delay in getting the plans to New England, but so great was the popular enthusiasm in the seaports that the local shipbuilders to whom contracts were awarded made their own plans, following the dimensions that Congress prescribed, and went right ahead. Two frigates, *Warren* at Providence and *Raleigh* at Portsmouth, were actually launched in the spring of 1776. *Raleigh* was built in only sixty working days but she never got to sea until August 1777, for want of men and guns. Several others were never completed, or were bottled up at their building yards by the British, or destroyed on the stocks to avoid capture. Almost all were badly built of timber that had not been sufficiently seasoned.

The fate of this new Navy is an awful example of what happens to an inferior fleet opposed to a strong sea power. Yet it might have done better with skilled officers, well-disciplined crews, competent top command and good planning. The few and far between efforts to organize task forces were a lamentable failure, Paul Jones alone bringing victory out of defeat in the case of *Bonhomme Richard*. Almost all the successes of this Navy were in commerce-destroying and in single ship action.

In addition to the warships that were built in the United States, Congress acquired a number of foreign-built vessels such as *Queen of France* (28 guns) and *Deane* (32 guns). Those that Paul Jones commanded, or was concerned with, will be mentioned in due course. The older, converted Continental Navy of Esek Hopkins was gradually swept off the sea by battle and marine disaster.*

Thus, if Paul Jones had been given command of one of the new frigates, as he ardently wished, he would have had less than an even chance of getting her out to sea. It was fortunate that he was passed over and given the sloop of war *Ranger*.

---

* *Alfred*, captured by British 9 March 1778; *Columbus*, driven ashore at Point Judith 1 April 1778 when trying to run the blockade, burned by her crew; *Cabot*, driven ashore March 1777 and salvaged by the British; *Andrew Doria*, burned in the Delaware Nov. 1777 to prevent capture; *Lexington*, captured by the British Sept. 1777; *Hampden*, condemned after running aground in Narragansett Bay; *Reprisal*, foundered on the Grand Bank Oct. 1777; *Fly*, burned in the Delaware 1778; *Wasp*, blown up to prevent capture 1777 after grounding in Chesapeake Bay; sloop *Providence*, last survivor of the 1775 Navy, blown up by her crew to prevent capture in the Penobscot, 1779.

4. "Amphitrite" to "Ranger"

His command came in a roundabout way. In March 1777, after realizing that he could never obtain the promised fleet, he went to Philadelphia and spent a month there lobbying.

Congress on 25 March voted that their agents were to purchase and convert three ships, one of which to be given "to Captain John Paul Jones, until better provisions be made for him." John Hancock was lavish in compliments, promised to rectify the rank list of 10 October 1776, and asked for Jones's captain's commission of 8 August to be returned in order to make out a new one dated 10 May (when Hopkins appointed him to sloop *Providence*); then pretended to have lost the 8 August document and issued him a new Captain's commission with the fatal date of 10 October, and with the Number 18 and the old sloop as ball-and-chain. At least that is what Jones wrote three years later, and the story is so consistent with Hancock's way of doing business that it is probably true.

In April of 1777, while Jones was still in Philadelphia, the French armed merchant ship *Amphitrite*, Captain Fautrel, entered Portsmouth, New Hampshire, with a valuable cargo of munitions. She was under French orders to proceed to Charleston, South Carolina, there load a cargo of rice and return to France. It occurred to some bright spirit on the Marine Committee that here was a golden opportunity to get Paul Jones across the Atlantic, where he could take command of one of the new ships to be purchased in France. Over there, it was thought, he would not be hampered by local prejudices, or quarrel with superiors and subordinates. So on 9 May the Marine Committee issued to him the strangest set of orders ever received by a captain of the Navy. He is to go on board *Amphitrite* "appearing or acting on suitable Occasions as the Commander," and with as many extra seamen and petty officers as he deems necessary to fight the ship. En route to Charleston, and thence to France, he is to take prizes and split the proceeds three ways: one third to the French owners, master and crew, one third to Captain Jones and his merry men, one third to Congress. Upon arrival in France, Captain Jones will proceed to Paris, where the American Commissioners will have been instructed to procure him a "fine ship." This he is to man and fit out "with the utmost Expedition," follow the Commissioners' orders for a cruise in the narrow seas, and eventually sail her to America.

Captain Jones, desperate for a command, was agreeable. Upon receiving these orders at Boston on 21 May, he rushed to Portsmouth to visit *Amphitrite* and her French master. Captain Fautrel, who was no fool, flatly declined to take Jones on board under the conditions made by Congress. One rather wishes that he had accepted, since the story of a cruise in a French armed ship under joint command of Jones and staff and a French master and crew, the deciding of "suitable occasions" when Jones should take command, and the splitting of prize money three ways, would have afforded an hilarious episode in our naval history.

The master of another French merchant ship in port, *Le Mercure*, offered to take Jones across as a passenger; but he declined, as she was too lightly armed for his taste. He played with the idea of fitting out his prize ship *Mellish* as a man-of-war. Then Colonel John Langdon of Portsmouth came to his rescue. He offered to send Jones across in command of a new sloop of war of 20 guns which had just been launched. That really led to something.

John Langdon, formerly on the Marine Committee of Congress, was building this vessel on the Committee's orders. He had designated to her command an elderly merchant mariner named John Roche, who had also been employed "to advise and assist about the building." This character, who hailed from Cork, had entered Portsmouth some time before the war as master of a ship from Quebec laden with furs, which he appropriated and sold, alleging that they were his property. He then set up as a merchant and made himself solid with Langdon. But in 1777 his act of barratry caught up with him; and upon official complaint by the State of Massachusetts Bay that he was "a person of doubtful character and ought not to be entrusted with such a command," Congress took action.

On 14 June 1777, Congress

Resolved, that Captain Roach be suspended.
Resolved, that Captain John Paul Jones be appointed to command the said ship *Ranger.*

Symbolically, although doubtless accidentally, the Roche suspension and Jones appointment appear in the *Journals* of Congress immediately after:

Resolved, That the Flag of the thirteen United States be thirteen stripes, alternate red and white; that the union be thirteen stars, white in a blue field, representing a new constellation.

Thus, the most glorious part of Paul Jones's career in the Navy began on the birthday of the Stars and Stripes.

VI

"Ranger" and Her Maiden Voyage

July-December 1777.

1. Fitting-out Troubles

Captain Paul Jones received his new orders at Boston on 1 July 1777. After giving Captain Roche, whom he had met in Boston, time to pack his bags and leave, and after writing to friends in various New England ports to drum up recruits, he journeyed about 12 July to Portsmouth, where sloop of war *Ranger* and frigate *Raleigh* were fitting out.

Portsmouth, at the mouth of the Piscataqua River, which drained the principal American source of tall pine trees for masts and spars, was one of the leading shipbuilding centers of North America. Several local families such as the Wentworths, Wendells, Langdons and Pepperells, having made fortunes exporting timber to England and the West Indies, had built commodious Georgian mansions and formed a genial and cultivated society that revolved around the royal governor and his little court. Portsmouth was a northern counter-part to Annapolis, Maryland. Until his cabin was ready in *Ranger*, Paul Jones probably stayed at the Marquis of Rockingham tavern. Portsmouth had a well-established Saint John Lodge of Masons which afforded Captain Jones a circle of brethren. He made friends among the gentry and fascinated their young ladies. From his letters one gains the impression that he was happier in Portsmouth than anywhere else short of Paris, both in 1777 and when he returned years later to fit out *America*, although most of the time he was fighting with Colonel Langdon.

Ranger was called *Hampshire* until her launching. She was re-named in honor of the famous outfit called Rogers' Rangers, in which many Portsmouth men had served, although Major Rogers himself was now working for the British. No more appropriate name for a ship commanded by John Paul Jones could have been devised. Designed by William Hackett, she was built on Rising Castle (now Badger) Island in the Piscataqua, facing the town of Portsmouth. Thence frigate *Raleigh* had been launched in 1776, and there *America* was built later in the war. Tobias Lear, Langdon's son-in-law, had the general oversight of construction.

Neither plan nor picture of *Ranger* has survived; from the register of the Royal Navy, to which she eventually belonged, we learn that she measured 97 feet 2 inches on the gun deck (which would mean about 110 feet over all), 77 feet 9 inches keel, 27 feet 8 inches beam, 12 feet depth of hold; and her tonnage was 318.5. By way of comparison, she was about 25 feet shorter than the sloop yacht *Ranger* which defended the *America's* Cup in 1937, the same length as the standard submarine chasers of World War II, and one-seventh the length of the aircraft carrier that was named after her in 1933. Rated as a sloop of war, *Ranger* was square-rigged on all three masts, carried royals as well as topgallant sails and a full set of studding sails. Her bulwarks were pierced for 20 nine-pounder guns, a num-ber that Captain Jones reduced to 18 because he rightly felt that she was too light to carry more to advantage. Her topsides were painted black with a broad yellow stripe, which harmonized with a figure-head of the same color. Captain Gurley, an English seaman who had a close look at *Ranger* in the Irish Sea, described her as "Hake built and Hollow Counter'd," which meant that she had a fine, sharp bow and an undercut stern to give her a clean run. And her dimensions which we have quoted confirm that. He added that she looked like a Bermuda-built vessel, which was a compliment, since Bermuda invented the sharp and rakish vessel that made for speed.

"The *Ranger* taken altogether will in my Judgment prove the best Cruizer in America," wrote Paul Jones to the officers whom he sent to drum up recruits. "She will always be able to Fight her Guns under a most excellent cover and nothing can be better calculated for sailing Fast or making good Weather. . . . Since the establishment of our Navy no persons in it have had so good, so fair a prospect of success as ours is at present." With later acquaintance he learned her faults. Her masts, which had been intended for a much larger vessel, were too long and heavy; the mainmast, for instance, had a diameter of 21 inches, which was the proper size for a 64-gun warship of 1400 tons' burthen, and her sail plan was too ample for her hull.

Ranger had been launched two months before Paul Jones took over her command in mid-July, but there was a world of work to do before she could be fit for sea. All the cordage, sails and cannon procured for her had been turned over to *Raleigh;* Jones had a bare ship to dress. Like all devoted shipmasters, he was very particular about turning out his mistress in proper style; and that was not easy in Portsmouth.

Congress by this time had appointed agents in every leading Eastern seaport, as well as two Navy Boards of three men each, the Eastern at Boston and the Middle at Philadelphia, "to execute the business of the Navy," under the direction of the Marine Committee. This, according to Paul Jones, made confusion worse confounded. What the Navy wanted, he wrote to Robert Morris and Benjamin Franklin, was "a man of Abilities at its head" who could make a proper selection of officers, and "Commissioners of Dock Yards to

Superintend the Building and Outfit of all Ships of war—With power to appoint Deputies to provide & have in constant Readiness Sufficient Quantities of Provisions Stores Slops &c. so that the small number of Ships we have may be constantly employed and not Continue Idle as they do at present." All that would come in good time; but Congress was far too much harried by the critical military and political situation in 1777 to pay much attention to the Navy. Jones could expect no help from Philadelphia in fitting out *Ranger*. And he had little help from the leading citizen of Portsmouth, Colonel John Langdon, former member of the Marine Committee of Congress, local Navy Agent, and responsible for building *Ranger*.

Colonel Langdon was an able man of forceful character; a prominent merchant-shipowner and also Speaker of the New Hampshire Assembly. After the war he served in the Federal Convention, the United States Senate, and was elected Governor of New Hampshire. But in 1777 he was only Navy Agent, not even a member of the Eastern Navy Board; and in the loose system, or lack of system, of naval administration that prevailed, he could not exercise the powers of a modern commandant of a naval district with an ample staff. For over a year before Jones arrived in Portsmouth, Langdon had been wrestling with the problem of getting frigate *Raleigh*, first of the new Navy to be launched, ready for sea. It had taken him all that time to procure guns for her, and she did not sail until mid-August 1777. Now he had Paul Jones on his neck.

Jones was one of those captains who must have everything "shipshape and Bristol-fashion." From his knowledge of warships he saw that *Ranger* was oversparred and too light for her guns. He could leave guns on the beach, but he could not get a smaller set of spars out of Langdon, despite Portsmouth's being the mast emporium of North America; he had to cut down those that she had, in France. Jones had insisted on her equipment being of the best, and on having plenty of spare parts. It was up to Langdon to procure them, but the Colonel became so exasperated with the Captain's repeated demands that he burst out with the declaration that he knew as well as

Jones "how to Equip, Govern, or Fight a Ship of War." Imagine that!—wrote Jones to the secretary of the Marine Committee of Congress—instead of giving me the necessary assistance required of an agent, "he thinks himself my Master—and he, who was bred in a shop and hath been about a voyage or two at sea under a Nurse, had once the assurance to tell me that he knew as well as myself how to fit out, Govern and Fight a Ship of War!" That was a very silly statement; Langdon had been master of four different merchantmen before settling down as a shipowner.

Jones's particular grief was that Langdon provided *Ranger* with less than thirty gallons of rum—a commodity not exactly scarce in New England—for a crew of 150. And the Colonel would give him no boatswain's whistle—probably thought the boatswain should bellow his orders, as in the merchant marine. But Jones got ahead of him on that point. Before sailing he purchased two silver "Boatswain's Calls" at Boston for twelve dollars and charged them to his expense account; and in France he obtained a third. Another and more serious complaint was over the quality of *Ranger's* sails. Instead of good Russia duck or English canvas, he had to accept an inferior hemp-and-jute material called hessians that was generally used for bagging; and he had to make her topmast staysails and studding sails out of scraps of canvas that were too heavy for such light sails.

We have Jones's account of his disbursements in fitting out *Ranger*. He sent a midshipman shopping in Boston for various items impossible to find in Portsmouth. He invested $198.66 in "Live Stock &c. provided for the voyage to Europe, a part whereof" (the chickens) "being destined for the use of the sicke on Board." He had learned in the merchant marine the importance of having a good supply of "slops"—readymade clothing—to issue to the crew, and now "paid the Taylors for making up Slops" $192.66.

The Captain had little say in the appointment of *Ranger's* officers. With Langdon and William Whipple, another New Hampshire congressman, he was one of a committee of three to select the commissioned and warrant officers. But no friend of his, nor any officers who had served under him before, was acceptable to his Portsmouth colleagues. The principle of "localitis" was applied right down the line:* every officer was a local character, newly commissioned for this cruise; the Marine Committee had furnished Whipple with a pack of blank commissions for that purpose. For first lieutenant, corresponding to the modern exec., *Ranger* was given Langdon's brother-in-law Thomas Simpson, a merchant mariner nine years older than Captain Jones. The second lieutenant, Elijah Hall, five years older than the Captain, was a shipbuilder and merchant of Portsmouth. David Cullam, the master, a rough local character, had good merchant marine experience. *Ranger's* surgeon, Dr. Ezra Green, a Harvard graduate from Dover, New Hampshire, had served for two years in the Army and wanted a sea-change. His mate, Jacob Walden, who doubled as steward, came out of a Portsmouth apothecary's shop. Lieutenant Samuel Wallingford USMC also belonged in the neighborhood. At the request of John Wendell, Captain Jones's best friend in Portsmouth, his son David Wentworth Wendell obtained a midshipman's billet. David's qualifications are related in a letter from his father to Captain Jones, who was expected to repeat them to Benjamin Franklin: he was a grandson of old Colonel Wendell and Pascal Wentworth of Portsmouth, a nephew of Colonel Quincy of Braintree, and a cousin of John Hancock and John Adams. Despite these impressive connections, Dave Wendell proved to be a modest youth who asked for no favors.

Not one of these officers, except Captain Parke of the Marine Corps, had served in the Navy. Paul Jones was under a triple handicap as a naval officer who expected naval discipline, a stranger to Portsmouth, and a Scot. If Scotsmen were disliked in Virginia, where they were known, they were detested in New England, where few people had seen one before the Highland regiments came over to fight. Moreover, a consistent Whig propaganda

* The only exception was Captain Matthew Parke USMC, the one friend Jones was allowed to appoint; but the other officers ganged up on Parke and virtually forced Jones to dismiss him in France.

GREAT
ENCOURAGEMENT
FOR
SEAMEN.

ALL GENTLEMEN SEAMEN and able-bodied LANDSMEN who have a Mind to diftinguifh themfelves in the GLORIOUS CAUSE of their Country, and make their Fortunes, an Opportunity now offers on board the Ship RANGER, of Twenty Guns, (for France) now laying in Portsmouth, in the State of New-Hampshire, commanded by JOHN PAUL JONES Efq; let them repair to the Ship's Rendezvous in Portsmouth, or at the Sign of Commodore Manley, in Salem, where they will be kindly entertained, and receive the greateft Encouragement.---The Ship Ranger, in the Opinion of every Perfon who has feen her is looked upon to be one of the beft Cruizers in America.---She will be always able to Fight her Guns under a moft excellent Cover ; and no Veffel yet built was ever calculated for failing fafter, and making good Weather.

Any Gentlemen Volunteers who have a Mind to take an agreable Voyage in this pleafant Seafon of the Year, may, by entering on board the above Ship Ranger, meet with every Civility they can poffibly expect, and for a further Encouragement depend on the firft Opportunity being embraced to reward each one agreable to his Merit.

All reafonable Travelling Expences will be allowed, and the Advance-Money be paid on their Appearance on Board.

IN CONGRESS, March 29, 1777.

Resolved,

THAT the Marine Committee be authorifed to advance to every able Seaman, that enters into the Continental Service, any Sum not exceeding FORTY DOLLARS, and to every ordinary Seaman or Landfman, any Sum not exceeding TWENTY DOLLARS, to be deducted from their future Prize-Money.

By Order of Congress,

JOHN-HANCOCK, President.

DANVERS: Printed by E. Russell, at the Houfe late the Bell-Tavern.

line throughout the war was to blame all the woes of the Empire on Lord Bute and other Scots "carpetbaggers," who were supposed to be a secret cabal behind George III and Lord North.

Colonel Langdon was of no assistance in getting *Ranger* a crew. Jones had to do that himself, with the help of the handbill here reproduced in facsimile. He wrote to Captain Parke at Providence to send around "a Drum, Fife and Colours" to attract enlistments there. Parke managed to sign on twenty-two men but Captain Hopkins of frigate *Warren* snaked them away from under his nose. Midshipman Charrier was asked to beat the bushes for recruits along the North Shore of Massachusetts. Lieutenant Wallingford tried to entice local lads to join, but *Ranger* was in competition with *Raleigh,* which still lacked a hundred men of her full complement, and also with local privateers. William Whipple of the officer procurement committee wrote to Josiah Bartlett from Portsmouth after *Ranger* had sailed:

> There is at this time 5 Privateers fitting out here [and, he might have added, some of them owned by John Langdon] which I suppose will take 400 men. These must be by far the greater part Countrymen, for the Seamen are chiefly gone, most of them in Hallifax Gaol. Besides all this, you may depend no public ship will ever be manned while there is a privateer fitting out. The reason is plain: Those people who have the most influence with Seamen think it their interest to discourage the Public service, because by that they promote their own interest, viz, Privateering. In order to do this effectually, every officer in the public service (I mean in the Navy) is treated with general contempt.

And he goes on to say that if nothing is done by Congress to remedy this state of affairs, the United States Navy will be "officered by Tinkers, Shoemakers, and & Horse Jockeys, and no Gentleman worth employing will accept a Commission." That is just what Paul Jones had been writing, somewhat more politely, to the Marine Committee; and just about what happened.

The advances paid by Jones to seamen who enlisted in *Ranger* amounted to $713, and the expenses of recruiting them to $542.12½. But some deserted to privateers after receiving their advance and signing the roll; Captain Jones paid out $82.66 for "expenses in pursuit of deserters." At the end of August he petitioned the New Hampshire government to let him enlist "matrosses" (an old word for cannoneers) from the forts of Portsmouth Harbor. At that time *Ranger* had neither sails nor men; not until 20 September could enough hessians be assembled to make even one suit of sails. On the same day Paul Jones renewed his plea for matrosses. Three weeks later he was so exasperated as to write an angry letter to Colonel Langdon, who had refused to pay for *Ranger's* yawl boat or cutter. He, Captain Jones, was authorized by Congress to "Equip, Officer and Man the *Ranger*," and he expects his orders "to be duly honored." Langdon paid no attention. The Captain, evidently facing a dim prospect of returning alive from the forthcoming cruise, made his will, appointing Robert Morris and Joseph Hewes his executors, each to have "a Mourning Ring" valued at £100. The balance of his property was to go to his mother and sisters in Scotland.

2. Fox's Ferry

October also brought good news. General Burgoyne surrendered his entire army at Saratoga on the 17th. *Ranger* was made bearer of duplicate dispatches from Congress to Benjamin Franklin announcing the event; but the French merchantman *Penet*, carrying the original dispatches, beat her across the Atlantic.

Burgoyne's surrender, causing Paul Jones to hope that the war would soon be over, made him revert to his earlier dream of a plantation in Virginia. Major John Gizzard Frazer, sometime assistant quartermaster general in Washington's army, had met Jones at the tavern where both stayed in Boston. They conceived a great liking for each other. Jones, after failing to persuade Robert Morris to give the

Major a commission in the Marine Corps, invited Frazer to sail in *Ranger* to France, where possibly he could pick up something. Having given this invitation, he received a request from the Major to bring his "field beds" and his "Girl" on board; and that this girl was not the Major's daughter may be inferred from the next clause in his letter, requesting Jones to find lodgings for her "in some decent private house" in Portsmouth; and, as "I wish to have as much of her Company as I can, let none of my acquaintances there know of it."

Major Frazer soon came to Portsmouth complete with girl, for whom, no doubt, Captain Jones found a discreet lodging. And from Portsmouth, the Major writes to Carter Braxton Esq. of King William County, Virginia, to enlist his aid in buying for Captain Jones a "small landed estate on the Mattapony called Foxes Ferry." Jones, he says, is so impressed by his "truly Elysian" description of Fox's Ferry that he wishes to buy it for the asking price of twelve hundred pounds; will Mr. Braxton try to obtain it for that sum? But, for reasons unexplained, the deal fell through. Possibly Carter or Jones discovered that Fox's Ferry was under litigation between the Fox and Frazer families, so that no clear title could be had. It is still known as "Frazier Ferry."

About this time, to fit his character as an officer and gentleman and possible Virginia planter, Paul Jones ordered to be painted for himself an achievement of arms, and had an heraldic seal cut. The arms are the stag used by several Jones families of Wales, quartered with those of a Paul family of Gloucestershire. The crest is the Jones stag; and the motto, the only original part, is *Pro Republica*.

Did the Captain plan to renew his suit to Dorothea Dandridge? "Captain J. P. Jones USN of Fox's Ferry, King William County," would sound much better to the Dandridges than "Master John Paul *alias* Jones, brother to the late town tailor of Fredericksburg." Actually it was too late; Dorothea had already married Patrick Henry. But, in my opinion, Jones never gave Dorothea a thought after his naval career began. She occupied no place in his heart, and only for a short time in his calculations. One of the truest maxims of La

Rochefoucauld is, *"On passe souvent de l'amour à l'ambition; mais on ne revient guère de l'ambition à l'amour."** Paul Jones's feet were now on a ladder that might lead anywhere, and he would not descend from it for anyone. If he could obtain a bride who would help him to rise socially, so much to the good. But rather than be tied to some provincial belle, he preferred to amuse himself with a succession of mistresses. And in France he found them.

A lady of another color with whom he had become acquainted in Boston was Phillis Wheatley, the former slave whose poetry was considered one of the wonders of the age, and who received compliments even from George Washington. Jones, who considered himself no mean poet, wrote some verses which he sent via Captain Hector McNeill to "the Celebrated Phillis the African Favorite of the Nine and of Apollo."

As a final commission from William Whipple of Portsmouth, with whom Jones always remained friendly, he was asked to purchase for Mrs. Whipple in France several dozen pair of gloves, and enough black cloth to make several cloaks and dresses. And his Boston friend Abraham Livingston gave him a more extensive order—twelve cases "Exceeding Good Boardeaux Claret," "One sett Tea China" to cost about five pounds, "One Sett Table Ware such as is commonly used among the French," not to exceed ten pounds; and sundry "Table Cloaths," decanters, glasses, almonds, anchovies, capers and olives; but only six pounds of tea. Boston no longer cared much for tea.

3. Passage to France

Warships of the Revolutionary Navy had no opportunity for a shakedown cruise to test their performance, followed by a period of upkeep to correct errors and replace faulty gear. They had to nip out to sea as soon as they were ready and the wind served, and make time off shore to escape prowling enemy frigates.

---

*"One often proceeds from love to ambition; but one seldom returns from ambition to love."

On 30 October Paul Jones wrote to Joseph Hewes and Robert Morris, again complained of the way he had been treated by the Navy, declaring that several captains ranked above him were "altogether illiterate and Utterly ignorant of Marine affairs," and denying "the dirty and Ungrateful insinuations" of Commodore Hopkins respecting him.

Ranger was then ready to sail, but the wind was in the east, so Jones had time to write one more letter to John Brown, secretary of the Marine Committee of Congress, complaining that "the outfit of this small ship hath given me more anxiety and Uneasiness than all the other duty which I have performed in the Service." But, he added, *Ranger* has "the best disposed crew in the world."

At last, 1 November 1777, when a northwest wind blew down the Piscataqua, *Ranger* could sail. Her crew hove the anchor cable short, Master Cullam bellowing orders and the boatswains piping shrilly on their new silver calls to annoy Colonel Langdon. Topsail yards were braced sharp, precisely at nine o'clock a gun was fired, the Marines' drums and fifes beat a merry tune while the men heaved on the capstan bars to break out the anchor, and as *Ranger* whipped around under the fresh breeze from the White Mountains, with a strong ebb current under her keel, Captain Jones on the quarterdeck in his best blue uniform and Major Frazer in continentals waved their cocked hats to the ladies ashore. The ship gathered speed as she squared away, nipped around Fort Point "with a bone in her teeth," set lower courses, topgallant sails and studding sails as she passed Jaffrey Point, hauled up sharp on the port tack to pass the Isles of Shoals, and before night lost sight of the American shore. Bound away at last!

There were about 150 officers and men, all told, on board *Ranger*. Jones messed with Major Frazer, who came on board minus girl but with Negro servant and a private supply of wines and liquors which he used liberally, and which the Captain barely touched. Jones would have done better to have messed in the wardroom with the other officers and endeavored to win their friendship and loyalty by his charm and conversation; but that was not Navy practice, and Jones refused to make concessions to democracy. The enlisted men, whom he described before sailing as "orderly, well disciplined and spirited," numbered 140. Most of them hailed from the Piscataqua region or Essex County, Massachusetts, from families such as Hutchins, Jackson, Odiorne, Parsons, Low, Shapleigh, Sherburne and Sargent. There were also several Irishmen, one French Canadian, and a Swede, Edward Meyer, who proved to be more loyal to Captain Jones than most of the local lads. And there were two local free Negroes, Cato Carlile and Scipio Africanus.

Surgeon Green's diary tells us of a gale on 14-16 November during which a tiller rope parted, with consequent danger of the ship broaching; of taking brigs *Mary* and *George,* bound from Malaga to England with fruit and wine, and of dogging a British convoy without success. But the best account of *Ranger's* passage to France is in a gay letter from the Captain to John Wendell of Portsmouth. It shows, as does no other letter of Paul Jones, the joy that every true sailor derives from a fair wind when he has a good ship and a willing crew:

Ranger, NANTES *11ᵗʰ Decʳ 1777*

MY DEAR SIR,

The *Ranger* was wafted by the Pinions of the gentlest, and most friendly Gales, along the Surface of the Blue profound of Neptune; and not the swelling bosom of a Friend's nor even of an *Enemi's Sail,* appeared within our placid Horizon, untill after we had passed the Everlasting Mountains in the Sea, (called Azores) whose Tops are in the Clouds, and whoe's Foundations are in the Center. When lo! this Halcyon Season was interrupted! the "gathering Fleets o'erspread the Sea" and Wars alarms began! Nor ceased day or night untill, aided by the mighty Boreus, we cast Anchor in this Asylum the 2ᵈ Currᵗ but since I am not certain that my Poetry will be understood, it may not be amiss to add, *by way of marginal note,* that after leaving Portsmouth nothing remarkable happened untill I got to the Eastward of the Western Islands; and that from that time untill my arrival here, I fell in with Ships every day and sometimes every Hour; within Eighty Leagues of

Ushant, I met with an Enemies fleet of Ten Sail bound up Channel, but not withstanding my best endeavours, I was unable to detach any of them from the strong Convoy under which they sailed. I met with and brought too a variety of other Ships none whereof proved British Property, except two Brigantines from Malaga with Fruit for London, which became Prizes, the one is arrived here, the other I am told in Quiberon Bay; as I have met with and brought too several Ships in the Night, I had the most agreeable Proof of the Active Spirit of my Officers and Men.

I have forwarded my dispatches to Paris, by Express, and determine not to go myself unless I am sent for. I understand that in Obedience to Orders from the Secret Committee, the Commissioners had, some time ago, provided One of the finest Frigates for me that can be imagined, calculated for Thirty two, Twenty four Pounders, on one deck, and longer than any Ship in the Enemies Fleet; but that it has been found necessary to give her up, on account of some difficulties which they have met with at Court. My Heart glows with the most fervent Gratitude for this, and every other unsolicited and unexpected instance of the favo'r and Approbation of Congress; and if a Life of Services devoted to the Intrests of America, can be made Instrumental in securing its Independance; I shall be the happiest of Men, and regard the continuance of such Approbation, as an Honor far superior to the empty Peagantry, which Kings ever had Power to bestow.

I esteem your Son as a promising and deserving young Man, I have just now had some Conversation with him and am much Pleased with his diffidence and Modesty, he would not he says accept of a Commission untill he thinks himself equal to the duty of the Office of Lieutenant; there I think he shows a true Spirit: in the mean time, he tells me [he] is perfectly satisfy'd with his present Situation, any thing within my Power to render his Situation happy and Instructive, shall not be wanting.

I must rely on you to make my best Compliments acceptable to the fair Miss Wendell, and to the other agreeable Ladies

of my acquaintance in Portsmouth. The Captain of the *Raleigh*
I understand is well, and has lately been figuring it away at
Paris, whereof please to acquaint my *Sister* Officer.* I should
be exceedingly happy to hear from you, but as my destination depends on what I am to hear from the Commissioners,
I cannot at Present give you my Address, but will drop you
another, How do you do, shortly.

I am with Sentiments of Respect & Regard

My dear Sir,

Your Obliged,

very Obedient,

most humble Servant:

JNº P. Jones

John Wendell Esqʳ.
Portsmouth

From 26 November, when her surviving log or sea journal begins,
Ranger encountered "fresh gail" from the SW, then "fresh Breze
and Dirty Weather" from the NE and SE, "shipd a grate Deal of
Water"; then (29 November) "hard Gaile and Dirty Weather from
the SE, blowing very hard and a large Sea a-Going, Ship abundance
of water. At 3 lay by Under ref'd Main Course, Struck the top Gallant Mast. At 8 P.M. Moderate. Set the Four Sail Got up the top
Gallant Mast & lett 2 Refs out the Top Sails."

Sunday 30 November dawned fine, *Ranger* tearing along ESE at
9 knots under reefed topsails. At 5:00 P.M. she hove-to, sounded
and found bottom at 88 fathoms. The wind moderated, reefs were
shaken out, staysails and studding sails set, and in "Light Are and
pleasant Weather" she worked up toward the coast of Lower Brittany. Land was sighted at daylight 2 December, and at 10:00 A.M.
Ranger was off St.-Nazaire, standing in toward the mouth of the
Loire. At 4:30 P.M. a pilot came on board and conned her to an

---

* A sly allusion to Capt. Thomas Thompson and his wife. Thompson wrote good-naturedly to
Jones from Paris, 26 Dec. 1777, thanking him for buying a pair of shoes for Mrs. T., and hoping that
the Captain would soon enjoy the "pleasure which paris afourds."

anchorage in four fathoms off Paimboeuf, the deep-water port for Nantes, at midnight. The passage had taken 31 days, two or three of them spent in chasing prizes.

Captain Jones, not yet knowing that snow *Penet* had beaten *Ranger* in the race to bring news of Burgoyne's surrender, had the cutter hoisted out at once, and he, Surgeon Green and Major Frazer were rowed many miles upriver to Nantes.

A willing crew, we have said; apparently they behaved well on this passage and (wrote Surgeon Green) "arrived in good spirits." To William Whipple of Portsmouth, Jones wrote that taking the prizes afforded "excellent opportunities of exercising the Officers and Men especially in the Night, and it is with much pleasure that I assure you their behavior was to my entire Satisfaction." This feeling, as we shall see, was not reciprocated. The only person on board who gave the Captain any trouble on this passage was his passenger Major Frazer, who did nothing but drink "to intoxication," and staggered ashore at Nantes to make a tour of the inns and *estaminets* of Northern France.

Captain Jones's first official report to the Marine Committee of Congress declared that *Ranger* had not proved an effective warship —even though French naval officers who came on board called her *un parfait bijou*—a regular little jewel. She was "crank" (what we now call "tender"), meaning that her oversize spars and sail plan made her heel over too much in a moderate wind. It was bad for a warship to heel over like a yacht, because then her weather broadside fired up in the air and the lee gun ports had to be closed to keep out the water. *Ranger's* bottom was foul, as she had not been careened since her spring launching; and her sails were made of cheap stuff. Captain Jones promised to correct all this by heaving her down for a graving, obtaining new spars and sails, and ballasting her with thirty tons of lead.

"As America must become the first Marine Power in the world, the care and increase of our seamen is a consideration of the first magnitude, and claims the full attention of Congress," wrote Jones to Robert Morris shortly after *Ranger* made port. And he exemplified this himself. No officer in the Navy was more considerate of his crew than Jones, or kept them in better health; but he insisted on good discipline and a proper subordination. His first care, upon arrival at Paimboeuf, was for the people and the ship, even though at that time he expected to be relieved. He advanced spending money out of his own pocket, since Congress had made no arrangements for the men to draw pay in France. Before leaving for Nantes he ordered Lieutenant Simpson to buy bread, fresh meat, greens and a cask of brandy for the men, and to charter a lighter for ship's service to and from shore, so the people would not be continually hoisting out boats and getting them on board. There are many complaints on record against Captain Jones by his officers and men; but not one about the food. This I regard as significant, since food is the first thing that sailors growl about.

Preparations were made to heave *Ranger* down, to make necessary alterations in her rig, and obtain new sails to replace the now worn and baggy suit of hessians. At Paimboeuf Paul Jones found good company in his Philadelphia friend John Young, captain of U.S. armed sloop *Independence,* which was being converted to a brig. At Nantes he found a little American colony—Joshua Johnson of Maryland, whose daughter married John Quincy Adams; Franklin's nephew Jonathan Williams, the Continental agent there; his partner Thomas Morris, a half-brother of Robert Morris, and John Ross, a Scottish merchant who sympathized with the Americans. Also he ran into Benjamin Hill, who as pilot of sloop *Providence* had been her navigating officer during the raid on Nova Scotia. Hill wished to ship again under his old captain, and did so; but as *Ranger's* complement of officers was filled, he had to come as a volunteer midshipman without pay. Ben Hill proved to be a loyal and valuable officer.

Captain Jones had important objects in view. As he had written to Wendell, Congress had promised him a new command in France. And in seeking it, he was thrown for the first time into the toils of diplomacy.

VII

From the
Loire
to the
Solway

December 1777-April 1778

1. Paris and "L'Indien"

It was understood by Jones before he left Portsmouth that the
American Commissioners in Paris were to build or buy a new frigate for him in Europe. He carried a letter from the Marine Committee to the Commissioners, stating that this was the purpose of their
sending him to France. What they had in mind was a 40-gun, 154-
foot ship known as *L'Indien,* which was being built in a private shipyard at Amsterdam for American account. But by the time *Ranger*
arrived in France the Commissioners, hard up for funds and despairing
of persuading the Dutch government to let them take possession, had sold *L'Indien* to the French government. Jones did everything in his power to get this ship, even appealing over the head
of Benjamin Franklin to the French Minister of Marine, but international politics were too much for him. The British government,

apprised of his intention by spies in Paris, protested to the Dutch government, whose position, had it not listened to these protests, would have been similar to that of the British cabinet in 1862-1863 with respect to the famous C.S.S. *Alabama*.

Captain Jones was eager to obtain command of *L'Indien*, not only for the possibilities he saw in her, but to be relieved of *Ranger*. Frigate *Raleigh* (Captain Thompson) and his old ship *Alfred* (now under Captain Hinman) had preceded him to France with orders to load supplies for America, and Jones was afraid that the Commissioners would put *Ranger* into a task force under Thompson, who was twelve numbers ahead of him on the seniority list. But they had no such intention. They packed off *Raleigh* and *Alfred* before the end of the year. On the way home, *Alfred* was captured in a running fight with H.M.S. *Ariadne* and *Ceres*, *Raleigh* escaped without making any effort to support her, and as a result Captain Thompson was court-martialed and broken. Jones expected this; he liked Thompson as a good-natured fellow and able shipbuilder, but regarded him as unfit for a sea command.

Having ascertained that *Penet* had already arrived with the Burgoyne dispatches, Captain Jones decided not to go to Paris until invited, and returned on board *Ranger* at Paimboeuf on 9 December. On the 15th the summons came. Jones lost no time in proceeding to Paris by one of the fast post-chaises that the French government maintained for quick communication with its outports. By traveling day and night, one could make the capital in forty-eight hours, provided the weather was fair; but the regular coach journey required the better part of five days to cover less than three hundred miles.

Where Captain Jones put up on this, his first visit to Paris, we do not know, although we have a pretty good idea; nor have we a word from him on the "pleasure·which paris afourds," held forth by Captain Thompson. No doubt he reported immediately at the suburb of Passy, where Benjamin Franklin, already the most talked-about man in Paris, lived in a pavilion attached to the Hôtel Valentinois. The thirty-year-old naval officer and the septuagenarian diplomatist took to each other immediately. Franklin never failed to support the

Captain against his rivals; Jones admired and almost worshiped the Doctor. He also became intimate with Franklin's confidential secretary, Dr. Edward Bancroft, F.R.S. and Fellow of the Royal College of Physicians, who was actually receiving one thousand pounds a year as a British spy and transmitting the Commissioners' secrets to London. But if Jones found a friend in Franklin, he made an enemy of Arthur Lee, the second Commissioner, who hated Franklin bitterly, lost no opportunity to vilify him behind his back, and, with the help of his brother Richard Henry Lee and Sam Adams in Congress, tried to have him recalled in disgrace. Lee, too, had a secretary who was a British spy. Silas Deane, the third Commissioner, was a smooth character from Connecticut who had been on the Marine Committee of Congress and took a great interest in naval matters. Jones got on well with Deane and became a warm friend of his secretary William Carmichael, who by exception among the secretaries was faithful to his master and loyal to America. And Deane eventually went over to the enemy.

It cannot have taken Paul Jones long to size up the political and diplomatic situation. Franklin, by the gentlest and most delicate methods, was propelling the French government toward full recognition of American independence, and an offensive-defensive alliance with the United States. It was an amazing and amusing situation, as Thomas Carlyle noted in his *French Revolution:* "The sons of the Saxon Puritans, with their Old-Saxon temper, Old-Hebrew culture, sleek Silas, sleek Benjamin . . . among the light children of Heathenism, Monarchy, Sentimentalism, and the Scarlet Woman. A spectacle indeed!"

The news of Burgoyne's surrender helped Franklin immensely, because the Comte de Vergennes, the foreign minister, feared that if France did not act promptly some sort of compromise peace would be patched up. And if France did become a full-fledged ally to Congress, many new possibilities would open up for naval action.

The situation at Passy was not only confused by the rivalry between the American commissioners, but by Franklin's friends of the opposite sex. The Doctor's two most devoted ladies were Madame

Helvétius, to whom, at the age of seventy, he proposed marriage; and Madame Brillon de Jouy, who was willing to sit on the philosopher's lap and to let him play chess with her when she was in the bathtub, but who steadfastly refused to grant the additional favors that he craved. Probably Paul Jones did not meet these two ladies, as he never sends them his compliments in his letters to Franklin. The one lady whom we know that he did meet at this time was Madame Le Ray de Chaumont, wife of the man who owned the Hôtel Valentinois and who lived in the main part of that vast edifice.

Jacques Donatien Le Ray was a bourgeois who, after making a fortune in the East India trade, bought the sumptuous Hôtel Valentinois and the Château de Chaumont on the Loire, whence he adopted the title Sieur de Chaumont. Louis XV chose him for his privy council and gave him two other honorary appointments. He owned a fleet of merchant vessels and did a great deal of business procuring supplies for the French Navy. More, it would seem, from hatred of England than from love of America or of liberty, he had placed his money and influence behind the revolted colonies and handled a large part of the unofficial aid sent to them before the final Franco-American alliance. Having Dr. Franklin and the other Commissioners and their secretaries live on the grounds of his splendid residence was a convenient means for conducting Franco-American relations informally and discreetly. Ferdinand Grand, the banker who handled the American accounts, lived nearby. Chaumont had a finger in every pie that concerned America; and he seems, from all one can find at this distance, to have been honest though not very wise. His relations with Jones oscillated between the most affectionate trust and appreciation on both sides, and a feeling on Jones's part that Chaumont was using him as a means of making money.

Jones always quarreled with people like Colonel Langdon or Commodore Hopkins who were in a position to control his movements or restrict his supplies, so he would probably have broken with Chaumont anyway. But their relationship was complicated by a love affair. The Captain had observed, or had been told by Franklin, that the best way to get things done in France was through the ladies, and that the quickest way to learn French was to find a "sleeping dictionary." Accordingly, he made love to Madame de Chaumont. *Née* Thérèse Joguer, she was several years junior to her husband, although a few years older than Jones. It was natural that the handsome young naval officer should be invited to stay in the Hôtel Valentinois when he visited Passy, and that when Monsieur had to go on a business trip, Madame should become intimate with the Captain. This was very pleasant for a time, but Paul Jones later found the relationship embarrassing when he had to depend on Monsieur for outfitting a fleet and selling his prizes. And he also discovered— what Franklin could have told him—that mistresses are easier to acquire than to shake off.

With respect to *L'Indien,* Jones got nothing but evasive promises. The business was in hand, but the French government could not be pressed while other and more delicate negotiations were under way. So, now that Thompson had sailed in *Raleigh,* the Captain returned on board *Ranger* at Paimboeuf, on 28 January 1778, with several plans in his head for her profitable employment, and a credit of five hundred louis d'or—about twenty-five hundred dollars in gold—to pay the people and buy supplies and equipment.*

2. A Sullen Crew and a Saucy "Scheem"

During the Captain's absence, agreeably to his orders, *Ranger* was careened on the beach and her bottom cleansed. "Chips" and his gang took 14 inches off the heel of the mainmast, stepped it 18 inches further aft, and lowered the floor of the powder magazine. "Sails" was established in a sail loft ashore to make a new suit, and to cut up the old suit of hessians to make bread bags. With these and other

---

* The French currency of the Old Régime was in *livres* (pounds), *sols* (shillings), and *deniers* (pence); but the livre was worth only about tenpence sterling, or 20 cents. A louis d'or was a gold coin worth 24 livres, equivalent to a sovereign or $4.80 in gold.

routine jobs, the people were kept busy; but they were not happy. Liberty at Paimboeuf offered few allurements, and they wanted (so they said) to get to sea and take prizes. Captain Jones's liberal supplies* of fresh provisions and brandy, and spending money advanced out of his own pocket, had no effect on their morale; when he returned on board he found a sullen crew and heard mutterings and rumblings.

The trouble was endemic. The crew had been encouraged by Lieutenant Simpson to believe that Captain Jones was little more than a passenger and would leave *Ranger* forever in France; here he was back again, working them like hell and planning God knows what crazy scheme, in which there would be no prize money. One or two, it seems, had kept copies of the recruiting poster, which promised "an agreable Voyage in this pleasant Season of the Year." This evoked sarcastic comment, now that snow was falling on deck and ice running down the Loire. They had been promised that they would "make their Fortunes," but so far had taken only two prizes and had not received a penny from either. In the poster they were addressed as "Gentlemen Seamen," but they had been treated like scum by this foreign captain, a Scot at that. New Englanders did not take kindly to naval discipline. They wanted officers whom they knew personally, or at least knew of; local characters who mixed with their men and swapped stories about Sairey Ann the town trollop, old Deacon Smith's young wife, and the dreadful way local farmers had raised prices. They were not appeased by draughts of brandy and promises of glory. "Every one was seized with the Epidemical malady of Homesickness," wrote Jones; and before they left Brittany Lieutenant Simpson told him that the people refused to obey orders. Pleasant prospect for the Captain!

As soon as Jones concluded that there was no immediate chance

---

* *Ranger's* log shows the following amounts of brandy received on board after the initial cask on 4 Dec.: "30 pot of brandy for the people" 15 Dec.; "a Cask of Brandy" and "a Hoghd of Brandy for the Ship's Use" 17 Dec.; "a Hoghd. of Brandy" 23 Dec.; "15 hoghd of Brandy and four Barrels of Old Brandy" 17 Jan. But this seems not to have been enough, as they "Got from on Board the *Independence* a Cask of Rum" 30 Jan., "1 Hamper & 2 casks of Ginn" 11 Feb. "5 hampers Bordeaux wine" on 7 Feb. was doubtless for the wardroom.

of obtaining *L'Indien,* he sought and obtained from the American Commissioners blanket orders, dated 16 January 1778. These instructed him, "after equipping the *Ranger* in the best manner for the cruise you propose, that you proceed with her in the manner you shall judge best for distressing the Enemies of the United States, by sea or otherwise, consistent with the laws of war, and the terms of your commission." He was given names of agents at Lorient, Bordeaux, Bilbao and Corunna to whom he could consign prizes. If he makes "an attempt on the coast of Great Britain," state the orders—evidence that this is what Jones proposed doing—he is advised not to return to France immediately, because France is still nominally neutral. He is cautioned against giving offense to the subjects of France or Spain or to any neutral power.

These orders, signed by Franklin and Deane but not by Lee, were indeed a blank check. Note, particularly, "by sea or otherwise"; Jones could, if he chose, have marched *Ranger's* crew inland to burn a city. "I have in contemplation," he wrote to the Marine Committee of Congress, "several Enterprizes of some importance—the Commissioners do not even promise to Justify me should I fail in any bold attempt; I will not, however, under this discouragement, alter my designs. When an Enemy thinks a design against them is improbable, they can always be surprised and attacked with advantage." How true that is! One has only to think of Pearl Harbor.

The immediate "scheem," as he called it in his letters, was a hit-and-run raid on an English port to destroy shipping. The Commissioners seem to have understood that something of the sort was in the wind because they promised Jones to recommend that Congress give *Ranger's* crew a bonus in lieu of the prizes they might otherwise have taken.

Paul Jones, obviously, shared the strategic ideas of Robert Morris: that the most effective employment for "our Infant fleet" would not be commerce-destroying—that could be left to the privateers, which were good for nothing else—but "to attack the enemies' defenceless places" and so pin down forces that would otherwise be used to blockade or invade the United States. Morris was thinking of a raid on the English West Indies, but Jones had the bolder conception of surprising some important town in the British Isles. That is what he tried to do with *Ranger* and with *Bonhomme Richard*. In addition to what he proposed to do himself, he drafted, on 10 February 1778, a plan for a French naval attack on Admiral Lord Howe's fleet in Delaware Bay. Ten or twelve sail of the line, with frigates, he predicted, could capture the British squadron in the Delaware, then mop up their next strongest squadron at New York; lie in wait for Admiral Byron's fleet, which was on the way over, and take that too. He even predicted that the British seamen were so tired of "salt horse" that they would be glad to join the French Navy to get better food. Apart from the last clause, which was plain silly (British tars did desert, but not to eat "frog" food), Jones's strategy was sound; the King of France thought so well of it that he presented Silas Deane (who claimed the plan as his own) with a diamond-studded miniature of himself. But Louis XVI and his ministers were unwilling to initiate hostilities with England, and the execution of the plan was too long delayed. The Toulon fleet under Lieutenant-Général le Comte d'Estaing departed 18 April 1778 and reached the Delaware only on 8 July, to find that Howe had concentrated his fleet at New York. D'Estaing proceeded thither, but could not persuade the local pilots to take his ships through the Narrows. Jones always regarded D'Estaing's plan as his own, and there is support for this claim: the translation of his proposal in the French naval records is annotated, in a contemporary hand, *Cette insinuation a pu déterminer l'envoi de l'escadre du comte d'Estaing.**

The precise plan Jones had in mind for his own action when he returned on board *Ranger* we do not know, but it required coöperation from the French Navy. He spent two weeks at Paimboeuf (28 January-12 February) fitting-out. New topmast staysails were cut, "swiffel" guns were mounted in the fighting tops and arms chests

---

* "This suggestion probably decided the dispatch of the Comte d'Estaing's squadron."

placed there; studding-sail booms were rigged, the great sweeps (used to propel her in a flat calm) shortened, bow ports cut so that guns could be trained ahead in a chase. Quantities of marlin, spun yarn and all kinds of ship chandlery were bought; barrels of gunpowder, reams of "carterage" paper and fathoms of match stuff were provided. "Buckshot, Sliding Shot, Star Shot, Round Shot and Swevil Shot," 230 pair boots and shoes, 100 greatcoats, dozens of pistols, cutlasses and even blunderbusses were brought on board, together with "'5 dozen fowles,'" half a ton of cheese, two tons of hardtack, 40 sugar loaves and other provisions. Thomas Morris, the Continental agent at Nantes, died and Paul Jones attended his funeral, during which *Ranger* fired thirteen minute-guns in his honor.

There was jubilation on board when Morris's successor Jonathan Williams came down from Nantes and distributed prize money from the sale of one of the fruiters. With Williams on board as passenger, and in company with U.S. armed brig *Independence, Ranger* departed Paimboeuf at 5:00 A.M. 13 February 1778.

Now began a coastal cruise in which Jones became familiar with all the murmuring passes of the sea that lead to the granite shores of Brittany.

3. The Flag Saluted

At Quiberon Bay, where *Ranger* anchored at seven in the evening of 13 February, a squadron of line-of-battle ships and three frigates, under Chef d'Escadre La Motte Piquet, was waiting to escort an American-bound convoy a safe distance from the coast.

The presence of this squadron gave Paul Jones an opportunity he had long coveted, to exchange salutes with a French flag officer. From *Ranger* he sent a note by cutter to William Carmichael, Silas Deane's secretary, who was then at Quiberon, asking him to present his respects "to the French Admiral whom I mean to salute with thirteen guns under American Colours—provided he will Accept

the Compliment and Return Gun for Gun." Carmichael delivered
the message so promptly that the same evening Jones received the
following autograph reply from La Motte Piquet, who seems to
have had e. e. cummings's aversion to the use of capitals and
punctuation:

MONSIEUR
    si la frégatte la ranger et le brique l'independence saluent le
pavillon du roy 13 coups de canon en cas qu'ils soient com-
mandés par des officiers du congrés je leur rendray neuf coups
ils sont au surplus très fort les maitres de ne point salüer
    j'ay l'honneur de vous assurer des sentimens respectueux
avec lesquels je suis
                          Monsieur
              Votre très humble et très obeissant serviteur
                                LA MOTTE PIQUET
ce 13ᵉ fᵉʳ 1778
    je seray enchanté de voir mr. villiams voulés vous bien
monsieur luy faire mes remercimens et a mr. carmicael, j'ay
l'honneur de souhaitter le bon soir a mr. le marquis de vienne.*

Jones was disappointed; he wrote to Carmichael next day (14
February), somewhat irritably, that even "the haughty English return
Gun for Gun to foreign Officers of equal rank, and two less only to
Captains by flag officers." Thus, *Ranger* should have at least eleven
guns returned for thirteen; a mere nine he would not accept. Carmichael advised him not to hold out for more, since nine guns was
all that the American privateer *General Mifflin* received from Admiral
du Chauffault when she entered Brest the previous summer; and
even that was thrice the ordinary acknowledgment by a French rear
admiral to a thirteen-gun salute.

Jones did not like being compared to a privateer, but he sensibly

* "Sir, if the frigate *Ranger* and the brig *Independence* salute the royal ensign with thirteen guns,
and they are commanded by officers of the Congress, I shall return nine guns. They may, however, choose
not to salute. I have the honor to assure you of my respectful sentiments, etc. I shall be delighted to see
Mr. Williams; will you, Sir, kindly send my thanks to him and to Mr. Carmichael. I have the honor to bid
M. le marquis de Vienne good-night." This last clause was probably added as an excuse for making the
note so curt.

gave in. *Ranger* weighed anchor at 4:00 P.M. 14 February, and in
"Very Squaly weather," according to Dr. Green, beat into Quiberon
Bay, passed the stern of the French flagship at 6:00 P.M., fired thirteen guns and received nine. It blew so hard that even with two
anchors down and cables "out to all 4 shackles,"* *Ranger* dragged
and her lower yards had to be housed. Next morning, the 15th,
Captain Jones went on board brig *Independence,* commanded by
his friend Captain John Young. Again he sailed past the French flagship, repeated the salute and received the same nine-gun acknowledgment. Possibly he had hoped that on second thoughts La Motte
Piquet would give him another gun or two.

This was not the first time that any American flag had been saluted
in France, as Jones later claimed; but *General Mifflin* must have
been flying the Grand Union Flag, not the Stars and Stripes. The
salutes to *Ranger* and *Independence* on 14-15 February 1778 symbolized the secret alliance which had been signed between the two
countries a week earlier.

Now snugly anchored near the head of Quiberon Bay in 8 fathom
with 70 fathom of cable out, *Ranger* spent ten days not unpleasantly
despite dirty weather and snow squalls. Nearby was the little town
of Auray, where the waterfront (now called *quai Franklin* because
Ben once stopped there) is unchanged since the eighteenth century.
Independence sailed to Carnac and returned with a supply of livestock, two oxen and three calves for *Ranger.* Ten more tons of lead
ballast were stowed. A group of French naval officers, whom Jones
described as "a very well Bred set of men," were entertained on
board and the yards manned in their honor. In return, Captain Jones
and Mr. Carmichael were received on board the French flagship
"with every mark of respect and Gladness and saluted with a Feu
de Joie"—a musketry volley by French Marines. The "Empty Pa-
geantry of Kings," which Jones in an earlier letter to the Committee
had said that he despised, was beginning to take effect.

---

*When a ship's cables were faked on deck for quick paying out, they were stopped at regular
lengths, such as 25 fathom, to ring-bolts which at that time were called shackles.

Apparently it was part of Jones's first "scheem" for *Ranger* to sail with La Motte Piquet; but the Chef d'Escadre got his fleet under way during the morning of 25 February without saying a word to Captain Jones, much to his chagrin. Since there was no point in tarrying in Quiberon Bay, *Ranger* weighed and without a pilot stood out, in a high wind, toward the northern cape of Belle-Île. The wind was very squally from the northwest, and she could not weather the cape. Jones then wore ship and headed back for Quiberon Bay, but was unable to weather the rocks in the narrow passage between the mainland and La Teignouse reefs, the nearest entrance. *Ranger* narrowly escaped capsizing when a squall struck her sails, and in the midst of righting her the dreadful cry of "Fire!" was raised; but the flames were soon quenched. Jones signaled for a pilot, but none would come out in that weather; so, with night coming on, he ran to leeward of Belle-Île and jogged off-and-on under close-reefed topsails until morning. Next day, 26 February, *Ranger* arrived back in Quiberon Bay, "after a short but very tedious & unprofitable Cruize," Surgeon Green well remarked.

Jones now decided to sail to Brest, hoping that the French naval authorities there would do something for him. It was a cold, rough season of the year to be sailing along the reef-studded coast of Lower Brittany, and Jones properly waited for a good chance when the wind was fair. *Ranger* again departed Quiberon Bay 3 March in a fine ESE breeze, and as soon as she had "haw'ld round the Rocks" set topmast and topgallant studding sails, passed Île de Groix and Lorient, where Paul Jones was destined to spend many months of his life; and, passing inside the Îles de Glenan, where she picked up a pilot, came to anchor in the roadstead of Benodet. Next morning (5 March) Captain Jones sent a young boy of his crew named Joseph Ratcliff, who had broken out with smallpox pustules, in the ship's boat to Pont l'Abbé, with Surgeon Green in attendance. Lodgings were procured for the lad, and a local physician engaged to attend him. "We were treated with great respect, as we were Americans," wrote Dr. Green; "were waited on near half a mile to the Boat, and on parting gave them 3 cheers which was answered with Vive Le Congrès!"

Departing Benodet in the early hours of 6 March, *Ranger* with a NNE wind stood well off shore to be clear of the Penmarch rocks, then tacked and stood toward the land. All night she beat to windward, but at 8:00 A.M. on the 7th, having got a good slant, she just managed to weather the Pointe du Raz, observing a French frigate astern which failed to make it. After crossing Iroise Bay in a fresh gale, Jones found it too squally to beat up to Brest and anchored in the Bae de Davie on the north side of the Goulet de Brest for the night of 7-8 March. Next day he stood across the Goulet to the little port of Cameret, about eight miles below Brest.

At that time Brest was a purely military port, and the inner and outer harbors were so crowded with the great fleet of Lieutenant-Général le Comte d'Orvilliers* that there was no room for little *Ranger*. So at Cameret she stayed.

Captain Jones visited Brest every few days in the cutter, made his number with the Comte d'Orvilliers, and was promised a frigate and tender to accompany *Ranger* to sea. In the meantime all hands were kept busy. Experience along the coast of Brittany in squally winter weather proved that radical measures were necessary to increase her speed and seaworthiness. The entire rig was altered. "Chips" and his gang stripped the main and mizzen masts and set the one 5 feet, 9 inches and the other 6 feet farther aft; the yards, too, were shortened. The sailmakers took 69 yards of canvas out of six different sails and made a new suit of topgallant studding sails. The ballast, too, was shifted to give her better trim. Nor did Jones neglect his people's comfort; he had "Sails" make new hammocks for them. Lieutenant Hall afterward declared that these alterations were "to little or no purpose"; but actually they increased *Ranger's* speed and maneuverability. And although she spent the winter of

---

* The flag ranks in the Royal Navy of France, according to an Ordonnance of 1765, were: *Amiral* (=Admiral RN); *Vice-Amiral* (=Vice Admiral); *Lieutenant-Général des Armées Navales* (=Rear Admiral); *Chef d'Escadre* (=Commodore). Charles de la Roncière *Histoire de la Marine Française* (1934) p. 151.

1778-1779 in her home port, it is significant that nothing was done to alter the rig and sail plan as redesigned by Captain Jones.

Eight of the crew deserted at Cameret, but the police returned seven of them. The Captain, Lieutenant Simpson and Surgeon Green made a sightseeing trip to Brest on 14 March. Jones passed the night there, as he wished to discuss plans with d'Orvilliers; and in his absence Dr. Green received Madame de Chaumont and her two sisters on board. Imagine Jones's chagrin at having missed his *chère amie!* However, the ladies returned three days later, when the Captain was on board to do the honors.

On 23 March *Ranger* sailed up the Goulet to Brest and saluted flagship *La Bretagne* with thirteen guns. The Admiral "returned the Compliment," states the log without mentioning the number, and assigned *Ranger* to a naval mooring dolphin. Two days later, Jones wrote to Silas Deane: "I have had the *Ranger* in Disguise at Cameret but I have now pulled off the Masque as the face of Affairs are altered." But on the last day of March he is taking on, obviously as camouflage, "Red Cloth to Cover the Sides," as well as 4018 gallons of fresh water, more bread and beef. All hands "exercise the great guns" on 1 April and are given liberty after a barber has come on board to shave them clean, as the French associated beards with Russians and Turks. To the local *intendant de la marine*, with whom he had a "Tate a Tate" conference (as he calls it), Jones wrote that a convoy of twenty ships, his "principal object," was about to depart, which would render his project impracticable. What did he have in mind? My guess is that the twenty ships were a fleet of English merchantmen in some French harbor (England and France not yet being at war); that he had expected to work *Ranger* in among them, disguised as a peaceful freighter with the red cloth covering her telltale gun ports, and play fox in a flock of geese. D'Orvilliers, who was privy to the project, had promised to detail a frigate to escort *Ranger* past the British warships which were watching Brest, but apparently he did not do so in time.

At Brest, Captain Jones dismissed Captain Matthew Parke USMC, whom he had brought over to command the Marine guard of *L'Indien*. His junior officers resented sharing their prize money with Parke, and as Jones had to admit that two Marine officers were one too many for so small a ship, he let him go. As a substitute he accepted Lieutenant Jean Meijer of the Swedish Army, who was eager for action under the Stars and Stripes.

The Comte d'Orvilliers, who became Paul Jones's best friend in the Royal Navy of France, entertained him and Surgeon Green on board his flagship, and consented to forward a letter to M. de la Sartine, Ministre de la Marine, asking him to get *L'Indien* for Jones when he returned from his present mission. When *Ranger* departed Brest 2 April for Cameret, to be careened and graved once more before sailing, Jones saluted the French ensign with thirteen guns and received eleven in return—two more than La Motte Piquet had rendered; for by this time the two countries were allies. D'Orvilliers sent frigate *Fortunée* and a tender to accompany *Ranger* to sea. From Brest, on the 8th, Jones wrote to John Ross: "This morning the weather looks promising and we shall again proceed. The loss of time here will perhaps make it necessary for me to alter my plan agreeable to circumstances—as Milton said of Adam, 'The World lays all before me.' "

It certainly did; and two days later, 10 April, Paul Jones was on his way to fame and glory.

4. The Brush with "Hussar"

Captain Jones now reverted to his original scheme to raid an English seaport, destroy shipping and capture some important person as hostage, in order to force the British government to exchange American sailors taken prisoner. The raid he may have looked upon as proper retaliation for General John Vaughan's wanton burning of Esopus on the Hudson in early October 1777. Through the French secret service, he may also have known that the British government

had ordered the burning of American seaports as a military policy.*
Jones's first object, he said, was the exchange of prisoners; and his
second, "to put an end of burnings in America by making a good
fire in England of *Shipping*."

The release of American seamen from English prisons was very
close to the Captain's heart. Although the war had been going on
for three years, and the two enemies frequently exchanged Army
prisoners, the British government treated everyone taken in American armed vessels as a rebel and pirate. This was a sore point with
American sailors; and one of the results of *Ranger's* cruise was to
change the British practice, if not the policy.

Fortunée escorted *Ranger* for four days, then returned to Brest.
On 14 April Jones took brigantine *Dolphin* carrying flaxseed from
Ostend to Wexford. After taking her master and crew prisoner, the
Captain scuttled her, probably because she was of slight value and
he did not wish to reduce his own crew, already weakened by desertion. *Ranger's* trim was still down by the head; the Captain had
twenty-eight pigs of lead removed from the forepeak and stowed
in the run of the ship. On the 16th, *Ranger* raised Old Head of Kin-
sale, and, turning easterly, ran for St. George's Channel.

Off Wicklow she encountered the 250-ton ship *Lord Chatham* of
Dublin, bound to that city with a cargo of mixed merchandise and
a hundred hogsheads of prime English porter—which one would
suppose to have been a drug on the market in the home of Dublin
stout. She was captured without a fight, manned with a prize crew
under John Seward of Portsmouth, and sent into Brest, where she
arrived 22 April. Jones later had difficulty securing some of the porter for himself and his friends.

---

* Lord George Germain instructs Sir Henry Clinton, 8 March 1778, that if he cannot bring General
Washington to a decisive engagement shortly, he is to organize an amphibious operation "to attack the
Ports on the Coast, from New York to Nova Scotia, and to seize or destroy every Ship or Vessel in the
different Creeks or Harbors, wherever it is found practicalle to penetrate, as also to destroy all Wharfs and
Stores, and Materials for Ship-Building, so as to incapacitate them from raising a Marine, or continuing
their Depredations upon the Trade of this Kingdom." (B. F. Stevens *Facsimiles* XI no. 1062.) Documents
in Stopford-Sackville Collection record the King's pleasure over these depredations (Historical Mss.
Commission *Ninth Report* [1884] III 96-8).

The Irish Sea. *The compass rose displays the seal of Jones.*

From off Wicklow Head, *Ranger* stood north into the Irish Sea. By ten in the morning of 18 April she was off the Point of Ayre, the northern cape of the Isle of Man, ready to make the crossing thence to Whitehaven, when she was challenged by H.M. revenue wherry *Hussar*. The commander of this vessel, Captain Gurley, thought *Ranger* looked suspicious and decided to investigate. *Hussar* pursued her in a northeasterly direction and got almost alongside off the Big Scares ledges at the entrance to Luce Bay, Scotland. The Captain, reported Gurley, was "dressed in white with a large Hat Cocked." This is interesting and puzzling; white was the dress uniform of the French Army, not Navy, nor did merchant captains wear white; what could it have been? Possibly Jones was wearing his blue-and-white uniform without the blue coat; but it was not like him to appear thus before a foreign naval officer. I suspect that Jones wore a white coat for mere bravura, just as Nelson invited enemy sharpshooters to make him a target by wearing all his medals and orders at Trafalgar.

Gurley reported that the officers "appeared like Frenchmen, but spoke good English." One of them, dressed in blue (Master Cullam probably), hailed the revenue wherry and asked if she could spare him a pilot? Gurley replied that he could not and asked what ship she was. The officer in blue said, "The *Molly* of Glasgow." "Where from and whence bound?" asked Gurley. Jones then replied, "Bring to, or I'll sink you directly!" Captain Gurley said, Very well, he would. Upon which the blue-clad officer dropped his speaking trumpet and fired a musket and "the man in White cryed out, 'Up all Ports,' on which they run out a tier of Guns; but the *Hussar* being on the knuckle of her Bow, the Ship's Guns could not bear on her, but they played small arms on the *Hussar* who immediately put about to the Southward."

There was a strong wind blowing. *Ranger* tacked, fired a broadside at the cutter, scored one on her stern and holed her mainsail twice. Gurley then escaped by a maneuver that must have galled Jones, since it was the sort of trick he used to play on square-riggers with sloop *Providence*. Gurley beat to windward northeasterly, the only way he could gain on the *Ranger*, which "far outsailed the *Hussar*," he admitted. As soon as *Ranger*, after tacking, filled away, gathered speed and prepared to give her a broadside, *Hussar* promptly tacked and spoiled her aim, and in every tack the fore-and-aft sloop gained over the yard-swinging ship. When they neared the Scares, with a fast-running tide, Jones evidently felt he could not risk entering shallow Luce Bay and turned back. The cutter "slipped through our fingers," recorded Surgeon Green.

5. The Raid on Whitehaven

Next morning, 19 April, off the Mull of Galloway, *Ranger* intercepted a Scots coasting schooner bound for Irvine with oats and barley, sank her, and took her crew prisoner. From them Jones learned that there was a fleet of merchantmen in Loch Ryan, around the Rinns of Galloway. He decided to give these a working over, but a change of wind prevented. He pursued an armed cutter as far north as Ailsa Craig at the entrance to the Firth of Clyde, but could not catch her; then fell in with a sloop from Dublin in ballast, which he sank "to prevent intelligence."

Ranger now turned about and reëntered the North Channel between Ireland and Scotland. On 20 April, off Carrickfergus on Belfast Lough, Jones detained a small fishing vessel, whose crew informed him that a ship he had sighted at anchor in the Lough was H.M.S. *Drake*, a 20-gun sloop of war. Jones wished to sail right into the Lough "and cut her out," but his crew absolutely refused. They consented, however, to surprise her that night by crossing her bows and anchoring just to windward of her, so as to sweep her decks and then grapple and board. This plan miscarried for the simple reason that *Ranger's* anchor caught on the cathead, and the anchor detail, under a quartermaster who had been drinking, was unable to free it until the ship had overshot *Drake*. She came to on the

British warship's port quarter, only a hundred feet away. Since *Ranger* was still disguised as a peaceful merchantman, and *Drake* made no hostile move, Jones made the best of a bad situation, cut his cable and sheered off, intending to return and try again the following night. But it came on to blow great guns, so that *Ranger* barely weathered the Mew, the lighthouse at the southern entrance to Belfast Lough; the sea ran so high that she was forced to take shelter "under the south shore of Scotland." The crew were "very much fatigued," recorded Surgeon Green, and obviously disgruntled.

The 22nd of April dawned fair and cold; snow could be seen on both sides of Solway Firth and on the Isle of Man—"in three kingdoms," as Jones observed. He now decided to carry out his earlier plan for a descent on Whitehaven to burn the shipping. It was in no military sense an invasion, but a surprise hit-and-run raid to do as much mischief as possible. Paul Jones had no animosity against Whitehaven, the port whence he first sailed for Virginia at the age of thirteen. He chose it simply because he knew it so well that he could find his way in and out in the dark. The United States Navy, for want of something better to do, had elected to fight a commerce-destroying war, and here was an opportunity to destroy more shipping in one night than the entire Navy had taken at sea in a year. Captains Lambert Wickes and Henry Johnson had sailed *Reprisal* and *Lexington* around the British Isles, taking many prizes, in 1777; but it had not occurred to them to make a landing. No enemy had dared to do that to an English harbor within the memory of man. The Royal Navy was there to prevent it. Well, we'd see what the Royal Navy could do about Paul Jones!

Ranger's home-town crew did not see the Whitehaven enterprise in the same light. They had enlisted in the hope of big prize money, and so far they had taken nothing, or rather saved nothing, except the two fruiters on the passage to Nantes, and *Lord Chatham*. Now the Old Man was bent on sinking prizes instead of sending them in, and proposing to burn ships ashore—no prize money out of that, not even loot. Yankee sailors carried their notions of civil government to sea with them, and felt that the Captain should have called a New England town meeting to decide by majority vote whether or not they should engage a ship or raid a town! "A wise officer of mine," wrote Jones—he meant Surgeon Green—denounced the plan as rash, and remarked, "*Nothing could be got* by burning poor people's property." The Doctor, we must admit, "had something." Neither prize money nor military advantage was to be gained by burning the little coasters, fishermen and colliers that were lying in Whitehaven waiting for their summer's work; but nobody except the Captain seems to have appreciated the propaganda value of raiding an English seaport. Lieutenant Simpson (so Jones later believed) had encouraged the murmurs against his authority, and even gave some of the more surly and complaining sailors to understand that if it were not for that damned Scotsman they would be on their way home, and capturing prizes. This feeling had already boiled up in a near-mutiny. Lieutenant Meijer, the Swedish volunteer, tipped off by sailor Meyer in the crew as to what was cooking, warned the Captain, who, when Master Cullam rushed at him as a signal for the mutiny to start, put a pistol to his head and stopped it then and there. And when Jones exposed his Whitehaven plan to the officers and men, and called for volunteers, both lieutenants begged off because "overcome with fatigue."

The raid got off to a bad start. As *Ranger* was crossing Solway Firth, the wind grew faint and finally petered out, so that at midnight she was still many miles from Whitehaven. Two boats' crews were made up, with a total force of 40 officers and men. Paul Jones commanded one, with Lieutenant Meijer as his second in command; Lieutenant Wallingford USMC commanded the other, with Midshipman Ben Hill as his mate. At midnight they left the ship, and, only after three hours' hard rowing against the tide, reached the harbor. Day was already breaking.

Whitehaven Harbor is divided by a stone pier into two parts, the North Harbor and the South, each side defended by a battery. Both boats carried combustible "candles" made of canvas dipped in brimstone, to be ignited with flint and steel and thrown on board the ships, which were moored or grounded board-to-board. The Wallingford-Hill boat party landed at the Old Quay slip, where they entered the nearest pub and "made very free with the liquor, etc." While these fellows were carousing, Captain Jones and a few men scaled the wall of the south battery by climbing on each other's shoulders, spiked the guns, found the sentinels asleep in the guard-house and secured them. Then the Captain, taking only Midshipman Joe Green with him, spiked the guns at the north battery. Meijer, in the meantime, stood by the Captain's boat to insure that he was not left on the beach; and it was lucky he did, because the rest of the boat's crew told him that that was exactly what they intended to do.

Jones had to cope not only with insubordinate and mutinous be-havior, but with a traitor. This fellow, an Irishman named David Freeman alias David Smith, had enlisted in Portsmouth in order to get home. He now proceeded to do a Paul Revere act, rushing from house to house banging on the doors and warning the people to turn out to prevent their ships and houses being burned by the "pirates." And there were plenty of ships, too; Jones estimated 150 on the north side of over 200 tons' burthen, and 70 to 100 aground on the south side of the harbor. Presently half the town was swarming down to the water's edge; but Jones coolly placed sentinels while one of his men got fire from a house, lighted one of the "candles," and threw it on board collier *Thompson*. This was followed by rolling a barrel of tar on board, and soon the collier was blazing merrily.

It was now almost five o'clock, "the sun was a full hour above the horizon, and as sleep no longer ruled the world it was time to retire," as Jones (vaguely remembering Young's *Night Thoughts*) put it poetically in his official report. Hundreds of townsfolk, bewildered or belligerent, were swarming down to the harbor and doing their best to smother the flames. After releasing all but three of the prison-ers, the two boats' crews, minus the traitor, reëmbarked, Captain Jones the last. As they rowed out to *Ranger*, they were followed by wildly inaccurate gunfire from cannon which had been overlooked by the spiking parties. By six o'clock they were on board, *Ranger* having sailed toward shore to meet them. The raid was over, and the fires were soon quenched by the inhabitants, aided by a shower of rain. No blood had been shed on either side.

The damage done was inconsequential—British estimates ran from £250 to £1250—but the moral effect was stupendous. Nobody had done that sort of thing to an English seaport since 1667, when the Dutch burned Sheerness. Where was the Royal Navy, supposed to protect the coasts with its "wooden walls"? Every neighboring seaport was alerted. Lieutenant Governor Dawson of the Isle of Man called out the Manx militia, asked gentlemen to volunteer, and required local forces to provide a twenty-man guard to protect Castle Rushen, his official residence, every night until further notice. London newspapers rang changes on the "defenceless" state of the coast and the "inexcusable" laxness of government. An extra edition of the Whitehaven paper giving a blow-by-blow account of the raid was reprinted in the London *Morning Post*. On 28 April a local correspondent wrote to that paper, "We are all in a bustle here, from the late insolent attack of the provincial privateer's men"; people were cleaning old rusty swords and muskets, running bullets and making up powder cartridges. The deserter David Freeman made an affidavit, printed in the Whitehaven extra, to the effect that *Ranger* was a privateer "commanded by John Paul Jones, fitted out at Piscataqua, in New England"; and someone who saw him ashore identified the Captain as John Paul who had served his apprenticeship in *Friendship* of Whitehaven, and was "well known by many people in this town." The reprinting of this statement in the London *Morning Post* on 28 April was the first time that the name of Paul Jones came before the English public; it was far from being the last.

Few were able to share the humorous point of view of Horace Walpole, who wrote that he considered Jones ungrateful, since America owes her independence to the Scots; "though, to be sure, in strictness it was not what the Scots intended for them."

VIII

The
Raid on
St. Mary's
Isle

23 April 1778

That night's work at Whitehaven was a disappointment to Paul Jones, nor did he have the consolation of knowing that Freeman's treachery was largely responsible for his failure. So far as he could tell, it was owing to the late start and the lukewarm attitude of his officers and men that more ships were not burned. This promised ill for the success of *Ranger's* cruise; but there was nothing that the Captain could now do about it except go ahead and hope for the best.

For the very same day that opened at Whitehaven, he planned a raid which for originality surpassed anything hitherto conceived. He would descend on St. Mary's Isle in Kirkcudbright Bay across Solway Firth, and abduct the Earl of Selkirk as a hostage, to compel the British ministry to authorize an exchange of prisoners. This raid developed in so unexpected and dramatic a manner as to prove an important point of Jones's career, striking the imagination of friend and foe alike, and making his name feared or admired in every British harbor.

St. Mary's Isle, so called from a priory founded there in the twelfth century, is not an island but a peninsula stretching out into Kirkcudbright Bay, and the Selkirk "castle," so called in various romances about Paul Jones, was a rambling brick mansion, partly Jacobean and partly early Georgian. The Isle, which covers several hundred acres, was the seat of Dunbar Hamilton of Baldoon, who became the fourth Earl of Selkirk in 1744. His wife, whom he married in 1758, was Lady Helen Hamilton, granddaughter to the Earl of Haddington. In his childhood Jones may have seen Lord Selkirk as a guest at Arbigland (for he was a friend of Mr. Craik), or in Kirkcudbright when he called there during his service in the merchant marine. Selkirk was a generous and public-spirited but unimportant Scots peer: to Paul Jones, however, he was a very great lord, the possession of whose person, he naïvely supposed, would force the British government to do anything he asked in order to obtain his release.

Ranger covered the twenty miles across Solway Firth in a remarkably short time. By ten o'clock on the same morning as the raid on Whitehaven—23 April—she made Little Ross, the island that marks the entrance to Kirkcudbright Bay. Here the bay is a mile and a half wide, and for the same distance beyond Little Ross there is deep water, in which *Ranger* could safely maneuver under reduced sail while waiting for the Captain to perform his mission. That had to be by boat, since the course to the nearest point of St. Mary's Isle lay through an intricate channel that is bare at half tide. The channel was not then marked, as today, by buoys and perches, but Paul Jones knew it well from the many voyages he had made in and out of Kirkcudbright, which lies another two and a half miles up the Dee estuary. He knew all the landmarks—Torrs Point where Dutch William had set up a battery, the wood of Clauchandolly, Cairnsmore rising above the western shore, the "Inch" or islet off the southern point of St. Mary's Isle. It was springtime in Galloway and the fields were all tender green, the oaks and beeches which the Earl had planted on the Isle were in early bud, and the air was filled with a tumult of birdsong.

The ship's cutter was lowered into the water, Jones himself took command, and brought with him David Cullam the master, Lieutenant Wallingford of the Marine Corps, and a dozen sailors. At 10:30 or 11:00 the cutter, completely undetected, grounded at the Point of the Isle. Leaving one or two men to guard it, Jones and his two officers and a squad of well-armed sailors marched up the path toward the mansion. In so doing they encountered the head gardener and cleverly gave out that they were a press gang seeking recruits for His Majesty's Navy. This report no sooner spread than the undergardeners "and all the stout young fellows" ran off to the town. And from this gardener Jones learned that the Earl was absent, taking the waters at Buxton in Derbyshire. His mission was frustrated.

Back he started to the cutter, intending to return to *Ranger* without more ado. But Cullam and Wallingford expostulated, saying that they and the crew should be allowed to loot the mansion, considering that they had returned empty-handed from Whitehaven, and that some of their friends' houses in New England had been burned by British sailors. Jones, who knew when to insist and when to yield with these independent fellows, made a quick decision. The two officers and some of the men could go to the mansion, demand the family silver, and carry it off; but they must not search the house, molest the people or do any other pillage.

His orders were carried out to the letter. In the Selkirk mansion were the Countess, an eight-year-old son, and several younger daughters, Mrs. Mary Elliot their governess, and four guests: Mrs. Wood, widow of a former governor of the Isle of Man, with her three young daughters. And, of course, numerous domestics, male and female.

Shortly after eleven the Countess, who had just finished breakfast, observed some "horrid-looking wretches," armed to the teeth and dressed in no recognizable uniform, surrounding the house. She took them first for pirates. Mrs. Wood and her daughters and the maid-servants, fearing the worst, retired to the top story with the young children, while Lady Selkirk, Mrs. Elliot and Daniel the butler remained below to face the intruders. Cullam and Wallingford entered and spoke to the Countess. They told her (as she wrote to the Earl next day) that they were from frigate *Ranger,* "Captain Paul Jones Esq." commanding; that they were instructed to carry away her household silver; and if she complied they would neither search the house nor make any further trouble. The Countess, a lady of great charm, dignity and presence of mind, quickly decided that she had better do as they wished, since she had nobody to defend her. She entered the pantry, where the butler was trying to secrete some of the plate in a maid's apron, told him to drop it and hand over the lot. The officers called for sacks—proof, if Jones's word were not sufficient, that plunder had not originally been his mission. The Countess said that the senior officer, Master Cullam, who was clad in a blue suit which did not look like a uniform, "had a vile blackguard look, still kept civil as well he might"; but the junior officer "was a civil young man in a green uniform, an anchor on his buttons which were white" (the uniform of the United States Marine Corps), and wore over it a blue greatcoat. He "seemed naturally well bred and not to like his employment." When the sacks were filled, Cullam called for an inventory of the plate, apparently to ascertain that he had missed nothing. The Countess produced it and Cullam, after a quick glance, said, "Where are the coffeepot and the teapot?" The butler, who had secreted these two, produced them on the Countess's order, the teapot still full of wet leaves from breakfast, and they were added to the loot, which later proved to weigh about 250 ounces.

In the meantime Mrs. Elliot, who thought it very "odd" that the men asked for neither watches nor jewelry, chatted with the "horrid-looking wretches" about the door, and "asked them a thousand questions" about America; "they behaved with great civility," so she wrote to a cousin in Roxburghshire.

All this took only fifteen to twenty minutes. The Master and the Lieutenant, eager to decamp before the neighborhood was aroused, did not insist on taking small articles listed in the inventory that were in other parts of the mansion. When the Countess coolly requested a receipt for what they were about to carry off, Wallingford started to write it; but when he had got no farther than "This is to cert . . . ," Cullam told him to break it off. He and the Lieutenant each accepted a glass of wine offered by the Countess, courteously took their leave, formed up their men and marched in good order to the cutter, where Captain Jones was waiting, no doubt anxiously. They rowed the boat a good three miles to join *Ranger,* which promptly made sail and was last seen standing past Burrow Head. A King's cutter from Whitehaven—probably our old friend *Hussar*—dogged her all day, but lost her in the dark off the Mull of Galloway.

Lady Selkirk certainly acted the thoroughbred. She correctly estimated how to deal with the intruders, and avoided provoking them by sneering or indignant remarks; neither she nor the governess screamed or fainted, although they fully expected to be dragged on board *Ranger* in lieu of the Earl. They were not long alone after the sailors departed. Within half an hour, volunteer defenders, aroused by a servingman who had escaped the cordon of sailors and given the alarm at Kirkcudbright, began to swarm about the house. An old cannon, dragged from the town to the Point of the Isle, blazed away at a rock in the bay which in the setting sun bore some resemblance to a boat. Scotland had been deprived of her militia after the Forty-five; some of the local gentlemen, in fact, used this raid as an argument for reorganizing the local yeomanry.

From her tardy defenders the Countess learned that her assailant, as she promptly wrote to Mr. Craik, was John Paul, "born in your grounds and a gardener's son of yours"; a "great villain," she added in a letter to the Earl, who, when writing on 9 June to Lord Le Despencer, declared, "We were perfectly unacquainted with him till his landing at my house." This should effectively dispose of the yarn that Paul Jones had once lived on St. Mary's Isle as somebody's bastard and had been dismissed for trying to rape a maidservant in the buttery.

The rape of the plate by no means ends this story. Paul Jones, when he learned from his men how the Countess conducted herself, was filled with admiration for her. With great care, and doubtless after many false starts and rough drafts, he composed a letter to her, dated at Brest 8 May 1778, and dispatched it under cover to Lord Le Despencer, the Postmaster General of Great Britain, who with some reluctance forwarded it to the Countess. She received it within a month. Although the letter repeats some of the events already described and anticipates others, it is so characteristic of Jones, and so faithfully reflects the romantic streak in his character, that I have reprinted the whole from the original that the Countess received. It is written more smoothly and legibly than most of his letters, and without an erasure; but all in his hand.

Ranger, BREST, *8th May, 1778*

MADAM:—

It cannot be too much lamented that in the profession of Arms, the Officer of fine feelings, and of real Sensibility, should be under the necessity of winking at any action of Persons under his command, which his Heart cannot approve:—but the reflection is doubly severe when he finds himself Obliged, in appearance, to countenance such Action by his Authority.

This hard case was mine when on the 23$^{\underline{d}}$ of April last I landed on St. Mary's Isle. Knowing Lord Selkirk's intrest with his King, and esteeming *as I do* his private Character; I wished to make him the happy Instrument of alleviating the horrors of hopeless captivity, when the brave are overpowered and made Prisoners of War.

It was perhaps fortunate for you Madam that he was from home; for it was my intention to have taken him on board the *Ranger,* and to have detained him till thro' his means, a general and fair Exchange of Prisoners, as well in Europe as in America had been effected.

When I was informed by some Men whom I met at landing, that his Lordship was absent; I walked back to my Boat determining to leave the Island: by the way, however, some Officers who were with me could not forbear expressing their discontent; observing that in America no delicacy was shown by the English; who took away all sorts of movable Property, setting Fire not only to Towns and to Houses of the rich without distinction; but not even sparing the wretched hamlets and Milch Cows of the poor and helpless at the approach of an inclement Winter. That party had been with me, as Volunteers, the same morning at White Haven; some complaisance therefore was their due. I had but a moment to think how I might gratify them, and at the same time do your Ladyship the least Injury. I charged the Two Officers to permit none of the Seamen to enter the House, or to hurt anything about it—To treat you, Madam, with the utmost Respect—to accept of the plate which was offered—and to come away without making a search or demanding anything else.

I am induced to believe that I was punctually Obeyed; since I am informed that the plate which they brought away is far short of the Inventory which accompanied it. I have gratified my Men; and when the plate is sold, I shall become the Purchaser, and I will gratify *my own feelings* by restoring it to you, by such conveyance as you shall be pleased to direct.

Had the Earl been on board the *Ranger* the following Evening he would have seen the awful Pomp and dreadful Carnage of a Sea Engagement, both affording ample subject for the Pencil, as well as melancholy reflection for the contemplative mind. Humanity starts back from such scenes of horror, and cannot but execrate the vile Promoters of this detested War.

> For *They*, t'was THEY unsheath'd the ruthless blade,
> And Heav'n shall ask the Havock it has made.*

---

*Nobody has been able to identify this couplet as a quotation, and I believe that Jones composed it himself.

The British Ship of War, *Drake*, mounting 20 guns, with more than her full complement of Officers and Men, besides a number of Volunteers, came out from Carrickfergus, in order to attack and take the American Continental Ship of War, *Ranger*, of 18 guns and short of her complement of Officers and Men. The Ships met, and the advantage was disputed with great fortitude on each side for an Hour and Five minutes, when the gallant Commander of the *Drake* fell, and Victory declared in favor of the *Ranger*. His amiable Lieutenant lay mortally wounded besides near forty of the inferior officers and crew killed and wounded. A melancholy demonstration of the uncertainty of human prospects, and of the sad reverse of fortune which an hour can produce. I buried them in a spacious grave, with the Honors due to the memory of the brave.

Tho' I have drawn my Sword in the present generous Struggle for the rights of Men; yet I am not in Arms as an American, nor am I in pursuit of Riches. My Fortune is liberal enough, having no Wife nor Family, and having lived long enough to know that Riches cannot ensure Happiness. I profess myself a Citizen of the World, totally unfettered by the little mean distinctions of Climate or of Country, which diminish the benevolence of the Heart and set bounds to Philanthropy. Before this War began I had at an early time of Life, withdrawn from the Sea service, in favor of "calm contemplation and Poetic ease." I have sacrificed not only my favorite scheme of Life, but the *softer Affections of the Heart* and my prospects of Domestic Happiness:—And I am ready to sacrifice Life also with cheerfulness—if that forfeiture could restore Peace and Goodwill among mankind.

As the feelings of your gentle Bosom cannot but be congenial with mine—let me entreat you Madam to use your soft persuasive Arts with your Husband to endeavor to stop this Cruel and destructive War, in which Britain can never succeed. Heaven can never countenance the barbarous and unmanly Practices of the Britons in America, which Savages would Blush at; and which if not discontinued will soon be retaliated in Britain by a justly enraged People.—Should you fail in this, (for I am persuaded you will attempt it; and who can resist the power of such an Advocate?) Your endeavours to effect a general Exchange of Prisoners, will be an Act of Humanity, which will afford you Golden feelings on a Death bed.

I hope this cruel contest will soon be closed; but should it continue, I wage no War with the Fair. I acknowledge their Power, and bend before it with profound Submission; let not therefore the Amiable Countess of Selkirk regard me as an Enemy. I am ambitious of her esteem and Friendship, and would do anything consistent with my duty to merit it.

The honor of a Line from your hand in Answer to this will lay me under a very singular Obligation; and if I can render you any acceptable service in France or elsewhere, I hope you see into my character so far as to command me without the least grain of reserve.

I wish to know exactly the behavior of my People, as I determine to punish them if they have exceeded their Liberty.

I have the Honor to be with much Esteem and with profound Respect,

Madam,

Your most Obedient and most humble Servant

JNº P. Jones

Exactly what did Jones suppose that he could accomplish by this letter? Apparently he thought he had such expert knowledge of the female heart that he could appeal to the Countess by enlarging on his hatred of war, his disappointment in love and his solicitude concerning the conduct of his men. Or, as he expressed it, by his "sensibility," which he used in the contemporary sense of a delicate, refined taste. Most of all, he wished to establish himself as a gentleman in the minds of the Selkirks, with a view to returning to Galloway after this "cruel and destructive War" was over. An example of this wishful thinking appears in the account of the raid that he wrote for his *Mémoire* of 1786 to the King of France. He there states that the Countess was so eager to meet him that she proposed to accompany Cullam and Wallingford to the beach and invite him to dinner!

Jones was so proud of this letter that he not only sent Lady Selkirk three different originals in his own hand, by different intermediaries, in order to be certain that she would receive one, but had numerous copies made to flourish about. One was sent to Franklin, one to Arthur Lee, one to Van der Capellen, and one to the Marine Committee of Congress. He even included it among the *pièces justificatives* in his *Mémoire* to Louis XVI.

The Earl himself undertook to answer Jones's letter to the Countess. He was unable to have it delivered, as Lord Le Despencer refused to forward "a letter to such a Rascal and Rebel as this Jones." Passages from it, however, are worth preserving as a cool and politely contemptuous reply to the Captain's rodomontade; a letter which paid tribute to Jones's sensibility but was a good deal stronger on sense:

A Monsieur J. P. Jones,
Capitaine du Vaisseau Americain, *La Ranger*, à Brest
DUMFRIES, *June 9th, 1778*

SIR:—
   . . . You certainly are in the right, Sir, in saying that it was fortunate for Lady Selkirk that I was from home, as you intended to carry me off and detain me a prisoner, for had that happened, I dread what might have been its effect on my Wife, then well advanced in her pregnancy. I own I do not understand how a man of *Sensibility to fine feelings* could reconcile this to what his heart approved, especially as the carrying me off could have no possible effect for the purpose you mention which you say was, 'knowing my interest with the King, your intention was to detain me, until through my means, a general and fair exchange of prisoners, as well in Europe as in America had been effected.' Now, Sir, nothing can be more erroneous than these Ideas, for I have no interest whatever with the King, and am scarce known to him, being very seldom in London, scarce six months in whole, during these last one and twenty years. With regard to the King's ministers, I neither have nor can have any interest with them, as I have generally disapproved of most of their measure, and in particular of almost their whole

conduct in the unhappy and ill-judged American War. . . .

You must, therefore, be sensible on reflection, Sir, that you have proceeded on a very improper and mistaken notion, and that had your attempt succeeded, its only effect would have been to distress a family that never injured any person, and whose wishes have certainly been very friendly to the Constitutions and Just Liberties of America.

You exclaim on the barbarities committed in America, and say they will be retaliated in Britain if not discontinued. I have always been extremely sorry at the accounts of these things, no man can be a greater enemy to all ungenerous unhumanities in war than I am. God knows best which side began those things, and which has most to account for, but it is certainly the general opinion in Britain, that the Americans began the unusual and cruel practices complained of, and first against their own countrymen who adhered to the British Government.

In your letter you profess yourself a Citizen of the World, and that you have drawn your sword in support of the Rights of Man, yet you say you are not in arms as an American, nor in pursuit of Riches. If you are not in arms as an American, I do not understand in what character you act, and unless you have an American Commission, I doubt the laws of war and of nations would not be very favorable to you as a citizen of the World, which, however, ought to be a very honorable character, and you will do well to endeavor to act up to the humanity and honour of it. Consider then, Sir, the impropriety and danger to the Common Interests, and happiness of Society, in your departing from the established and usual practice of Modern War.

Nothing does more honour to Mankind, than the generous humanity and mildness introduced in War of late ages, through all the best civilized parts of Europe, and its violation is always disapproved of and generally resented by the Ministers of every State. I am therefore persuaded that neither the French Government nor the Congress, would have countenanced your carrying me off, nor would have permitted me to be detained. Their own coasts are as much exposed to such enterprises as ours, and they will not wish to introduce such things into the practice of war, as can have no effect upon the great and gen-

Lady Selkirk's Teapot

The Beach Where *Ranger's* Boat Landed

The Selkirk Mansion Raided by Jones

Kirkcudbright Bay and St. Mary's Isle, by Oppenheimer

Dupré Study for Portrait Medal of John Paul Jones

Dupré Study for Portrait Medal of Benjamin Franklin

eral operations of it, but would only add to its calamities. It certainly was fortunate both for Lady Selkirk and me, that I was from home, and it was also fortunate for you, Sir, that your officers and men behaved well, for had any of my family suffered outrage, murder or violence, no quarter of the Globe should have secured you nor even some of those under whose commission you act, from my vengeance. But, Sir, the Orders you mention in your letter were punctually'obeyed by your two Officers and Men, who in every respect behaved as well as could be expected on such an occasion. All the men remained on the outside of the house, were civil and did no injury, the two officers alone came within, and behaved with civility, and we were all sorry to hear afterwards that the younger officer in green uniform was killed in your engagement with the *Drake*, for he in particular showed so much civility and so apparent dislike at the business he was then on, that it is surprising how he should have been one of the proposers of it. What you mention is certainly so, that some of the Plate was left, but that was contrary to Lady Selkirk's intention and to her orders, but happened partly by accident, confusion and hurry, and partly by the improper inclinations of some servants, for which they were severely reprimanded afterwards. . . .

Your genteel offer, Sir, of returning the plate is very polite, but at the same time neither Lady Selkirk nor I can think of accepting it, as you must purchase it you say for that purpose, but if your delicacy makes you unwilling to keep that share of its value which as Captain you are entitled to, without purchasing, I would in that case wish that part to be given to those private men who were on the party, as an encouragement for their good behaviour.* You, Sir, are entitled to what is more honorable, viz: the Praise of having your men under good discipline, which on all occasions I take care to make known.

Your most obedient servant,

SELKIRK

---

* Nothing was missed from the mansion except the plate that the Countess handed over. But one of the sailors managed to lift, as "souvenir," a pair of gilt spurs from the entrance hall which he was guarding. A shipmate described later how he tried them on his hands, feet and neck, but finally tossed them overboard, saying that the "damned things were no damned use to anybody."

Paul Jones never received this, which is a pity, since it might have conveyed to him, as nothing else could, what a fool he had made of himself in writing as he did to the Countess.

*   *   *

As the Isle and Little Ross faded from Captain Jones's view on that April day in 1778, was he planning to return to Scotland after the war, invest his prize money in land, marry a well-born lass and shine in county society? One may so infer from his extraordinary letter to Lady Selkirk; and there is evidence that that is exactly what was in his mind. A London newspaper for December 1779 prints an "Extract of a Letter from Holland" of 1 November, stating that Captain Jones, in conversation with the writer, observed that he had ordered agents to purchase land for him on Solway Firth, where he intended to end his days. But if he ever hoped to return to Galloway as a landed gentleman he soon learned, from the furious attacks on his honor in the English press and by British officers in the Russian service, that he could not expect to be accepted socially in Great Britain. Never again did he set foot on Scots soil.

But he did return the plate, every bit of it, after the war was over; as Lord Selkirk (coming down from his high horse) acknowledged and even graciously announced in the Edinburgh newspapers. This restitution cost Jones much money and more trouble, but he saw it through. He had the plate examined at Brest, and when told that there was no sale in France for "old-fashioned" English silver, had it valued as bullion. It was estimated to be worth three thousand livres, or six hundred dollars. Fifteen per cent of that was the Captain's share; but the rest ($510) he paid out of his own pocket to *Ranger's* officers and crew. Most of the pieces are still in the possession of Sir Basil Hope-Dunbar, the Earl's descendant, at St. Mary's Isle.

A curious epilogue is afforded by a chance meeting of Paul Jones with the Earl's heir, Basil Lord Daer, at Paris in 1791.* Fellow guests

---

*Lord Daer as the Fifth Earl became famous as the organizer of the Red River settlement in Manitoba. In 1885 when the Sixth Earl died, he left St. Mary's Isle to Lady Isabella Hope, from whom the present owner, Sir Basil Hope-Dunbar, is descended. The title then reverted to the family of the Duke of Hamilton, whose third son is now the Earl of Selkirk.

at a party given by William Short, the American chargé d'affaires, they remained in the same room for two hours before being introduced. Daer, who was a fifteen-year-old schoolboy at the time of the raid, chatted amiably with Jones about the silver, expressing his father's gratitude for the restitution and for the good conduct of his men. "He seems a sensible little fellow," wrote Daer to the Earl. *"He is not as dark as I had heard."*

Incidentally, this is a significant statement about Paul Jones's appearance. The English newspapers had described him as dark and swarthy, such as pirates are supposed to be; that is why Daer was surprised to find him with light brown hair turning gray, and hazel eyes.

"He acknowledged," continued Daer in the same letter, "he was from Britain, but said he was *settled* in America before the war began, and it was then his country. I did not ask him from what part of the kingdom."

Thus, many years after the war, Paul Jones was still eager to make a favorable impression on the Selkirk family.

IX

"Drake"
Captured
and Cruise
Ends

April-May 1778

By the close of the eventful twenty-four hours, which included the raids on Whitehaven and St. Mary's Isle, Captain Jones might have been excused if he decided to return to France around the western coast of Ireland. The country had been thoroughly aroused. Letters from Whitehaven, Dumfries, Irvine, Glasgow, Belfast and other ports were pouring in on the Admiralty, which immediately sent H.M.S. *Stag* in pursuit of *Ranger* and ordered H.M.S. *Doctor* to cruise in the North Channel to protect the trade of Ayrshire.

These ships had about as much chance of intercepting slippery *Ranger* as our destroyer patrol of 1942 had of catching U-boats off the American coast. And Paul Jones showed his contempt for the Royal Navy by remaining in its home waters, since he had a score to settle with H.M.S. *Drake*.

Already by daybreak 24 April he had *Ranger* at the entrance of Belfast Lough, standing in toward Kilroot Point near Carrickfergus, when he sighted *Drake* standing out. Her commander, Captain Burden RN, a superannuated officer about to retire, had been warned about the American "privateer," as the British persisted in calling *Ranger,* but he could not be certain that this strange vessel entering the Lough was not a peaceful trader. The wind being high and contrary, he sent out his gig in charge of a lieutenant to reconnoiter. At the time numerous residents of villages on the Lough put out in yachts and other small boats, hoping, like true Irishmen, to witness a good fight. They certainly got their money's worth, for the battle of *Ranger* vs. *Drake,* which Jones described in such pathetic terms to Lady Selkirk, was a hot one.

Jones kept his crew below decks and *Ranger's* stern on the approaching gig, so that the British lieutenant could not see her gun ports, even with a spyglass. This officer was allowed to approach and come on board, when he was informed that he was a prisoner to Captain John Paul Jones of the United States Navy. This successful ruse, according to Jones, "tickled the caprice" of his surly crew, who had been holding a tumultuous town meeting below, presided over by Lieutenant Simpson, and were on the verge of mutiny. "Soothed again into good Humour" they decided to fight; and with the added prospect of a pocketful of prize money from a captured warship, they put up a "truely Gallant" fight, as their captain admitted.

The pleasure boats, seeing the gig taken in tow, and noting that *Drake's* recall signals remained unanswered, withdrew to a prudent distance, and alarm smokes began to arise on both shores of the Lough. Jones decided to bait *Drake* off shore, in order to fight where he would have room to maneuver. The Englishman worked slowly out of Carrickfergus Bay against a freshening northeast wind and flood tide, *Ranger* keeping ahead, then laying-to with lower courses clewed up and fore topsail backed to await her approach. After *Drake* had weathered the Mew, Jones allowed her to come within hailing distance. He was amused and somewhat puzzled to note how closely she resembled his old ship *Alfred,* her figurehead being a man in "Armour and on the same Attitude with *Alfred's"* figurehead, which was supposed to represent the Black Prince. Later he learned that she had been built in Philadelphia as a tobacco freighter shortly before the war, captured by the British, purchased for three thousand pounds by the Royal Navy in 1777, and converted to a 20-gun sloop of war.

Drake now raised English colors, *Ranger* displayed the Stars and Stripes, and the Englishman hailed, "What ship is that?" Master Cullam replied, as instructed by Jones, "The American Continental ship *Ranger*—that we waited for them and desired they would come on."

"The sun was now little more than an hour from setting, it was therefore time to begin," observed Jones. "The *Drake* being then astern of the *Ranger,* I ordered the helm up." That placed her athwart *Drake's* bows, at right angles to her keel. From that position, he fired a broadside of grapeshot, with good effect, right along the enemy's decks.

"The action was warm, close and obstinate," reported Jones. The two vessels were well matched. Both were sloops of war, *Drake* mounting 20 six-pounders and *Ranger* 18 nine-pounders; *Drake* measured 275 and *Ranger* 316 tons. The Englishman had the more numerous crew, so it behooved Jones not to let him grapple and board. His tactics were to disable the enemy by concentrating cannon fire at pistol-shot range on men, masts, yards and sails, but to spare *Drake's* hull so as to save her as a prize. We have no details of the maneuvering; if Jones did what we think he must have done, he sailed around *Drake* to take the lee gauge so that *Ranger's* angle of heel would elevate her guns and enable grape and chain-shot to tear through sails, spars and rigging; while *Drake,* her guns depressed, could only hit *Ranger's* hull near the waterline with her light six-pound cannon balls. Perhaps Jones wore ship—turned her around—after fighting a glass, in order to let the guns of one broadside cool off and bring the other to bear; but that was a dangerous maneuver, as it exposed one's ship to being raked fore and aft when performing it. The only Americans lost were in the maintop, they were probably picked off by the British maintopmen.

After the fight had been going on for two glasses—one hour—and five minutes, Captain Burden was killed by a musket ball in the head (compliments U. S. Marine Corps); his exec. (Lieutenant Dobbs) received a mortal wound; the third in command, the master, seeing *Drake* so badly cut up aloft as to be unmanageable, cried "Quarters!" Gunfire then ceased on both sides, and Captain Jones sent over a boarding party in *Drake's* own boat.

The boarders found her headsails and the fore- and main-topsail yards shot away, the topgallant yard and spanker gaff hanging along their respective masts, the British ensign trailing over her stern, sails and rigging cut to pieces, and the hull "very much galled." A member of the boarding party added that he stumbled over the dead body of an English Army officer "who had come to see the Yankees whipped," and that the decks were running with blood and rum, since a keg of liquor, brought out to celebrate the victory, had been demolished by a cannon ball.

The men killed on board *Ranger* were Samuel Wallingford, her courteous Lieutenant of Marines, and two seamen; five were wounded. The official account of *Drake's* losses were four killed and nineteen wounded. No fewer than 133 officers and men, including the cook and the cook's wife, were taken prisoner. Captain Burden and Lieutenant Dobbs, who died of his wounds, were buried at sea with full military honors.

Jones was always punctilious in observing naval amenities. When he received, at Brest, a letter from a British firm at Bordeaux addressed to Lieutenant Dobbs, he replied:

> It gives me real Pain to inform you that he is no more: he survived the Engagement only 36 hours. In the Course of that time I paid him two Visits on board the *Drake* and found him

in such spirits that I had no apprehension of what so soon followed. I freely consented to land him among his Friends the
day after the Engagement when we passed Belfast; but the
Surgeons as well as himself thought the Risque was too great,
after a loss of Blood. His Boy was therefore at his desire sent
ashore. He was buried in the Ocean with the Honors due to the
Brave and the respect due to his private Character. I would
write to his Brother, but wish to avoid the too tender Subject. I am convinced that he was shewed all possible care and
tenderness. Consequently his Hurt exceeded the Art of the
Surgeon and the Skill of the Physician. You are at liberty to
Communicate this Account to his Relations.

As *Drake* was now incapable of sailing, *Ranger* took her in tow,
and the two vessels were seen at sunset by gentlemen of Donaghadee
to be passing through the narrow channel between Copeland Island
and the southern headland of Belfast Lough. The following day, 25
April, they lay-to off Ballywater, County Down, about fifteen miles
to the southward, where *Ranger's* crew and the prisoners from *Drake*
worked hard at refitting the prize brigantine *Patience* of Whitehaven, bound to Norway, which had sailed so close that *Ranger* cast
off and made prize of her. The wind now veered south, so Captain
Jones decided to return to France northabout, around Ireland, which
offered the best chance to escape pursuers. Off Belfast Lough that
evening he set ashore, in one of his own boats, the fishermen he had
taken prisoner the previous week, with a new sail, and money in
their pockets. "The grateful fishermen were in raptures; and expressed their joy in three huzzas as they passed the *Ranger's* quarter."

This incident enhanced the popularity of Paul Jones in the British
Isles, and helped to build up a legend of him as a seafaring Robin
Hood. For example, it is firmly believed on the Island of Islay, which
Ranger and *Drake* passed on 28 April, that Jones sought shelter in
Lochindael, impressed two fishermen whom he later released, and
intended to kidnap the Campbell of Islay, whose seat was at the
head of the Loch. When informed by the fishermen that the Camp-
bell was not at home but was expected shortly in a vessel carrying

treasure from the Far East, Jones intercepted the East Indiaman and relieved her of her cargo. There is nothing in *Ranger's* log or Jones's narrative to support this story. He did not enter Lochindael and he captured neither the Campbell nor an East Indiaman.

Drake was again in condition to sail after the people had worked on her all night at sea, lying-to in the North Channel between Torr Head and the Mull of Kintyre. On the 28th, off Islay, Captain Jones appointed Lieutenant Simpson the prizemaster, with the following orders:

LIEUTENANT SIMPSON,
SIR,

You are hereby appointed Commander of our Prize the English Ship of War *Drake*. You are to keep Company with me and to pay punctual Attention to the Signals delivered herewith for your government. You are to Superintend the Navigation and defence of the Ship under your Command and to support me as much as possible, should we fall in with and engage any of the Enemies Ships.

The Honor of our Flagg is much concerned in the preservation of this Prize, therefore keep close by me and she shall not be given tamely up.

You will take your Station on the *Ranger's* Starboard Quarter at or about the Distance of a Cable's length. Should bad weather or any Accident Separate you from the *Ranger*, you are to make the best of your way to France, and I recommend the Port of Brest to your preference.

So much for the memorable fight of 24 April 1778 off Belfast Lough. H.M.S. *Drake* was not the first vessel of the Royal Navy to be captured by an American,* but her battle with *Ranger* was the most spectacular one up to that time between ships of the rival Navies. And it had the further interest of being fought between two

---

* H.M. sloop of war *Lynx* was taken by Continental privateer *Cromwell* in May 1776; and H.M. frigate *Fox*, 24 guns, was taken by *Hancock*, Capt. Manley, and *Boston*, Capt. McNeill, on 7 June 1777. *Fox* was later recaptured by the British, and then re-recaptured by French frigate *Junon*, which brought her into Brest in Sept. 1778 when Paul Jones was there; he thought he might take command of her.

ships of very nearly the same size and strength. An article in the *London Morning Chronicle* of 9 May 1778, summing up all possible excuses for *Drake's* defeat, such as weak gunpowder, death of the captain, and the difference in striking power between six- and nine-pounders, candidly admitted that in "engagements with the French and Spaniards such a superiority would have been laughed at; but the case is different when we engage with our own countrymen; men who have the same spirit and bravery with ourselves."

The Admiralty did its best to catch Paul Jones. In addition to H.M.S. *Stag* and *Doctor,* which were sent in search of him before the battle, *Thetis,* a 36-gun frigate, was dispatched from Glasgow to cruise in the North Channel; sloop of war *Heart of Oak* sailed from Liverpool to patrol the Irish Sea, and by 1 May *Boston* (32 guns) from Waterford, and a few smaller warships, were looking for him.

By that time *Ranger* and her prize were on their way around Northern Ireland. Everything went well during the return passage until 4 May when they were approaching the French coast and running into danger of attack. *Drake* was making such poor progress with her jury rig that Jones decided to take her in tow again. Next morning, when Ushant bore SE by S, distant 45 miles, the Captain spied a ship to leeward that looked like a good prize and, eager to please his men by a capture, cast off the towline, hailed *Drake* and ordered Lieutenant Simpson to follow him in the chase. Everyone on board *Drake* later testified that this order was heard so indistinctly that Simpson hailed *Ranger's* quarterdeck and asked if he was to make the best of his way independently to Brest, and that Lieutenant Hall answered, "Aye, aye!" Consequently, Simpson held his southerly course for Ushant while *Ranger* came about and chased the strange ship downwind, northward. After ascertaining that she was a neutral Swede, Jones turned south again and caught up with *Drake* on the 6th. He was furious with Simpson, having made up his mind that the Lieutenant had deliberately disobeyed his command to follow *Ranger.* He ordered *Drake* to heave-to, sent Lieutenant Hall on board to take over the prize command, suspended

Simpson from duty and placed him under arrest. It was a sour note on which to end a successful cruise.

The two ships entered Brest on the evening of 8 May, *Drake* "with English Colours inverted under the American Stars," and 200 prisoners on board. In a cruise of only 28 days *Ranger* had performed one of the most brilliant exploits of the naval war—a land raid, two merchantmen taken prize, others destroyed, and a British man-of-war captured. Captain Jones naturally expected to be treated as a hero, but nobody except his friend the Comte d'Orvilliers took much notice of him.

Nevertheless—not that it was any consolation—he did become a sort of hero to the British people; and one of the numerous ballads about him dates from this cruise.

> You have heard o' Paul Jones?
>   Have you not? Have you not?
> And you've heard o' Paul Jones?
>   Have you not?
>
> A rogue and a vagabond;
>   Is he not? Is he not? *(bis)*
>
> He came to Selkirk-ha',
>   Did he not? Did he not? *(bis)*
>
> And stole the rings and the jewels a',
>   Did he not? Did he not?
>
> Robbed the plate and jewels a',
>   Which did his conscience gall,
>   Did it not?

X

In
Irons

May 1778-February 1779

1. Prisoners and Prizes

When a square-rigger loses headway coming about and her sails are caught aback so that she makes sternway, she is said to be "in irons." That was Paul Jones's situation from his arrival at Brest with his prize, on 8 May 1778, to February of 1779 when he was given command of *Bonhomme Richard*. He could neither advance nor retreat. He gave up *Ranger* but was unable to get another command. He was stuck at Brest, unwilling to go to Paris and amuse himself because he feared to miss something at sea, and mortified because in the sight of French naval officers he was being humiliated. Things were not so bad as they seemed, and eventually Paul Jones squared away on a cruise that brought him undying fame; but in the meantime his talents were completely wasted for a crucial nine months of the war, and he suffered more chagrin than at any other time between the outbreak of the War of Independence and his Russian command.

His immediate problems were money, prisoners, prizes and Lieutenant Simpson. A few days after his arrival he wrote out and partly cashed a draft on the American Plenipotentiaries at Paris for a thousand louis d'or—forty-eight hundred dollars—to distribute "among the officers and Men to whom I owe my late success," as he explained, and "that they may be furnished with the means of procuring little comforts and necessaries for themselves" as well as supply to their "suffering Families in America." Very considerate on the Captain's part, but irregular as well as unnecessary; for, as he later admitted, his earlier letter of credit from Paris for 500 louis d'or was still unused. The first word he had from Paris was the dishonoring of this draft. That bad news caught him so short of cash that only through friendship with a French merchant at Brest, who took a mortgage on the prizes, and by favor of the royal abattoir, could the Captain obtain meat and drink for his sailors. To a proud and sensitive man such as Jones, this was "a Deplorable & disgraceful Situation in the sight of the French Fleet." And the humiliation was even worse than the inconvenience. Dr. Franklin finally wrote him a soothing letter on 1 June which raised his hopes for a fine new command; and means were found to supply *Ranger's* crew and the prisoners.

These prisoners—the 133 or more taken in *Drake,* and those from *Patience, Lord Chatham* and the vessels sunk—were indeed a problem. France and England were still nominally at peace. England had withdrawn her ambassador on 17 March, but hostilities did not open until 17 June, when frigates *La Belle Poule* and *Arethusa* fought to a finish. D'Orvilliers advised Jones to ship his prisoners to America in *Drake,* or the French government would order them released. That did not suit Jones, as he planned to use them to exchange for American sailors who were being kept in English jails. On 1 September 1777 there were 123 of these Americans in Fortin Prison near Portsmouth, and 234 at Mill Prison, Plymouth; more had come in since. D'Orvilliers consented to say nothing about Jones's prisoners to the French authorities, placed them under guard in a prison hulk in

Brest harbor, and assumed responsibility for feeding them. But when D'Orvilliers put out to sea in July to give battle to Admiral Keppel, the senior French naval officer at Brest informed Jones that he had no men available to maintain the guard. Jones was in consternation lest the prisoners escape; but he managed to find some means to keep them from slipping away.

The unpleasant subject of the treatment of American naval prisoners during the war afforded fuel for American Anglophobes for a century or more, and there is no point in stirring it up again. The British government allowed Army officers and soldiers to be freely exchanged but insisted on treating all Americans taken prisoner in privateers or other armed vessels as rebels or pirates who had no belligerent rights. One and all were indicted for treason and committed to jail. This could be done with impunity, since American armed ships captured few prisoners and kept still fewer, simply because they did not know what to do with them; we have already seen how Paul Jones let most of his go at Canso in 1776. Local authorities at Halifax and perhaps elsewhere did occasionally exchange naval prisoners, but that was irregular and unauthorized.

Paul Jones was very much concerned over this situation. Now, with a parcel of British naval prisoners that really counted, he had cards in hand. And he used them very cannily, working through Franklin to break down the Admiralty's intransigence. In February 1779, an exchange was arranged, by which Paul Jones's prisoners to the number of 164, including *Drake's* cook complete with wife, together with over 60 others taken by the French, were exchanged for 228 American sailors. And many of these enlisted in *Bonhomme Richard.* That broke the ice; but it was still irregular and illegal from the British point of view, and not until the spring of 1780 did Parliament pass an act permitting the Admiralty to exchange American naval prisoners, of whom there were then almost 1100 in British jails, for British sailors held prisoner in the United States or France.

Prizes were the next problem with which Jones had to deal. The French government vacillated. Early in 1778 it had raised no objection to *Ranger's* fruiter prizes being sold in Nantes and Bordeaux;

but in May, when France and England were on the brink of war, it made difficulties about selling *Drake, Lord Chatham* and *Patience*. Paul Jones was determined not to send them to America lest they be recaptured en route, and because his men wanted their prize money right away. On his first visit to Paris after *Ranger's* return, Jones went directly to the French authorities and obtained permission "to dispose of our Prizes to the best Advantage" without any rake-off to the French Admiralty. Yet, even after France and England were formally at war, he had plenty of trouble. Brest as a purely military port, was not a good place to sell prizes; Nantes would have been much better. But, because of a shakeup in the American mission to France, Jones's friend Jonathan Williams, the Navy agent at Nantes, had been relieved by a Swiss merchant there named Schweighauser, who was Arthur Lee's man and would not even release to Captain Jones his share of the barreled porter in *Lord Chatham*. Eventually *Patience* and *Lord Chatham* were sold, but they did not fetch as much as they should have (so Jones reported) because the sale was not properly advertised. *Drake*, although a really valuable prize, brought only thirty-six thousand livres, about seventy-two hundred dollars. Jonathan Williams as a private merchant helped Jones by purchasing in advance the shares of *Ranger's* crew, 85 per cent of the total. That was a common practice in the eighteenth century; seamen often sold their shares in a prize before the vessel was sold, rather than wait months or years to receive their just due. *Ranger's* men naturally preferred a few louis d'or in hand to a hatful of Continental currency in the American bush.

2. The Case of Lieutenant Simpson

But the Captain's prime personal problem was Lieutenant Simpson. He had been placed under arrest for insubordination without being given a chance to clear it up, and Jones was unwilling to admit his error. This was not Simpson's only offense; he had encouraged the crew of *Ranger* in their mutinous attitude toward their Captain and, if Lieutenant Meijer may be believed, had even connived to throw Jones overboard or leave him on the beach at Whitehaven. The Captain naturally wished to air the whole matter in a court-martial. But there were then no senior American naval officers in France to set up a court-martial. Horatio Nelson later had the same problem in H.M.S. *Pegasus*. He had to place an offending lieutenant under arrest and managed to get rid of him only by transfer to another ship. The only thing that Jones could have done, consistent with Navy regulations and sound discipline, was to place Simpson under arrest. To his democratic crew that was plain tyranny—contrary to Magna Carta and the Bill of Rights—worse than George III!

Actually, it was no great hardship for Simpson to be under arrest. He kept his cabin on board *Drake* and had the run of the quarterdeck until Jones found that he was undermining the prize crew's discipline. He was then transferred to a private cabin on a French prison hulk in the harbor. There again he made so much trouble that D'Orvilliers—not Jones—had him placed in the naval prison ashore to cool off. This was described by *Ranger's* crew as "a Lousey, Dirtey French Gaol" unfit for a "Faithful, true & Fatherly Oficer, our First Lieutenant."

That statement formed part of a petition which 77 sailors, calling themselves "the Jovial Tars Now on board the Continental Sloop of war *Ranger*," sent to Benjamin Franklin. Warrant and petty officers to the number of twenty-eight signed a similar petition, as did Lieutenant Hall, Master Cullam and Dr. Green; only the midshipmen and about thirty of the crew appear to have been loyal to their Captain. This strong support of Simpson created a serious situation for Jones. After Franklin, Lee and John Adams (Deane's relief as commissioner) had begged him to be less inflexible, he consented on 10 June to free Simpson on parole. Five weeks later he released the lieutenant from his parole so that he could command *Ranger* on her homeward passage, making the face-saving excuse that no other competent navigator was available.

Simpson returned on board *Ranger* 27 July, "to the joy and Satisfaction of the whole Ship's Company," according to Surgeon Green, and assumed the command.

This did not end the matter. Simpson swaggered about Brest declaring that Jones was discredited and out of a job; and the furious Captain demanded that he be court-martialed. But Navy regulations required for a court-martial at least three captains not involved in the dispute, and three such were not available until Captain Abraham Whipple entered Brest about 15 August 1778 in command of frigate *Providence,* together with frigate *Boston,* Captain Samuel Tucker. Jones, who had returned to Brest on the 10th, urged Whipple to call a court-martial, which he refused to do, pointing out that Jones's letter releasing Simpson from his parole was equivalent to wiping out all charges against him.

It is the commonest thing in the world for sailors to think themselves ill-used and to blame everything they dislike, even the weather, on the "Old Man." In the case of *Ranger,* this state of affairs was aggravated by the insubordination of the officers. In their petitions in favor of Simpson, both officers and men adverted very severely on Paul Jones. Elijah Hall went so far as to say that he was "the cause of the Disorder" because "his mode of Government is so far from ours that no American of spirit can ever serve with Cheerfulness under him." I interpret this to mean, not that Jones was another Captain Bligh, but that he insisted on naval, not merchant marine, discipline; and that he embarked on operations with a military rather than a monetary object. Jones himself summarized the situation in a letter to the Commissioners:

> When *Gain* is the ruling principle of Officers in an Infant Navy—it is no wonder that they do not cultivate by their precepts nor enforce by their Example the principles of *Dutiful Subordination, Cheerful unrepining* Obedience in those who are under their command, nor is it strange that this principle should weaken the sacred bonds of order and Discipline, and introduce the Mistaken and baneful Idea of Licentiousness and Free Agency under the specious name of "Liberty."

A particular grievance of these people was a clause added to the terms under which they enlisted: "For twelve months, or more if absent from the Eastern States," or words to that effect. Captain Jones put this in the roster book at Portsmouth to protect himself from what had happened to Captain Biddle. When frigate *Randolph* put in at Charleston, South Carolina, after her Pennsylvania crew's twelve-month enlistment was up, they jumped ship in a body, and months elapsed before he could get another lot. Jones had expressly ordered Simpson to read this clause aloud and explain it to every man before he signed on; but now, encouraged by Lieutenant Hall, they claimed they had never heard of it. The people even accused Jones of obstructing the sale of their prizes, when he was making every effort to move the French government to allow the sale, as well as to obtain from the Navy agent at Bordeaux the proceeds of the second fruiter taken the previous November. And he had risked his footing with Franklin, as we have seen, by borrowing so that his crew could have spending money and buy goods to take home to their families.

Captain Jones's efforts on behalf of his people continued throughout the summer, in spite of their unfortunate attitude toward himself. He saw to it that the American Plenipotentiaries recommended Congress to give each man of the landing party at Whitehaven a bonus, and to allow the entire crew to receive prize money in advance.

If Paul Jones was well rid of *Ranger,* her ship's company were glad to be free of him. The warrant and petty officers in one of their petitions declared, "His Government arbitrary his Temper & Treatment insufferable, for the most trivial matters threatening to shoot the Person or Persons whom he, in sallies of Passion, chooses to call Ignorant or disobedient." Captain Jones, like other naval officers of renown, did lose his temper at times, and no doubt he lost it frequently with this sullen, danger-dodging crew, some of whom had even plotted to kill him. He hated laziness, slackness and disobedience at all times. Midshipman Fanning of *Bonhomme Richard* tells how one day Captain Jones had a dispute with a lieutenant, ordered him below and assisted him down the ladder with several kicks in the rear, but half an hour later sent his orderly to invite the lieutenant to dine. That, he observed, was just like Jones; "passionate to the highest degree one minute, and the next ready to make a reconciliation." Fanning was an embroiderer of the truth; but one may believe this story because later, on board *Ariel,* the deck log notes that "Mr. Fanning, Midshipman," was the one kicked, and Midshipman Potter "ordered in irons by the Capt. for a Thermometer being broke in his Cabbin."

It is a pity that the Simpson business never became thoroughly ventilated; but there was nothing exceptional about it. The Revolutionary Navy was no band of brothers. All successful captains during the war had trouble with their crews and several quarreled with one another. Wickes had a mutiny on his hands in France, Biddle's crew deserted at Charleston, Barry was troubled by indiscipline; the only commanding officers of frigates who had no trouble were those who never got to sea, or who lost their ships early in the war. Captain Jones wrote letters to the Marine Committee denouncing Captains Manley and Hacker; Captain Nicholson lobbied in Congress against Jones's promotion; Captains Whipple and Thompson ventilated their personal enmity in the newspapers; Captain Hector McNeill of frigate *Boston* felt obliged to write to her master's mate that his "orders placarded on the bulk Head in common view" are to be obeyed by "you and every other Officer." He adds, "The misfortune has been that yourself and many others of the late Officers of the *Boston* fancied yourselves totally independent of me."

Ranger sailed from Brest 21 August 1778 under Simpson's command and in company with frigates *Boston* and *Providence.* On 16 October she made Portsmouth after an uneventful passage and there spent three winter months. Simpson, armed with a new captain's commission from Congress (which Jones thought outrageous), took her to sea around 1 March 1779, and in company with frigates *Warren* and *Queen of France* made a number of captures. The following year she was taken with Commodore Whipple's squadron at Charleston and became H.M.S. *Halifax* for a brief period. The Royal Navy either did not like *Ranger* or (as is more likely) found her full of dry rot; for in October 1781 they sold her for a merchant ship, for the small sum of £650. And so this little sloop that had once terrified the British Isles ended her days quietly under the Red Ensign.

Captain Simpson, after being released by the British, returned to the merchant marine and was lost at sea. Elijah Hall made his peace with Paul Jones, who offered him the first lieutenant's billet in the new *America*. Master Cullam invested his prize money to such good purpose that after the war he was one of the richest citizens of Portsmouth. Steward Walden also did well; as a leading Portsmouth merchant he presided over the local reception committee to President Washington in 1789. Walden lived fourscore years, but was outdone in longevity by Dr. Ezra Green, who died just three days short of attaining his one hundred and second birthday. The surgeon never altered his opinion that Paul Jones was a poor commander and that Lieutenant Simpson had been unjustly treated. In 1845, sixty-seven years after the events that we have been describing, Dr. Green was visited by Jared Sparks, the historian, who loved to take down tales from Revolutionary veterans. The Doctor told Sparks that he considered the descent on Whitehaven "rash," because the boats' gunwales were so low in the water that they would have swamped if the sea had made up.

Ranger's officers, with the exception of Lieutenant Wallingford and Midshipmen Hill and Wendell, were a pretty sorry lot. At a time when their captain most needed their loyalty and support they acted in a manner that can only be described as yellow. As Captain Hector McNeill justly observed, "God and Nature has said, that one head is indispensibley Necessray on board of a ship."

3. Farewell to "L'Indien"

One of Paul Jones's praiseworthy traits was his constant desire to improve his professional knowledge. Wishing to study French battle tactics and fleet evolutions at first hand, he requested D'Orvilliers to take him on board when he sortied to attack the English Channel

Fleet. The Count was delighted—he seems to have loved Jones—but dared not invite him without an order from the Minister of Marine. Application was made, but Sartine did not deign to reply until it was too late. Paul Jones had dinner with the Count on board flagship *La Bretagne* the day she sailed, and even accompanied him into the roadstead; but he then had to drop down the ladder into a boat and go ashore. And at Brest he stayed, biting his nails during two weeks of fleet evolution and the Battle of Ushant of 27 June 1778. D'Orvilliers had 27 ships of the line; Admiral Keppel, in H.M.S. *Victory*, had 30, not counting frigates and smaller warships. After maneuvering for four days to get the advantage, the two columns deployed in battle line, converged on opposite tacks, banged away at each other as they passed, and then retired, each claiming victory. It was a good illustration of a witty French definition of a naval battle: "Do you know what a naval combat is? One maneuvers, one encounters, one fires cannon; then each of the two fleets retires. And the ocean is as salt as ever!"

Neither side won much credit from this battle. Keppel was court-martialed but acquitted; D'Orvilliers lost face, and the Duc de Chartres, commanding the French blue squadron in *Saint-Esprit* (80 guns), with La Motte Piquet by his side to keep him well advised, was accused of failing to obey signals and deprived of his naval command. That was bad for Paul Jones, as he had cultivated both the royal rear admiral and his fascinating Duchesse, and it was worse for Chartres, who hoped to make a reputation so that he could succeed his father-in-law the Duc de Penthièvre as Grand Admiral of France.*

These vexations were nothing to the disappointment and chagrin that Paul Jones suffered from being put off again and again about a

---

* Actually, as Capt. de V. Pierre Guiot explains in *Neptunia* No. 45 (1957) p. 16, the fault was that of La Motte Piquet and the C.O.'s of two leading ships. But Chartres (the future Duc d'Orléans, "Philippe Egalité"), who was unpopular at court, took the blame. The Comte de Rochechouart in his *Souvenirs* tells the following anecdote. The Queen asked the Duke about the ladies he had met at the races. He said that they were of two kinds, *"des passables ou des passées."* The Duchess de Brionne, overhearing this and believing that by *passée* he meant her, remarked to the Duke, *"Monseigneur se connaît mieux en signalements qu'en signaux!"* Shortly after, it became the Duke's duty to hold open a door for the Duchess, to whom he quipped, *"Beauté, passez!"* But the Duchess had the last word: *"Comme votre réputation, Monseigneur!"*

new command. His orders from Congress before he left America were to take a new frigate to be purchased by the American Commissioners at Paris, and then operate under their direction. He had, as we have seen, tried to obtain *L'Indien* before he set sail for Whitehaven, and now he warmly renewed these efforts at Paris and at Passy, the proper places to get the business done. Franklin wrote to him on 1 June that he positively would have *L'Indien*. On the 10th he wrote that it was all "settled." On Franklin's invitation he came at once to Passy and remained until 7 August 1778, spending *la belle saison* in the Hôtel Valentinois, where, doubtless, Madame de Chaumont afforded him a certain consolation for his manifold disappointments. Yet, despite her influence with her husband, and his with Sartine, and Franklin's favor at court, Jones seemed to get nowhere. He did persuade Sartine to write a letter requesting Franklin to order him to remain in France, for a prospective command and mission, rather than return to America. But what command, and what mission?*

L'Indien, now French property, lay at Amsterdam, all but ready for sea, and, according to a correspondent of Jones, wanting only a fortnight's work on her rigging, and pontoons to float her out of the Zuider Zee. The French Court had sent an international adventurer, the Prince de Nassau-Siegen (apparently chosen because of a remote kinship to the Prince of Orange), to try to reverse the attitude of the Dutch government; and Jones promised that if he effected this he should have a commission under him. Franklin told Jones to "make preparations for all possible despatch for a voyage to America," presumably in *L'Indien*, although he did not mention her by name. It was on the strength of that assurance that Jones released Simpson from his parole, so that he could take *Ranger* home. But Nassau-Siegen accomplished nothing and the Dutch were obdurate. Their government wanted no trouble with the Mistress of the Seas.

* In Paris, Jones had cut for himself two heraldic seals to replace the one he brought from America. The Jones-Paul arms are in an oval shield, supported by an infant Neptune holding a trident, and with flags and other emblems appearing on the dexter side. In the one, the motto PRO REPUBLICA appears on a ribbon under the shield, together with the Masonic square and compass; in the other, the shield rests on waves and the motto is over it.

Paul Jones missed something good when he failed to get command of that ship. *L'Indien* was a long, slim vessel, unlike the stubby frigates of the War of Independence. Eventually she got clear of Dutch waters, but not under Jones. France sold her to the Duc de Montmorency-Luxembourg who, having no use for a frigate, chartered her to "Commodore" Alexander Gillon of the South Carolina Navy. This character had been in France for over a year trying to obtain a ship, and had offered to buy *L'Indien* through Chaumont. Apparently Luxembourg let him have her in return for a share in any prizes she might capture. Since by that time the Netherlands were in the war on our side, Gillon was allowed to arm her with 32 thirty-six pounders and 12 twelves, to man her with 300 "Volontaires de Luxembourg," as he called them, as well as with American deserters from *Alliance,* and take her to sea in the summer of 1781, renamed *South Carolina.* Her career in that state's navy was short and inglorious, but she was a fine ship and Jones made another attempt to obtain her in 1782.

To Sartine, Jones wrote from Paris on 17 July 1778 acknowledging an offer to command *L'Épervier,* a captured British corvette of 16 guns. Jones declined, on the ground that he expected shortly to return to America and there receive "the Chief Command the first squadron destined for an Expedition . . . and when Congress see fit to appoint Admirals, I have Assurances that my Name will not be forgot. These are flattering prospects to a Man who has Drawn his Sword only upon principles of Philanthropy and in support of the Dignity of Human Nature. But as I prefer a solid to a shining Reputation, an useful to a splendid Command, I hold myself Ready, with the approbation of the Commissioners, to be Governed by you in any Measures that may tend to Distress and Humble the Common Enemy."

Sartine now invited the Captain to express his views; and of course, being Paul Jones, he had plenty of views—a raid to be pressed right up the Clyde to Glasgow; a raid on the West Coast of Africa, with interception of British East Indiamen; a raid on the Newfoundland fisheries, to be pursued into Hudson's Bay; an attack on the English convoys from the Baltic. Each plan required that he be put in command of a task force of two or three French frigates with attendant cutters or tenders. Sartine listened to everything, but promised nothing. There was talk of allowing Jones to break his flag in frigate *Renommée* as nucleus of a raiding force; but she was given to a French naval officer. He was invited to take command of a few small armed vessels operating out of St.-Malo to break up the English privateer fleet based on the Channel Islands, but Jones declined after ascertaining that the Prince de Nassau-Siegen was to be placed over him, and Nassau-Siegen was completely routed. H.M.S. *Fox* was brought into Brest as prize by French frigate *Junon*, and Jones said he would settle for her; Sartine promised her to him but gave her to a French lieutenant. "Have patience," chided Franklin on 6 September; but Jones's patience was exhausted. Sartine now offered to return him to the United States by *une bonne voiture* (a good conveyance), meaning a suitable ship; but to Jones, who still understood French very imperfectly, this sounded like offering to send a drunk home in a hackney coach. He exploded with rage. "The minister," he wrote to Le Ray de Chaumont, "has treated me like a Child five successive times by leading me on from Great to little and from little to less." He even hinted at challenging Monseigneur le Ministre de la Marine to a duel, in vindication of his "sacred honor." So passionate and intemperate did Jones become that both Franklin and Chaumont made tentative efforts to get him out of the country. Chaumont offered to give Jones command of his own privateer *L'Union,* but the Captain replied proudly, "I am not my own Master, and as a Servant of the imperial Republic of America Honor'd with the Friendship and favor of the Congress, I cannot from my own authority or inclination serve either myself or even my best Friends in any private line whatsoever. . . . My Duty and my Sensibility cannot brook this unworthy Situation." And to John Ross he swore that he would never "seek for Fame" where his "desire is Infinite," save under "the American Flagg." Franklin passed Jones a hint via his secretary that he would do well to go home, to which the Captain replied, "Perish that thought. It is impossible. I would now lay down my life rather than return to America before my honor is made perfectly whole."

One thing Franklin did for Jones was to assign him a bilingual secretary, Lieutenant Amiel, whom the Captain kept busy writing letters. He wrote to everybody he could think of—to all three American Plenipotentiaries and their private secretaries, to Robert Morris and Joseph Hewes, to Jonathan Williams and John Ross, to the Duc de la Rochefoucauld, the Duc and Duchesse de Chartres; even to the King himself, complaining of having been "chained Down to shameful Inactivity for the space of Five Months," and assuring Louis XVI that he had drawn his sword "in support of the Violated Dignity and rights of Human nature." This letter was enclosed in one to William Franklin, who was to beg his grandfather the Doctor to ask the Duchesse de Chartres to present it to the King in person and to be present himself in case His Majesty asked any questions! Jones even tried to call himself to the attention of General Washington by sending him a pair of gilt epaulets.

Jones attributed his difficulties in some part to the American Plenipotentiaries in Paris. He felt that Franklin had let him down; he knew that Arthur Lee ("the Wasp," as he called him) was his enemy; and he got the idea that John Adams, whose attitude toward him throughout the war was consistently favorable, belonged in the same camp. It is painful to find Jones adopting toward Adams the "gentleman despises shopkeeper" attitude that he had earlier displayed toward Colonel Langdon. In a letter to William Carmichael he refers to honest John as "that wicked and conceited upstart"; and, in one to M. Dumas at the Hague, he wishes that "Mr. Roundface," as he called Adams, "were at home to mind his trade and his fireside."

Jones's exasperation is understandable, but he seemed to assume that Franklin, Adams and Lee had nothing to do except attend to his problems. They had heavy responsibilities in diplomacy, finance and logistics. They were the only official intermediaries with our new allies. They had to deal with a flock of unemployed European soldiers and adventurers who were as eager as Jones to draw their swords for

"the Dignity of Human nature." They were importuned by agents
of Virginia, Massachusetts, South Carolina and other States which
were trying to float their own loans, obtain their own supplies, and
even build their own navies. Under these circumstances the Plenipotentiaries may be excused for feeling that Captain Jones should handle his internal ship discipline without appealing to them, and that he
was becoming a bore and a nuisance.

Even so, Jones naturally felt humiliated when the Plenipotentiaries
ordered Simpson to take command of *Ranger,* and disappointed him
about *L'Indien*. From Brest on 15 August he wrote to them almost
desperately: "I beseech you, I conjure you, I demand of you to afford me Redress." The only redress he obtained was a face-saving assurance in writing, signed by Franklin and Adams, that Sartine had
formally requested that Captain Jones be detained in France for important naval plans, and that Simpson had taken command of *Ranger*
with his, the Captain's, consent.

Whatever the reason, and whoever may have been responsible, it
was the height of folly to keep Paul Jones unemployed throughout
the second half of 1778 and well into the New Year. D'Orvilliers
could easily have spared a few frigates from his fleet, lying inactive
at Brest after the drawn battle off Ushant, to give Jones the task
force he required to raid the British Isles or intercept English merchant convoys in the narrow seas. A little more pressure on the part
of the Americans at Passy could probably have got *L'Indien* out of
neutral waters and under Jones's command; Luxembourg was not
the only person who might have figured as her nominal owner.

On the American side of the Atlantic, the year 1778 was disastrous
for the new Navy. Frigate *Randolph* blew up, killing Captain Biddle
and all but four of her crew, when fighting H.M.S. *Yarmouth* in the
West Indies on 7 March. Frigates *Warren* and *Providence* escaped
to sea from Narragansett Bay but were mainly employed in fetching
Army supplies from France. Frigate *Virginia*, when trying to elude
the blockade of Chesapeake Bay, ran on a shoal and was tamely surrendered to the British by James Nicholson, senior captain of the

Navy. Frigates *Hancock* and *Delaware* were captured. Five other new frigates had to be burned or scuttled to prevent their falling into enemy hands. Captain John Barry, after relieving Captain Thompson in command of *Raleigh,* was forced to run her aground to escape capture by two British warships, a fate that had already befallen *Columbus* and *Cabot.* Except for the brief period in the summer of 1778 when D'Estaing's French fleet was operating in American waters, the enemy had almost complete control of American coastal waters; he moved troops and supplies from one port to another with little hindrance except the occasional loss of a supply ship to a privateer. By the end of the year the effective United States Navy consisted of five frigates anchored in Boston Harbor, frigate *Alliance* fitting out for her first cruise, *Ranger* back in her home port, and sloop *Providence.* It was the French Navy that pinned down the strongest elements of the British Navy in home waters, and prevented the enemy from carrying out Lord George Germain's policy of raiding and burning every American seaport from New England to the Carolinas.

During this distressing period of frustrated hopes, Paul Jones received no encouragement from America. Congress passed no resolution thanking him for capturing *Drake.* Neither Morris nor the Marine Committee wrote to him for months. American newspapers played up his raid on Whitehaven and gleefully discussed the consternation it had created in England; but that was no compensation for lack of official recognition. Consequently it was with unusual pleasure that Jones, on 12 November, received the following affectionate if illiterate letter from Thomas Bell, captain of an American privateer that had put into Lorient, and his old friend from Hopkins days:

> You Cant think of the pleashur I had in Phila^d when I heard of your success for tacking the *drack* & never More Angrey on my Arivel her when I heard of your Ill tretment by some Gentl^n Which I feal with you by Experience. poor Young had the misfortune to loss the Brig [*Independence*]

on Occacok Bar. on My Arivel at Edenton I had the Pleashur of Seaing your freands Mess.ʳˢ Hews & Smith they Speak of you with Rapturs & on my Arivel at Mʳ Morriss he did the saim. for Short the publick to the Southward thinks you the finest fellow belonging to America. I am supprised how Simpson got the Comᵈ or you Could Suffer it Without his being brought to A triel. I hope you have don nothing but you can Stand by. Some of your Northward Gentlⁿ told me the Gentlⁿ In Paris had set you Aside & Appointed Simpson to the Comᵈ I told them it must be A thing Emposibel for them to do without your Consent. The Other Day a northward Captain was hear from Brest in Compʸ with a Scoundrel of a brocker & his first Lieut. As to the brocker I have Ofended him so Viley that he thinks Me as bad as he dos you. As to the Capᵗ When I first saw him I tuck him for a Comedin of france not of America.* . . .

. . . One Lande A frenchman has got the finest Ship belonging to America She is Called the *Alience* bult I belive in Portsmouth it has Caused a great deal of disturbance amount the Captains to the Southward they are Dayly Getting Leve of Absence and thare pay is Stoped till they Return† but God Knows when that will be as the Gratest part is dissatisfied. . . . Lodgings in Philaᵈ is from to 7 to 8 pounds the Weack they have Raised the fregats** but God knows when they will be Repaird thaey have no Carpenters no Wood or Aney thing of the Kind. Philaᵈ looks Shoking no Ships or Sailors nor nothing dowing but What Mʳ Morris dos. my Brig belongs to him She mounts 12 six pounders & the Onley Squar Rigᵈ Vessell when I left it. . . .

P.S. Mr. Morris has left the Marien and Every thing is Going to the devel as fast [as it] can

Jones replied in one of his best letters—serious, prophetic and jocular:

---

* Abraham Whipple of frigate *Providence;* he had visited Paris and had been presented to the King.

† It was in consequence of these naval officers being laid off by Congress for want of employment that many of them, such as Gustavus Conyngham, accepted commands of privateers.

** Those scuttled in the Delaware to avoid capture.

MY DEAR SIR,

. . . Your account of the particular affection towards me of Mʳ Morris Mʳ Hewes and other worthy Characters affords me the truest pleasure. I would far rather have the Esteem and Friendship of a few such Men than the empty applause of Millions, who possess less liberal souls. Yet I confess to you that my Vanity is greatly Flattered by your account of the generous Public approbation of my past services—And I pledge myself to that generous Public that it shall be my first care and my hearts supremest wish to merit the Continuance of its approbation, by my future services and constant endeavours to support the Honor of Freedoms Flag. . . .

Your account of the Situation of Philadelphia and of our Poor Marine distresses much—but let us not altogether despond. Tho' I am no Prophet, the one will yet become the *first City,* and the other the *first Navy* within a much shorter space of time than is generally imagined. When the Enemies land force is once conquered and expelled the Continent, our Marine will rise as if by Enchantment, and become, within the memory of Persons now living, the wonder and Envy of the World. . . .

I am sorry and much disappointed by not hearing from Young, who said so much about his Wife's friend, my fair Mistress! By his silence I fear I have a Rival who by Opportunity and Importunity may make great and Dangerous advances towards the Heart before I can arrive to raise the Siege. I'm afraid this making Love by Proxy will not answer; and I shall Despair of its Success Unless I soon receive some Encouragement. . . .

Captain Bell's letter was forwarded by James Moylan, an Irish merchant at Lorient to whom Jones had written begging him to find some French ship, suitable for conversion to warlike uses, that he could buy on credit, if Sartine would not pay for her. Moylan replied on 10 November that he had found one. She was a French East Indiaman of about 900 tons, *Le Duc de Duras* by name. This is the vessel that is known to history as *Bonhomme Richard.*

XI

The "Bonhomme Richard" Squadron

November 1778-August 1779

1. A Ship at Last

Paul Jones did not immediately jump at the suggestion of buying *Le Duc de Duras;* he continued writing letters to Chaumont and Franklin and American agents in the outports, seeking the best ship for his purpose. Another East Indiaman called *Turgot* sounded better, but she was snapped up. He even played with the idea of having a frigate along the lines of the famous *La Belle Poule* constructed for him by a Bordeaux shipbuilder. Chaumont offered him a choice of several British prizes brought into Brest; he looked each one over and rejected her as a mere tub. For, he replied, "I wish to have no Connection with any Ship that does not sail *fast,* for I intend *to go in harm's way*. . . . I would rather be shott ashore than sent to Sea in such things as the Armed Prizes I have described."

Yet it was his fate never to command a ship fast enough to force battle on a foe that chose to flee.

By 7 December Jones is in Lorient, the port especially created for the Compagnie des Indes, rival to England's East India Company. There he decides that *Duc de Duras,* although built in 1766, "is the only Ship offered for sale in France that will answer our purpose." A spate of excited letters to Chaumont, urging him to purchase and arm this ship at once, follows; Jones would also have written to Madame, he says, "But unhappily I am not able to express myself in French in Language that would do justice to my Sentiments—& my Mind has been so perplexed that I have not been able to study." He assures the Reverend Father John Mehegen, Irish chaplain to the Comte d'Orvilliers, that he "has not been occupied either by Love or War" since his arrival in Lorient, and wishes he could have a chance to fight, since his mind is "unsuited to the gentle breathings and softer concerns of the former." The owner of *Duras,* one Bérard, is coy; he will sell, but must have an answer in ten days; matters are approaching a crisis and Jones cannot any longer be trifled with. He keeps Christmas and New Year's with James Moylan at Lorient, fearful lest *Duras* slip through his fingers, and she almost does, but in early February 1779 he has the happiness to learn that all is arranged.

M. de Sartine writes to him that the King "in consequence of the distinguished manner in which you have served the United States, and the complete confidence that your conduct has deserved on the part of Congress, has thought proper to place at your disposition the ship *Le Duras* of 40 guns, now at Lorient." The King is about to issue orders for her armament, she will sail under the American flag, and if her complement cannot be filled with Americans, Jones may enlist French volunteers. He may sail whenever he is ready, without further orders, and he will himself decide, according to circumstances, the course he will take, "whether in European waters or those of America."

At last, the glorious opportunity! But Paul Jones had over six months more of diplomacy, exasperation and plain hard work before he got to sea in *Bonhomme Richard,* as Sartine graciously consented that he rename the old East Indiaman. This was the French translation of "Poor Richard," Franklin's nom de plume for his famous almanacs. *Les Maximes du Bonhomme Richard,* translated from the almanacs, were all the rage in Paris; and among them Jones found one so very apt—"If he wishes to have any business faithfully and expeditiously performed, to go on it himself"—that he happily adopted this name for his ship, at the same time complimenting Dr. Franklin.

2. Naughty Susanna

The Captain made a hurried trip to Paris and Passy in mid-February, to pay his respects to Dr. Franklin and his devotions to Madame de Chaumont. There then took place an incident which caused Jones great embarrassment and afforded the circle of his friends at Passy many a good laugh.

We are able to laugh at it too, because, through a curious misunderstanding, it was recorded. Shortly after Jones's return to Lorient, Franklin wrote to him on various business, and in a postscript made a jocose allusion to clearing up a "mystery" in Jones's life, of which he assumed that the Captain had already been informed by Madame his *chère amie.* But Jones had not been informed and did not understand the allusion. He jumped to the conclusion that Franklin had heard gossip about the mutiny at Tobago in 1773, decided that he had better make a clean breast of it, and wrote the long letter which we drew upon in Chapter II as the only account of that affair which has been preserved. Upon receiving this lengthy confession, Franklin was puzzled. He had not the remotest knowledge of the Tobago affair; the "mystery" he had alluded to was a carnival prank which a naughty *femme de chambre* had played at Passy.

Here is what happened; and the reader is assured that this is no incident out of *Le Mariage de Figaro,* although Beaumarchais, who wrote the comedy that is the basis for Mozart's opera, was an intimate of the Franklin circle, and it may well have given him an idea.

Abbé Rochon, the curé of Passy, called on Dr. Franklin the day after Jones left for Lorient to inform him that the gardener of the Hôtel de Valentinois accused the Captain of having attempted to rape his wife the evening before. The Abbé was relieved that the Captain had departed, because the gardener's three sons had sworn to kill him! This story, wrote Franklin, "occasioned some Laughing; for the old Woman being one of the grossest, coarsest, dirtiest & ugliest that we may find in a thousand, Madame Chaumont said it gave a high Idea of the Strength of Appetite and Courage of the Americans!" One can imagine the scene in Franklin's little study—the half serious, half-jocular priest, the venerable Doctor trying to look horror-struck, his secretaries attempting to stifle laughter, and Madame bursting out, "*Mon Dieu,* these Americans! Savages! red Indians!"

The explanation, which Madame must have suspected or she would not have laughed, was this. On Shrove Tuesday, the last evening of the carnival, Mademoiselle de Chaumont's *femme de chambre* had amused herself by dressing up in one of Jones's uniforms which he had left behind. Thus disguised as the Captain, she encountered the old hag in the garden after dark, and "took it into her head to try her Chastity, which it seems was found Proof." Thus was the "mystery" explained.

What later happened to this naughty Susanna does not appear; but one gathers from Paul Jones's farewell letter to Madame de Chaumont before sailing in *Bonhomme Richard* that he, at least, was not amused. He had been made a fool of, not only by the maid's escapade, but by telling Dr. Franklin about the Tobago affair. It made the Captain angry with himself to have placed in other hands a story that might be used against him. He could imagine the Chaumonts, Dr. Bancroft and young Franklin, the Doctor's secretary, snickering over his naïveté. He never again alluded to either episode.

The Captain's farewell letter to Madame de Chaumont is the first from him to any of his lady loves of which he kept a draft. It is certainly a model of polite stuffiness and insolent civility. One wonders whether Madame, after reading it, fell into a rage and tore it to bits, or laughed it off as a piece of gross impertinence, and looked about for a new lover. Probably the latter; for, as soon as the French Revolution made divorce possible, Chaumont divorced her.

ON BOARD THE *Bon Homme Richard*
L'ORIENT, *June 13th, 1779*

Altho' my pen has hitherto been Silent yet my thoughts have done ample Justice to the Affectionate Friendship of Madame de Chaumont. Since I last had the honor of seeing her I have indeed had very little time to write, yet had I been Sufficiently Acquainted with her Language, she would have heard from me frequently. As I have been so long under involuntary Silence, you have a Just right to expect me to say something that can make atonement in this letter, and I ardently wish not to disappoint you. I feel however, that I never had more to say nor less power to express myself. I am on the point of proving again the uncertain fortune of War. If I survive, I hope to return with Laurels. I hope this I say, because I am sure to take with me your good wishes, and because I know that my Success would afford you pleasure. To Support the Cause of Human Nature, I sacrifice all the soft emotions of the Heart at a time of Life, too, when Love is my Duty. But my Soul's Supreme Ambition is to merit the partial praises of my Friends which I know I have not yet done by my Services. I can only add that whatever my future fortune may be, I shall carry with me thro life the most Constant and Lively sense of your polite Attentions and of your delicate and Unreserved Friendship.

I am with Sentiments of real Esteem Affection and Respect

Madame

yours

&c

MADAME DE CHAUMONT
Passy

In other words, Jones was through with her. "Love 'em and leave 'em," the eternal sailor's motto, was his too. But he was far from through with that lady's husband.

3. "Bonhomme Richard" and Her Consorts

Exact information about *Bonhomme Richard* is hard to find, for she sank after her one moment of glory, all engravings of her are posthumous, and the existing models, like those of most historic ships, are simply the best that a good marine archaeologist can do with the few facts at his disposal.* Registering 850 to 900 tons, at least twice the burthen of any ship previously commanded by Jones, she was a rather tired old craft, having made two round voyages to China under the Compagnie des Indes, two more under the Crown (which had owned her once before), and several more under private owners. Her owner in 1778, M. Bérard, proposed to convert her to a privateer and managed to extract 6 eighteen-pounders from the French Navy for that purpose. Before she was ready for sea, Sartine bought her for the asking price of two hundred and twenty thousand livres (forty-four thousand dollars), 60 per cent more than the Crown had sold her for in 1771. The King charged himself with the entire expense of fitting out, for which Sartine gave Chaumont carte blanche; and he also took responsibility for the payroll.

Paul Jones's first concern was to find enough guns of sufficient caliber to make *Richard* a proper fighting ship. A cannon foundry at Nantes could do nothing for him. Another at Périgueux was not interested. He journeyed to Angoulême in March and there made a contract for a number of guns. A firm at Bordeaux named Louis Sezerac l'aîné et fils promised to cast the rest, but none arrived in time; Jones had to pick up what he could, and he was lucky to get 16 new-model twelve-pounders out of the French Navy. As finally armed, *Bonhomme Richard* mounted 6 nine-pounders on the forecastle and quarterdeck, 16 new and 12 old twelve-pounders on the covered gun deck as main battery, and the 6 old eighteen-pounders

---

* As all French East Indiamen were of similar build, it is likely that *La Paix,* the model of which in the National Maritime Museum at Greenwich is here shown, was very similar to *Le Duc de Duras;* they were built within a year or two of each other. *La Paix* was 145 feet long, stem to sternpost, 35 foot beam and had ports for 46 guns. Note the similarity of her stern to *Richard's* as shown on the Dupré medal.

mounted à *la Sainte-Barbe,* i.e., in the gunroom, the junior officers' messroom under the after part of the gun deck. New ports had to be pierced for these eighteen-pounders, which proved to be a liability in battle.

Jones enjoyed fitting out more than anything except fighting and making love. There was plenty to be done to *Bonhomme Richard.* Since his first orders looked to her becoming the flagship of an amphibious operation with Lafayette, he had to have space for troops, and on deck he built a roundhouse or caboose to accommodate the General and staff. Had he known the sort of operation he eventually had to perform, he would have "razeed" *Richard*—cut her down one deck to obtain better speed, and mounted one battery of 30 eighteen-pounders on the open gun deck rather than a composite battery of three different calibers, which is what he obtained. And he adds, characteristically in this letter to Franklin of 4 July 1779, "I have saluted the sun last evening & this morning and shall again this evening. This I hope will be done to the latest posterity where ever the Flag of Freedom is Displayed!"

Before long, Jones's command was enlarged, as he had always hoped, by the addition of several more vessels. For this, Lafayette seems to have been largely responsible. The Marquis, now Major General U.S. Army, returned to France in early February of 1779 in the hope of inducing the King to put more effort into the American war. The dispatch of Rochambeau's expeditionary force and of De Grasse's fleet was, in part, a result of his efforts. Before going back to the United States, Lafayette hoped to distinguish himself in the European theater. The plan that he had in mind was a full-fledged amphibious assault on a major seaport like Liverpool. Franklin, with whom Lafayette discussed this plan, suggested Paul Jones as the proper man to command the task force. "There is honor enough to be got for both of you if the expedition is conducted with a prudent unanimity," he wrote to Jones, adding the benevolent caution that Lafayette, being a major general, must command the landing force. Lafayette wrote to Jones that he would be happy to divide with him "whatever share of glory may await us," and Jones replied with equal enthusiasm, both to Lafayette and to Franklin, whose "liberal and nobleminded instructions," he said, "would make a coward brave."

The City of Liverpool, which somehow got wind of what was cooking, became terrified at the prospect of a raid by Paul Jones. The city council begged the British government to complete a fort on the Mersey, to send them a thousand stand of arms and to remove French prisoners to a safe place in the interior. In the Isle of Man, Lieutenant Governor Dawson alerted the militia on 19 May "that Paul Jones lately sail'd from Brest with four of five sail of armed vessels with Land Forces aboard," that "this Isle is the most probable place of rendezvous." The Manx militia must be prepared to assemble at short notice, a horse and rider must be kept ready to carry word to the Castle, and beacon fires should be laid to communicate with similar beacons on St. Bee's Head, Cumberland, if suspicious vessels are sighted.

To have had two such young, ardent and brave officers as Jones and Lafayette commanding a combined operation would have added a bright page to the history of that war. But it was not to be. On 22 May Lafayette informed Jones that the King had made other plans, and he greatly regretted being deprived of being a witness to the Captain's "Success, abilities and Glory." And, he added, "What will be further determined about your squadron is yet uncertain, and the Ministers are to consult with Doctor Franklin."

For a squadron it already was. The new American-built frigate *Alliance*, which brought Lafayette back to France, had been assigned to Jones by Franklin at the request of Sartine. She was under the command of a strange, half-mad Frenchman named Pierre Landais, who was destined to be a greater enemy than the British to Paul Jones. A member of an old seafaring family of St.-Malo and Jones's senior by ten years, he had served in the French Navy since youth, had been wounded in the Seven Years' War, commanded a small vessel in Bougainville's voyage around the world, and risen to the rank of Capitaine de Brulôt.* In 1775 he refused an appointment as Lieutenant of the Port of Brest, knowing that to be a dead-end command, and was discharged from the French Navy; but in 1777 he persuaded Silas Deane to send him to America in command of a supply ship, with a letter of introduction to Congress recommending him for a commission in the United States Navy. The Marine Committee of Congress promptly appointed him captain of frigate *Alliance*, then building at Salisbury on the Merrimac. Proceeding to New England, he was taken up by Sam Adams, who persuaded the General Court at Boston to make Landais an honorary citizen of Massachusetts—the sole honor of that kind bestowed by the Bay State during the war. This may have been a naïve way of disarming local prejudice and making Landais a Yankee by legislation; but it fits in neatly with other evidence that the Lee-Adams faction intended to build up Landais as a naval Lafayette and rival to Jones. That was a rôle which the Frenchman was only too ready to assume, without the slightest capacity to fill it. He had a mutiny on his hands during his first ocean crossing; and John Adams, who saw a good deal of him on board and ashore at Lorient, wrote in his diary that Landais "is jealous of every Thing, jealous of every Body, of all his officers, all his Passengers; he knows not how to treat his officers, nor his passengers, nor any Body else. Silence, Reserve, and a forbidding Air will never gain the Hearts neither by Affection nor by Veneration of our Americans. There is in this man an Inactivity and an Indecisiveness that will ruin him. He is bewildered—an absent bewildered man—an embarrassed Mind."

Alliance, with as many twelve-pounders as *Richard*, and two more nine-pounders, was the strongest ship placed under Paul Jones's command, but not the only one. The French government assigned to him three armed ships. The most important was frigate *Pallas*, armed with 26 nine-pounders, commanded by Capitaine de Brulôt Cottineau de Kerloguen. Built as a privateer in 1778, she had sailed, laden with warlike stores, to North Carolina, where, while waiting

---

* Capt. de Brulôt (fire ship) was a grade equivalent to captain of infantry, usually given to masters of merchant vessels or privateers to honor some particular exploit.

for a return cargo, Cottineau and his sailors helped the State to build Fort Hancock on Point Lookout. On the return passage, *Pallas* acquitted herself so well in an action with H.M.S. *La Brune* that she and her commanding officer and men were taken into the French Navy. They proved to be the most loyal and valuable addition to Jones's task force.

Next in order comes brig *Vengeance* (Lieutenant de Vaisseau Ricot), armed lightly with a dozen four-pounders; and, last, a smart, fast King's cutter captured from the British named *Le Cerf* (Enseigne de Vaisseau Varage), armed with 2 eight-pounders and 16 six-pounders. All three French commanding officers were given captain's or lieutenant's commissions in the United States Navy, of which Dr. Franklin apparently had a supply in blank. All except *Alliance* were outfitted, paid and maintained by the French Navy without expense to the United States. Paul Jones calculated that this squadron cost France some three million livres (six hundred thousand dollars). A curious arrangement, necessary because of the penury of Congress, but one which gave rise to a sea of trouble. Arthur Lee, we may say, began to agitate the waters of doubt and calumny by writing to Sam Adams that it was a "shameful and illegal business" to place *Alliance* under Paul Jones's command, and that the *Bonhomme Richard* task force was simply "a project of Chaumont and Williams" (Franklin's nephew) to make money for themselves. This libel—that the Jones squadron was nothing but a bunch of French privateers—kept popping up in Paris, Holland and Philadelphia, to the Commodore's annoyance and disgust.

When the plan for a descent on Liverpool by Lafayette and Jones was abandoned in May, Sartine ordered the Commodore to lead his squadron in a diversionary operation against Scotland or northern England, with the object of pinning down enemy forces that might oppose a major landing in southern England. That landing was to have been the major naval operation in 1779; but Jones's diversion turned out to be more successful than the main show.

This invasion of England, for which two French divisions of 20,000 men each were assembled, was to have been prepared by the combined fleets of France and Spain annihilating or neutralizing English naval forces in the Channel. D'Orvilliers' fleet sortied from Brest 3 June 1779 to rendezvous with the Spaniards. For six weeks he cruised back and forth off Corunna and Cape Finisterre, waiting for the Dons to appear. When they finally joined, on 26 July, the combined fleet numbered 64 ships of the line with 4774 guns (not counting frigates, corvettes and smaller craft), whilst Admiral Sir Charles Hardy RN, commanding the Channel Fleet, could collect only 38 ships of the line with 2968 guns; the rest of the Royal Navy was in American waters or the Mediterranean. The Spanish ships were so slow that the Allies raised the Lizard only on 14 August. By that time the French fleet was ravaged by smallpox, scurvy and typhus. D'Orvilliers, sixty-nine years old, lost heart after his only son died on board, and allowed his chief of staff, Capitaine de Vaisseau Pavillon (whom Paul Jones considered the best naval strategist of his time) to carry on. The combined fleet anchored in Plymouth roadstead 16 August, in a flat calm; no enemy had yet appeared, as Hardy wisely declined battle. Water and food were now giving out, the sick list increased daily, the officers were in despair; but orders from Versailles were to range the south coast of England, and if Hardy still refused battle, to establish a beachhead somewhere in Cornwall. On the last day of August, D'Orvilliers encountered Hardy off the Scilly Isles and pursued him for two days without coming to grips. The situation on board the French fleet was now so desperate that Sartine ordered it to return to Brest; the Spanish ships then sailed home and the invasion force broke up. A fantastic number of men died at sea, or in hospitals ashore; flagship *Ville de Paris* lost 61 dead and 560 sick out of 1100 men; and the total number of sick landed at Brest reached 7000. England had been saved from invasion without a battle. The total failure of this Franco-Spanish operation explains to some extent the tremendous acclaim given in France to Paul Jones's victory off Flamborough Head which occurred only two days after thwarted D'Orvilliers entered Brest.

With five ships to man and get ready for sea, Jones was driven to exasperation. Since France paid the piper, she called the tune; and Le Ray de Chaumont, as paymaster general of the squadron, soon occupied a place in Jones's catalogue of villains alongside Colonel Langdon of Portsmouth. He imagined that *Le Commissaire*, as he persisted in calling this distinguished French official, was taking revenge on him for the amours of his wife. His specific complaints, however, do not seem very substantial; for instance, he made much out of being sent to sea without a supply of irons to secure prisoners—recalling the boatswain's whistle episode in *Ranger*.

A running picture of the vicissitudes of manning and fitting out this mixed squadron is given in letters from Messieurs Grandville and Thévenard, successively Captain of the Port of Lorient, to the Paris Minister of Marine, as well as in Jones's letters to Franklin.

Grandville writes from Lorient on 5 April that Commodore Jones has been to Nantes and recruited some sixty French volunteers, "wretches picked up on the street and absolutely good for nothing." Why does he not recruit men from Comte Walsh's Irish regiment in the French service? Irish soldiers would be delighted to take a crack at England. He predicts that *Bonhomme Richard* will be ready for offensive action in two weeks—actually she and the squadron required four months more to get to sea. *Alliance,* which anchored 12 May in Penmarch roadstead, also needs sailors. Many of the crew who sailed her across, sick men released from D'Estaing's fleet, are to be discharged—they are "almost naked and in very bad shape"; and the English prisoners on board who volunteered for American naval service proved to be unruly and mutinous. There is a great bustle in port when the French frigate *Le Sensible* embarks two distinguished passengers, John Adams returning to Philadelphia after his first foreign mission, and the Chevalier de la Luzerne, first French minister plenipotentiary to the United States. Luzerne insists on tossing twelve tons of cargo out of *Le Sensible* to make room for his personal effects, and her captain borrows two charts of the American coast from Commodore Jones.

4. Preliminary Cruise

On 12 June 1779 Thévenard reports that most of Jones's squadron is ready to sail. But before starting on his diversionary operation, he is ordered by Sartine to escort French merchant vessels to various ports on the Bay of Biscay, so that they would not be picked up by British cruisers and privateers.

The squadron sailed 19 June to perform this temporary escort duty. First night out, when only a few miles off the coast, *Bonhomme Richard* and *Alliance* collided during a squall and damaged each other, though not enough to cause them to return. *Richard's* officer of the deck was court-martialed and broken for this accident, but the real culprit was Captain Landais of *Alliance,* who refused to yield right of way to the flagship, and who went below to load his pistols at the time of the crash instead of directing operations on deck. British warships approached the convoy on more than one occasion, but hauled off when they observed the escort's strength; and Paul Jones discovered, to his chagrin, that *Bonhomme Richard* was not fast enough to force them to fight against their will. All four ships gave chase to three frigates which proved to be a French light squadron from Rochefort under the Chevalier de la Touche. *Cerf* had a fight with two English cutters in which Lieutenant Varage handled her so well that the King gave him a bonus of six hundred livres, and presented swords to his two lieutenants.

When the squadron returned to Lorient 1 July, Paul Jones found plenty of trouble awaiting him besides making repairs. M. Salomon, gentlemen's tailor of the port, was on the dock waving a bill for one thousand, seven hundred and seventy-six livres (about three hundred and forty-four dollars) for uniforms that he had made for ten officers of *Richard.* New orders had arrived from Sartine, countersigned by Franklin. In them there was no mention of a diversion to the big invasion of England. Jones is to conduct a mere commerce-destroying cruise. He is to make the best of his way with the vessels under his command to the west of Ireland, sail north to the

Orkney Islands and across the North Sea to the Naze and the Dogger Bank, "in order to take the enemy's property in those seas." Prizes are to be sent into Dunkirk, Ostend or Bergen. The cruise is to be terminated about 15 August at the Texel, in Holland, where Jones will await further orders.

Jones always thought that the order to terminate his cruise at the Texel was a bit of Chaumont's dirty work; but there was a sound reason for it. The French Navy was dependent on the Baltic for spars, tar, hemp and sailcloth. A merchant fleet carrying these naval stores from the Belts to France had put into neutral Dutch waters in November 1778 for protection from English cruisers, which were lying in wait for them in the North Sea, and had been there ever since. Jones's squadron was wanted to escort this Baltic fleet to Brest.

But Sartine did not trouble to explain, and the Commodore lost no time in protesting. His ships were too slow to overtake enemy privateers, he said—but he had not been asked to do that, only to capture merchant ships. Couldn't the Lafayette plan be revived? Or, relieve him of this command and get him a really fast ship, *L'Indien* for instance? Franklin promptly replied, "I observe what you write about a Change of the Destination; but when a thing has been once considered and determined on in Council, they don't care to resume the Consideration of it, having much Business on hand, and there is not now time to obtain a Reconsideration. . . . As the Court is at the Chief Expense, I think they have the best right to direct."

So that was that. But Paul Jones still entertained the same notions of the proper strategy for a weak naval power that he had when he commanded *Ranger:* "It appears to me to be the province of our Infant Navy to Surprise and spread Alarm, with fast sailing ships. When we grow stronger we can meet their Fleets and dispute with them the Sovereignty of the Ocean." His strategy of hit-and-run raids was adopted by England against Germany in 1940, culminating in the famous raid on Dieppe in August 1942. Paul Jones and Lord Mountbatten would have understood each other perfectly.

There was plenty more to be done to ready these ships for their cruise. *Alliance* had lost her mizzenmast in the collision and *Richard's* bowsprit, a spar vital to uphold the intricate skeleton of a square-rigger, was found to be rotten and had to be replaced. In the meantime *Pallas, Vengeance* and *Cerf* were sent to cruise off Belle-Île, to capture or chase away British privateers infesting those waters. Two returned dismasted, and none made a prize. The careening and graving of *Alliance* were completed by 13 July. A sound old mast was shaped and fitted as *Richard's* new bowsprit.

On 21 July M. Thévenard reports that the Commodore has been ill, and is having trouble with his sailors. He was right on both counts. Worn out by his efforts and torn by exasperation, Paul Jones suffered his first illness in years. His difficulties with the crew were unending. The French volunteers and the American sailors came to blows, and the English prisoners who had signed on were mutinous. In consequence of a plot that was discovered among them to capture *Richard* and carry her to England with Jones as a prisoner, a series of courts-martial were held. The ringleader, Quartermaster Towers, got 250 lashes "on his bare back with a Cat of nine Tails at the Gangway" and was thrown into a French prison; an armorer with the respectable name of William Lawrence Sturgis was found guilty of disobedience but released, as he had already spent six weeks in "the Cashoe" (the brig); a French volunteer with the eminent name of Jean Rousseau was found guilty of theft and given 33 lashes.

The Minister of Marine, probably at the Commodore's request, now ordered a hundred English prisoners who had been enrolled in *Richard's* crew to be discharged as untrustworthy and to be replaced by others. The Commodore duly discharged 77 English prisoners, together with 23 bad actors among his crew who were deserters from the Royal Navy, and 6 Englishmen who were in hospital ashore. Jones wished to replace them by Portuguese sailors who had arrived in French cutter *L'Épervier*. Sartine disapproved of Jones's shipping the Portuguese because *Richard* had no Catholic chaplain, and suggested that he substitute Hollanders; but the Commodore preferred Portuguese in the hand to Dutch in the bush. He sent a courier to

Franklin at his own expense to beg him to order a captured King's cutter added to his task force; but if Franklin tried, he was unsuccessful.

On 28 July when the squadron was ready to sail, foul wind detained it in port. Jones sent his two lieutenants to Nantes to engage some of the American prisoners lately released from English prisons; Midshipman Nathaniel Fanning was one of them. And 38 Portuguese, Danish and Dutch sailors from *L'Épervier* were placed at his disposition.

At this juncture, on the first day of August, Le Ray de Chaumont returned to Lorient with full powers from Sartine to put on the heat. According to Thévenard, *Richard* then had for crew: 177 officers, seamen and others; 121 volunteers, officers and soldiers; 30 Portuguese and 9 other foreigners, and 43 American sailors from English prisons who were expected any day from Nantes; they arrived a few days later. This total of 380, Sartine agreed, was ample. According to French naval regulations, a 30-gun ship was entitled to 280 men, and a 50-gun ship to 439 men; *Richard*, about halfway between the two, rated only 360, so the Commodore should not complain. But of course he did complain; he thought himself ill used to be given no more men. The Minister of Marine, in this same letter, expresses the wish that the squadron may sail at the earliest possible date, and he accords Commodore Jones the singular privilege of using the Franco-Spanish code of flag signals, trusting that he will see that its secrecy is not compromised.

5. Task Force Completed

On 9 August *Bonhomme Richard*, *Pallas*, *Cerf* and *Vengeance* sail from Lorient to join *Alliance* off the Île de Groix. Two French privateers named *Monsieur* and *Granville*, whose masters have decided to join Jones, are already there. On the 10th all seven ships are at anchor in the roadstead, awaiting the arrival of United States privateer *General*

Mifflin, which Jones has invited to join. She arrives, but the master has other orders and declines. Le Ray de Chaumont "is almost always on board some vessel of this division to regulate its affairs," writes Thévenard. That infuriates Jones, especially since Chaumont issues to each ship's officer a copy of Sartine's orders instead of giving them to the Commodore to endorse and distribute.

Finally, on 14 August at 4:00 A.M. the task force sets sail from Groix Roadstead. Thévenard gives its composition at that time as follows:

	No. of Officers and Men	Commanding Officer	Ordnance					
			18s	12s	9s	8s	6s	4s
Frigate *Bonhomme Richard*	380	Capt. John P. Jones USN	6	28	6	—	—	—
Frigate *Alliance*	215	Capt. Pierre Landais USN	—	28	8	—	—	—
Frigate *La Pallas*	253	Capt. de B. Denis-Nicolas Cottineau	—	—	26	—	—	6
Corvette *La Vengeance*	66	Lt. de V. Philippe-Nicholas Ricot	—	—	—	—	—	12
Cutter *Le Cerf*	157	Ens. de V. Joseph Varage	—	—	—	2	16	—
Privateer *Monsieur*	357	Guidloup	—	26	—	—	—	12
Privateer *Granville*	100	Dumaurier, or Demauriec	—	—	—	4	6	—

Paul Jones, as we have seen, was Captain U.S. Navy with the courtesy rank of Commodore; Landais, Ricot and Cottineau had U.S. captains' commissions, and Varage claimed the same temporary rank, although he was only Enseigne de Vaisseau in the French Navy. Corvette *Vengeance* and cutter *Cerf* were rigged as brigantines; the others, except possibly privateer *Granville,* were square-rigged three-masters.

On the advice of Le Ray de Chaumont and (as he later asserted) against his own better judgment, the Commodore executed a *Concordat* or agreement with him and the four naval captains before sailing. Jones later declared that it was unheard of and improper for a commodore of a task force to have any other relation with his captains than that of their commander. But the captains of Esek Hopkins's squadron, all Americans, had made a similar agreement before sailing for New Providence and something of the kind was needed by this heterogeneous task force. The Concordat provided that all the ships would be considered as belonging to the United States Navy, would fly the American ensign and operate under United States Navy regulations, especially in the matter of splitting prize money. All prizes are to be consigned to M. de Chaumont, and the portion of each ship in prizes taken by any vessel of the squadron will be determined by the American minister at the Court of Versailles and the French Minister of Marine. These two provisions created trouble later; but as the French, through Chaumont, provided all the expense, it was reasonable that they should have a say in the disposal of prizes.

Monsieur and *Granville* were not included in this contract because they were privateers; and also, no doubt, because Jones expected they would quit whenever it suited them, which is exactly what they did. *Monsieur,* a ship only slightly less powerful than *Bonhomme Richard,* stayed with the task force but a few days, and *Granville* but a week longer. Jones, noting their departures, observed that privateersmen were unreliable in military operations and devoid of honor or good faith, which was true enough.

Thus, inauspiciously, began a cruise which brought undying fame to our hero and to the officers and men of *Bonhomme Richard.*

XII

A Mad Cruise

August-September 1779

1. Commodore, Officers and Men

Now that "the Honourable Captain John P. Jones, Commander in Chief of the American Squadron now in Europe," as he styles himself, is at last clear of the land, let us take a good look at him, and at his officers and crew.

We are fortunate in having a lively impression of Paul Jones in the diary of John Adams when living on board *Alliance,* awaiting passage for America. He and sixteen other officers and gentlemen were given an "elegant dinner" by Jones at L'Epée Royale in Lorient on 13 May 1779. The conversation, says Adams, was "not very instructive," except for one good bit of advice that he noted down, that there were two ways of learning French, "take a Mistress and go to the Commedie." Apparently this observation came from the Commodore. Surgeon Brooke of *Bonhomme Richard* wouldn't let off Adams from giving his opinion as to which method was preferable, and John replied "Both at once!" But he added, somewhat stuffily, in case Abigail should inspect his diary, "The language is nowhere better spoken than at the Commedie." He continues:

> After Dinner walked out, with Captains Jones & Landais to see Jones's Marines—dressed in the English Uniforms, red & white; a Number of very active & clever Sergiants & Corporals are employed to teach them the exercise, and Manevous & Marches, &c. After which Jones came on Board our Ship. This is the most ambitious and intriguing officer in the American Navy. Jones has Art, and Secrecy, and aspires very high. You see the Character of the Man in his uniform, and that of his officers and Marines—variant from the Uniforms established by Congress. Golden Button holes, for himself—two Epauletts —Marines in red and white, instead of Green.
>
> Eccentricities and Irregularities are to be expected from him—they are in his Character, they are visible in his Eyes. His voice is soft and still and small, his eye has keeness and Wildness and softness in it.

The Marines, however, were French, not American Marines, and were wearing their proper uniform of red coat with white waistcoat and breeches. Gilt-edged buttonholes (or gilt buttons) were in the uniform regulations agreed to by the naval captains at Boston in 1777, and Jones probably assumed a second epaulet because he was now a commodore. He appreciated better than anyone else in the United States Navy at that time the importance of taut, clean uniforms and good manners for the morale and efficiency of a ship's company. He dressed his officers in the blue uniform with white lapels, waistcoat and breeches which had been adopted in 1777, partly because it was much smarter than the dingy blue-and-red of 1776, and partly to be a help in deceptive warfare. By "intriguing," Adams meant Jones's efforts to improve his seniority, of which he had been cognizant in Congress, and his zeal to obtain command of *L'Indien*. As for Jones's voice, everyone who commented on it, in ordinary social contacts, agreed with Adams's impression that the Commodore spoke soft and low. They never heard his quarterdeck voice.

Within a year of the time of which we are speaking, there were made in Paris the two best life portraits of Paul Jones. These are the mezzotint head and shoulders by Moreau *le jeune,* and the life-sized bust by Jean-Antoine Houdon, a photograph of which we have reproduced. Houdon sculptured many distinguished characters like Washington, Voltaire and Franklin. He worked from life and followed exact proportions and dimensions, using characteristic poses of his subjects, so that his busts are speaking likenesses. Note Jones's high cheekbones, his sharp, wedge-shaped nose, his mouth and lips, which could curl with scorn or anger, break into a brilliant smile, frame polite conversation in that soft, low voice that John Adams heard, or hurl a loud, stern command against the thunder of battle and the breeze. Note the strong, well-molded chin and jaws. Observe the neat uniform, the ribbon and cross (conferred on him after this cruise), the carefully arranged neckcloth; the hair neatly dressed, brushed back from the forehead and tied behind in a queue. It is a strong, resolute countenance; proud, uncompromising, defiant, ambitious, and (from long experience) on the defensive against fools and intriguers.

Let the reader make up his own mind as to the manner of man Paul Jones was by studying this noble portrait of him. To me, it is a passionate, not a calm face; the face of a man who is not at peace even with himself, but at war with society and the world; yet that of a man who longs, even yearns, for peace. I see no sense of humor in his countenance, but a look of impatient irony. It is the face of a man who exacts everything that is due to his rank and his accomplishments, but is ungenerous, even to the women whom he loves and discards. A man incapable of giving himself completely to a friend or a mistress, but who identifies himself completely with his cause—PRO REPUBLICA.

Paul Jones was moderate in his tastes. Until after the end of the war his body was spare and taut; he never ate or drank to excess.

Midshipman Fanning, who acted as the Commodore's secretary on the forthcoming cruise and shared his cabin, testified, "I never knew him to drink any kind of ardent spirits. On the contrary his constant drink was lemonade (lime juice and water, with a little sugar to make it the more palatable)." After dining at sea, in fair weather, "he made it a custom to drink three glasses of wine." Unlike Nelson he was never troubled with seasickness, but exposed himself recklessly both to the weather and to enemy fire in battle; the frequent soakings and chill eventually undermined his health, but no British bullet ever found a mark in him. As he once gallantly remarked to a lady, "he had only been wounded with arrows that no enemy discharged."

Next, a brief look at the officers of *Bonhomme Richard*. Jones had good men to choose from among the naval lieutenants and privateer officers stranded in France or released from English prisons.

For First Lieutenant of *Bonhomme Richard,* the Commodore chose Richard Dale of Virginia, who though twenty-two years old had been at sea for eight or nine years. He had served under Captains John Barry and Henry Johnson in armed brig *Lexington,* which accompanied *Reprisal* in her cruise around the British Isles in 1777. On her way home, *Lexington* was captured and Dale was thrown into Mill Prison, Portsmouth. He escaped, was recaptured and given the "black hole" treatment, but escaped again and made his way to Lorient, where he volunteered for *Bonhomme Richard*. Paul Jones loved Dale as a younger brother; he was one of the few officers with whom he was glad to share credit for a victory. He served in the French war of 1798 as Captain U.S. Navy and later became Commodore of the Mediterranean squadron.

Next junior to Lieutenant Dale were two men from Newburyport in Massachusetts. Henry Lunt, twenty-six years old, a seaman in *Alfred* on the New Providence expedition, had transferred with Paul Jones to sloop *Providence* for his first independent cruise. When that was over, he shipped with his cousin, Cutting Lunt, in a privateer, which was captured on Christmas Eve 1776. After more than two years spent in Mill Prison, the Lunts were exchanged and arrived at Nantes in a cartel in March 1779. Jones was overjoyed to meet his old shipmate, and promptly appointed him second lieutenant of *Bonhomme Richard,* and his cousin Cutting, aged thirty, master. Dr. Lawrence Brooke, a physician of an old Virginia family, volunteered as surgeon; he impressed John Adams with learned conversation, but Midshipman Fanning wrote that Dr. Brooke was more butcher than surgeon. Matthew Mease, a shipowner of Philadelphia who happened to be in France, accepted the post of purser after all other billets had been filled and in action took charge of a battery, behaving "with distinguished coolness and intrepidity," according to the Commodore.

For midshipmen's billets Jones accepted ten young men from different parts of the country. Three were South Carolinians, all "brave, steady officers"; John W. Linthwaite, Robert Coram and John Mayrant, "a young gentleman of fortune, whose conduct in the engagement did him great honor." A fourth midshipman, Nathaniel Fanning of Stonington, Connecticut, had been captured when serving in privateer *Angelica,* and was exchanged. His courage in action made him a favorite with the Commodore, but the feeling was not reciprocated, and Fanning's later *Narrative* of his sea experiences is a source of unpleasant and untrue stories about Paul Jones. A fifth midshipman, Beaumont Groube, whom Jones picked up from the American colony at Nantes, acquired meretricious fame as the "Lieutenant Grub" of the chapbooks, supposedly shot by Jones for striking the ensign.

There were three Irish officers in the wardroom, Lieutenant Eugene Macarthy and Sub-lieutenants James Gerald O'Kelly and Edward Stack. These were volunteers from the Irish regiment of marine artillery in the French Army, commanded by Colonel le Comte de Walsh-Serrant. Young Stack was particularly commended for his conduct in the battle by the Commodore, who succeeded in getting him promoted and given a pension; and Jones exerted himself to have both Irishmen elected to the Society of the Cincinnati. Occupying the roundhouse built for Lafayette were two lieutenant

colonels of French Marines, Paul de Chamillard de Varville and An-
toine-Félix Wybert. Both were towers of strength to the Commodore; Wybert, who had been around the world with Bougainville,
subsequently obtained a commission in the Engineering Corps,
U.S. Army. Our old friend Major Frazer pled for an invitation, but
Jones had had enough of him; instead, he accepted, on a volunteer
basis, as liaison with the French Marines, Captain Alexander Dick
USA, whom John Adams describes as "of good family and handsome
fortune in Virginia."

The officers of *Bonhomme Richard*, accordingly, were a more ho-
mogeneous group than the crew; and, as volunteers accepted by
Jones, they were personally loyal to the Commodore.

As for the crew, Jones himself observed, in his *Mémoire* to the
King, that it looked like as bad a one as you could find anywhere;
yet it turned out to be one of the best he ever commanded. Thévenard and Paul Jones agree as to the numbers; the Commodore wrote
to Sartine on 11 August that it then consisted of "380 officers, men
and boys, inclusive of 137 Marine soldiers, 36 Landsmen and 32
Boys." The earliest detailed list is one "from an official source" (now
lost) in Sherburne's biography. This breaks down by ranks and na-
tionalities as follows:

	Officers	Petty Officers	Able Seamen	Ordinary Seamen	Boys	Total
Americans	17	16	17	2	27	79
Irish	3	6	6	5	1	21
English	—	20	19	10	10	59
Scotch	—	1	2	1	—	4
Swedish	—	—	7	—	—	7
Norwegian	—	—	2	1	—	3
Portuguese	—	—	6	22	1	29
Swiss	—	—	1	—	—	1
Italian	—	—	—	1	—	1
East Indian	—	—	—	1	1	2
French	—	—	—	—	1	1
	20	43	60	43	41	207

With the addition of three cooks, whose nationality is not given, this adds up to 210, which falls short by 170 of the total given by Thévenard and by Jones himself; but the 36 French "landsmen" (three of whom were probably the cooks) and 137 French Marines make up the difference. Thus, when *Bonhomme Richard* finally sailed, she had on board 20 naval officers, mostly American; 43 petty officers, a majority British, and 144 seamen and boys, of which 46 were American, 54 British, and the rest belonged to seven different nations; together with 137 French Marines and 36 French "landsmen," who were mostly peasants or fishermen from Brittany. Over a hundred of these men, including almost all the Americans, had been released from English prisons largely through Jones's efforts. They were willing recruits, partly because they landed in France with neither money nor jobs; and partly, as John Kilby admitted, because "revenge sometimes is quite pleasant to men." These veteran seamen liked Jones, despite the fact that the first impression that some of them had of *Bonhomme Richard* was the spectacle of the coxswain and crew of the Commodore's barge being triced up to the rigging and flogged. That was their punishment for deserting the boat ashore and getting drunk, so that the Commodore had to hire a fisherman to get himself back on board his flagship—an insult to his rank and dignity not easily forgiven.

This was a setup far superior to what Paul Jones had had in *Ranger;* and from that experience he had learned a good deal about handling men. Colonel Wybert, one of the French Marine officers on board, later testified "that Commodore Paul Jones, far from commanding with haughtiness and brutality, as certain persons have endeavored to circulate, was always (though very strict and sharp in the service) affable, genteel, and very indulgent, not only towards his officers, but likewise toward the sentries and soldiers, whom he ever treated with humanity." Instead of a crew of spoiled home-town boys who were looking for easy money, Jones now had a hard core of professional seamen who wanted to fight and who recognized their Captain as the great seaman and leader that he was.

Both from his own experience under Commodore Hopkins and from D'Orvilliers' mishaps in the Battle of Ushant, Jones had learned the importance of a sound system of naval signaling. So he drew up a set of day and night recognition signals for use in his own squadron; and he also had the flags and the code-book so that he could use the Chevalier de Pavillon's system of communication. But none of Jones's commanding officers except Cottineau seem to have paid any attention to them. Standing orders were issued to the officers and men "on board the American Ship of War the *Bon Homme Richard*." The officer of the deck and the duty officer of the French Marines were always to wear a gorget on their breasts. The Marine guard was always to be ready at a moment's warning, and all Marines not on guard must stand watch with the seamen and assist them "particularly in Cleaning and Working the Ship." Midshipmen on watch were to be divided between quarterdeck, waist and forecastle. Masters' mates were to attend to the rigging and to give special attention to the preventer braces on the yards, and stoppers on topsail sheets. These were additional lines for use in case the main braces and sheets were shot away.

2. Off Ireland and the Hebrides

We are fortunate to have a detailed account of this cruise in the Commodore's fourteen-page official report to Dr. Franklin dated 3 October 1779. It is written with his usual verve and skill, a model of what an action report should be, but seldom is. In addition, we have personal accounts by Lieutenant Dale, Midshipman Fanning and Gunner's Mate Kilby. And Jones's progress around the British Isles was closely followed and reported by the British press.

The squadron, comprising *Bonhomme Richard*, frigates *Alliance* and *Pallas*, cutter *Cerf*, corvette *Vengeance* and privateers *Monsieur* and *Granville*, sailed from Groix Roadstead on 14 August 1779. For several days *Richard's* logbook notes nothing but pleasant weather

Cruise of
BONHOMME RICHARD
around the British Isles
Aug.-Sept. 1779

0   100
Nautical miles

Foula I. SHETLAND
1800 2/9   3/9   Prizes sent to Bergen
ALLIANCE separates
PALLAS
rejoins   Fair I.
UNION   1/9   N.Ronaldsey
captured   1900 5/9
ALLIANCE   ORKNEY Is.   6/9
rejoins   7/9
1930 3/9
1400 30/8   NORTH   8/9
Flannan Is.   MINCH
9/9
St Kilda   10/9   NORTH

Dates of positions
are noon, unless
otherwise stated

SCOTLAND   SEA

Dundee   Inchcape Rock
15/9
Kilkaldy   14/9
17/9   Leith   Dunbar 18/9
Edinburgh   Holy I.
Bamburgh
Kirkcudbright   19/9
Dumfries June R.   Newcastle
Londonderry   Scarborough
Flamborough Hd.
Belfast   Whitehaven   23/9   1100 25/9
B.RICHARD sinks
ALLIANCE and
I. of Man   Hull   PALLAS rejoin
R. Humber   1800 12/9
IRELAND   ENGLAND
Anglesey   Liverpool
Dublin
Wicklow
Head
ALLIANCE & PALLAS   SEA   WALES
separate
26/8 Blasket I.   Waterford
Dingle Bay   Ballinskellig Bay   R. James
Skelligs   Cork   London   Goodwin
Mizen Hd.   Sands
GRANVILLE   Portsmouth   Dover   Dunkirk
departs   MAYFLOWER taken   Calais
I. of Wight   Gris Nez
19/8
MONSIEUR   Lands End   English Channel   Dieppe
departs   Scilly Is.
17/8   C. la Hague   Cherbourg   Le Havre
CHANNEL Is.   R. Seine
16/8
Ushant   Brest
Raz Pt.   FRANCE
Penmarch   Lorient
Groix I. 14/8   Raisz

and moderate winds. The Commodore, hoping to capture a few prizes off the English Channel, was in no hurry, and took eight days to cover the 350 miles between Ushant and southwest Ireland. On the 16th, a vessel from London bound for Madeira was spoken and her master and supercargo "dined on board the *Richard,*" but she was not detained, as under a neutral flag. On the 18th, *Monsieur* took a prize. According to the Concordat this should have been shared by the whole squadron; but the privateer master refused to let the Commodore set a prize crew on board, and deserted him next day after returning his signal flags. A large ship was chased on 19-20 August, but she got away. On the 21st, brigantine *Mayflower,* bound from Liverpool to London laden with provisions, surrendered after two shots had been fired. Midshipman Reuben Chase and four men were placed on board as prize crew, and she was sent to Lorient.

Mizen Head, Ireland, lay abeam at 8:00 A.M. August 23, and with a "fine Breese of Wind" astern, the squadron stood northwesterly along the ironbound coast of Kerry. At noon it was five miles SSW of a rocky island, the Great Skellig, which marks the southern entrance to Dingle Bay. Here began a chapter of accidents. At 4:00 P.M. when *Richard* was three miles off the Skelligs, and in sight of the Blaskets at the northern entrance of Dingle Bay, the wind fell to a flat calm. At the same time, brig *Fortune* was sighted and the Commodore sent two armed boats to take her, which they did easily. She was bound from Newfoundland for Bristol with a cargo of staves and whale oil. A prize crew under one of *Granville's* officers was placed on board and she was sent to Nantes or St.-Malo.

That same evening of 23 August, in a flat calm, the swell and current began to set *Richard* so close to the Skelligs that the Commodore ordered his barge—the biggest boat that he carried—to be lowered and manned with a coxswain and six seamen in order to tow the ship clear of danger. Master Lunt made the mistake of appointing as coxswain the one who had been flogged at Lorient, and manning the boat with Irishmen who, seizing a chance for home, cut the tow-rope at 10:30 P.M. and rowed rapidly shoreward. Upon seeing them make off, Lunt lowered the jolly boat, and with himself in command, and two other officers and nine men, chased the deserters. They pursued with such zeal that they got lost in a fog mull which hung over southwest Ireland that night and next day, the 24th.

On the afternoon of the 24th, Captain Landais came on board the flagship, and, in the presence of the two ranking French officers, addressed the Commodore "in the most gross and insulting terms" which (according to Wybert) he promptly translated into French for the benefit of Colonel de Chamillard, who did not understand English. Landais was angry because Jones, anticipating the calm, had forbidden him to chase a vessel the previous day close to shore; he told the Commodore that "he was the only American in the squadron"—owing, presumably, to his honorary Bay State citizenship—and that he would henceforth chase "when and where he thought proper, and in every other matter." That is exactly what he did.

Jones now sent cutter *Cerf* to reconnoiter the Irish coast and recover the missing boats, while the squadron stood off and on; that is, sailed back and forth at a safe distance from the reefs. On the afternoon of the 25th, it closed and ranged the coast, but no *Cerf* was seen. Next day, too, the Commodore drew a blank. A gale was now making up. Taking Landais's advice for once, the Commodore gave up the search and shaped a northerly course under reduced sail. Although he showed a light at the masthead and fired a gun every hour of the night, in the morning he found himself accompanied only by little *Vengeance*. Landais had made off on his own and was not again seen until the last day of August. About the same time, *Granville* retired with a prize and never turned up; *Pallas* had broken her tiller and was repairing it. Jones later learned to his sorrow that by following Landais's advice and standing north he missed a chance at a fleet of East Indiamen bound for Limerick.

As for cutter *Cerf*, Lieutenant Varage had made a mess of his mission. Upon sighting Master Lunt's boat he showed English colors and fired a gun. Lunt, naturally supposing her to be an enemy cutter (she had been H.M.S. *Stag*, and the weather was foggy) made his best efforts to escape, and in so doing got lost, landed at Ballinskelligs Bay in the hope of finding something to eat, and was promptly captured by the Kerry Rangers. *Cerf* never rejoined the Commodore but returned to Lorient. Varage excused himself because "in the blow of 26 August the devil himself could not have kept the sea," and claimed that her mainmast broke and that he had been attacked by an English cutter.

Not only had Jones lost an 18-gun cutter, two boats, a good officer (and Lunt did not survive his second stretch in an English prison) and 16 men; the country was now aroused against him. For the next two weeks the London papers were printing letters from Counties Cork and Kerry, giving a complete task organization of the enemy furnished by the deserters, and reporting that Jones's mission was to burn Limerick or Galway. The Admiralty ordered H.M.S. *Ulysses* and *Boston* to sail in search of him, but they searched the wrong coast of Ireland, assuming that Jones intended to take another crack at Whitehaven.

For the next few days the wind blew fair, brisk and puffy; the only entries in *Richard's* log are about cracking on topgallants, royals, mizzen-topmast staysail and studding sails, and shortening sail in the squalls. In four days she logged 450 miles. Jones was now entering a region of magnificent scenery. Perhaps he recalled some lines of Thomson's *Seasons,* his favorite poem, when he saw the surf boiling around "utmost Kilda's shore."

At 2:00 P.M. 30 August, *Bonhomme Richard* and *Vengeance* sighted the Flannan Islands off the Outer Hebrides. That evening they left the Butt of Lewis astern, and at the entrance to the North Minch, as the sun rose next morning, "saw 3 sail to windward and two to leward & Hoisted our Englisch Ensing. Att 7 tak Ship and gave Chase for the Sail to Windward. At 8 P.M. took two Reefs in each top Sail. Shifted the Pt. Cabbin & lower Deck Gunes on Middle Deck. Att 11 A.M. Came up with our Chace & hailed her she hauled down her Curllers."

In such fashion the logkeeper of *Richard* records the capture of

Union, a valuable letter-of-marque ship bound from London to Quebec with a cargo of clothing for the British Army in Canada. This was at noon 1 September when they were off the northwest point of Scotland, appropriately named Cape Wrath. Commodore Jones having named this cape as rendezvous, here *Alliance* caught up, with prize ship *Betsey,* similar to *Union,* which she had taken. All four ships, with *Vengeance,* now lay-to and drifted in "a frich gail of wind and Drisely weather." Captain Landais was still in an ugly mood, and although Jones gave him the privilege of manning *Union* (which *Alliance* had had no part in taking), he refused to obey orders or even to acknowledge signals. He sent these two rich prizes into Bergen, according to Chaumont's orders but against the Commodore's wishes; when Jones sent Purser Mease, Colonels Wybert and de Chamillard and Captain Cottineau on board *Alliance* to remonstrate with Landais, he "Spoke of Capt. Jones in terms highly disrespectful and insolent, and said he would see him on shore when they must kill one or t'other, etc," according to Mease.

On the night of 1-2 September frigate *Pallas* caught up with the squadron and next afternoon little *Vengeance* took an Irish brigantine, homeward bound from Norway. Foula Island, off the Shetlands' Mainland, was in sight at sundown. At noon 3 September the squadron attained its farthest north, lat. 59° 55' according to the flag navigator's not too reliable noon sight; and then turned south past the Skroo on Fair Isle.* *Richard* hove-to or sailed back and forth among the rocky Shetlands for the better part of three days, and *Alliance* took a couple more small prizes. Captain Landais was ordered to board the flagship for a conference, flatly refused, and presently parted company again.

On 4 September the weather turned tempestuous. *Bonhomme Richard,* with *Vengeance* and *Pallas* in company, did not sight land between 5 and 13 September, when the Cheviot Hills loomed up from off Dunbar. Next day Jones took two colliers from Leith bound

---

* My interpretation of the puzzling log for 4 Sept. is that they mistook Sumburgh Head for Fair Isle, but at 6:00 P.M. on the 3rd got a good fix on Fair Isle and North Ronaldshay.

to Riga, and put Midshipman Linthwaite on board one of them with a prize crew.

3. Up the Firth of Forth

"Though much weakened and embarrassed with prisoners," wrote Jones in his *Mémoire* to Louis XVI, "I was anxious to teach the enemy humanity by some exemplary stroke of retaliation, to relieve the remainder of the Americans from captivity in England." And also, though he had not been so ordered, he wished to pin down British troops in the north and so help the landing of D'Orvilliers in the south of England; for he had not yet heard of that fiasco. *Alliance* being over the horizon as usual, the captains of *Pallas* and *Vengeance* were summoned on board the flagship to discuss the Commodore's plan. A bold one it was indeed: to land at Leith, the seaport of Edinburgh, and lay it under a heavy ransom as an alternative to sacking and burning the town. Jones admits that after arguing all night with Captains Cottineau and Ricot, "all his arguments on the side of honour and humanity failed"; so, about midway in the morning watch, with first coffee, he brought up the possibility of squeezing a ransom of two hundred thousand pounds out of Leith, and "was now heard with attention; and they entered warmly into his project." The wind was fair for the Firth of Forth and the Commodore was ready to start; but *Pallas* and *Vengeance*, in the absence of their captains, were chasing prizes far to the southward; and by the time lumbering *Richard* had arrived within signaling distance of them the wind had changed. Fortunes of War!

Commodore Jones decided nevertheless to beat up the Firth of Forth against the wind. He drew up a landing bill for 130 men in six boats, and even composed an ultimatum "To the Worshipful the Provost of Leith," which Colonel de Chamillard was to present, and articles of capitulation for the town fathers to sign. Half the ransom, the amount of which was not specified (but Jones told Chamillard to settle for fifty thousand pounds) was to be paid on the nail within an hour, and the rest secured by six hostages, or Leith would be laid "in ashes." This formidable sum, Colonel de Chamillard was to explain, should be regarded as a contribution toward the indemnity "which Britain owes to the much Injured Citizens of America. Savages Would blush at the Unmanly Violation and rapacity that has marked the tracks of British tyranny in America, from which neither virgin innocence nor helpless age has been a plea of protection or Pity."

Sad to relate, the Colonel never had a chance to deliver this eloquent document. The savages blushed in vain, nor were the innocent virgins revenged; and it was all due to the wind.

We must not, however, assume that Paul Jones's indignation over British "atrocities" in America was insincere. The "virgin innocence" refers to the unfortunate Jane M'Crae, scalped by Burgoyne's Indians. Jones had certainly heard, before sailing, of General Vaughan's burning of Esopus, New York, in 1777, and of Commodore Sir George Collier's depredations in the Chesapeake in May 1779; for all these events were played up by the English opposition newspapers and satirical prints. And he may well have heard of General Tryon's burning and plundering expedition by 2600 troops in a fleet of warships and tenders, on the coastal towns of Connecticut. In these raids, in early July 1779, hundreds of dwelling houses, mills, shops and even churches were burned, and the village of Fairfield was almost completely destroyed, without the excuse of a military objective. Congress seriously considered ordering Franklin to hire incendiaries to burn London in retaliation, starting with the Royal Palace; but fortunately thought better of it. Even so, the opposition press in London used these events as a stick to belabor the North ministry, and praised Jones for his moderation. The *London Evening Post* declared editorially:

> Many of the particulars of the burning the two towns in Connecticut, viz. Fairfield and Norwalk, have been received; but they are too shocking to relate. The brutality and cruelty of the soldiers, in several instances, are too dreadful, as well as unfit, to be printed.

Another opposition paper remarked:

Paul Jones is a pirate indeed, a plunderer, but he is not a Barbarian; he does not hold his commission from the Administration of Britain, and therefore he has no order to ravage and lay waste the dwellings of the innocent. Perhaps, indeed, as soon as the reports of Sir George. Collier's conduct have reached him, he will think it his duty to retaliate upon us; and since neither the laws of war, nor the dictates of humanity, can restrain us from going into all the extremes of bloodshed, he will try what the force of retaliation can effect. Good God! What fools and madmen are those who venture to destroy the towns of the Americans in so lawless a manner. Their horrid example brings desolation on this country.

The War of Independence had reached a strategic deadlock, a situation that recurred in both World Wars of the twentieth century. Each party, unable to reach a decision by fleet action or pitched land battles, resorts to raids and to haphazard, desultory operations which have no military effect but arouse bitter hatred on the receiving end and a smug satisfaction on the other side. This deadlock in the War of Independence was not broken until 1781, when De Grasse defeated a British fleet off the Capes of the Chesapeake; that led to the surrender of Cornwallis.

We can follow the progress of Commodore Jones's three-ship task force in letters addressed to Captain Napier, senior British naval officer in Edinburgh. On the morning of 14 September a 40-gun ship (*Richard*) is sighted six miles off Dunbar, coming up from the southward (where landfall had been made on the Cheviot Hills), and a smaller ship (*Vengeance*) which had been reconnoitering the Firth of Forth runs down and speaks her. "It is the opinion that they are both ships belonging to the enemy." *Pallas* then appears. Lieutenant Younghusband is sent post-haste to Dunbar to take a look at the ships, and reports, "They are certainly the squadron of PAUL JONES."

Horrors! Midlothian, East Lothian and Fifeshire are thrown into consternation; everyone asks, "Where will the arch-pirate land?"

The uproar is humorously described in a mock heroic poem printed the same year, called "Paul Jones, or the Fife Coast Garland":

Pray, tell us good neighbors, whence all this affray?
(Quoth Trim), all this packing and posting away,
With cart-loads of luggage, aunts, sisters, and wives
All driving as if 'twas a race for their lives?
Has d'Orvilliers' vast navy invaded our coast?
Is Amherst cut off at Coxheath with the host?. . .
Cox-coxcomb! yield the road, or I'll break all your bones,
The pi-pirate, trai-traitor comes, d——m him, Paul Jones! . . .

You've heard what amazement has fill'd all the coast,
Since the tidings of Jones by the last Wednesday's post,
When the *Mercury, Courant,* and *Ruddiman's Gazette*
Made the bravest to tremble, and the leanest to sweat; . . .

At the brawl of some children the multitude runs,
And casts away prospects as they'd soon do their guns;
My Lord rang for tea, but was told it was late,
That Tom, Jack, and Susan kept guard at the gate
And their Lady had pack'd up all china and plate.
All was then hurly-burly from Leith to Dunbar,
With trenches, pallisadoes, and long guns to shoot far;
Out march'd the brisk sailors to man their platoons,
All sweat, dust, and foaming, in march'd the dragoons,
In dread of Paul Jones and his horse-stealing loons.

After their appearance off Dunbar on 14 September, *Richard, Pallas* and *Vengeance* stood north to the famous bell buoy off Inchcape Rock (did Jones bless the Abbot of Aberbrothok?); then south again, past the Isle of May, to the entrance of the Firth of Forth. That afternoon *Richard* made prize of outward-bound collier *Friendship* of Kirkaldy, and detained her master as a pilot for the Firth. From him Jones learned the defenseless state of Leith and Edinburgh. The great guns in the Castle could not reach out to sea.

Richard's delightfully illiterate log-keeper notes briefly the greatest practical joke of the cruise, one that put all hands in good humor. At 4:00 P.M. September 16 "There Come A Shore Boat a Bord with 5 Men in hit. At ½ peast 5 P.M. sent 4 of them a Shore again and sent 1 Cask of Powder withem."

Here is what happened. Sir John Anstruther, Bart., of Elie House, Fifeshire, became very fearful when he heard that the terrible Paul Jones was approaching. He had a brass cannon and ball to protect his mansion on the north shore of the Firth, but no powder. So he sent out his yacht *Royal Charlotte*, with orders to speak H.M.S. *Romney* and ask for the loan of a barrel of gunpowder. Unable to locate *Romney*, then many leagues distant, the master spoke and boarded the first "British" ship he met, which happened to be *Bonhomme Richard*, tacking close to the Ainsters rocks. His story, as told to Captain Napier at Edinburgh, is worth quoting, as it even tells us how Paul Jones and his merry men were dressed:

They run nigh to the largest ship and when within hail of hir were desired to keep off, which they did, but upon their tacking from them were called back and no sooner alongside than Andrew Paton was ordered on board and carried down to the Caben where he continued about two hourse. Stevens while on the Gunnel observed that all the officers on the quarterdeck were drest in Blew turn'd up with white the same as in the British Navy. The ship had three boats & a Norway Shaft* belonging to her, one of which boats were out, and armed with four Serwivels & Small Arms, two Officers a Cocksween & eight men. They think the boat is Spanish or Frensh build by having apron bow. . . . The lower deck ports being Eight of a side were all fast caulht in. She had fifteen ports on Each Side on the upper deck with three guns on Each Side of the quarter deck. . . . The officer on the quarter deck ask't Patton what force was in Lieth Road & was answered two armed ships and two cutters soon after which they put into the

* A type of ship's boat.

boat a bagg containing 100 weight Gun Powder with a letter addressed to Sir John Anstruther with Captain Johnston of the *Romley's* compliments to Sir John and that he had retained Patton as a Pilot for Lieth Roads and sent him (Sir John) the powder for his own defense desiring the payment might be made to [blank] house in Edinburgh when demanded. The whole Crew were Clean drest and seemed all to be British that nothing but English was spoken while they were along side.

This yacht hand was a more accurate observer than others who approached *Richard* near enough to see the officers and crew. One such described the Commodore as "dressed in the American uniform, with a Scotch bonnet edged with gold; is of a middling stature, stern countenance and swarthy complexion." Here is the origin of the popular prints showing Jones scowling darkly under the "bonnet" of his fatherland, as became a pirate.

After the yacht shoved off, Jones had a little sport with her impressed pilot. He asked him, "What's the news?"

"Why, that rebel and pirate Paul Jones is off the coast, and he ought to be hanged."

"Do you know whom you are addressing?"

"Are you not Captain Johnston of H.M.S. *Romney?*"

"No, I am PAUL JONES."

The poor pilot dropped to his knees and begged for mercy. Jones, laughing, said, "Get up! I won't hurt a hair on your head, but you are my prisoner."

Late in the afternoon of 16 September the task force, beating up the Firth, was sighted by telescopes from the ramparts of Edinburgh Castle. Leith and the capital are in a turmoil. All day drums are rolling, bugles blowing and pipes skirling; frightened citizens pack off their wives, children and baggage to the hills, and the stouter fellows, armed with pikes, claymores and fowling pieces (for Scotland had been deprived of her militia since the Forty-five rising), march fearfully to the waterfront. Leith begged for a hundred muskets from the Castle, and her police (appropriately called the *Sederunt*) were put on a twenty-four-hour alert. It was in consequence of Paul Jones's visit that a fort was built at Leith in 1780, and a sort of National Guard, the "Defensive Band of Volunteers," organized by the gentlemen of Edinburgh. Sir Walter Scott well remembered the bustle; it hurt his "pride as a Scotsman" to reflect on how defenseless the capital had been.

On the morning of 17 September the squadron, conned by the pilot impressed from Sir John's yacht, stood boldly up within a mile of Kirkaldy. From the shore it looked as if they were about to attack "the lang Toon," as Kirkaldy was called. The inhabitants were gravely alarmed; but the local minister, the Reverend Mr. Shirra, had a chair brought down to the edge of the beach and supplicated the Deity as follows:

> Now deer Lord, dinna ye think it a shame for ye to send this vile piret to rob our folk o' Kirkaldy; for ye ken they're puir enow already, and hae naething to spaire. The wa the ween blaws, he'll be here in a jiffie, and wha kens what he may do? He's nae too guid for ony thing. Meickle's the mischief he has dune already. He'll burn their hooses, tak their very claes and tirl them to the sark; and wae's me! Wha kens but the bluidy villain might take their lives? The puir weemen are maist frightened out o' their wits, and the bairns skirling after them. I canna thol't it! I canna thol't it! I hae been lang a faithfu' servant to ye, Laird; but gin ye dinna turn the ween about, and blaw the scoundrel out of our gate, I'll na staur a fit, but will just sit here till the tide comes. Sae tak yere wull o't!

And there was every appearance that his odd prayer was answered. For, shortly after it was delivered, the American squadron came about on the starboard tack and stood across the Firth, past Inchkeith Rock. It had almost arrived within cannon shot of Leith, and the Commodore was ready to hoist out boats and embark the landing force, when "a Very severe gale of Wind came on, and being directly Contrary obliged me to bear away after having in Vain Endeavoured for sometime to Withstand its violence,'' he wrote. *Richard's* topgallant masts had to be housed, one of her small prizes went to the bottom; the other, *Friendship,* was ransomed for a sum of money and her master given a safe-conduct, and the squadron was driven under short sail to the mouth of the Firth. The gale abated by evening, but the Commodore rightly felt that, surprise being lost, he must abandon his rash project.

Thus Scotland was spared the spectacle of the Mayor and Corporation of Leith, like the famous Burghers of Calais, begging Colonel de Chamillard to spare them, and trying to beat down the ransom. It is likely that, if the men had landed, they might have bluffed and frightened the authorities into paying something, since the town was virtually defenseless except for a hundred muskets in the hands of frightened citizenry. The one small cutter stationed to defend Leith weighed anchor and fled when her skipper sighted Jones's squadron approaching; H.M.S. *Romney* was far away, and not until 24 September did H.M. frigate *Emerald* and armed ships *London* and *Content,* dispatched from the Nore to seek out Paul Jones, arrive before Leith. They must have passed him in the night on the way to his glorious but almost fatal rendezvous off Flamborough Head.

XIII

The
Battle off
Flamborough
Head

23 September 1779

1. From the Forth to the Humber

"Jones was a man to be obeyed," remarked Lieutenant Mackenzie, his early naval biographer. But he was often disobeyed. He had been disobeyed off the Blaskets, and so lost two boats, some good men, and the cutter. He had been disobeyed by Landais off Cape Wrath and Fair Isle. He had had to argue the French captains into the raid on Leith, and so lost a fair wind and surprise. Again, the Commodore was thwarted as his squadron sailed southward along the rugged coast of Northumberland.

In order to elude British warships which were searching for him off shore, Jones sailed close aboard the Holy Isle of Lindisfarne, and stood into Skate Roadstead. When Bamburgh Castle loomed up, he playfully shot a cannon ball at the ancient edifice; it landed in a private garden and is treasured by the owner's descendants to this day.

His intention was to raid Newcastle-on-Tyne in order to cut off London's winter coal supply. On Tuesday, 19 September, he had his boats' oars muffled and next morning the Marines were readied for executing the Leith landing plan. Newcastle was gravely alarmed. A respectable inhabitant wrote to the Admiralty, "Paul Jones's squadron is *actually* off here, he stood in for Tynemouth Castle this *morning* with five ships—but seeing a Fleet of Colliers to the Southward he sent three of his smallest after them, the event of which we don't know. I have had the mortification of *seeing* him also this Afternoon with three prizes, the one a Brig that sail'd from this Port in the morning called the *Union* with other two small Sloops. His force is said to be [of] 86, 20, 28, 20 & 16 Guns *and nothing in the World to oppose him.*"

Actually, Jones had only three warships with him—the two others were prizes—and Captain Cottineau, with whom Jones consulted, had no stomach for another shore raid. He argued that if the squadron tarried on the Northumbrian coast after the alarm it had created in the Forth, it would certainly be taken. Cottineau even told Colonel de Chamillard that unless the Commodore turned southward, both *Pallas* and *Vengeance* would desert him. Jones considered attacking Newcastle with one ship only, and the officers of *Richard* were all for it; but he decided that the risk was incommensurate to the possible gain. So he abandoned the attempt when *Richard* was so close to shore that the houses of South Shields were clearly visible.

We must not judge Jones's captains by World War II standards. In the eighteenth century, even in the grand fleets of England and France, deliberate misunderstanding of the commanding officer's signals, unauthorized action by individual ships, and plain insubordination, were frequent. Hood let Graves down in the Battle off the Capes of the Chesapeake; Bougainville disobeyed De Grasse in the Battle of the Saints; and the Bailly de Suffren, the greatest French naval officer of his day, was never able to obtain proper coöperation in his Indian Ocean operations. The more daring and original a commander might be, the less chance he had of being followed and obeyed. The naval historian De la Roncière remarked on Suffren's experience, "New strategy and tactics, principles directly opposed to those of his time, impeccable concept from start to finish; that was the contribution of this great seaman. Feeble execution, total incomprehension, insufficient coöperation—such were the common faults of his lieutenants." This was certain to be the case under Paul Jones, an officer who never fought by the book but was alert to profit by opportunities, with a squadron whose commanding officers at best did not understand him, and one of whom was eager to destroy him.

But there was no insubordination on board the flagship; none of the caballing and surly disobedience that had frustrated Jones in *Ranger*. During the few months that he had commanded *Bonhomme Richard*, he welded her officers and men into a fighting man-of-war's crew. The officers were of his choice; and the enlisted men fought gallantly because they liked fighting and were devoted to their commander, even if he did lose his temper at times. Paul Jones was like a temperamental orchestra leader who enrages almost every musician under him, yet produces a magnificent ensemble.

A collier in ballast and sloop *Speedwell* taken off Whitby were now stripped of compasses and other valuables and ordered to be scuttled. Cottineau, however, let the sloop go upon payment of ransom, a practice of French privateers that Jones disapproved.

Passing Scarborough on the starboard hand, the squadron chased all night a fleet whose masts were seen over the southern horizon. Around 1:00 A.M. 22 September, Jones captured a Scarborough collier in ballast, forced another vessel ashore between Flamborough Head and the Spurn, and took an English brigantine from Rotterdam. Scarborough hoisted a red flag as signal that an enemy was off the coast; all maritime Yorkshire was in consternation. The militia beat to arms and went on twenty-four-hour duty, expecting a landing. The gentry packed off their women, children and valuables; desperate letters were dispatched to the Admiralty, demanding protection. Hull was equally alarmed; a "general meeting," called by the mayor to decide what to do, decided there was nothing they could do, as the fort was decayed and its cannon dangerous only to the cannoneers. The Northumberland militia were called out and marched to Bridlington and Beverley. These preparations to repel a landing force continued long after Jones had fought the battle and sailed away.

By 8:00 A.M. on the 22nd, the squadron was off the Spurn, the northern cape to the Humber estuary. Commodore Jones, wishing to chase a merchant convoy that he had sighted, hoisted the British signal for a pilot—the Union Jack at the fore-topgallant masthead. That brought out two pilot boats. One pilot boarded *Richard*, thinking her to be British; the other boarded the prize from Rotterdam. He, too, was brought to Jones and detained, together with one of the boats which was taken in tow. Jones tried to entice some of the ships anchored in the Humber to come out and fight, but in vain; and the wind became too light and variable to risk *Richard* inside the estuary. So, during the evening, when Spurn Light bore WNW distant 18 miles, *Richard* turned north again toward Flamborough Head, to rejoin *Pallas*, which had already turned back to chase prizes in those profitable waters.

Shortly before midnight two sail were sighted from the flagship. All hands were called to quarters, and the night recognition signals —lanterns at the three mastheads—were hoisted. At 5:30 A.M. of the fateful 23rd, when day was breaking, the two ships were made out to be *Alliance*, which had not been seen for over a fortnight, and frigate *Pallas*. Counting little cutter *Vengeance*, the Commodore now had four ships under his command.

The squadron sailed slowly before the light wind toward Flamborough Head. At 2:00 P.M., when the wind had almost died, the Commodore sent one of the captured pilot boats under command of Lieutenant Henry Lunt to take a brig sighted to windward, which he suspected to be the one that he had formerly run ashore. An hour later, the Commodore realized that his long-sought opportunity had arrived. A fleet of 41 sail appeared off Flamborough Head, bearing

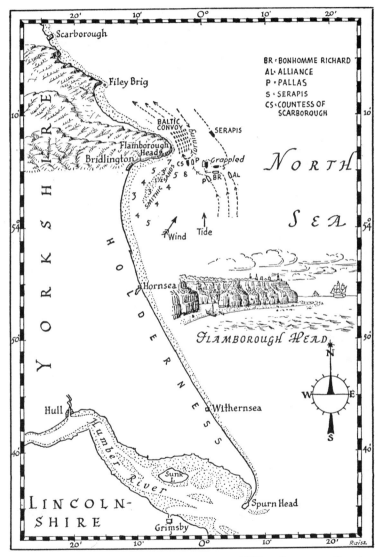

The Yorkshire Coast to Illustrate Action off Flamborough Head,
25 Sept. 1779

north-northeast from *Richard* and standing in her direction. From what the captured pilots told him, Jones knew that this was a convoy from the Baltic escorted by frigate *Serapis* (44 guns) and sloop of war *Countess of Scarborough* (20 guns).

2. The Battle Begins

H.M.S. *Serapis* (pronounced Se-ray´pis; the keeper of *Richard's* log called her "Searuppus"), commanded by Captain Richard Pearson RN, was a new copper-bottomed frigate.* Rated at 44 guns, actually she had 50; a main battery of 20 eighteen-pounders on a lower gun deck (compared with *Richard's* 6 of that caliber); 20 nine-pounders on an upper covered gun deck (compared with *Richard's* 28 twelve-pounders), and 10 six-pounders on the quarterdeck (where *Richard* had 6 nine-pounders). Captain Pearson had arrived at Elsinore 19 August with a convoy from the Nore, and was there joined by H.M.S. *Countess of Scarborough*, Captain Thomas Piercy, to escort a convoy of 70 sail to England. The convoy departed Elsinore 1 September, anchored near Christiansund during an easterly gale, departed 15 September and made landfall near Whitby on the 23rd. At that time the convoy numbered 44 sail, as the ships bound for Scottish ports had parted company. Captain Pearson was much pleased with his new fast frigate, his only complaint being with the old eighteen-pounders that the Admiralty had furnished. Their vents were so big that too much gunpowder exploded through them, and their muzzles were so long that when the guns were drawn in there was no space left to coil down his hawsers properly. But there is no doubt that *Serapis* was a newer, faster and more nimble frigate than *Richard;* and in fire power, owing to her far greater number of eighteen-

---

* Copper sheathing for ship bottoms had been introduced in the British Navy at the beginning of the war, and the French, learning about it from a captured ship in 1778, were beginning to use it in their Navy. These thin copper plates, nailed to the bottom, discouraged marine growth and added as much as a knot to a ship's speed. Jones tried to get copper plates for *Richard* in 1779 but did not succeed.

pounders, she was definitely superior. In terms of recent warfare, it was as though a 14-inch-gunned battleship, with an additional advantage of speed, engaged an 8-inch-gunned heavy cruiser.

Flamborough Head, off which the famous night action was fought, is a broad headland of chalk cliffs rising 450 feet above the sea, cut by deep gullies with tiny beaches at the foot, and honeycombed by numerous caves which were favorite resorts of smugglers. The tide splits at the Head; half the flood, running from north to south, sweeps seaward off a sandbar called the Smithics; the other half, running between the Smithics and the shore, makes a great "boil" over a reef jutting out from the Head, known as the Flamborough Steel. Just before low water, a strong inshore current sets northerly and the ebb current outside the Smithics starts two hours later than the ebb inside. It is dangerous ground for a stranger; the ten-fathom line is about three miles off the Head. At Flamborough Head today, only a lighthouse and a few small cottages on the cliff alter its 1779 profile, which was the last glimpse that over a hundred brave seamen had of the land to which they hoped to return. And *Bonhomme Richard* in her long career had never looked so beautiful as she did that last full day of her life, when the westering sun gilded her towering pyramid of sail and touched up the high lights on her elaborate quarter galleries and carving.

Captain Pearson was expecting Jones, since the bailiffs of Scarborough had sent out a boat to warn him; but his primary duty was to protect the convoy. Ordering it to sail as close to shore as the merchant captains dared, he stood off shore to cover. Shortly after noon on the 23rd, the convoy, which so far had ignored Pearson's signals, sighted *Richard, Alliance,* and *Pallas* and promptly tacked inshore, "letting fly their topgallant sheets and firing guns" as an alarm signal and then turning north to seek refuge under the guns of Scarborough Castle. Light airs were blowing from the southwest. *Serapis* cracked on sail to get between her convoy and the enemy, and succeeded in so doing. "At one o'clock," wrote Pearson in his report, "we got sight of the Enemys ships from the masthead, and about four we made them plain from the Deck to be three large ships and a brig; upon which I made the *Countess of Scarborough* signal to join me, she being in shore with the Convoy, . . . I then brought too, to let the *Countess of Scarboro* come up, and cleared ship for Action; at ½ past five she joined me, the Enemy's ships then bearing down upon us with light breeze at SSW; at six Tacked and laid our Head in shore, in order to keep our Ground the better between the Enemy's ships and the Convoy." Brave Pearson did not flinch from engaging an enemy that appeared to be double his strength; and the timid, uncertain maneuvering of the three smaller American ships made him the more brisk to offer battle.

Commodore Jones, who had always wanted to break up a Baltic convoy, knowing its importance for supplying the Royal Navy, made every effort to close; but the wind was so light that it took him three and a half hours to cover the ten or eleven miles between himself and *Serapis,* and he realized that he would have to take or sink the two escorts before he could get a crack at the convoy.

At 3:00 P.M. Jones sighted the enemy; at 3:30 *Richard* fired a gun (which Lieutenant Lunt did not hear) to recall the pilot boat, hoisted the signal General Chase, crossed royal yards and set all three royals. At 4:00 studding sails were set on both sides and the gunners, seamen and officers quietly took their assigned stations aloft, on deck and below. At 5:00 the Marine drummers marched up and down beating the roll for General Quarters. At 6:00, just as the sun was setting, the Commodore made the agreed signal "Form Line of Battle"—a blue flag at the fore, blue pendant at the main truck, and blue-and-yellow flag at the mizzen. Nobody paid any attention to it. *Alliance,* in the lead, prudently hauled her wind, leaving *Richard* alone to engage *Serapis; Pallas,* astern of *Richard,* sheered off, but later redeemed herself by engaging *Countess of Scarborough; Vengeance* simply sailed about, looking on.

By 6:30 *Richard* had hauled up her lower courses for better visibility and rounded-to on the weather (port) quarter of *Serapis.* Presently the two ships were side by side on the port tack heading west,

Richard to the southward and windward of *Serapis*, the wind then being southwest by south. Commodore Jones was on the quarter-deck, de Chamillard with about twenty French Marines on the poop, Lieutenant Dale had charge of the gun deck and the main battery, Lieutenant Stack commanded twenty sailors and Marines manning swivels and small arms in the maintop, Midshipman Fanning commanded the foretop with fourteen men, and Midshipman Coram the smaller mizzen top with nine men. Midshipman Mayrant stood by the Commodore to act as his aide. The guns were shotted and ready; the gunners of the starboard battery, with lighted match in hand for each piece, were awaiting the word to fire. *Serapis* triced up her gunports, revealing two decks of guns and making a formidable appearance. In Midshipman Fanning's words, "Just as the moon was rising, the weather being clear, the surface of the great deep being perfectly smooth, even as in a millpond," and the two ships being within pistol shot, Captain Pearson hailed, "What ship is that?" Paul Jones, in order to get into close action, was flying British colors. Playing for time, he caused Master Stacey to reply, "The *Princess Royal!*" "Where from?" asked Pearson. The answer, whatever it may have been, was not heard on board *Serapis*. She hailed again, "Answer immediately, or I shall be under the necessity of firing into you." Jones struck his British colors, caused a big red-white-and-blue striped American ensign to be raised, and gave the word to fire his starboard broadside. *Serapis* fired hers almost simultaneously (Battle Plan No. 1, p. 230). At the first or second salvo, two of Jones's eighteen-pounders burst, killing many gunners and ruining the rest of that battery, as well as blowing up part of the deck above.

"The battle being thus begun," wrote Jones in his narrative, "was Continued with Unremitting fury." Each captain strove to maneuver his ship across the other's bow or stern, in order to rake. *Serapis*, the faster by reason of her slippery bottom, several times gained an advantageous position "in spite of my best Endeavours to prevent it," admitted Jones. After exchanging two or three broadsides, the Commodore estimated that a gun-to-gun duel would be fatal for

Successive Positions in the Battle off Flamborough Head.

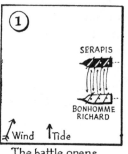

①

SERAPIS

BONHOMME RICHARD

Wind   Tide

The battle opens.

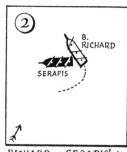

②

B. RICHARD

SERAPIS

RICHARD on SERAPIS' starboard quarter, hoping to board.

③

SERAPIS

B. RICHARD

"I have not yet begun to fight!"

SERAPIS tries to cross RICHARD'S bow, but has not enough headway. RICHARD'S bowsprit hits SERAPIS.

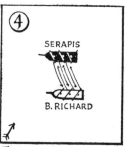

④

SERAPIS

B. RICHARD

They straighten out again. SERAPIS backs topsails to reduce speed.

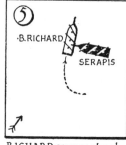

⑤

B. RICHARD

SERAPIS

RICHARD surges ahead, tries to cross SERAPIS' bow, her jib boom fouls RICHARD'S mizzen shrouds.

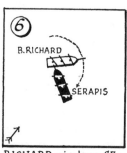

⑥

B. RICHARD

SERAPIS

RICHARD pivots on SERAPIS' bowsprit.

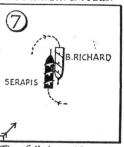

⑦

B. RICHARD

SERAPIS

They fall alongside, grappled. Night falls.

⑧

3rd broadside

B. RICHARD

SERAPIS

ALLIANCE

2nd broadside

Tide

SERAPIS, anchored and locked to RICHARD, swings 180° with tide. They fight for two hours, when SERAPIS strikes. ALLIANCE sails around them firing broadsides mostly at RICHARD.

him; he must attempt to board and grapple. He backed *Richard's* fore and main topsails, dropped astern on *Serapis's* port quarter, both ships firing furiously at a range of 80 to 100 feet, "filled again, put his helm a-weather" (to port), ran *Richard* up on *Serapis's* starboard quarter and attempted to board (Plan No. 2). This was a very disadvantageous position from which to carry an enemy ship by boarding; it was like attempting an amphibious assault on so narrow a front that the enemy could concentrate his fire on a thin line of men. The English sailors repulsed the boarders, and Jones sheered off.

The next move was Pearson's, an attempt to cross *Richard's* bow to rake her (Plan No. 3); but *Serapis* had not enough headway to make it; and Jones, following her movements, ran *Richard's* bow into her stern. It was at this juncture—not near the close of the battle as has generally been stated—that Captain Pearson called out "Has your ship struck?" and Paul Jones made the immortal reply:

I HAVE NOT YET BEGUN TO FIGHT

Nor had he. Unable to bring a single cannon to bear on *Serapis* from that position (Plan No. 3), *Richard* backed her topsails to get clear, *Serapis* wore briskly around "on her heel" from a northeasterly to a westerly heading, and *Richard* too pulled away and straightened out (Plan No. 4). *Serapis* being ahead, Pearson backed topsails to check headway and get broadside to *Richard* in order to bring his superior fire power to bear. Jones, divining his intent, ordered Master Stacey "to lay the enemy's ship on board." Taking advantage of a fresh puff of wind, which did not strike *Serapis* because *Richard's* sails blanketed hers, Jones ranged ahead, ordered helm a-weather (to port) and tried the same maneuver that Pearson had attempted on him. He laid *Richard* "athwart hawse"—as the cap of a T—in order to rake his enemy's decks (Plan No. 5).

"It did not exactly succeed to my wishes," admitted Jones, because, owing to some of the yards' braces having been shot away, the people could not trim them properly and maneuver quickly enough to clear. The two ships collided, bow to stern; *Serapis* thrust her jib-boom (tip end of the bowsprit) right into *Richard's* mizzen shrouds—the rigging that held up her after mast (Plan No. 5). The wind acting on the sails of both ships caused them to pivot (Plan No. 6) until they were on a north-south axis, bow to stern and stern to bow (No. 7). A fluke of *Serapis's* starboard anchor sealed this fatal marriage by hooking the bulwarks of *Richard's* starboard quarter, and the two ships' topsides clapped together so that the muzzles of their guns were touching. Paul Jones, joyfully accepting this new situation, shouted, "Well done, my brave lads, we have got her now; throw on board her the grappling-irons and stand by for boarding!" And while waiting for Master Stacey to rouse out a spare line, the Commodore with his own hands seized a forestay of *Serapis* which had parted and fallen across *Richard's* quarterdeck and made it fast to his mizzenmast. At this juncture the master appeared with the line, swearing horribly; the Captain checked him by remarking, "Mr. Stacey, it's no time to be swearing now—you may by the next moment be in eternity; but let us do our duty."

3. The Deadly Embrace

All this was as pretty a piece of maneuvering as you could see at the start of a modern yacht race, and the unforeseen clapperclaw was exactly what Jones wanted. He was outgunned even at the start of the action, and he had abandoned his eighteen-pounder battery—his only cannon of the same caliber as the main battery of *Serapis*—suspecting after two blew up the rest would follow. He knew that his only chance of victory, or even survival, was to disable the rigging of *Serapis* and kill off her crew by musketry and hand grenades, or to take her boarding; and as the British frigate had two covered gun decks, capture by boarding would be very difficult. Captain Pearson, on the contrary, had to shake off *Richard's* deadly hug if he were to bring his superior fire power to bear. To that end

Stern of French East Indiaman Model,
Contemporary with *Bonhomme Richard*

Battle off Flamborough Head,
from the Dupré Medal

Battle off Flamborough Head, from the Laponière-Fittle Engraving

John Paul Jones
as Seen by His Enemies.
Published in London
within a Month of the Battle

John Paul Jones
as Seen by His Friends.
Gouache Drawing of about 1781

he ordered the grappling hooks to be cast off or severed; but *Richard's* sharpshooters picked off the sailors who tried to do that. Pearson then dropped anchor in 15 to 20 fathoms of water,* hoping that the wind and tide would swing *Richard* clear. On the contrary, the two ships, spitting fire at each other, pivoted through a half circle, for all the world like one of those macabre dances of death by two skeletons in a medieval engraving. *Serapis*, now held by her anchor, headed south into wind and tide, while *Richard*, still fast grappled to her, pointed north (Plan No. 8, p.*230*).

It is now between 8:00 and 8:30; the harvest moon, two days short of full, rises over heavy clouds on the eastern horizon and illuminates the battle. "Flamborough reapers, homegoing, pause on the hillside; for what sulphur-cloud is that which defaces the sleek sea; sulphur-cloud spitting streaks of fire?" Spectators, attracted from Scarborough and Bridlington by the sound of the opening salvos, flock to Flamborough Head. They witness a naval combat the like of which has never been fought before or since. Here, for two long hours, *Bonhomme Richard* and *Serapis* are mortised together, snug as two logs in a woodpile, guns muzzle to muzzle. They are so close that the starboard gun ports of *Serapis*, shut during the first phase of the battle, cannot be opened outboard and have to be blown off by her guns; and the gunners, in order to load and ram their charges home, must thrust their staves into the enemy's gun ports. At one point the sails of both ships are ablaze, and killing is suspended while damage control parties fight the flames; then each ship resumes banging away at t'other. The Englishman wants to break off and fight at cannon range but cannot, the American clings desperately to him, knowing that only by maintaining the clinch can he survive. Deprived of his eighteen-pounder battery in the gunroom by the bursting of the guns, and of his main battery of

---

* Fanning says in 10-12 fathoms, but he agrees with other narrators of the battle that the position of *Serapis* when anchored was one league (3 nautical miles) E by S of Flamborough Head. According to the contemporary chart which is the basis of ours, the depth at that point was about 15 fathoms, and the modern chart makes it over 20. Probably there has been some scouring of the bottom in that strong tideway.

twelve-pounders by the blast from *Serapis's* two decks of eighteen-pounders, Commodore Jones has no cannon left except three nine-pounders on the quarterdeck, one of which he helps to trundle over from the port side and serves with his own hands.

Jones's one advantage, other than his own inflexible determination, is the good marksmanship of the French Marine musketeers on deck, and of the polyglot seamen and gunners in the fighting tops. Owing to their fast and accurate shooting with swivels, coehorns, small arms and tossed grenades, *Serapis* can keep no man alive on deck, and her open-deck battery of 10 six-pounders is deserted. But her eighteen-pounders, below deck, go on roaring and breaching through *Richard's* topsides, and Jones has no means to counter them. French shipbuilders must have put stout stuff into that old East Indiaman; for when the fight ended, only a few stanchions prevented her quarterdeck from falling into the gunroom, or her main deck from crashing into the hold, and her topsides were a mass of fragments and splinters. Jones's tactics of close grappling prevented the English guns from breaking his masts and yards, which continued to support his fighting men in the tops, even when the rest of *Bonhomme Richard* had been reduced to little more than a battered raft.

"During this time," reported Pearson, "from the great Quantity and Variety of Combustible Matters which they threw in upon our Decks, Chains and in short into every part of the Ship, we were on fire not less than Ten or Twelve times in different parts." It is a scene difficult to imagine, impossible to describe in detail. The yards of *Richard* so far overhang the deck of *Serapis* that her sailors are able to leap into the enemy's tops, throw out the English topmen, and then shoot directly down at her deck and even into the hatches.

Vengeance during the battle maneuvered at a safe distance; the boat commanded by Lunt stood by, not daring to come alongside; *Pallas* hotly engaged *Countess of Scarborough*, and Landais in *Alliance* played the rôle of a madman. During the early part of the clinch, he raked *Richard*, killing two sailors and driving others from their battle stations. He then sailed close to where the other two ships were fighting, but did nothing to help *Pallas*. After that he beat up to windward in very leisurely fashion and, about two hours after his first blast at *Richard,* crossed the axis of the two locked ships (Plan No. 8, p. *230*) to windward of them. Turning downwind, *Alliance* crossed *Richard's* stern, and "while we were hailing her," said Midshipman Mayrant, poured into her port quarter a broadside which holed her between wind and water and even under water. He then passed ahead, returned athwart *Richard's* bows and—despite the Commodore's hailing, "Lay the enemy on board!" the seamen shouting, "Don't fire—you have killed several of our men already!" and Lieutenant Stack calling from his fighting top, "I beg you will not sink us!"—Landais gave *Richard* a third and the most fatal broadside, fired into the forecastle where men driven from the gun deck had gathered. It killed several more, including a chief petty officer.

This cannot have been accidental, as Jones had his night recognition signals burning, the scene was illuminated by moonlight, gun flashes and fires; *Richard's* topsides were painted black, and those of *Serapis* bright yellow. The evidence is overwhelming that Landais did it on purpose. After the battle he confided to one of the French colonels that his intention was to help *Serapis* sink *Richard,* then board and capture the British frigate and emerge the hero and victor of the battle. Later he had the impudence to claim that his broadsides forced Captain Pearson to strike; and Pearson himself was not backward in claiming that he succumbed to two frigates, not one. But the testimony collected by Commodore Jones at the Texel is conclusive: *Alliance* was nowhere about in the last half hour of the battle, Landais having fired his last malevolent broadside around 10:00 P.M. and retired to a safe distance to think up more mischief. His crew suffered not one casualty, and his ship no damage. She was hit only thrice by *Scarborough* at long range; one of the balls stuck in her topsides and the other two bounced off.

The Commodore directed the nine-pounder guns on his quarterdeck and served one of them himself, since Purser Mease, the officer in charge of that one remaining battery, was badly wounded in the head. At one moment Jones became so exhausted that he sat down to rest on a hencoop, when a sailor came up to him and said, "For God's sake, Captain, strike!" Jones paused, then leaped to his feet and said, "No, I will sink, I will never strike!" and resumed his service of the nine-pounder.

His indomitable spirit, and the sharp work of his topmen and Marines, were the decisive factors in the battle. They picked off so many British gunners that the boy "powder monkeys" found few people on the gundeck of *Serapis* to receive the powder cartridges being brought up from the magazine, and dropped them on deck. An enterprising seaman of *Richard's* crew, a Scot named William Hamilton, took a basket of hand grenades and a live match out to the end of a yardarm that hung directly above an open hatch of *Serapis* and dropped a grenade right through it, which exploded the powder cartridges that the boys had left lying about. At least twenty men were killed and others frightfully burned. Jones followed up this lucky break by directing the fire of his three nine-pounders, loaded with double-headed shot, against the enemy's mainmast.

Immediately after the big explosion, Captain Pearson was at the point of calling for quarter when three of Jones's petty officers, two of whom had been wounded, put their heads together and decided that *Richard* would sink if she did not strike. The chief gunner, an Englishman named Henry Gardner, ran aft to haul down the ensign; but, finding that a cannon ball had carried away ensign and staff, he began bawling, "Quarters, Quarters, for God's sake!" At this the Commodore, pulling a pistol from his belt, hurled it at the chief and felled him to the deck.* Pearson, however, had heard the cry and called over to Jones, "Sir, do you ask for a quarter?" He replied, "No, sir, I haven't as yet *thought* of it, but I'm determined to make *you* strike." Pearson's reply to that was to command "Boarders Away!" But by the time his boarding party had crossed *Richard's* bulwarks, "They discovered a Superior Number lying under Cover with Pikes in their hands ready to receive them, on which our people" (admit-

---

* This is the origin of the yarn about Jones shooting "Lieutenant Grub" (Midshipman Beaumont Groube) for hauling down the ensign.

ted Pearson) "retreted instantly into our own ship, and returned to their Guns again."*

4. Victory

It was now 10:00 P.M. The battle went on for another thirty minutes, becoming even more bloody and desperate. *Richard's* master at arms liberated the prisoners from the hold, to the number of over a hundred, and assured them that they had better man the pumps if they valued their lives. Most of them did so; but one, the master of prize ship *Union*, leaped through an open port of *Serapis*, rushed on deck and told Captain Pearson that if he could hold out a little longer Jones would either strike or sink, for there were already five feet of water in the hold.

At this moment—five or ten minutes after ten—the situation of *Bonhomme Richard* seemed hopeless to almost every officer except the Captain. A sinking ship, on fire, all cannon silenced except three nine-pounders while the enemy's eighteens are still blazing away, prisoners at large, officers losing heart and chiefs bellowing "Quarters!"—all that, which to almost any other commanding officer would have added up to the ultimate in desperate circumstances, failed to break Paul Jones's will to victory. And victory was very near. A few minutes before 10:30, when the mainmast of *Serapis*, which Jones had been pelting with doubleheaded shot, began to tremble, Captain Pearson lost his nerve. Four of his eighteen-pounders were still firing, but he decided that it was time for him to strike. The Red Ensign, which he had caused to be nailed to its staff, he had to tear down with his own hands since no man near him was able to move.

---

* One of the strange things about this part of the action is that neither side attempted to board the other until near the end. The probability is that *Richard's* crew looked like such desperate cutthroats that Pearson did not dare board except as a last expedient; and that Jones, with his keen tactical sense, felt that his men could do more execution with firearms than with boarding pikes and cutlasses. It is also strange that both commanding officers, although in full view on deck throughout the action, and conspicuous by their uniforms, escaped without a scratch. Jones probably ordered his sharpshooters to spare Pearson so that he could have the honor of capturing a captain RN; and Pearson may have given similar orders in the hope of taking the "pirate."

This is the situation that the two nearly contemporary engravings of the action attempt to depict: *Serapis's* mainmast just going or gone. But the artists have altered the facts to suit Captain Pearson's excuses and explanations. The Red Ensign is still flying, because Pearson claimed that he did not strike until after the mainmast fell; and *Alliance* is firing broadsides at *Serapis* about half an hour after she ceased firing, because Pearson wished to believe that he had been conquered by two ships, not one. Of the two engravings, Peltro's is the least inaccurate, since it shows *Bonhomme Richard* heading downwind, and Flamborough Head and the escaping convoy at about the right bearing and distance. *Pallas* and *Scarborough* are still fighting in the left background, although Piercy struck at least half an hour before Pearson did; and on the extreme edge *Vengeance* is shown, sailing about aimlessly. Neither of the engravings indicates that *Serapis* had anchored; this fact appears only in Renaud's design for Jones's medal, which was engraved as a frontispiece for André's edition of the Commodore's *Mémoire*. The reverse of Dupré's medal, although it does not show *Serapis* anchored, is on the whole the best picture of the battle.

With the Commodore's permission, Lieutenant Dale now swung himself on board *Serapis* to take possession, followed by a boarding party in which Midshipman Mayrant was wounded by a pike wielded by a British seaman who had not heard that his Captain had struck. Nor had the first lieutenant of *Serapis;* he had to have the fact confirmed by Captain Pearson.

Lieutenant Dale now conducts Captain Pearson on board *Richard* and formally introduces him to Commodore Jones. At this point the tottering mainmast of *Serapis* cracks and falls overboard, carrying with it her mizzen topmast. The defeated captain hands his sword to Jones, who promptly returns it with a few gracious words about his gallant fight, and invites him below into his wrecked cabin to drink a glass of wine. Such were the ceremonial manners of eighteenth-century warfare.

This deadly duel was not the whole of the Battle of Flamborough

Head. *Countess of Scarborough,* several cable lengths ahead of *Serapis* when the action opened, was pursued and closely engaged a few minutes later by *Pallas,* Captain Cottineau. They exchanged broadsides for about twenty minutes, when *Pallas,* for reasons unexplained, dropped astern out of range. Captain Piercy of *Scarborough,* feeling that he had got off easily since he was greatly outgunned, sailed over to support *Serapis,* but decided not to get involved in that murderous mêlée. Cottineau then forced him to renew action a mile or more to leeward of the other antagonists. Captain Landais looked in briefly on them at this state of the battle, received a few random shots and fired at the wrong ship, but otherwise did not participate. Captain Cottineau, whom Jones considered the ablest of the French officers under his command, followed standard French tactics of aiming at the enemy's spars and rigging, and to such good purpose that at the end of two hours the *Countess* was disabled, although she had lost only four men. Captain Piercy then surrendered, and his ship made a valuable prize. This brought up the total bag of prisoners made by Jones's squadron to 504, including 26 officers of the Royal Navy and 18 masters and mates of merchant ships.

The fight between *Bonhomme Richard* and *Serapis* had lasted between three and three-and-a-half hours. The British frigate was in a deplorable condition; her spars, sails and rigging were cut away, and dead and dying men lay about her decks. But the state of *Richard* was even more frightful. Her rudder was hanging by one pintle, her stern frames and transoms were almost entirely shot away, the quarterdeck was about to fall into the gunroom, at least five feet of water were in the hold, and it was gaining from holes below the waterline (some of them made by *Alliance*), and her topsides were open to the moonlight. The timbers of her lower deck from the mainmast aft, "being greatly decayed with age, were mangled beyond my power of description," observed Jones in his "Narrative" of the battle, "and a person must have been an Eye Witness to form a Just idea of this tremendous scene of Carneg, Wreck and ruin that Every Where appeared. Humanity cannot but recoil from the prospect of such finished horror, and Lament that War should be capable of producing such fatal Consequences."

This last statement was perfectly sincere. Paul Jones, like many of the greatest admirals and generals of the English-speaking nations, loved fighting but hated war. He shared the belief of eighteenth-century philosophers that war was an outmoded and barbarous method of settling international disputes, and hoped that the particular conflict in which he happened to be engaged would be the last. The gods willed otherwise.

*   *   *

NOTE TO CHAPTER XIII

What Did Paul Jones Say during the Battle off Flamborough Head?

Captain Pearson in his Letter on the Action dated 9 October 1779, in Admiralty Records 1-2305, is my authority for the hails, and for *Richard's* reply, "The *Princess Royal*"; Fanning, writing in 1806, says that it was "Come a little nearer and I will tell you." Pearson says that he replied, "Where from?" but Fanning says that he said, "What are you laden with?" and Jones answered, "Round, grape and double-headed shot!"

In the account of the battle that he wrote especially for Sherburne's biography published in 1825, Richard Dale first gave the famous "I have not yet begun to fight." He states that Jones said this a few minutes after the first collision between *Richard* and *Serapis* and before the grapple. This is the obvious place for it, not at the end of the battle, which makes no sense.

That notion apparently began with Dr. Benjamin Rush. In his commonplace book written between 1800 and 1813, privately printed by Louis Alexander Biddle in 1905 as *A Memorial containing . . . Sundry Incidents in the Life of Dr. Benjamin Rush,* p. 121, the Doctor says that he heard Jones "give a minute account of his engagement with the *Serapis* in a small circle at dinner. . . . Towards the close of the battle, while his deck was swimming in blood, the Captain of the *Serapis* called him to strike. 'No sir,' said he,—'I will not,—we have had but a small fight as yet.'" This dinner must have taken place between 1781 and 1783, but at least 17 years elapsed before Dr. Rush recorded it. Dale's version was not recorded for 44 years, but I conclude that the naval officer who was present at the fight had a more accurate memory than the doctor who was not.

After Pearson's surrender, Thomas Berry, a British volunteer in *Richard*, and six other sailors, seized one of the undamaged boats of the frigate and escaped to the shore where they told a series of tall tales to the authorities. Here is the reproduction of one of their affidavits, in the London *Evening Post* of 30 September 1779, as quoted in Seitz p. 55:

"The Captain of the *Serapis* called out to Jones to strike, else he would sink him. To which the latter replied, 'that he might if he could; for whenever the Devil was ready for him, he would rather obey his summons than strike to anyone.' They add, that during the engagement Paul Jones (who was dressed in a short jacket and long trousers, with about 12 charged pistols slung in a belt around his middle, and a cutlass in his hand) shot seven of his men for deserting from their quarters; and to his nephew, whom he thought a little dastardly, he said, 'that d——n his eyes he would not blow his brains out, but he would pepper his shins,' and actually had the barbarity to shoot at the lad's legs who is a lieutenant in his ship." This is the description and story which was seized upon by writers of popular chapbooks. Jones fought in uniform, shot nobody of his own crew, and had no nephew on board; but Berry's yarn never died.

Fanning is the authority for Jones saying, as soon as the two ships were locked, "Well done, my brave lads," etc.; for Jones's reproof to Master Stacey for swearing; he also says that when the petty officers were bawling "Quarters!" he heard Jones say, "What d——d rascals are them [*sic*]—shoot them—kill them!"

The London *Public Advertiser* of 30 October 1779 gives the hencoop story, as coming from "One of the Men escaped from Paul Jones." It probably happened when the two ships were locked together and had been grappled for an hour. Jones, in one of his later accounts of the battle, said, "I was determined to conquer, or die in the attempt."

Finally, what did Jones himself say that he replied to Pearson near the end of the action, when the captain of *Serapis* inquired if he were asking for quarter? In his "Narrative" of 3 Oct. 1779 (Jones Mss. VI 7299) Jones does not give his exact words but says, "I having answered him [Pearson] in the most determined negative, they renewed the battle with double fury." He repeated his exact words in his *Mémoire* of 1786 to Louis XVI, but unfortunately we have this only in André's French translation (p. 99) as follows:

"Je répondis au capitaine anglais: *Je ne songe point à me rendre; mais je suis déterminé à vou faire demander quartier.*"

Now, what does this phrase translate? We have a clue in a letter from Amsterdam, 8 October 1779, printed in the London *Evening Post* of the 12th and the *Public Advertiser* of the 13th (Seitz pp. 87-8). The writer gives a straightforward account of the action, which he must have had from Jones himself or from someone near to him. He says, "Captain Pearson . . . asked Jones if he had struck? (At this time the flag was shot away.) 'No, sir,' says he, 'I have not yet thought of it, but am determined to make you strike.'"

Probably these are the very words that André translated as "Je ne songe point à me rendre," etc. Most writers on Jones, however, have repeated the version that appeared in an English chapbook of about 1830, *Life Voyages and Sea Battles of That Celebrated Seaman Commodore Paul Jones:* "I do not dream of surrendering; I am determined to make you strike!" But "I do not dream" strikes a false note. The London *Evening Post* statement, in my opinion, is what Jones said just before Pearson surrendered.

Fanning's statement, made in his *Narrative* of 1806, that Pearson said he hated to surrender to a man who "had a halter around his neck," is generally discounted, although it is consistent with the surly discourtesy that Pearson displayed toward Jones during their brief intercourse at the Texel.

XIV

Aftermath
of Battle

25 September-31 December 1779

1. Post Mortems

Lieutenant Dale, after cutting the anchor cable of *Serapis*, got her under way with such sails as were left on her foremast and the stump of her mizzen. For 36 hours she, as well as *Pallas, Alliance, Vengeance* and *Countess of Scarborough* with a French prize crew in charge, stood by crippled *Bonhomme Richard*, sailing very slowly in an easterly direction. The moon set at a few minutes before 4:00 A.M. September 24; sunrise came at 5:50, but the 24th was a dark, foggy day that broke on a scene of destruction.

For two nights and a day the survivors worked valiantly to save *Richard*, while Surgeon Brooke and his mates did their best for the wounded, and the dead were consigned to the deep. The fires were not quenched until 10:00 A.M. on the 24th. At 2:00 P.M. the chief carpenter told Captain Jones frankly and forcibly that the leaks could not be stopped even if men from the other ships helped with bucket brigades. Jones did not agree. In order to get *Serapis* organized, he had himself rowed over to her, leaving the first lieutenant of *Pallas* in command of *Richard* with orders to keep the carpenters at work and the pumps going. But at 7:00 P.M. 24 September, when he returned on board *Richard,* he agreed that she was past saving. He then gave orders to transfer the wounded to other vessels of the squadron, employing all ships' boats for this work. He himself left at 7:30 and formally transferred his flag to *Serapis*. At 10:00 P.M. he sent for Master Stacey and ordered Abandon Ship, which was carried out during the night with the ships' boats, while the pumps clanked and thumped away to prevent *Richard* from taking a sudden dive.

At 4:00 A.M. on the 25th, when the water was almost up to the lower deck, the weary carpenters belayed pumping; at 10:00 A.M. 25 September the last man left the ship; at 11:00 Commodore Jones "saw, with inexpressible grief, the last glimpse of the *Bonhomme Richard*" as her honored hulk sank, bow first, below the waters of the North Sea.

Casualties were heavy, for an eighteenth-century naval battle. Jones estimated his loss at 150 killed and wounded out of a total of 322, but unfortunately did not give the proportion of each. Pearson's list of *Serapis's* casualties, which he admitted to be incomplete, named 49 killed and 68 wounded; but Jones, after checking with the English surgeon, concluded that at least one hundred were killed.*

Although Captain Pearson had lost two warships, he had accomplished his mission; the Baltic convoy got through without loss. All the merchant ships escaped during the night and anchored under the guns of Scarborough Castle, which no hostile warship dared approach, and on the 24th they were further protected by thick fog. In his mortification over having lost a fine frigate, Captain Pearson may be forgiven for having declared that he had been attacked by *Alliance*

---

* *Richard's* crew numbered 322 instead of 380 as it did at the start of the cruise because diminished by desertion off the Blaskets, and by manning prizes. The crew of *Serapis* numbered about 325.

as well as by *Bonhomme Richard,* thus attempting to rob Jones of his glory; but the evidence is overwhelming that *Alliance* did more harm to friend than to foe. Jones, checking on board *Serapis,* ascertained that she had lost only one man to Landais's wild shooting. To quote the measured words of Captain Mahan, "The share taken by the *Alliance* . . . was used . . . to give to this affair a color not reconcilable with the facts. That an 18-pounder, two-decked ship should have struck to a 12-pounder vessel whose only claim to a second deck was the abortive battery of six eighteens, carried barely above the waterline, was a circumstance not to be admitted, if it could otherwise be represented."

There can be no doubt that Paul Jones won, and deserved to win. Pearson's seamanship and tactics were inferior to his, or he would never have allowed himself to be grappled; Jones, by clinching, neutralized the decided advantage of the enemy in speed, mobility and fire power. Pearson fought a brave fight; but the better man, in command of the worse ship, won.

Pearson and Piercy of the *Countess* were acquitted by courts-martial as having "done infinite credit to themselves by a very obstinate defense against a superior force." Both received the freedom of Scarborough and other cities, Pearson was presented with a magnificent silver vase by the Russia Company out of gratitude for saving them from heavy loss, and later he was knighted by King George III. Thus, the vanquished captain got more out of his defeat than did Jones from victory.

The Admiralty, upon its first news of the battle, sent ships scurrying in search of Paul Jones in every direction except the right one, to the coast of Holland. A squadron consisting of H.M.S. *Prudent* (64 guns), *Amphitrite* (28), *Pegasus* (28), *Medea* (28) and *Champion* (24) was detached next day from Spithead "in pursuit of Paul Jones to the Firth of Forth"; they were off Scarborough on the 28th and continued northward. For it was long before the Admiralty found out in which direction the American task force had retired. At Scarborough it was reported that Jones had gone to Norway. A letter from Fort William in the Scottish Highlands on 25 September declared that he was around Inverness. A letter from Yarmouth on 5 October brought a report from H.M.S. *Winchelsea* that Jones had been seen steering ENE with *Serapis* in tow. About 10 October the Admiralty finally learned his whereabouts from a merchant ship which had come from the Texel. It then set up a close blockade of that Dutch roadstead. As late as 1 December H.M.S. *Jupiter* of 50 guns and three frigates were detached from Spithead "to watch the motions of Paul Jones at the Texel."

If there had then been such a thing as a clipping agency, Paul Jones could have collected several hatfuls of amusing extracts from the British press. "Paul Jones resembles a Jack o' Lantern, to mislead our marines and terrify our coasts," said the London *Morning Post* on 1 October; "he is no sooner seen than lost." Paul Jones is still "the most general topic of conversation," according to the same paper four weeks later. Anecdotes of the battle were eagerly collected from the sailors who got ashore, and were printed. A correspondent was even sent to Kirkbean to collect anecdotes of Paul Jones's school days; one such relates how, in retaliation for a flogging administered for not learning his lesson, he beat the pedagogue senseless with a club and then took refuge on board a man-of-war; for which accident "are we indebted for having such a formidable and desperate pirate by sea."

The First Lord of the Admiralty, Lord Sandwich, was needled, under his nickname "Jemmy Twitcher" (hero of *The Beggar's Opera*), in a ballad:

> If success to our fleets be not quickly restor'd
> The leaders in office to shove from the board,
> May they all fare alike, and the de'il pick their bones,
> Of Germain, Jemmy Twitcher, Lord North and Paul Jones.

Sandwich was also the target of an amusing fake letter from Paul Jones to "Jemmy Twitcher," printed in the London *Evening Post*. The Commodore therein thanked the First Lord for the opportunity afforded him to take prizes and raid the coast. He ventured to say that this singular complaisance was derived from a similarity of tastes—"Your Lordship and I do, both of us, heartily despise all the musty rules of religion; Your Lordship and I do, both of us, love a bottle and a wench," etc. Reprints of this squib are still being circulated as genuine.

It is not surprising that Jones's character and career were bitterly attacked in certain quarters, especially by officers of the Royal Navy; for he had foiled them and flailed them and made monkeys of them.

Englishmen, in their rage over the humiliation, denounced him as a mere pirate and published fictitious anecdotes of his alleged cruel humor. This was natural enough. During the American Civil War, Captain Semmes of the *Alabama* was denounced as a pirate, and Northern newspapers demanded that he be hanged if caught. It is not true, however, that the British government ever put a price on Paul Jones's head. Officially it regarded him, as it did every American naval or privateer officer, as a rebel and pirate. But the amazing thing about the English reaction to Jones is the admiration that he aroused, especially among the common people. If, on the one hand, we have the uncomplimentary picture of "Paul Jones the Pirate," we have an English mezzotint which is almost flattering.

Ballads of which Paul Jones is the hero were composed and printed. The first that can be dated is a broadsheet printed at Pocklington, Yorkshire, not far from the scene of the battle, before the end of 1779. Countless copies of it appeared in later years, with variants. This ballad must have been composed by an American sympathizer; and it bears marks of the author's having talked with the wounded pilot, or the men who got away in a boat immediately after the battle. The first edition, in the Firth collection at the Bodleian Library, reads as follows:

PAUL JONES

An American Frigate, call'd the *Richard* by name
Mounted guns forty-four, from New York she came,
To cruise in the channel of old England's fame,
With a noble commander, Paul Jones was his name.

We had not cruised long, before two sails we espied
A large forty-four, and a twenty likewise,
With fifty bright shipping, well loaded with stores,
And the convoy stood in for Old Yorkshire's shore.

'Bout the hour of twelve, we came alongside,
With a long speaking trumpet, whence came you he cried,
Come answer me quickly, or I'll hail you no more,
Or else a broadside into you I will pour.

We fought them four glasses, four glasses so hot,
Till forty bold seamen lay dead on the spot
And fifty-five more lay bleeding in gore,
While the thund'ring large cannons of Paul Jones did roar.

Our carpenter being frightened, to Paul Jones did say,
Our ship leaks water, since fighting today,
Paul Jones made answer, in the hight of his pride,
If we can do no better we'll sink alongside.

Paul Jones he then smiled and to his men did say
Let every man stand the best of his play,
For broadside for broadside they fought on the main,
Like true British heroes we return'd it again.

The *Seraphis* wore round our ship for to rake,
Which made the proud hearts of the English to ache,
The Shot flew so hot we could not stand it long,
Till the bold British colours from the English came down.

Oh now my brave boys we have taken a rich prize,
A large forty-four and a twenty likewise,
Help the poor mothers that have reason to weep
At the loss of their sons in the unfathomed deep.

Not all the ballads were so complimentary to Jones. "A New Song of Paul Jones, the Cumberland Militia and Scarborough Volunteers" begins:

> Come, each loyal Briton of courage so bold
> As annals can shew, you would ne'er be controul'd;
> It vexes my patience, I'm sure, night and day
> To think how that traitor *Paul Jones* got away.
> > *Derry-down, down, hey! derry down.*

It goes on to rake up the old Mungo Maxwell affair, and to tell how the local militia marched down to the Spaws, expecting a landing.

The ballad that we have already quoted about the raid on St. Mary's Isle was also dressed up with new verses, such as:

> You have heard o' Paul Jones?
> > Have you not? have you not? [*bis*]
> How he came to Leith Pier, and he fill'd the folks with fear,
> > And he fill'd the folks with fear,
> > > Did he not?

> He took the *Serapis*
> > Did he not? Did he not? [*bis*]
> He took the *Serapis*, tho' the battle it was hot;
> > But a rogue and vagabond,
> > > Is he not?

Another poetaster published a turgid poem in heroic couplets called *Elegiac Epistles on the Calamities of Love and War, Including a Genuine Description of the Tragical Engagement between H.M.S. Serapis . . . and Paul Jones.** But the most amusing product of the Paul Jones tradition, which received renewed impetus at Flamborough Head, was a series of penny-plain and twopence-colored chapbooks purporting to tell *The True History of Paul Jones the Notorious Sea Pirate;* or, more elaborately and for sixpence, *The Life, Voyages and Sea Battles of that Celebrated Seaman, Commodore Paul Jones still remembered by some of the Old Inhabitants now living in Wapping, he being originally in the Coal-Trade.* There was something about Jones's dashing character that appealed to the sporting instincts of the ordinary Englishman,

---

* Senior Collection Naval Academy Museum.

and the large number of these chapbooks indicates that he became a popular hero like Robin Hood and Dick Turpin. Many of these ephemeral "histories" have a frontispiece showing Paul Jones with a ferocious scowl on his face, clad in a uniform the like of which was never seen, saving the American ensign from an ignominious strike by shooting down the unfortunate "Lieutenant Grub"—"the reader is assured of the fact, which came from the most undoubted authority, that of William Grub's widow." Why innocent Midshipman Groube, who survived the battle and shipped with Jones in *Alliance* and *Ariel,* was substituted for the cowardly gunner, nobody has been able to explain.

An incident that did much to make Paul Jones popular in England was his generous treatment of Pilot John Jackson from the Humber, whom he had detained, and who lost an arm during the action with *Serapis.* From Holland Jones returned him home in his own boat, with "smart money" of 100 ducats (about $250) in hand. In addition, the Commodore wrote to the Mayor and Corporation of Hull that Jackson had been subjected to *force majeure;* and that if they would semiannually certify to the American Minister at the Court of France that he was alive, he would receive half pay for life. This promise was not honored by Congress, to whom Thomas Jefferson referred the matter; and the pilot, who lived until 1836, never obtained anything from America beyond his hundred ducats.

In France, the impact of Jones's victory was immense, for France badly needed news of a victory after the Combined Fleet's expensive fiasco. "For some days after the arrival of your express," wrote Franklin to Jones, "scarce anything was talked of at Paris and Versailles but your cool Conduct & persevering Bravery during the terrible Conflict." John Adams wrote, "the cry of Versailles and the Clamour of Paris became as loud in the favour of Monsieur Jones as of Monsieur Franklin, and the inclination of the Ladies to embrace him almost as fashionable and as strong." An enterprising printer at Rouen got out a *Relation* of the battle, as early as 7 October. And it is interesting to note that our hero, accepting the name by which he was known throughout Europe, now begins to sign himself "Paul

Jones" instead of "Jnọ P. Jones," which he had used since joining the Navy.

In America, too, the news was received with particular acclaim because the year 1779 was a bad one for the cause—Georgia lost to the British, disastrous Penobscot expedition, and British coastal raids in the Chesapeake and Long Island Sound. But the victory off Flamborough Head was unpleasing to the Arthur Lee-Sam Adams faction. One of their members in Congress, James Lovell, wrote nastily to General Washington: "The Stories of the Display of our 13 Stripes in Holland may be perhaps pleasing to certain classes here, but I have some Proofs that Things have been conducted rather in Conformity to Dutch Politics, and in a manner that will be productive of more solid Benefit than the Pleasure of indulging the little proud Affectations of our rising Navy." The "manner" that he wanted was for the Dutch to return *Serapis* and the *Countess* to the British, since that would finish Jones and give Franklin a black eye.

General Washington paid no attention to this sneer; he always kept hands off the Navy. And Congress in December 1779, when Jones was at the Texel, carried out one of his frequent administrative suggestions. It replaced the old Marine Committee by a Board of Admiralty, nominally of five members but usually consisting only of three—Francis Lewis, William Ellery and young James Madison of Virginia. When Paul Jones learned of this shortly after the British capture of Commodore Whipple's fleet at Charleston, he wrote to his friend Carmichael, "There is . . . a Board of Admiralty at last appointed. This ought to have been done long ago, . . . as we have now lost, I may say, all our Navy."

2. At the Texel

Commodore Jones, flying his flag in *Serapis*, sailed his squadron, now comprising *Alliance, Countess of Scarborough, Pallas* and *Vengeance*, straight across the North Sea into Dutch waters. Or, it would be more accurate to say, they sailed him; for the other ships, having been instructed by Chaumont that the cruise should end at the Texel, shaped their course for that roadstead, despite Jones's signals to put in at Dunkirk. He preferred Dunkirk as a French, not a neutral port, where he could land his more than 500 prisoners, exchange them promptly, and then proceed to the Texel; but since the prisoners were distributed among all four ships, he had to follow them. The passage across the North Sea took many days because of the crippled condition of *Serapis*. Under Jones's energetic direction, the people got up a jury mainmast on 28 September (three days after *Richard* went down) and bent a new mainsail next day. At 2:00 P.M. October 2, *Serapis* raised the coast of Holland, at 4:00 a pilot came on board; the squadron for safety stood off shore in a fresh gale from the northwest until midnight, then tacked, and by noon on the 3rd all were anchored in Texel roadstead.

The Texel, where Jones's squadron was destined to spend the rest of the year 1779, is the largest island of the chain that blocks off the Zuider Zee, and also the name of the roadstead behind the island which served as the deep-water harbor for Amsterdam. That city, 75 miles distant, could be reached in those days only by a shallow, tortuous channel through the Zee. There seems to have been a dockyard and repair facilities at the Texel, but little else. Fresh water and provisions had to be brought from Amsterdam.

Chaumont, in ordering the squadron thither, was merely obeying the orders of Sartine, who wanted Jones to escort to France the convoy from the Baltic then waiting in the Texel. But it was an unwise order which led to infinite trouble and vexation. The French government did not wish to embarrass the Netherlands or drag it into the war; on the contrary, French policy was to keep the Dutch neutral and use their merchant marine to keep up lines of trade denied to the French by the British Navy. Now the Netherlands government was gravely embarrassed by the arrival of Jones's squadron, Jones himself was hampered in his operations, and his prolonged stay at the Texel—his "purgatory" as he called it—did nobody any good except the Amsterdam ship chandlers.

The government of the Dutch Republic was a peculiar one which seems to have been devised for the purpose of avoiding decisions. At the head of it was an hereditary president, the Stadtholder, William V of the House of Orange; but the real power in the Republic was the States General, a senate consisting of one delegate from each of the seven United Provinces. The system was complicated by the fact that Holland was as wealthy and populous as the other six provinces put together; thus her prime minister, known as the Grand Pensionary, was almost if not quite as powerful as the Stadtholder. And all treaties had to be ratified by the assembly of each province before being submitted to the States General. It was as if the dream of Aaron Burr and Timothy Pickering had come true, and a Northern Confederation had been formed of New York and the New England States, in which the presidency was hereditary in the Roosevelt family, a jealous Senate exercised the sovereign power subject to a "Bricker Amendment" on states' rights, and the Governor of New York had a veto on the President.

The Dutch Republic was divided into two parties, the Orangist and the Patriot. The former, led by the Prince, was definitely pro-English; the other, of which J. D. Van der Capellen was a leader, was pro-French and pro-American. The Republic was allied to England, which had the right to call on her for aid if attacked; but both political parties were trying their best to keep clear of the present struggle. Important personalities with whom Jones had to deal were this same Van der Capellen, the French Ambassador (le Duc de la Vauguyon), and a Swiss *philosophe* and man of letters, Charles-Guillaume-Frédéric Dumas. This gentleman, whom Franklin knew before the war, was keenly interested in America and devoted to her cause, apparently because it represented the same "principles of general philanthropy" that appealed to Paul Jones. In Amsterdam, too, was Stephen Sayre, an American adventurer, inventor and mischief-maker, sometime banker in and sheriff of London. He had been Arthur Lee's secretary and quarreled with him, but retained from that association a bitter hatred for Franklin and all his works. Through his friendship with Van der Capellen, Sayre was trying to sell to the

Dutch wild lands in America which he did not possess. Dumas, who knew something about the American West—he had translated Colonel Bouquet's narrative of his expedition to the Ohio Country—seems to have exposed this scheme, which enraged Sayre, who refers to him in letters to Van der Capellen as "that little insignificant Shoemaker." Sayre now spread a rumor, greatly to Paul Jones's annoyance and disgust, to the effect that *Richard, Pallas* and *Vengeance* were Le Ray de Chaumont's privateers, and he even had the impudence to propose himself as captain of the *Alliance* when Landais was relieved of her command. Dumas did not like the French Ambassador, whom he referred to sarcastically as "the Great Man." Thus, all Americans and friends of America in the Netherlands were jealous and distrustful of one another. It was very much as at Passy, only worse.

What Paul Jones and the French Ambassador wanted was permission for the Commodore to repair and replenish his ships, land and exchange his prisoners, and, in short, do everything that he might have done in an allied port. But the British government demanded that Jones be treated as an outlawed pirate, and his prizes, if not his person, handed over to them. The British Ambassador, Sir Joseph Yorke, argued that since the United States were not a recognized government but a group of rebellious provinces, they had no belligerent rights; American armed ships were no better than pirates and all their captures were illegal. That reasoning appealed to the Danish government, which released the three prizes that Jones sent into Bergen; but it did not go down in the Netherlands. The United Provinces remembered that they had been rebels once, and the Patriot Party was strong enough to neutralize the Orangists under the peculiar checks and balances of the government. Even in England, the opposition London *Evening Post* on 28 October inquired whether the Court had taken steps to punish the British outrages in Virginia and Connecticut. And, "If it has not, with what propriety or justice does it now demand Captain Paul Jones? Is not the requisition to the last degree ridiculous and absurd? And will not the

HIER KOMT PAUL JONES AAN.

(Liedje op de komst van den Amerikaanschen kaperkapitein Paul Jones in ons land, 1779).

Niet te snel.

1. Hier komt Pau-wel Jo-nes aan, 't Is zoo'n aar-dig vent - - je! Zijn
2. Hier komt Pau-wel Jo-nes aan, 't Is zoo'n aar-dig vent - - je! Een
3. Hier komt Pau-wel Jo-nes aan, 't Is zoo'n aar-dig vent - - je! Het

schip is na de grond gegaan,   Op een Engelsch ent-je![1]
ge-bo-ren A-me-ri-kaan,   Gantsch geen Engelsch vent-je! { Hadden wij hem hier,
doet zoo vee-le hel-dendaên Tot wel-stant van zijn vrint-je! |

hadden zij hem daar, Hij wist het te pro-bee-ren, For-tuin kan anders kee-ren.

[1] Het schip van PAUL JONES was in Oct. 1779 in een strijd met de Engelschen bij kaap Land-send Engelsch endje gezonken. Hij heesch toen zijne vlag aan boord van het veroverde schip *Serapis* en liep met zijn smaldeel Texel binnen.

inflammatory and diabolical proceedings of the British troops in America excite retaliation, and make poor Old England (once famed for mercy and sound policy) contemptible in the eyes of every nation on earth?"

There can be no doubt that Paul Jones was popular in Holland. When he visited Amsterdam a few days after his arrival at the Texel, to obtain permission to establish his wounded and prisoners on shore, he was followed on the street, ballads were composed in his honor, and he received a public ovation when he attended the theater. Indeed, the earliest authentic portrait of Paul Jones subsequent to the 1776 silhouette is the etching here reproduced, made by Simon Fokke of Amsterdam when the Commodore was attending the theater on 9 October.

"When Paul Jones appeared in the 'Change of Amsterdam," wrote the correspondent of another London paper, "all business seemed for a while suspended in order to gaze and follow him. He was dressed in a blue frock coat, metal buttons, white cloth waistcoat and breeches, with a broadsword under his arm. When he quitted the 'Change the Crowd followed him to his Lodgings and huzzaed him all the way home."

There was even a ditty written in his honor by some member of the Patriot Party who regarded his presence as an asset. Although a partisan song, it was so catchy that it has been added to the corpus of Dutch folksongs and is still sung by children in the Netherlands. The original music and words of three stanzas are here reproduced; a free translation is as follows:

HERE COMES PAUL JONES

Song on the arrival of the American Privateer Captain in our Land,
1779

Here comes Paul Jones; such a nice fellow!
His ship went down at England's End.

Chorus

Had we him here, had they him there,
He'd know what to do; fortune may turn.

Here comes Paul Jones; such a nice fellow!
A born American; no Englishman at all.

(Chorus)

Here comes Paul Jones; such a nice fellow!
He does many bold deeds for the good of his friends.

(Chorus)

The additional stanzas have the same first line and chorus, with these additions:

The prisoners whom he brought were from Britain and England.
He does things very skillfully; he has made a fine prize.
From Texel straight to Brest he went; let them see only his behind!
He's like a swan on the sea, shoots cannon balls like currants.
He carries a sword on his hip; but he looks like a student.

And the last stanza runs:

Here comes Paul Jones, he is such a nice fellow!
He's done his business well, and still acts the hero.

Chorus

White paper, yellow paper;
White paper, yellow paper;
Soon Paul Jones will be here!*

* The "paper" refers to the correspondence between the Dutch and British governments.

An indignant English gentleman in Amsterdam wrote to a London newspaper on 12 October:

> This desperado parades the streets, and appears upon 'Change with all the effrontery of a man of the first condition. No sooner was it known in France that he was in the Texel, than a courier was dispatched with orders for him to go overland to Paris, where he says he is to have the grant of a fresh commission, and a larger squadron, sufficient to make a descent on any part of Great Britain or Ireland, as occasion requires, or opportunity serves. . . . The Dutch look upon him to be a brave officer, and therefore bestowed many fulsome compliments during his stay here. Nay, they even go so far as to lay odds that before Christmas he lands a force in England or Ireland. Thus one desperate action has raised him high in the opinion of Holland and France, for a man of great courage and abilities, [but] he is desperate through fear, and has been successful without abilities.

Sir Joseph Yorke, to present his case, called on the Prince of Orange, the Grand Pensionary and the President of the States General. He obtained sympathy from the Prince but no promises from anyone. He tried to arrange to have Paul Jones arrested in the street for robbery, but the High Bailiff of Amsterdam would not allow it. As the Ambassador admitted, "The extraordinary Surprize and Embarrassment" occasioned by the appearance of Jones's squadron "has really deprived them of the Power of acting, as it was so unexpected, and out of the beaten track." And the checks-and-balances constitution prevented anyone from making a decision. The French Ambassador, the Duc de la Vauguyon, wisely advised Jones to keep quiet, give no offense, and play for time. The Dutch authorities, he predicted, would not force *Serapis* to go to sea in the state she was in, and if her repairs could be prolonged the British blockading squadron would return to port.

Commodore Jones's first object was to land the sick members of his crews and his 504 British prisoners. In this effort he was hindered rather than helped by Captain Pearson and the Dutch authorities, who were stuffy about having them ashore. Sir Joseph Yorke wrote to his government, "The Weather, the Fears of the infection on the shore, the difficulties of knowing how to treat with these Piratical people without committing His Majesty's Dignity, all have conspired to puzzle the Business. I hope, however, that the wounded officers are actually on shore, . . . for Jones has so far acted humanely."

This tribute to the "pirate's" humanity is significant. Jones offered to release the officer prisoners on parole, but Pearson would not agree, fearing lest his men, if left on board without their officers, join the United States Navy. Not until the end of October was Jones permitted to land even the wounded prisoners and to house them in a fort on Texel Island, guarded by French Marines.

Captain Pearson's attitude throughout these negotiations was surly and ungentlemanly. After he had been paroled and found a billet on shore, Jones at his request sent him his mess furniture and plate from *Serapis.* Pearson replied "that he could receive nothing from the hands of a rebel," although he had already accepted the return of his sword. Jones amiably sent him the effects as coming from Captain Cottineau of the French Navy, and they were accepted without a word of acknowledgment.

The Commodore would have been glad to release all British prisoners if an equal number of American sailors could have been let out of English jails. He was determined, however, to hang on to Captain Pearson as a hostage for the release, or at least the better treatment, of Captain Gustavus Conyngham, the most successful commerce-destroyer in the United States Navy and the most unfortunate. When stranded in Europe, in 1777, Conyngham was commissioned by Franklin to command first a privateer, and then the 14-gun Continental cutter *Revenge,* fitted out at Dunkirk. For eighteeen months he ranged the narrow seas, the Atlantic, and the West Indies in this little vessel with a mixed crew, occasionally slipping into a hospitable Spanish port for upkeep, and taking the incredible number of sixty prizes. When he finally arrived at Philadelphia early in

1779, Congress sold *Revenge* to a group of merchants, who promptly fitted her out as a privateer with Conyngham as master. On his
first cruise under letter-of-marque, he was captured and given "the
treatment" at Mill Prison, from which he dug his way out in November 1779 and escaped to Holland. Jones, who had never met Conyngham, greeted him warmly and welcomed him on board the
Alliance until he could obtain a new command.

Captain Landais went to Paris to be dealt with by Dr. Franklin,
who was supplied with a detailed account of his mad actions, attested
by many of *Richard's* officers, and even by some of his own. Either
Franklin suspended him from command, or he was induced to resign it; but Landais had another card to play, with the aid of
Arthur Lee.

Jones spent much time at Amsterdam, arranging through M. Dumas and the house of Neufville for supplies, and carpenters to fit
Serapis for sea. He also visited The Hague to call on the French Ambassador and leading Dutch officials. Van der Capellen, who well described himself as "an old and tryed friend of America," wrote to
Jones requesting an account of his life and exploits to counteract the
"despicable party spirit" of the Orangists. In reply, Jones sent him
a copy of his action report under cover of an interesting autobio-
graphical letter, declaring that he had drawn his sword "only in support of the Dignity of Freedom," that America was the country of
his "fond election" from the age of thirteen, and that he had been
the first to hoist the "Flag of Freedom" on the Delaware. He also enclosed a copy of his letter to the Countess of Selkirk. The Baron was
charmed to find that Jones was no "rough, unpolished sailor" but a
man of "sensibility," and even proposed to have the Selkirk correspondence printed; but M. Dumas warned the Commodore to be
"more reserved," and he gallantly forbade the publication of his letter to a lady without her consent.

That these trips to the cities of the Netherlands were not wholly
on business may be gathered from various allusions to a pretty
young girl, the daughter of M. Dumas. At Passy, Franklin and his
secretaries had described to Jones the charms of a certain lady in the

Netherlands and teasingly urged him to court her. From the Texel on 26 October the Commodore wrote to Bancroft:

> I have seen the *fine lady* of this country which I came to Europe to Espouse. She is really a fine Woman yet I have seen also a second sister equally a Belle who will soon be fit for a Man; and I should prefer this younger because one might prevent some little Errors from taking root in her mind which the other seems to have contracted. It is a great pity that two such lovely lasses should be watched with so much Jealousy; for they are not so comeatable here as they might be in France. I have left to me only Doct.ʳ Franklins remedy, Patience.

Rather coarse and coldblooded! But that was Jones's usual attitude toward women. Mademoiselle Anna Jacoba Dumas had only passed her thirteenth birthday when Jones was at sea in *Bonhomme Richard*. Nevertheless, and in spite of her being heavily chaperoned, the gallant Commodore managed to strike up a flirtation. He wrote to Neufville at Amsterdam on 5 November that although he longed to visit that city he would have to "defer bending the Knee to beauty until a more favorable occasion." Probably he managed to see Anna frequently during the next four weeks, for she wrote a song in his honor under the pseudonym "The Virgin Muse." Jones was too busy with one thing and another to reply immediately, except in a letter to her father: "The Virgin Muse has my Virgin Thanks for her Virgin Song!" Once safely off shore in *Alliance,* and clear of any serious involvement, he wrote this poem, carefully saving a copy for ammunition on a future target, and mailed it to the young lady.

> Were I, Paul Jones, dear maid, "the king of sea,"
>   I find such merit in thy virgin song,
> A coral crown with bays I'd give to thee,
>   A car which on the waves should smoothly glide along.
> The nereids all about thy side should wait,
> And gladly sing in triumph of thy state
>   "Vivat, vivat, the happy virgin muse!
>   Of liberty the friend, who tyrant power pursues!"

Or happier lot! were fair Columbia free
   From British tyranny—and youth still mine,
I'd tell a tender tale to one like thee
   With artless looks and breast as pure as thine.
If she approved my flame, distrust apart,
Like faithful turtles we'd have but one heart;
   Together then we'd tune the silver lyre,
   As love or sacred freedom should our lays inspire.

But since, alas! the rage of war prevails,
   And cruel Britons desolate our land,
For freedom still I spread my willing sails,
   My unsheathed sword my injured country shall command.
Go on, bright maid! the muses all attend
Genius like thine, and wish to be its friend.
   Trust me, although conveyed through this poor shift,
   My New Year's thoughts are grateful for thy gift.

Since young ladies are not critical of verses addressed to them, we may infer that Mademoiselle Dumas regarded this as wonderful poetry, and overlooked the fact that it contained more about the writer than about herself.

If Anna Jacoba and Paul Jones ever met again, there is no record of it. Before he returned to Holland she had married one Abraham Senserff, and bore him three children. But we may be sure that she never entirely forgot the Commodore, and that through all his later adventures he retained a tender memory of "The Virgin Muse."

This was the most innocent of his many love affairs.

3. Off Again in "Alliance"

It was a dull autumn and winter for sailors at the Texel. No shore recreations, no prize money except one ducat per man, which some of the sailors contemptuously tossed overboard. But when they looked out to sea from the flat island, the sails of the British block-ading squadron were plainly visible. Better boredom in Holland than Mill Prison in England.

By 4 November the weather turned foul, the Dutch carpenters re-fused to work on *Serapis*, "thick cloudy weather and hard rain" are noted in her log day after day. It was too rough to send boats to Amsterdam; even the supply of fresh water ran low.

The British Ambassador, finding he could not force the Dutch government to take such drastic action as handing over *Serapis* and *Scarborough* to George III, now exerted pressure to have Jones's squadron forced out into the waiting guns of the Royal Navy. The French Ambassador answered this argument by claiming that the entire squadron was French; surely their High Mightinesses would not offend His Most Christian Majesty? One Dutch official even came on board *Serapis* to get a look at Jones's alleged French com-mission; the Commodore was urged by the Ambassador to sign a paper declaring that he had one which had gone down in *Bonhomme Richard*, but he declined to be a party to such a falsehood. Since the French government decided to take responsibility for the entire squadron except *Alliance*, Jones shifted his flag to the frigate and transferred to her a certain amount of equipment from *Serapis*, from which he parted with great reluctance. She was not only the finest frigate he had seen, but "a proud trophy of his Valour"; and Landais, as sloppy a seaman as he was unreliable, had left *Alliance* looking more like a pigsty than a naval vessel. The armament and equipment had been allowed to deteriorate, the officers were drunken and in-subordinate, and the men, wallowing in their own filth, were shot through with epidemic diseases.

On 12 November the French Ambassador instructed Jones not to sail until further notice. The same day, Vice Admiral Pieter Hendrik Reynst of the Netherlands Navy, whom the Prince of Orange had sent to relieve a more tolerant naval commander, insisted that Jones depart with the first fair wind, and moved a squadron of Dutch seventy-fours to the Texel. He sent Jones so many insistent, even insulting messages, that the Commodore offered to fight any three of his ships if he would sail outside the harbor. This invitation was not accepted. Five days later, the government of Holland decided by a close vote that Jones must be forced out. At that the French Ambassador ordered *Pallas* and *Vengeance* to show French instead of American colors. In a conference with Jones at Amsterdam, the Duke induced the Commodore to agree that *Serapis* and *Scarborough* also raise the royal ensign of France, so that they might act as cartel ships to take the British prisoners to England. *Scarborough*, together with *Vengeance* and two French cutters, did return 191 of these prisoners. To Jones's great and justified indignation, they were exchanged in England for Frenchmen, not Americans.

As part of this French camouflage scheme, Sartine offered Jones a French letter-of-marque as captain of privateers. At that, the Commodore exploded with wrath. He was sick of being called a corsair by the French and a pirate by the British. And now for an ally to offer him, Captain in the United States Navy, a privateer's commission, was too much. He declined, with no thanks; and dispatched a spate of letters to his friends at home and in France, complaining of "a most impertinent proposal," and of "so unworthy a proposition" as to be offered a "dirty piece of Parchment."

Completely disgusted with the way the French had let him down, Jones wrote to Robert Morris on 5 December that he proposed to sail home; and to Samuel Huntington, President of Congress, he sent a sixteen-page letter—the "Texel Memorial"—recapitulating his services to the country since 1775, concluding that he hoped to be employed under the "immediate direction" of Congress, without diplomatic or other foreign intermediaries.

Another menace of whom Jones remained unaware was "Commodore" Gillon of the South Carolina Navy. This character, then in Paris, proposed to Chaumont to buy *L'Indien* on credit for 600,000 livres and to combine her with Jones's ships at the Texel under his own command, "to do something clever."

It was indeed time to depart; but as yet Jones had no orders from

Franklin or from Congress as to what he should do or whither he should sail. Westerly gales kept *Alliance* windbound. The Royal Navy was still "laying" for him; the First Lord's exasperation is revealed in a letter of 23 November to Captain Francis Reynolds RN: "For God's sake, get to Sea instantly, in consequence of the orders you have received. If you can take Paul Jones, you will be as high in the estimation of the public as if you had beat the Combined Fleets."

Foul weather in December drove off the British blockading squadron temporarily. Jones employed the time to get *Alliance* properly cleansed and rerigged. Her logbook notes the arrival of more provisions from Amsterdam, including "one Pipe of Gin"—a double hogshead. On 21 December she was careened and her bottom scrubbed. Two days later, 7710 pounds of hardtack, 82 barrels of salt beef and pork, and sundry other provisions including coffee, sugar and "liquor" were struck below. The Dutch seventy-fours were anchored close to her, with Admiral Reynst sending pointed inquiries as to when Jones would leave' but he waited in the Texel until he was good and ready.*

Finally, on 27 December, the wind came fair for *Alliance* to sortie. Paul Jones, rigging a springline on a second anchor in order to let the wind fill the sails promptly and gain headway in the crowded roadstead, slipped that cable, raised American colors and departed. At 11:00 A.M., when clear of the land, he dropped his pilot.

Alliance sortied at a time when the British blockaders had been blown off station by a brave east wind, which was just what Jones wanted to tear through the narrow seas; he disdained to take her by the long and safe route, around Scotland. Hugging the Flemish banks so as to hold her wind, by 1:00 P.M. she had passed Camper-

---

* The convoy carrying French naval stores from the Baltic, which had been waiting for months for Jones to escort it to Brest, waited a little longer until the Netherlands Navy furnished an escort. In spite of its neutral character, the British Navy pounced on it in the Channel and captured several ships, whereupon Holland and England decided to declare war on each other.

down, the coastal village that gave its name to Duncan's victory in
1797. By 4:00, when the first dogwatch was set, the wind had become a full gale and Jones ordered the fore and main topsails to be
close-reefed; in so doing the fore topsail split and had to be unbent
for repairs. Even so, *Alliance* had more sail than she could carry,
and the reefed main topsail had to be furled. On she rushed, and at
6:00 P.M. the lights at the mouth of the Meuse were sighted; she
had logged 65 to 70 miles in seven hours.

During the midwatch, at 3:00 A.M. 28 December, the wind moderated, reefs were shaken out of the main and mizzen topsails, the
mended fore topsail was roused aloft and bent to the yard. Staysails
and fore-topmast studding sails were then set, and, after sundown,
as *Alliance* was approaching Goodwin Sands, the riding lights of a
British fleet at anchor were seen twinkling in the Downs. At 9:00
A.M. land was sighted on both sides of Dover Strait; at 10:00 Calais
slipped astern, and at noon Cap Gris Nez bore SE by S, distant six
miles. *Alliance* was well out of the lion's mouth.

The easterly wind now moderated, the rest of the studding sails
and the driver were set, and the weather grew thick, a welcome
screen from patrolling British frigates. As a precaution, Captain
Jones at 10:00 A.M. on the 29th set General Quarters, gave the word
"up all Hammocks," and "Exercised the Cannon." She was then
off the Isle of Wight. Cap la Hague on the Cherbourg peninsula
bore WSW distant 15 miles at 1:00 P.M.; by that time Jones was
feeling so saucy as to chase a ship and a brig. By noon next day,
the 30th, when *Alliance* had passed the Channel Islands, she caught
up with these vessels and found that one was a Swede from Stockholm and the other a Danziger, both neutral. That afternoon the
sea became so rough that all guns had to be run inboard and the
ports battened down. Topsails were close-reefed to a strong southeast gale at noon on the last day of the old year; and by the time
16 bells ushered in 1780, *Alliance* was off Ushant, clear of the English Channel.

Paul Jones was feeling the elation that every sailor experiences
when getting out to sea after long detention ashore. He little sus-

pected that his era of achievement was at an end, and that another period of frustration lay ahead. But some good times lay ahead, too.

4. Epilogue

Now, what became of the ships that took part in this memorable cruise, and the prizes they took; and how much did they bring their captors?

Countess of Scarborough was sold at Dunkirk for a merchantman. *La Vengeance* was also sold cheap by the French Navy, which apparently had no more use for her. Chaumont wanted *Pallas* made a dispatch boat under the Imperial flag, to protect her from capture; but whether or not this was done I have been unable to ascertain. Commandant Cottineau sailed *Serapis* to Lorient, where by Chaumont's orders (and to Jones's indignation) she was stripped of her armament, razeed, and sold to a merchant of Paris for two hundred and forty thousand livres—about forty-eight thousand dollars. From him she was purchased by the French Navy, which newly coppered her bottom, rearmed her and sent her to the Indian Ocean under command of Lieutenant de Vaisseau Roche. In July 1781, when she was anchored at Ste.-Marie de Madagascar, her exec., Lieutenant de Vaisseau Lhéritier, undertook to "cut" some very high-proof brandy at nighttime, to make the French equivalent of the British Navy's grog. A sailor who was holding an open signal lamp, to throw light on the process, dropped it into the tub of strong brandy, an intense fire broke out, and the ship was completely destroyed.

The other prizes taken by Jones's squadron brought varying sums, and the grand total was divided among all ships of the squadron according to the formula that Jones had obtained from the British Navy. This worked out at 132,915 livres 12*s* 8*d*—about $26,583 in gold—as *Bonhomme Richard's* share. There is preserved in the National Archives at Washington a schedule of the proper division among her crew, after a settlement had been made with the French government in 1784.

Distribution of Prize Money to Officers and Crew of Bonhomme Richard

	livres	sols	deniers
Commodore John Paul Jones	13,291	5	6
Colonel de Chamillard, French Royal Marine Corps	8,179	4	9
Lieutenants Dale and Lunt, Masters Lunt and Stacey, each	4,089	12	5
Capitaine Wybert de Mézières, French Royal Marine Corps.	2,044	16	2
Surgeon Brooke, Purser Mease, Lieutenants Stack, Macarthy and O'Kelly of the Walsh Regiment, Lt. de la Bernerie of Marines, each	1,022	8	1
John Burbank, master at arms, and Joachim Hidaut, pilot, each	860	7	8
Two Top Sergeants of Marines, and 12 Midshipmen, each	511	4	0
Two Boatswains, each	537	14	10
Five Chief Petty Officers (Sails, Chips, Guns, Gunners' Mates), Clerk and Second Surgeon, each	645	5	9
27 other Petty Officers and Marine Corporals and Sergeants, each	430	3	10
168 Able Seamen and French Marine Privates, and 2 Cooks, each	215	1	11
Five other Petty Officers (Cooper, Cook, Gunsmiths), each	322	12	10
43 Ordinary Seamen, each	161	6	4
36 Boys and Cooks, each	107	10	11

Thus, Paul Jones received about $2658 in gold as Commodore's and Captain's twentieths, and no other American officer received more than $818—very poor pickings according to the naval standards of his day.

Apparently if a sailor died in action or from his wounds, his heirs got nothing. The shares of the living were subject to deductions for advances or debts, including those to M. Salomon the gentleman's tailor of Lorient. And the Commodore had advanced out of his own pocket five louis d'or (twenty-five dollars) to a considerable number of sailors.

One concludes that the famous cruise of *Bonhomme Richard* and her consorts was more profitable in terms of fame than in cold cash. But the money was soon spent, while the glory is everlasting.*

* By the Royal Navy formula which Jones applied, the share of every other ship in his squadron was as follows:

	livres	*sols*	*deniers*
Alliance	108,892	8	0
Pallas	68,858	7	7
Cerf	29,892	0	7
Vengeance	12,810	17	4

XV

Pinnacle
of
Fame

1780

1. Back to Lorient

We left Paul Jones off Ushant on New Year's Day 1780, as captain of
Alliance. Neither at that time, nor at any time until John Barry commanded her, was she a happy ship. There was bad blood between the
two sets of officers and men on board, the original *Alliance* crew
from New England and the polyglot survivors of *Richard*. The mer-
its of the two ships and the details of the action off Flamborough
Head were constantly being argued and discussed; there were fist
fights among sailors and threats of duels between officers. "Our
ward-room," recorded Fanning, "exhibited nothing but wran-
gling, jangling and a scene of disgust." It was perhaps this state
of affairs which caused Captain Jones to enter certain remarks on his
station bill for working the ship. The officers are to pass the word
of command without confusion, and "the People as is their place *to*

execute orders and never to speak loud except in Case of Necessity."
Jones liked orders to be carried out smoothly and silently; he hated
loud bawling, such as there had to be in any ship commanded by
Landais.

From off Ushant *Alliance* sailed south to the latitude of Cape Finisterre in the hope of taking prizes, but almost every ship that she
spoke—a Prussian galliot, Dutchmen bound to Cadiz and Surinam—
turned out to be friendly or neutral. Only one small English brig,
bound from Liverpool to Leghorn, was taken and a prize crew
placed on board.

Dutch brigantine *Berkenbosch,* intercepted but released, nevertheless caused trouble. *Alliance* brought her to on 9 January 1780, and
Jones ordered the skipper to come on board. After examining his
papers and finding that the ship was neutral although the cargo
was British, he let the vessel proceed; but he insisted on swapping
cooks (the one in *Alliance* being horrible) and he advised the skipper to make for an American port, where the ship would probably be
allowed to sell her cargo for a good price. But the *Berkenbosch,* as
Dumas wrote to Jones, was the last vessel he should have molested,
because she belonged to a Dutch V.I.P., nephew of the Grand Pensionary, who also happened to be a good friend to America. The
brigantine was subsequently captured by the British in the West Indies and condemned as a prize, the Dutch then being at war with
England. But the Dutch skipper entered a "protest" against Jones's
action, asserting that *Alliance's* unwanted cook was an American
prizemaster who was responsible for the loss of the ship! Jones denied this roundly; but two years later Robert R. Livingston was calling on him for a statement to satisfy the Netherlands government.

On 16 January 1780, which opened with "Fresh Gales and Dirty
Weather" according to the logbook of *Alliance,* Jones decided to
put in at Corunna, the celebrated seaport in northern Spain. There
he took on more wood, water and provisions, and set Chips and
crew to work reducing the length of the main yard. Here, too, an
incipient mutiny boiled up. The crew, asserting that the Captain had

promised to take them directly to Lorient where they would be paid, refused to work; but next day, according to the log, "the People were satisfied by the Captain, so as to appear chearfully to Duty." Under his direction they performed the difficult operation of careening the frigate, scrubbing her bottom, "Blacking the bends," and "sundry other Jobbs." The only other evidence in the logbook of trouble at Corunna is that boatswain's mate Darling was "Confined to his Cabbin" on 27 January. This may have had something to do with the previous entry, "Broached 1 Pipe of Gin"—a pipe, be it remembered, being a double hogshead.

That same day Captain Jones entertained the Governor of Corunna and a number of Spanish gentlemen on board, fired a thirteen-gun salute, and at noon got under way in company with French frigate *Le Sensible*. Midshipman Fanning asserts that next day Jones announced that he intended to cruise in search of prizes for three weeks before putting in at Lorient, and that the officers dissuaded him, partly on the plea that they had no winter clothes. The only recorded case of indiscipline was a brawl between Lieutenant Degge and the master carpenter, James Bragg. The Lieutenant knocked Chips down and kicked him in the belly because he had sent his mate to batten down hatchways in a heavy sea instead of doing it himself.

Logbook entries indicate that *Alliance* made her way slowly across the Bay of Biscay in foul weather and against contrary winds: "Saw a Fleet, to leeward. Hauled on Wind and made Sail from them, a Large Sea with Fresh Gales" (6 February); recaptured a French barque that had been taken by a Guernsey privateer but found her so leaky that she had to be sunk, saving her cargo of wine; picked up American merchant ship *Livingston* returning from Virginia with a cargo of tobacco, and escorted her into Groix Roads on 10 February. There *Alliance* remained for a week, the people largely employed in making gaskets and spunyarn; and after Jones had caused another anchor to be brought out, *Alliance* having only one left, the frigate weighed, stood into Lorient harbor and picked up one of the King's moorings on 19 February. Captain Jones, "about blind with sore eyes" as he wrote to Franklin, put up ashore with his friend James Moylan, who since his last visit had acquired a frisky and attractive seventeen-year-old French wife.

Altogether, this seems to have been a very unhappy cruise. The call at Corunna resulted in several cases of venereal disease, one of the few instances of sickness in any of Jones's ships. Henry Lunt, the first lieutenant, who had been with Jones in *Providence* and volunteered in *Bonhomme Richard*, now demanded his discharge. In a simple, honest note to the Captain he said: "Sir you have treated [me] with disrespect all the Late Cruze which Makes My Life Very unhappy when I think of it & that amost all the Time. I have often Said it & say it still, I would Sooner Go in a Warlik Ship with Cap.ᵗ Jones than any Man Ever I Saw if I Could be treated with Respect, But I Never Have Been; wich Makes me Very uneasy & Discontent." Here is good evidence of the faultfinding, nagging and perfectionism on Jones's part which, coupled with his unpredictable temper, made him disliked by so many shipmates. One is relieved to find that in this case he managed to placate Lunt, who stayed with him until the end of the war.

Alliance was no exception to the rule that Jones was never satisfied with any ship until he had completely rerigged her. He submitted to Franklin a detailed list, supported by Chips Bragg's report, of what should be done before she would be fit to cross the Atlantic. The cutwater (the timber under the bowsprit) was badly wrenched and strained. The bowsprit was too long and low, and loose at that. Her tops were too small to accommodate fighting men. She was heavily oversparred, like *Ranger*. The storerooms were small, inconvenient and impossible to keep clean or free of vermin. The powder magazine was so insecure from fire that twenty casks of powder had to be stored in the hold, where they were spoiled by seawater leaking in. The galley brickwork had disintegrated, the copper had a big hole in it, and the deck underneath was burned. There were useless hatchways on the gun deck that obstructed the working of the guns. The distribution of the iron ballast, done according to some odd notion of Landais, made her pitch and plunge. The mizzenmast was too close to the mainmast, which in turn was stepped too far aft. She wanted a coat of the new copper sheathing to protect her bottom. Dr. Franklin threw up his hands at this last item and wrote Jones that he could have no copper; but he opposed no necessary repairs.

The logbook of *Alliance* shows that all these defects were remedied by the work of her own crew, with some help from carpenters of the American privateer *Luzerne* and from French sailmakers, bricklayers, tinsmiths and plumbers.* Captain Mackenzie, Jones's naval biographer of over a century ago, pronounces these alterations to have been "eminently judicious and expedient"; and he remarks, interestingly enough, that many of the same defects "are still found in our ships of war at the present day"—1841—including the drooping bowsprit, the excessive weight of spars, the faulty stepping of the mizzenmast and the defective arrangement of storerooms. Jones had the hatchways sealed while several iron pots of brimstone and other combustibles were slowly burned below, to kill the rats and other vermin that had multiplied since the Texel. He certainly did hate dirt on board ship.

Franklin had already received orders from the Congressional Board of Admiralty to send *Alliance* home as quickly as possible with arms, uniforms and other supplies urgently needed by Washington's Army. He wrote to Jones on 19 February urging him to sail quickly, after taking on 16,000 stand of arms that Lafayette had been the means of procuring, and 120 bales of uniform cloth purchased by John Ross at Nantes. He was to take as passengers Samuel Wharton, a merchant of Philadelphia, and two roving American diplomats—quarrelsome Arthur Lee and hot-tempered Ralph Izard of South Carolina. Jones must have known that Lee was his and Franklin's enemy (if he did not, Dumas had just written him to that ef-

---

* A plumber in those days was a man who worked in lead, which was wanted to prevent chafe in hawse pipes and protect the deck from the galley stove. Neither *Alliance* nor any other ship then had plumbing in the modern sense. The officers had a "seat of ease" on each quarter galley, and the men used the head of the ship, under the bowsprit.

fect); but he welcomed him to his ship and promised Franklin to be brisk and saving in fitting the frigate for sea.

These passengers were not slow to turn up at Lorient and get in Jones's way. Arthur Lee—the great incorruptible, the exponent of republican simplicity, the denouncer of "jobbery" and smeller-out of "corruption"—had acquired a *berline* or traveling coach, big as a modern trailer, for his completely fruitless visits to the courts of Europe, together with an enormous quantity of baggage and a number of body servants. These, he demanded, must be shipped to America in *Alliance*. Since a frigate, if she is to preserve her fighting quality, has very little room for cargo—*Alliance* had not half enough space for the arms and bales of clothing which Franklin wished to send—Jones refused Lee's request and thereby enhanced his enmity, of which he was to feel a flagrant example in no short time.

In the meantime the crew of *Alliance* were becoming more and more discontented at receiving neither pay nor prize money. Franklin managed to scrape up twenty-four thousand livres (about forty-eight hundred dollars) from which, the logbook says, "the People Received one Months Pay" on 22 April—the first they had had since leaving America almost a year earlier. Their sensibilities were aroused by seeing *Serapis* dismantled within view of their moorings. The delay about paying prize money was due largely to Chaumont, who had it all in his hands. He promised Franklin that he would place one hundred thousand livres with his banker at Lorient for preliminary distribution among the men; but when Jones called for it at the banker's, no money was there, nor did it ever come, since Chaumont was deep in speculation. But the men themselves were partly responsible for the delay. The Ministry of Marine wished to buy both *Serapis* and *Countess of Scarborough* for a fixed price, so much per gun, which the King was accustomed to pay for prize warships; but the officers and men of *Alliance* regarded this as a cheat and insisted that the ships be sold at auction. That took time for making complete inventories, advertising the sales, and so forth; and in the end they fetched less than if the royal offer had been accepted.

Dr. Bancroft, Franklin's disloyal secretary, wrote to Jones on 15 April that the twenty-four thousand livres for the crew "ought to do for a time," and that he hoped *Alliance* would sail "next week." But by that time Jones, faithful to "Poor Richard's" motto not to send but go yourself, was on his way to Paris in hope of lighting a fire under the Ministry and Chaumont. *Alliance* did not sail next week, nor indeed for twelve weeks, and then after more fuss and bother than anyone could have anticipated.

2. Glory in Paris

In mid-April there began for Paul Jones what he looked back upon as the happiest time of his life. He became the lion of Paris, honored by everyone from the King down. He was initiated into a famous Masonic lodge, his bust was done by the leading sculptor of Europe, he was invited to dine with great men, lovely women threw themselves into his arms. It cannot be denied that this attention somewhat turned his head and made it difficult for him to settle down when the war was over; but we would be niggardly to deny our hero the honors, the applause and, as Captain Thompson put it, the "pleasure which paris afourds."

During his six weeks' stay in the capital, Jones was the guest of Dr. Bancroft in a house at Passy near Dr. Franklin's, and the great man himself introduced the Commodore to the French court. He conducted Jones to the King's next levee at Versailles, and on the following day the Prince de Beauveau, captain of the palace guard, presented him personally to Louis XVI. From Jones's failure to mention any conversation between himself and the monarch, it is probable that Louis merely smiled pleasantly and bowed his head, as he was used to do, but said nothing. There is no record that Jones was ever especially presented to the Queen, whom he described in a letter as "a sweet girl"—much as if one should refer to Queen Elizabeth II as a "cute kid." But he must have seen her at the public levees.

Mission accomplished, as far as promises could do it, Jones on 20 April is about to return to Lorient and his ship (judging from what appears to have been intended as a farewell letter to Franklin of that date), when pressure is brought upon him to prolong his stay. His brother Masons wish to induct him into the Lodge of the Nine Sisters, the most famous in France. The King intends to decorate him, and it would be uncivil to absent himself. M. le Baron de Castille, Count Sarsfield, and the distinguished old Maréchal Duc de Biron, invite him to dine. The Prince de Nassau-Siegen, who had mismanaged the affair of *L'Indien,* writes that he is at liberty to call on "Mlle. Guimard," probably a well-known courtesan; Captain Cottineau proposes a shipmates' reunion. A certain M. de Monplaisir reminds Paul Jones that he has promised to attend a reception chez Madame la Présidente d'Ormoy, a noted bluestocking. He must of course renew his acquaintance with the Duc de Chartres (now Duc d'Orléans) and his beautiful Duchesse at the Palais Royal. Artists and sculptors want opportunities to do a portrait of the valiant Paul Jones, and several ladies of rank and fashion wish to see more of him, intimately.

Thus the Captain's departure was postponed from day to day. The weeks slipped by very quickly in May, most beautiful of seasons in Paris, when the chestnut and plane tree leaves are freshly green, the gardens full of flowers, twilight lasts almost to midnight, and dawn comes much too soon. Jones was a celebrity, acclaimed and applauded by people in the street, at the Opéra and at the Comédie Italienne, which was close by the present Théâtre Français. Once at the opera, it is said, the manager arranged for a "prop" laurel wreath to hover on a string over the Captain's head as he sat in a box, and descend upon his brow; but Jones had the good taste to decline such a piece of claptrap. (John Ledyard, however, heard a few years later that he appeared twice at the opera crowned with laurel.) Baron Grimm, the German diplomat who knew everyone in the literary and fashionable world, took him up, and in his memoirs expressed his astonishment that *"l'intrépide Paul-Jones,"* after having given abundant proof of his firm and courageous spirit, should be *"l'homme du monde le plus sensible et le plus doux"*—a man of the world the most mild and the most full of sensibility, who wrote verses "full of grace and sweetness." Sensibility paid in Paris, even though it got one nowhere with the Selkirks.

Paul Jones also found a congenial family which he could visit on terms of intimacy, to replace the now alienated Chaumonts. These were the Genets. François Genet, head of the clan, had an important post under Vergennes in the French foreign office. One of his daughters was Madame de Campan, dame d'Honneur of the Queen; and his son, Edmond-Charles Genet, who entered the foreign service, later became famous as the "Citizen Genet" sent by the Girondin ministry in 1792 to the United States.

In his person, Jones dramatized the French love of valor and victory, and the victory over *Serapis* was the only important Allied success at sea in 1779. He was thirty-two years old, handsome, strong and virile, with a compelling glance; and he had the good sense to observe French *politesse* in his social intercourse. No smell of tar, no quarterdeck abruptness followed him into the salon or the boudoir. Nobody ever made this more clear than Mrs. John Adams, the excellent Abigail, in a letter she wrote to her sister some years later:

> From the intrepid character he justly supported in the American Navy, I expected to have seen a rough, stout, warlike Roman—instead of that I should sooner think of wrapping him up in cotton wool, and putting him in my pocket, than sending him to contend with cannon-balls. He is small of stature, well proportioned, soft in his speech, easy in his address, polite in his manners, vastly civil, understands all the etiquette of a lady's toilette as perfectly as he does the mast, sails and rigging of his ship. Under all this appearance of softness he is bold, enterprising, ambitious and active. He has been here often and dined with us several times; he is said to be a man of gallantry and a favorite amongst the French ladies, whom he is frequently commending for the neatness of their persons, their easy manners and their taste in dress. He knows how

often the ladies use the baths, what color best suits a lady's complexion, what cosmetics are most favorable to the skin.

M. de Bachaumont, whose diary was published some twenty years later, described Jones's initiation into the Lodge of the Nine Sisters, to which Franklin and Voltaire and many philosophers, liberals and future leaders of the French Revolution belonged. Brother Dixmerie pronounced the welcoming oration. He compared Jones with the greatest heroes of ancient and modern times, and concluded with a quatrain comparing the Commodore's actions to that of a coquette whom one thinks to capture, but instead is captured by her. No sooner had he been initiated than the brethren of the Nine Sisters commissioned Jean-Antoine Houdon to do a superb portrait bust, which was exhibited at the Salon of 1781, and of which several contemporary replicas have been preserved.

Although Jones's greatest pleasures were afforded by the ladies, his most exalted honors came from the fountain of honor, the King. The delighted Commodore was informed that Louis XVI wished to invest him with the Order of Military Merit. Since, according to international etiquette, no officer could accept a decoration from a foreign prince without the consent of his own government, Jones could not be invested with the order at Versailles. But Sartine wrote to the President of Congress on behalf of the King, requesting the necessary permission; and as we shall see, it was granted.

This *Ordre du Mérite Militaire* had been created by Louis XV as a means of decorating Swiss and other foreign officers in the French service who as Protestants were ineligible for the more exalted Orders of Saint-Louis, Saint-Esprit, Saint-Michel and Saint-Lazare. There were three grades, of which Paul Jones was given the lowest, that of Chevalier; but even that was equivalent to the old plain K. B. (Knight of the Bath) in England. The decoration, which appears (somewhat prematurely) on the Houdon bust of Jones, was an eight-pointed gold star with fleur-de-lis in the angles, the obverse charged with a shield bearing a sword, point up, and the motto PRO VIRTUTE BELLICO. On the reverse was a laurel crown with the device LUDOVICUS

XV INSTITUIT 1759. It was attached to a dark blue ribbon and worn in the buttonhole.

Subsequent to receiving this honor, Jones had a new heraldic seal cut—his third or fourth. The Jones and Paul quarterings are sur-mounted by a coronet, indicating his rank as chevalier; and the coro-net, somewhat incongruously, is topped by a screaming eagle. The cross of his French decoration hangs under the shield, which an infant Neptune, complete with trident, supports.

An even greater honor conferred on Jones by the King was the presentation of a gold-hilted sword, with an inscription on the re-casso in bad but euphonious Latin: VINDICATI MARIS LUDOVICUS XVI REMUNERATOR STRENUO VINDICATI. This apparently is intended to mean, "Louis XVI rewards the Stout Vindicator of the Freedom of the Seas." One side of the grip is adorned with a medallion of Mars, the other with Hercules; Neptune is on the pommel, Mars and Mi-nerva on the guard plate, and there are flags, fleur-de-lis, floral designs and dolphins as well. Paul Jones was overcome with joy and pride over this sword, which was delivered to him at Lorient in a suitable case; but his education in ancient history had been so neglected that he had to inquire of Genet as to what the human figures represented. After his death his niece presented it to Robert Morris, who gave it to Commodore John Barry, as a transmittendum to the senior officer of the United States Navy. Barry, however, bequeathed it to Jones's old friend and shipmate, Captain Richard Dale, one of whose descend-ants has lent it to the Naval Academy. There it is appropriately placed near Paul Jones's tomb, and there may it long rest, but never rust.

3. The Pursuit of Madame de Lowendahl

This sword might have come into the keeping of a certain fair lady to whom Jones paid court, had she been willing to confer favors in re-turn. Madame la Comtesse de Lowendahl was of royal blood—Jones aimed high, as usual. Born Charlotte-Marguerite de Bourbon, daugh-ter of Prince Charles de Bourbon Condé, she was married to Général de Brigade le Comte François-Xavier de Lowendahl, a son of the old Maréchal de Lowendahl. Twenty-six years old, beautiful, fascinating and gifted, she was a good amateur singer and a passable miniature painter, as proved by the one that she did of Paul Jones.

The Captain seems to have met her through the Genets. It so happened that an English lady named Caroline Edes, or Edes-Herbert, who wrote letters to a London newspaper, was sitting out the war with the Genets, yet feeding social gossip of Paris to her English readers by way of Holland. One of her installments stated, in part: "The famous Paul Jones dines and sups here often. He is a smart man of thirty-six, speaks but little French, appears to be an extraordinary genius, a poet as well as a hero; a few days ago he wrote some verses extempore, of which I send you a copy. He is greatly admired here, especially by the ladies, who are all wild for love of him, as he for them, but he adores Lady——who has honored him with every mark of politeness and attention."

A second installment in the Edes society column, written after Jones had returned to Lorient in June, reads in part:

> Since my last, Paul Jones drank tea and supped here. If I am in love with him, for love I may die; I have as many rivals as there are ladies, but the most formidable is still Lady——who possesses all his heart. This lady is of high rank and virtue, very sensible, good natured and affable. Besides this, she is possessed of youth, beauty and wit, and every other female accomplishment. He is gone, I suppose, for America. They correspond, and his letters are replete with elegance, sentiment and delicacy. She drew his picture (a striking likeness) and wrote some lines under it, which are much admired, and presented it to him, who, since he received it, is, he says, like a second Narcissus, in love with his own resemblances; to be sure he is the most agreeable sea-wolf one could wish to meet with.

When these spicy bits bounced back to Paris, everyone knew that Lady——meant the Comtesse de Lowendahl, and that lady was not pleased. She had been playing cat-and-mouse with Jones because her husband the Brigadier was out of a job and she imagined that the Commodore might help him to obtain a command under Washington. But, unlike many ladies of a later day, she did not court publicity and was careful to afford Edes no more chitchat.

Before these journalistic revelations appeared, the Comtesse went through a somewhat guarded exchange of letters with the Commodore. The first, undated, is a short note. She declares that what she said yesterday *"n'était qu'un badinage";* was only fun. She could not respond to his sentiments, flattered as she is by them, *"sans tromper un galant homme avec lequel je vis"*—in other words, without deceiving her husband. One may easily guess the nature of the proposition that Jones had made to her the day before, and her immediate reply. But Paul Jones was not one to take "No" for an answer. He spent his last evening before leaving Paris with the Comtesse at Versailles. From Nantes on 7 June he writes to her that nothing short of the Glorious Cause of Freedom which he serves could induce him to part from her; he cannot attempt to describe his feelings toward her, so full is he of Gratitude and Sensibility; she has made him in love with his own picture because she had "condescended to draw it." (Miss Edes had that bit of gossip straight.) He is sending her a cipher so that they can correspond secretly, together with a lock of his hair, and would gladly send her his heart; he will certainly return to France in order to see her again.

Madame de Lowendahl's next letter was delivered to Jones by no less a person than her husband, who came not to demand pistols for two and coffee for one, but to ask Jones to help him get a job! In this letter, a cool one evidently, Madame pretended that she had never received the secret cipher and that the letter had not been intended for her; it is true that Jones always spelled her name wrongly, La Vendahl. In Jones's reply of 14 July he declares himself honored by his visit from the Brigadier, with whom he would be happy to share the command of a Franco-American expeditionary force. He tells Madame about the King's presentation sword and begs her to

Profile of the Bust of John Paul Jones by Houdon, 1780,
Formerly Belonging to Thomas Jefferson

"Portsmouth, sur la côte de la Nouvelle Angleterre . . ."
From a Drawing by Ozanne, 1778. The Square-rigger
Leaving Port Is Very Similar to U.S.S. *Ranger*

Engraving of the Lowendal
Miniature of Jones, 1780

U.S.S. *Alliance* passing Boston Light, 1780.
From a contemporary Painting by Captain Matthew Parke USMC

Portrait of Chevalier Paul Jones
by Charles Willson Peale, 1781

House in Portsmouth, N.H., Where Jones Stayed in 1781-1782.
From a Painting of about 1860

keep it for him until his return to France; and if she declines a friendly correspondence with him by the secret cipher, "as Friendship has nothing to do with Sex" (a recent discovery by Jones!), "if you please to write me in French I shall be able to Read it."

Madame's next has not been preserved; but we may obtain an idea of its contents from Jones's reply, dated on board *Ariel* 21 September 1780. It is an extremely cool missive. He is honored by her "very polite letter of 5 August." He regrets her refusal to be the "deposite" of his sword, and so will keep it himself. The Comte de Maurepas is in favor of the proposed expeditionary force; Congress will surely fall in with the scheme. He hopes that they may continue to be friends, and to correspond. Jones was not so naïve as not to see that the lady had used him to serve her husband, and that he had received a polite but firm brush-off.

The Comtesse de Lowendahl's commendable virtue was unfortunate for Jones. She should have been our Commodore's Lady Hamilton. She had position, wit, intelligence and beauty. He was never to have a mistress like her.

Two ladies with whom Paul Jones had innocuous friendship were Madame d'Ormoy and Madame de Saint-Julien. The former, called Madame la Présidente because her husband had been presiding magistrate of a court of justice, was the author of romantic novels such as *Les malheurs de la jeune Émilie*, and *La Laura amoureuse*. She was addicted to writing long letters and sending her manuscripts to celebrities such as Jean-Jacques Rousseau, who remarks in his *Rêveries du promeneur solitaire* that Madame la Présidente had pursued him for years, goodness knows why! As a widow in reduced circumstances with young daughters to bring out, she had to keep up with society; and her favorite method of entertaining her friends was to give parties at which ladies clothed in diaphanous white sang choruses to Madame's own words and music. Jones was taken to one of these doubtfully enjoyable affairs by M. de Monplaisir about 10 May. Madame la Présidente, delighted to have roped a new lion, invited both Jones and Franklin to sup with her, rue des Blancs

Manteaux, on the 18th, promising that "the ladies are practising some new couplets to sing to him." It can hardly be doubted that these couplets celebrated the exploits of Jones. Happily they have not been preserved; and the chorus, we gather, was composed of respectable ladies, neither young nor pretty, who did not interest the Commodore. There was no sentimental attachment here; but Jones, thinking that Madame la Présidente might be useful to him, frequented her salon, lent her his carriage when he was not using it himself, and presented her on parting with an inkstand which he hoped she would make use of to "instruct Mankind and support the Dignity and Rights of Human Nature." One feels that she would have preferred to make a more romantic and less philosophical use of it. He wrote to her no fewer than three farewell letters from French seaports, giving her a rough outline of his movements and ambitions; she in turn flattered him by mentioning his name to Frederick the Great, who was one of her unwilling correspondents.

Another acquaintance of whom Jones had a right to be proud was Madame de Saint-Julien, an intelligent, well-bred lady who watched over the aged Voltaire like a broody hen over a chick. On 17 May she writes to Jones regretting that she was not at home to receive *"son cher et brave Monsieur Paul Jones,"* and hopes that he will call again; eleven days later she sends him a sprightly note, referring to a conversation between them, in which she remarks what a pity it is that Jones cannot command words as he does action, since the two go as well together as promises and performances.

Paul Jones had two other acquaintances at this time with whom he corresponded. One was a certain Madame Tellisson (as he addresses her) of whom little is known except that she was a highly respectable lady and an acquaintance of Dr. Franklin. Jones wrote to her a sober, matter-of-fact letter from Lorient on 24 July at her request, giving an account of his "late expedition." The other was Aglaé de Hunolstein, lady-in-waiting to the Duchesse d'Orléans and a *chère amie* of Lafayette. Her correspondence with Jones seems to have been largely on business—her brother-in-law the Comte de Vauban wanted passage to America to join Rochambeau; and Jones wanted Mademoiselle's influence at court to obtain a better ship than *Ariel*.

4. Delia

The Commodore's letters to these ladies cannot by any stretch of imagination have been written by a lover to his mistress, but it was otherwise with those of "Delia." On her side at least there was passion. Née Nicolson, of a Scots family long resident in Holland, this young lady married another Scots expatriate named Count William Murray, who added his wife's maiden name to his own; she was generally called La Comtesse de Nicolson. Jones called her Delia, after a favorite song of his, written by Major André at Philadelphia, which begins:

> Return, enraptured hours
> When Delia's heart was mine.

The Murray-Nicolsons had lived abroad so long that they wrote English with difficulty, and Delia always addressed her lover in erratic French.

The first indication of this friendship is in an undated note, probably of May 1780, from M. de Charlary, evidently a secretary, inviting the Commodore to spend a day and night with the Nicolsons in their château at Sennonville, near Pontoise; if he cannot do so, they will hope to see him again in Paris. They had a *hôtel* in the Chaussée d'Antin, the newest fashionable quarter. Apparently Jones made the visit and the liaison began then and there; the Commodore and the Countess fell in love at first sight.

It was an old Spanish custom, which the French court followed, for a lover to promote the careers of his mistress's brothers, cousins and even husbands. Thus, we have a note in Frenchified English from the Count, hoping that Jones will gather a new "cargo of laurels." That is followed by one from Lieutenant-Général le Marquis de Puységur, a very important person, stating that he has heard that Jones has accepted the Countess's brother the Chevalier William Nicolson into his service, which gives him (the Marquis) great pleasure, as Nicolson has had no military command since the Scots regiments in the French Army were reorganized at the end of the last war. This letter of the Marquis was brought to Lorient by William Nicolson, who was accompanied by his sister the Comtesse; and she spent five tender and loving days with Paul Jones at a place she calls "Lherbon." Delia's spelling is very eccentric; but we can identify this place as Hennebont on the Blavet River, a discreet six miles from Lorient.

Here are a few extracts from these wildly passionate letters, all written after the rendezvous, which probably took place near the end of June or in early July, 1780. They are undated, with neither address nor signature, nor beginning nor end, so the sequence is a little problem. What appears to be the first letter runs as follows:

> Je suis dans la plus cruelle inquiétude sur votre santé, mon unique amour! . . . mon ange, mon adorable Jones! Quand serons nous rejoint pour ne plus étre séparés? . . . Ne vous faites aucun reproche sur le voyage à L——. Jamais une démarche ne m'a fait autant de plaisir. . . . Je ne compte avoir existée dans toute ma vie que les cinq jours qui ont passés, hélas, comme un songe. . . . Mon seul regret est d'avoir emmené mon frère qui non seulement a perdu son temps mais qui a dépensé beaucoup d'argent et fort mal comme il fait toujours et sans égard aux circonstances. . . . Excuse ta malheureuse Delia, pardonne sa faiblesse, songe qu'elle t'adore et qu'elle meurt si elle te perd ou si tu l'oublie. . . .
>
> Je reçois ta lettre du 18 et 19, et je vous avoue que je suis embarassée parce que je voudrais vous conseiller. . . . J'ai peu songé à ma fortune . . . je ne puis vous rendre heureux par là, ni vivre avec toi d'une manière opulante. Pour moi une cabane et mon amant je serais trop heureuse! Mais jamais je

n'exigerais de toi des sacrifices, Tu n'est pas fait pour vivre dans la retraite, et je n'oserais jamais vous le proposer. . . . Je t'aime avec idolatrie et pour toi seule. . . . Si vous êtes absolument sans fortune et que vous fussiez obligé de quitter le service par mécontentement, il faut vous rendre aussitôt en France, et compter sur mon coeur qui t'adore et qui s'empresserait par tous ce qui depend d'elle à te faire oublier les injustices des hommes. . . . Si vous voulez que je quitte Paris je serais moins riche mais j'aurais fait ce que vous désirez. . . . Je compte malgré tout sur votre probité, que jamais personne ne verrait le marques que je vous ai données d'un sentiment, hélas plus fort que moi, plus forte que ma raison. . . .*

Jones had evidently confided to her his difficulties about paying the crew; for in her next, she makes him a touching proposal:

Je n'ai jamais osé t'en parler, mais on m'a dit que l'on ne trouvait pas [de quoi] payer ton équipage. Au nom de tout l'amour dont je suis consumée, mande-moi si je puis y être utile. J'ai des diamants et effets de toutes espèces; je trouverais facilement une somme; commande ton amante c'est faire son bonheur. . . . Vingt fois, étant dans tes bras, j'ai voulu t'en parler, mais j'ai craint de te déplaire.†

---

* "I am in the most cruel uncertainty over your health, my only love! My angel, my adorable Jones! When shall we meet never to be separated? Do not reproach yourself over the journey to L——. Nothing ever gave me so much pleasure. I feel that I never lived except those five days which passed, alas, like a dream. My one regret is to have taken my brother, who not only lost his time but spent a lot of money, badly as he always does and regardless of circumstances. Excuse your wretched Delia, pardon her weakness, think that she adores you and that she dies if she loses you or if you forget her. I received your letter of the 18th and 19th, and I confess that I am embarrassed because I would like to consult you. I have little thought of my fortune. I cannot render you happy with it, nor live with you in an opulent manner; for me a cabin and my lover, and I would be too happy! But never would I exact of you sacrifices; you are not made to live in retirement, I would never dare propose it. I love you with idolatry and you only. If you are completely without fortune and were obliged to quit the service through discontent, you must immediately return to France, and count on my heart which adores you and will try by all that depends on it to make you forget the injustice of men. If you wish me to leave Paris I would be less rich but I would do what you wish. I count above all on your probity, that nobody will ever see the marks I have given you of a sentiment which, alas, is stronger than me or my reason."

† "I never dared to speak to you of this, but I have heard that you couldn't find the money to pay your people. In the name of all the love with which I am consumed, command me if I can be useful. I have diamonds and effects of various kinds; I could easily find a sum; command your mistress, it would make her happy. Twenty times in your arms I wished to speak to you of this, but I feared to displease you."

After making this generous offer, which we are glad to say Jones refused to accept, she goes on in rapture:

> À l'instant de te quitter a Lherbon, ce soir cruel ou j'ai eu te quitter . . . au moment ou tu me pressais de reçevoir l'objet dont tu a su que j'avais besoin, et dont j'aurais pu me passer; combien de fois j'ai maudit le Chevalier. Cela m'a privé de te voir au moins deux heures, ah Dieu! moi qui comptait tous les moments! . . . L'instant ou je t'ai perdu de vue, j'ai cru expirer de désespoir! . . . Je voulais terminer toutes mes souffrances! . . . Cher et trop adorable Jones . . . Dieu! je meurs de désir de te joindre pour ne plus te quitter. . . . Ciel! Jones me oublieras! il pourrait cesser de m'aimer! . . . Non, son grand coeur n'est pas capable de tant de cruauté! et je comte sur lui comme sur le ciel même! Excuse cher amant le désordre de mes écrits. . . . Tu me demande grace pour tes vers, adorable Jones! que ta modestie est cher à mon coeur. . . . Jamais mortel ne fut adoré comme tu l'est de mon coeur!*

In the third of this series, Delia complains of receiving no letter from Jones, and threatens that if she does not hear from him by Tuesday she will never write to him again. She is bringing Jones's new heraldic seal, and the sword belt that she has made for him, to Dr. Bancroft to forward to Lorient. But she does write again, pouring out her love, declaring that it is unworthy of his glory, thanking him for what he has done for her brother. And then another letter:

> Six postes et point de nouvelles . . . que dois-je penser d'une aussi cruelle oublie? Serriez-vous malade, auriez-vous cessé de

---

* "At the moment of leaving you at Hennebont, that cruel eve when I had to leave you, at the moment when you urged me to receive the object that you knew I needed and which I could have gone without; how many times I have cursed the Chevalier [her brother] who deprived me of seeing you for at least two hours. God! I who counted every moment! At the instant when I lost sight of you I thought I would die of despair! I wished to end all my sufferings! Dear and too adorable Jones, God! I die of desire to join you and never to leave you. Heavens! Jones will forget me! He could cease to love me! No, his great heart is incapable of such cruelty! And I count on him as on Heaven itself! Excuse, dear lover, the disorder of my writing. You ask pardon for your verses, adorable Jones! How dear to my heart is your modesty! Never mortal was adored as you are by my heart!"

m'aimer? Dieu! cette idée me fait frissoner! Non, je ne puis
vous croire si barbare, vous ne voudriez pas mon mort, . . .
je suis trop sensible et craintive; l'aimable et tendre J—— est
aussi fidel amant que vaillant guerrier et zélé patriote!*

Her next is the only one we can approximately date; she is writing
on "the 22nd" and has received one from him on Sunday the 20th,
so this must be August of 1780. His letter, she says, is spotted with
traces of tears, which moves her to a torrent of weeping when she
thinks of the fatal moment when they first met. If Jones is not satisfied with things in America he must return to his faithful mistress.
Her brother the Chevalier is going down to Lorient; if his sister
could only accompany him! *Elle voudrait être le dernier de vos sujets*—
"she would willingly be the lowest member of your crew." And
there is one more letter, thanking Jones for a tender one from him,
and hoping that he will leave her his portrait. That he never did.

During most of the time that he was receiving ardent letters from
Delia and assuring her of his undying love, Jones was doing his best
to make up to the Comtesse de Lowendahl.

Among his papers is the draft of an affectionate letter to Delia,
written at Portsmouth on Christmas Day 1781; but his love for her
did not survive an absence of two years. Upon his return to Paris
late in 1783 she was still there, loving and receptive, living in an
apartment on "the Boulevard," and apparently a widow. But her
"adorable Jones" did not respond; he was probably afraid that if he
did, he might have to marry her. And the last we hear of Delia is a
tender, sorrowful note in which she implores him, "O most amiable
and most ungrateful of men, come to your best friend, who burns
with the desire of seeing you. . . . Come, in the name of Heaven!"

Delia's last appearance in the records of history is an entry in the

---

* "Six posts and no news . . . what am I to think of such cruel forgetfulness; could you be sick,
would you have ceased to love me? God! This idea makes me shudder! No, I cannot think you so barbarous, you do not wish my death. I am too sensitive and fearful; the amiable and tender Jones is as faithful lover as valiant warrior and zealous patriot."

official register of *émigrés* of the French Revolution: *Comtesse de Murray et ses trois enfants, originaires de l'Escaut, et émigrés.* This surely is Delia, since she came from the region of the Scheldt. It means that she left France in time to escape being guillotined. We know nothing further about this lady, the most ardent and disinterested of Paul Jones's mistresses, who offered to give up her husband and her social position to live with Jones "in a cabin."

What with honors, friendship and amours, the beautiful month of May slipped rapidly by. We have several records of Jones in the memoirs of the time. M. Bachaumont, in his diary for 20 May, tells of a dinner given in his honor by the Maréchal Duc de Biron, at which Jones made a reputation for wit, although, says the diarist, he had to use an interpreter since he was "completely incapable" of expressing himself in French. It was on this occasion that the Commodore, upon being informed that Captain Pearson, late of H.M.S. *Serapis,* had been knighted, remarked, "Let me fight him again, M. le Maréchal, and I'll make him a lord!" And when someone asked him whether he had attended a military review and had followed the maneuvers of the French Guards Regiment, Jones replied that he would prefer to see them manuevering in St. James's Park in London instead of safely in Paris.

On 1 June the Captain received a peremptory note from Dr. Franklin, enclosing a copy of a dispatch from the Congressional Board of Admiralty. They directed that *Alliance* set sail forthwith, as Washington's army was in dire need of the weapons and clothing, and Franklin ordered the Captain to "carry the same into Execution with all possible Expedition."

So Jones departed Paris, but he did not go immediately to Lorient. Nantes awaited him; the brethren of the Masonic Lodge there, which he had doubtless frequented when commanding *Ranger,* wished to entertain him, and the ladies were not to be denied. He spent there a week of continual fête. Anecdotes of his gallantry were told; Mademoiselle de Menou, daughter of the Comte de Menou, asked him if he had ever been wounded? "Never at sea," he replied, "but I have been hit by arrows that were never discharged by the English!" The young lady thought this so charming that she presented him with a cockade, which he promised to wear in every battle.

This was over all too soon for the Commodore. Back again to Lorient he went, to encounter a sea of troubles.

XVI

"Alliance"
and
"Ariel"

June 1780-February 1781

1. Plans and Projects

Paul Jones had not passed all his time at Paris in gay dalliance. He kept pressure on Sartine to sell the prizes, and on Chaumont to release the money due. His excuse for remaining there so long was a good one, that he did not wish to face the officers and men of *Alliance* without money in hand for them. But that is what he eventually had to do.

In addition, Jones was trying to persuade Franklin, Sartine, and Vergennes, the Minister of Foreign Affairs, to accept an aggressive plan for future naval activity. He wished to repeat the *Bonhomme Richard* cruise on a larger scale, using as flagship either *Alliance* or *America*, the ship-of-the-line then being built in New Hampshire. With several French frigates under his command and a strong landing force (which Lowendahl might command if the Comtesse were kind), Jones felt he could accomplish something important. When he broached this project to Sartine, he was told that the French Navy had suffered so heavily from disease in the abortive cross-Channel operation of 1779, and had recruited so many sailors for the Chevalier de Ternay's fleet, that it could not man all its frigates. Jones then conceived the idea of sailing home in *Alliance*, obtaining the command of *America*, and returning to France with double crews to serve the French frigates which had no men. The Minister of Marine agreed in principle, doubtless expecting that Jones would get neither *America* nor the sailors.

An immediate object of the Commodore was to obtain a ship to carry the arms and uniforms for which there was no room in *Alliance*. James Moylan had written to him on 17 April that the frigate was already full, and four hundred chests of arms were awaiting shipment. Moylan owned brig *Luke*, which he was ready to charter for that purpose; but Dr. Franklin then had no money to pay freight, so Jones had to seek the unsatisfactory substitute of a naval vessel. Sartine, on 3 June, assured Franklin that he had given the necessary orders; and that is how Jones obtained corvette *Ariel*. In the end, *Luke* and a second merchant vessel had to be procured, and even they could not get all the supplies across.

Many people had ideas about what Jones should do next. Franklin hoped to work off on him the fleet of American privateers which he had been persuaded to organize in French ports, and which gave the American minister infinite trouble and vexation; but the very word "privateer" was a red rag to Jones. And an unknown well-wisher drew up a fantastic plan for him to capture the island of St. Helena.

One of the first operations suggested by Paul Jones, after the New Providence expedition, had been to take St. Helena. That remote island, now associated with Napoleon's exile, had strategic value as a port of call and replenishment for the British East Indiamen. In Allied possession it would have been an excellent base for privateering against these ships, from whose cargoes Britain derived a substantial part of her financial strength.

In 1780, when Jones was in Paris, one of his French admirers had the same thought. To the Foreign Minister he delivered an outline plan for Jones to capture St. Helena by stealth, a project so comic and wildly impractical that Vergennes placed it in his archives to amuse posterity.

Under command of *"l'intrépide et intelligent Paul Jones,"* a squadron of five ships with 1500 troops on board is to be assembled. Instead of sending them directly to St. Helena, they are to call at Boston to recruit twenty-five youths between sixteen and eighteen years old, less than five feet tall, *sveltes et nerveux,* to be disguised as women. *Le sang est beau à la Nouvelle Angelterre,* declares this ingenious naval planner; *on y trouvera aisement de jolis visages, des cheveux, du teint de la peau.* These lads with the rosy cheeks, blond hair and pretty features will be disguised as English officers' wives and daughters returning from the East Indies, in bright cotton prints, big straw hats, crêpe de chine, Cashmere shawls and crimson parasols. To complete the deception, some New England Negroes should be enrolled and disguised in robes and turbans to pass as dark-skinned Moslem servants.

The squadron will proceed directly from Boston to St. Helena. It will anchor in the roadstead, flying the British flag, with all soldiers and most of the sailors below decks. When the port officer's boat comes out, an American with a convincing English accent should cry out, "Don't board us, sir; we are infected with a terrible epidemic. All our soldiers are down with it. Strangely enough, it has not affected our ladies or their oriental servants. So we crave your permission to send both ladies and blacks ashore to set up a hospital tent where our poor fellows may be nursed back to health." The "ladies" during this colloquy will be much in evidence, and ply the English boat's crew with liquor. If the port officer is slow to be convinced, some asafetida, saffron and other pungent disinfectants should be lighted below to raise a nasty stink and suggest the presence of foul disease.

When the English port officer accedes to these pleas of humanity, as it is assumed he will, the "ladies," with loaded pistols and hand grenades concealed under their skirts, will enter the English boat.

While they are being rowed ashore, boats will be lowered from the French ships, supposedly to take ashore sick soldiers but really for the landing force. If the English on the beach become suspicious, the "ladies" will cover them with pistols and toss out a few hand grenades to hold the beachhead, as it were, until the landing force can touch down. As it does so, the Commodore, in the leading boat, will cry out in a loud voice:

"I am Paul Jones and you are prisoners of your Anglo-American brothers!"

At the dread name of Jones, the English soldiers are expected to drop all weapons and throw up their hands; and the twenty-five pretty Yankee boys in disguise, with their black squires, will enter the fort, confront the Governor in his audience chamber, and receive his surrender.

"Thus, St. Helena will be conquered without shedding a drop of blood!"

Jones probably never heard of this unconscious tribute to his reputation. He was destined never to have so easy a conquest.

2. Lee and Landais Score

At Lorient, where he arrived about 9 June 1780, Jones found a sad state of affairs on board *Alliance*. Captain Landais, after failing to persuade Franklin to reinstate him in command ("If, therefore, I had 20 ships of war at my disposition, I should not give one of them to Captain Landais" wrote Franklin), had obtained passage money to return to the United States and face a court-martial. To Lorient he had come, apparently to take passage in *Luzerne*, a privateer belonging to Robert Morris. But there he met Arthur Lee, who sold him a much better plan—to regain command of *Alliance* by argument and stealth.

Lee drew up a document which would have been a credit to any forecastle sea-lawyer, asserting that Landais, by his Congressional commission, was still the rightful captain of *Alliance* and that neither Jones nor Franklin had the authority to deprive him of it. Lee's object was to discredit Franklin and Jones, both of whom he hated. As a sample of the slant of Lee's mind, he wrote to James Warren, one of the New England members of his faction, "It is perpetually Dr. Franklin's practice to employ his wicked tools . . . to accuse others of the crimes of which he is guilty." To Lee's diseased brain, Jones was not a distinguished American officer but one of these "tools." And, to justify his faith in Landais, Lee wished to afford him another chance to prove himself the naval Lafayette.

Another troublemaker in port was "Commodore" Gillon of the South Carolina Navy. Having obtained control of *L'Indien*, Gillon now wanted sailors, hoped to snake away discontented members of *Alliance's* crew, and did.

Lee and Landais profited by Jones's absence in Paris to work on the *Alliance* people. By the evidence of the logbook, they had completed most of the repairs and improvements by early May and had nothing to do but paint, stow sea stores, "cleaning Ship and other Sundry Jobbs." And, of course, to brood over their wrongs. Some word of Jones's gay doings in Paris must have reached them and aroused their envy and resentment. While the Commodore was making love to countesses and sleeping with scented courtesans, they hadn't enough money to buy a drink or command the services of such poor trollops as a seaport provided for enlisted men. They saw *Serapis* being dismantled instead of sold. The word got around that Jones and Chaumont were in cahoots to rob poor Jack of his due; and when Landais appeared, promising with Lee's support to get them their pay and prize money, they flocked to his standard. In addition, they knew that under Jones's command there would be more fighting and slaughter, whilst under Landais in a fast ship they had every expectation, judging from his past performances, of getting home without a scratch. The original *Alliance* crew, most of whom were still on board, were home-town boys from the Merrimack Valley of the same breed as those who had manned *Ranger*. The *Bon-*

homme Richard survivors on board, who despised them, messed apart and had as little to do with them as possible.

Things had gone so far by 29 May, the day that Jones was saying a tender farewell to the Comtesse de Lowendahl at Versailles, that Landais was able to send to Franklin a mutinous document which he had written himself, and to which he had procured signatures from 115 officers and men of the *Alliance* crew. They declared that they would not sail from Lorient until they had six months' wages paid on the nail, all their prize money, including that for the ships sent into Bergen, and "until their legal captain, P. Landais, was restored to them." Fourteen officers of *Alliance*, including those who had earlier deposed that Landais had fired more on *Richard* than on the enemy, now signed a statement belying themselves, representing that the conduct of their captain in the battle had been beyond reproach. In answer to this document, Franklin sent a letter to the crew advising them to do their duty under Captain Jones, and warning them that if they did otherwise, people would say that the real reason was "that Captain Jones loved close fighting," whilst "Captain Landais was skilful in keeping out of harm's way." He advised Landais not to meddle with the command, and wrote to Jones, who had left Paris before the 29 May letter arrived, telling him about it and adding, "You are likely to have great trouble. I wish you well through it."

Jones, upon arriving at Lorient, should have boarded *Alliance* and stayed on board. Instead, he lodged ashore—probably this was the period of Delia's five-day visit—and by his own account went on board only once. He addressed the officers and men, told them the true state of affairs about prize money and pay, and invited complaints. Nobody spoke up, and the Captain went ashore convinced that they were satisfied. A day or two later, on 12 or 13 June, Landais pulled off the coup that he and Lee had planned. According to the *Alliance* logbook, "Capt. Landy came on board, and took command, he said by Order of Congress, his Orders were read to the Officers & People. Capt. Landy Ordered all the Officers that belonged to the Late *Bon Homme Richard*, Capt. Jones, on Shore, and any other Officers that would not Acknowledge him Capt. of the *Alliance*. Capt. Jones' Officers came on Shore. Capt. Jones set out for Paris.''

That is just what Captain Jones did. As Lieutenant Mackenzie remarked, he should have gone on board at once and regained possession of his ship. ''From the relative conduct of the two ships in battle, we cannot but think that Landais would have quailed before his eye. If he ventured on personal violence, Jones, being in the right, would not have been blamed for the consequences.'' But, instead of bearding the false Frenchman on his own quarterdeck, Jones bustled off to Paris to seek fresh authority from Franklin and Sartine.

Both he obtained; but both were successfully defied by Landais and Arthur Lee, whose traveling carriage and baggage had now been stowed in the hold, with Landais's connivance, while supplies badly wanted by Washington's Army were left on the beach.

Jones did not return from Paris until 20 June. He found that, a few hours before his arrival, *Alliance* had been warped from Lorient harbor to nearby Port Louis. To get out to sea, she would have to pass through a narrow strait enclosed by rocks and commanded by French batteries. In answer to a written plea from Jones before his return, to his friend Thévenard, Captain of the Port, the French military and naval authorities of that district caused a boom to be moved across *Alliance's* only possible exit, and issued orders to the commander of the Port Louis citadel, and of two forts, to fire on the frigate if she attempted to pass. Similar orders were given to three French warships then in port, and their armed boats were readied to board the American frigate with a hundred French marines. A French gunboat, armed with 3 twenty-four-pounders and manned by 65 men, stood by the boom to protect it from being cut.

At this juncture, to the astonishment of his French friends and the relief of Lee, Landais and company, Commodore Jones gave up. He interceded with the French authorities to have their orders to fire upon *Alliance* reversed, and the boom removed. Jones's explanation and excuse, as he wrote to Franklin, was the danger of the loss of life and of a fine frigate, and of making bad blood between allies, to the profit of their common enemy. "Had I remained silent an hour longer the dreadful work would have been done," he wrote to the Doctor. "Your Humanity will I know Justify the part I acted in preventing a scene that would have rendered me miserable for the rest of my life."

A very unconvincing statement. There need have been no "dreadful work." The most intrepid of commanders, which Landais certainly was not, with a battle-hardened crew, which his could hardly be called, would never have risked running such a murderous gantlet as had been set up to stop *Alliance*. A couple of shots from the gunboat guarding the boom would have been enough to check Landais, and in that narrow harbor means could have been found to arrest him and put him en route to the Bastille, a warrant to that effect having been issued by Sartine in the King's name.

The conclusion is inescapable that Jones was not particularly eager to regain command of *Alliance*. He had to pretend that he was, of course; but actually he felt well rid of her, and of Landais too. As evidence of what was on his mind, in his next letter to Franklin reporting the affront to his and the Doctor's authority, he urged him to borrow *Serapis* (which the King had just purchased) and let her be fitted out as a transport to take the rest of the military stores, which Lee and Landais had left on the beach, to America, escorted by *Ariel* under Jones's command. In America *Serapis* could be refitted as an amphibious command ship of the expeditionary force that he hoped to organize.

Nor was he altogether candid about events at Lorient. To Robert Morris, now his principal friend in Congress, Jones wrote on 27 June, "My humanity would not suffer me to remain a silent witness of Bloodshed between Allied Subjects of France and America," and that Arthur Lee's actions were prompted by hatred of "the Venerable the Wise and Good Franklin," who is universally esteemed in Europe. "Envy itself is Dumb when the Name of Franklin is but mentioned." Yet on the same day Jones wrote, partly in cipher, to Dr. Bancroft, Franklin's secretary, that the officers of the port "acted rather like Women than Men"; that he suspects "a secret understanding between them and Lee"; and added, "If 299 [Franklin] sits still in this matter I shall pronounce him and 868 [Bancroft] philosophers indeed! I am no Philosopher here but am stung to the core to find that my honest endeavours are not supported."

Franklin's reply to Jones's demand for *Serapis* showed a remarkable degree of irritation for so calm a philosopher: "I am perfectly bewildered," he said, "by the different schemes to get the goods across. Now you have *Ariel*, for Heaven's sake load her as heavily as she can bear, and sail! I will see to moving the rest." And on 5 July, after receiving Jones's dispatches and reading the impudent letter to Bancroft, the Doctor wrote his cool, calm letter of reproof to the Commodore.

> If you had stayed on board where your duty lay, instead of coming to Paris, you would not have lost your ship. Now you blame them [the port officers] as having deserted you in recovering her; though relinquishing to prevent mischief was a voluntary act of your own, for which you have credit; hereafter, if you should observe an occasion to give your officers and friends a little more praise than is their due, and confess more fault than you can justly be charged with, you will only become the sooner for it, a great captain. Criticizing and censuring almost every one you have to do with, will diminish friends, increase enemies, and thereby hurt your affairs.

One can only explain the Commodore's actions at this juncture by the supposition that he was unstrung by having to manage Landais and the ladies simultaneously, and that he was torn between his immediate humdrum duty and his ardent desire to command an important amphibious operation.

As soon as the officers of the port removed the boom, Landais warped *Alliance* through the narrow strait into Groix roadstead, out of cannon shot from shore. *Alliance* loaded no other cargo but 76 chests of small arms and 216 barrels of powder, "all of which I don't know who they are to belong to," as Landais described them in his report to the Board of Admiralty. But she had as ballast the battery especially cast in Angoulême for *Bonhomme Richard,* which arrived too late for Jones's cruise. It was a joke on Lee that Landais threw Lee's seagoing carriage ashore to accommodate this much; but the great exponent of republican virtue did manage to get 550 guineas' worth of his own goods on board.

Landais was now confronted with the same difficulty that Jones had had—the crew of *Alliance* refused to weigh anchor until they were paid. But he was able to surmount this with the aid of Schweighauser, the Continental agent at Lorient who was Arthur Lee's man. Schweighauser advanced to Landais 31,688 livres 12s 3d (about $6334) for "supplies"—namely, for money to pay and placate the crew.

Franklin refused to honor this bill. Schweighauser attempted to get even by clapping a lien on the supplies that had not been shipped by the end of 1780; but that did not do him much good. During the French Revolution, the government seized all the arms, paying only ten livres apiece for 818 muskets in good order, and other military stores in proportion. Schweighauser's heirs, after running up a bill of about $12,500 for storage and interest, tried to recover the whole from the United States Government in 1807, but failed.

Paul Jones, too, had an expense account of posting to and from Paris since his arrival in *Ranger* in 1777, and for living expenses while in Paris "on the public business." It amounted to the goodly sum of $4249.23, which was paid by Congress two years later.

The passage of *Alliance* from Brittany to America was one of the maddest crossings of the Atlantic ever made. Landais was incapable of keeping discipline. He quarreled with officers, seamen, Marines and passengers. Captain Parke USMC, who (to the great grief of Paul Jones) had thrown in his lot with Landais, was put in the brig first day out for refusing to take an oath to obey the Captain no matter what happened. Survivors of *Bonhomme Richard* who refused to obey the usurped captain were clapped into irons and thrown into the hold with the rats and the ballast. On one occasion when the frigate's sails were filling to a fair breeze for America, Landais suddenly ordered them furled, and then set and trimmed for the wrong course. There were violent quarrels about fishing on the Grand Bank and about killing livestock which had been put on board for the passengers' use. No less a person than the Honorable Arthur Lee, who complained of the drinking water, was told he could drink from the common scuttlebutt like the sailors; and Landais threatened him with a carving knife for helping himself first to roast pig at the wardroom table. Finally, on 11 August, the officers and passengers, led by Lee, banded together and forced Landais, who was sulking in his cabin, to give over the command to Lieutenant Degge, who had earlier been placed under arrest. Degge, let out of the brig, took *Alliance* into Boston, not Philadelphia where Congress wanted her, on 19 August 1780.

Upon receipt of Landais's incoherent report of the voyage—"I cannot even trust my clerk who weep and cry. . . . Never before was such things seen or heard of," etc.—the local Navy Board ordered Captain John Barry to relieve Landais. The Frenchman refused to resign, and three stout Marines had to drag him, fighting and screaming, out of his cabin and ashore. At the court-martial even Arthur Lee testified that in his opinion Landais was insane. The Court found that Landais had no right to resume command of *Alliance* without Franklin's permission, that he was guilty of allowing private goods to be shipped in place of public stores, that he had proved to be incapable of handling a ship, and should be dismissed from further service in the United States Navy. Congress acted accordingly.

Landais wrote and had printed in Boston a feeble and incoherent defense of his actions, but he was now deserted by all his partisans except Samuel Adams. That politician, in a letter to Richard Henry Lee who also had "patronized" Landais "when he first came into this Country," represented the Frenchman to be a martyr to Republican Virtue, victim of "a Faction on the other side of the Atlantick," and urged Congress to vote back pay and prize money to him, instead of to "this Jones" or to others who had done their duty.

After hanging around New York and Philadelphia for several years in the hope of getting money from Congress, Landais returned to France and received a flag command in the Navy of the Republic. Retired by old age in 1793, he came back to New York. Through importunity, and with the support of a surviving member of the Adams-Lee faction, Congressman Joseph B. Varnum, he obtained in 1810 a grant of four thousand dollars for the prize money he might have had from *Union* and *Betsey* if Denmark had not interfered! With this, Landais was far from satisfied; but it enabled him to purchase a small annuity on which he lived in proud and solitary poverty. According to a tablet that he had previously provided for St. Patrick's Cathedral, New York, he "disappeared, June 1818, age 87."

3. In Command of "Ariel"

Ariel was a 435-ton sloop of war built for the British Navy in 1777 and captured off the Carolinas by the French frigate *Amazone*. The French Navy lent her to Franklin in order to help him get the goods across. When Captain Jones lost *Alliance* to Landais, *Ariel* had already arrived at Lorient. Franklin hoped that he would lade her promptly and depart. But she did not leave for four months. *Bonhomme Richard* survivors, whom Landais had released or expelled at Lorient, formed the nucleus of *Ariel's* crew. Lieutenant Lunt and Master Stacey managed to get their effects off *Alliance* to serve in the corvette, and on 20 June, "Capt. Jones arrived from Paris," according to the log, assumed command, and began rerigging as usual. The rest of the crew was made up partly by Americans whom Jones hired, "Commodore" Gillon shanghaied, and the French police recovered. He also enlisted some English prisoners taken by the French, and was given a guard of French Marines.

Jonathan Williams, Franklin's nephew and Jones's friend, advised

Jones on 10 July that, owing to the depreciation of Continental currency, there was no hope "of joining any Ship to the *Ariel*" and that he had better make best speed to America—might even beat *Alliance*. But that could not be done. In order to accommodate even a part of the military supplies awaiting shipment, which amounted to 11,000 muskets, uniforms for 10,000 men, 120 bales of cloth and 800 barrels of powder, adding up to 300 tons' volume, *Ariel* had to be rerigged and rearmed *en flute*. This meant radically reducing both armament and crew in order to make room for cargo. *Ariel* as a warship had a battery of 26 nine-pounders and a crew of 120 to 150 officers and men. She was now reduced to 16 nine-pounders and a crew of 60 to 80, and carried provisions for only two months; yet, even so altered, she could carry only 200 tons of cargo. France furnished everything except the ship's stores and the payroll. Jones finally induced Franklin to charter two merchant brigs, *Luke* and *Duke of Leinster,* to help; but even they were unable to carry the balance of the supplies.

On 18 July *Ariel* began to load. Toward the close of the month, supposing her to be ready for sea, Franklin forwarded his dispatches for Congress by the Comte de Vauban who was to take passage in her. The logbook notes consistently fine weather. "People Employed about the Nettings for the Waist and other Necessary Jobbs," cleaning ship and taking on stores and spare parts.

August passed away, but no departure. Jones attributed the delay to contrary winds, but the logbook indicates that the wind was from the east a good part of the time. Probably the real reason was to await the loading of the two brigs which *Ariel* was to escort. But Jones was not sorry for the delay because he did not wish to leave France until the combined amphibious operation that he craved to command had been set up. His letters of 2 August to the Comte de Vergennes, Minister of Foreign Affairs, and Comte de Maurepas, the Prime Minister, prove that this was very much on his mind. He outlines possible attacks on England's home coasts and colonies and on her Baltic trade. On 9 August he writes to his friend Genet that *Ariel* is nearly ready to sail, but will not depart until he knows upon what bankers in Paris to draw, when she arrives in America, for the prize money that Chaumont is still holding back. And, "I am Uneasy at not hearing from my fair Friend Lady Lowendahl." The Comtesse was through with him; but Delia sent him on 22 August the farewell letter in which she wished she could embark as a member of his crew.

By 25 August *Ariel* was ready for sea, but still she tarried in Lorient. The crew were employed on 1 September, according to the logbook, in rigging the quarterdeck for a "Grand Entertainment," and 16 cases of wine were received on board. Next evening the festival took place—"Fired Salute, Exercised Great Guns and small arms," says the log. This laconic note is followed by one more interesting: "The Capt. Kicked Mr. Fanning, Midshipman, and Ordered him below." Fanning got his revenge in his *Narrative* of 1806,* by describing this entertainment as an extravagant affair, with silk awnings, "indecent" French paintings, hired plate worth twenty-two hundred pounds, a dinner of several courses prepared by a French chef, a lavish outlay of wines, and a French lady "gallanted on board by Captain Jones the evening before" to superintend the feast and the decorations. A prince of the royal house and three admirals, according to Fanning, "with more ladies of the first quality," were among the guests and the dinner lasted from 3:30 until sunset. Then the fireworks and gunfire commenced and went on until the ladies cried, "Enough!" At midnight all guests were set ashore, and the ship's officers saw everyone safely home. Fanning does not tell us at what point in the festivities he was kicked in the pants by Jones; and, in my opinion, these sumptuous details are all products of the outraged midshipman's imagination.

More credible are the stories he tells about Jones's shore activities in Lorient. James Moylan, who did a good deal of business for Congress at that port, was a rude, ugly man of about sixty, with a pretty

---

* Fanning tells several fantastic and incredible stories about Jones, one representing him as raving and screaming over Landais's action; the other, abusing a Marine officer named Sullivan both aboard and ashore. Since this Sullivan was a nephew of General John Sullivan, who remained on the most friendly terms with Jones, and as the fracas is mentioned by no other contemporary, I have no hesitation in rejecting these stories as untrue.

wife of about seventeen. Jones flirted with her, and they had been surprised "in a very loving position" by the husband without finding the opportunity that they craved. Accordingly, one day when Jones was going ashore and knew that Moylan would board *Ariel* to do business with the purser, he gave orders that after Moylan arrived no boat should leave the ship until he, the Captain, returned. About 8:00 P.M. the jealous husband began to feel uneasy and asked to be set ashore, but the officer of the deck obeyed his Captain's orders and the other officers so plied him with wine that he had to be put to bed on board, "drunk as a beast." Thus Jones was able to spend an undisturbed night with Madame.

Fanning tells with great gusto of the trick that he and two other midshipmen played on the Captain at Lorient. Jones took "a lady of pleasure" to the theater and retired with her during the entr'acte to a house of assignation, where he forgot his gold watch. A midshipman later assigned to the same room recognized and retrieved the watch; and then, in conjunction with two other young scamps, pawned it at a coffeehouse for a dozen of the best old claret and returned the pawn ticket anonymously to their commanding officer.

Ariel departed Lorient 5 September and anchored in Groix Roads. There she stayed for over a month; largely, it would seem, because of a succession of westerly and northerly gales. Every ship seems to have been hung up in that roadstead after leaving the Breton port. On Saturday 7 October she put to sea in "fine pleasant weather," wind NNW, in company with brigs *Luke* and *Duke of Leinster*, laden with military stores. Jones would have done better to have left earlier or delayed a little longer, but there was no official weather forecast in those days.

On the 8th, before *Ariel* was clear of the coast, the wind chopped around to the WSW, backing to S by W, and blew great guns. Never before, wrote Jones after it was all over, did he "fully conceive the awful Majesty of Tempest & of ship Wreak. . . . The tremendous scene that Nature then presented . . . surpassed the reach even of Poetic fancy and the pencil." Great seas tossed and roared on the granite coast of Brittany; the myriad off-shore reefs were boiling;

lashing rain blotted out the land. *Ariel* double-reefed her topsails, sent down her topgallant yards and struck topgallant masts, then furled both topsails and jibs and housed the guns. With his ship under reefed lower courses, and on the port tack, Jones made every effort to weather the Penmarch peninsula. But when she was about three miles off the Penmarch rocks, one of the worst dangers to navigation on that coast, the gale blew with such violence that the reefed mainsail and crojick had to be taken in, leaving her under a double-reefed foresail only. It was now too dark to see the land, but the lead line showed that the water was rapidly shoaling. Jones wore ship to course SSE, hoping this would enable her to claw off the coast; but the wind, being now SW by W, kept pressing her toward the rocks. To add to the danger, she leaked badly and one of the chain pumps became choked. In this distress (states the log), at 11:30 P.M. October 9, "the ship making much Water, . . . Handed the Fore Sail, finding the Ship would not right let go the Lee Anchor in 30 fathom." The ship, deep in the water by reason of her heavy lading, was fairly smothered by the high seas and laid over on her beam ends, the lee fore yardarm frequently dipping under water.

Even the best bower anchor, with two spare cables bent on and paid out, did not bring her head to wind. So, at 2:00 A.M. October 10, Jones ordered the foremast cut away; and as the step of the mainmast had twisted off in the violent motion of the ship, causing it to reel about dangerously, he ordered the mainmast, too, to be sacrificed. Before the men could get at the weather shrouds with their axes, the chain plates that held the lee shrouds gave way and the heavy mast fell over the weather bulwarks, carrying the mizzenmast and a quarter gallery with it. *Ariel*, completely dismasted, now came head to wind.

In that position, to windward of a reef upon which, had she struck, all hands would have perished, *Ariel* rode for two days and nights, while the pumps were constantly manned. "Chips" on the 11th rigged a pair of shears with which the men stepped a jury mizzenmast and crossed one yard. When the wind began to moderate at midnight the cable was cut, and *Ariel* under jury rig sailed back to

Groix with a fair wind. She made it at 10:00 A.M. on the 12th, obtained a pilot and proceeded to Lorient.

There the French volunteers in the crew, who according to Fanning had behaved badly during the crisis, drafted a petition to the Minister of Marine. Captain Jones, they say, "has deceived us, and that in the most horrible manner." He took advantage of their having anchored in Groix roadstead, and wanting spending money ashore, to make them sign on "for the duration" in return for two months' wages. They now want Sartine to release them "from slavery to the government of a nation which shows no consideration for Frenchmen except when it has absolute need of their help." They got no satisfaction.

Ariel was in a sad plight, but everyone was astounded that she had survived. The entire Breton coast was strewn with wrecks and the bodies of drowned men; even in landlocked harbors vessels had dragged ashore. To save his ship under these circumstances proved that Jones was a consummate seaman, and that he kept a cool head in face of danger. Thévenard, captain of the port of Lorient, wrote to the Minister of Marine: "The Commodore showed in this gale the same strength that he had exhibited in battle. . . . The crew and passengers all credit him with saving the ship." Even Fanning praises his captain's presence of mind and skill in escaping the "Pin Marks," as he calls the Penmarch rocks. Jones had observed one of the first principles for safety at sea, one of which Admiral Nimitz reminded the Pacific Fleet of—in 1945—"the time for taking all measures for a ship's safety is while you are still able to do so."

Unfortunately, the damage sustained in the gale required another postponement, for over two months as it turned out, of *Ariel's* departure. Jones did his best to get away earlier in a better ship, the French frigate *Terpsichore*. He resumed writing letters, not only to the ladies but to anyone who could or might help him. The Comte de Vauban, a passenger in *Ariel* during the great gale, went to Paris at Jones's request to use his friendship with Monseigneur le Duc d'Orléans to procure the French frigate; but Vauban found Monseigneur to be absent from Paris and out of favor at Versailles. Silas

Deane (now back in France) and the Maréchal de Castries, the new Navy Minister, were importuned; even the Chevalier Nicolson, whom Jones had made Captain of Marines in *Ariel*, worked on the problem, but Nicolson wrote that if Jones wanted the frigate he had better come to Paris himself. Jones had learned the lesson not to leave his ship, and he never came within a cable's length of substituting *Terpsichore* for *Ariel*.

On 12 December he wrote the last of three farewell letters to Madame la Présidente d'Ormoy, stating that *Ariel* would sail as soon as a messenger arrived from Paris with dispatches. And she actually did sail on the 18th. Almost seven months had elapsed since Franklin had urged Jones to depart at once. Brig *Luke*, a faster and handier vessel than *Ariel*, got clear of the coast before the gale struck in, returned to Lorient, sailed unescorted and was captured by the British. The Board of Admiralty in Philadelphia reported that this was the fault of the brig's owner, Moylan, who without cause refused to await *Ariel's* final sailing.

Because *Ariel* was armed *en flute*, laden largely with gunpowder and carrying important dispatches from the French government and from Franklin, Captain Jones had no desire to fight his way across. With a view to avoiding unwelcome contacts, he took the southern route along the northern edge of the tradewinds. At lat. 26° N, long. 60° W, a few hundred miles northeast of the West Indies, a large sail was sighted. The stranger, which Jones guessed to be British, gave chase. Jones tried to escape under cover of night, but the ship was on top of him the next morning. Since it was evident from the Englishman's superior speed that *Ariel* could not flee but must fight, Jones prepared one of his best stratagems. He cleared *Ariel* for action but kept her gun ports closed and the French Marines below decks, and showed British colors so that she could pass as a corvette of the Royal Navy (which she had been originally), and work up to a position for close action.

When the strange ship ranged up on *Ariel's* beam and to leeward, Captain Jones adopted the authoritative manner of an officer of the Royal Navy and bluffed the captain into giving an account of himself and his ship. His name, he said, was John Pindar; and his ship, the *Triumph,* British privateer of 20 guns, four more than *Ariel's.* She had originally been an American privateer owned by Nathaniel Tracy of Newburyport and commanded by a son of Commodore Hopkins. She had been captured, carried into New York and fitted out under the Red Ensign by an association of local Loyalists.* Jones even tried to persuade the captain to come on board *Ariel* with his papers to prove the truth of his statements; but at that Pindar demurred. Jones gave him five minutes to change his mind, then raised American colors, opened his ports, wore ship across *Triumph's* stern, and engaged at pistol range, continuing the action on the Englishman's lee beam. Captain Pindar, taken by surprise, made but a feeble resistance and after ten minutes' sharp work by *Ariel's* gunners struck his colors and called for quarter. Jones then ceased fire and his crew gave three cheers. While they were preparing to lower a boat to board, Pindar cleverly worked his ship to a position on *Ariel's* weather bow, then suddenly clapped on sail and forged ahead. Jones pursued in vain; the prospective prize got away. He considered this ruse to be base and cowardly; but considering that he had masqueraded as friendly up to the moment of opening fire, it is difficult to see why Pindar should not have pulled another ruse out of a seaman's bag of tricks.

This was Paul Jones's last battle under the American flag. It is much to his credit; because if he had not worked up to close range and obtained surprise his ship would probably have succumbed to superior force and speed.

Shortly after this action with *Triumph,* Captain Jones discovered a plot among the English volunteers in *Ariel's* crew to get possession of the ship. Twenty incipient mutineers were placed in irons under Marine guard, and there was no further trouble. And on 18 February 1781, three and a quarter years since Paul Jones had left his adopted country in *Ranger,* he brought *Ariel* to anchor in the harbor of Philadelphia.

* We can now identify her as the former Massachusetts privateer *Tracy,* John B. Hopkins commanding, of 200 tons, 16 six-pounders, which had been captured off Bermuda by H.M.S. *Intrepid* and *Cyclops* the previous September.

XVII

"America" Gained and Lost

February 1781-November 1783

1. Triumphant Homecoming

It was lucky for Paul Jones that *Alliance* preceded him to America and that the findings in the court-martial of Landais were in the hands of Congress before *Ariel's* arrival. The report of that mad voyage, coming from John Barry, the most popular captain in the Navy, took all the wind out of the sails of Arthur Lee and Sam Adams. These gentlemen had intended to make an issue of the delay in sending over munitions and uniforms. On 19 February 1781, the day after *Ariel* dropped anchor in the harbor of Philadelphia, Thomas Bee of South Carolina moved and James Varnum of Rhode Island seconded a motion to summon Captain Jones to Congress for a public investigation. After a debate, Samuel Adams moved to postpone further consideration of the motion, and it was dropped. Sam, a consummate politician, obviously did not care to have the doings of his friends Lee and Landais given further publicity, especially from a sharp-tongued witness such as Paul Jones. For the public hearing there was substituted an order to the Board of Admiralty to examine Captain Jones privately. Accordingly, John Brown, secretary of the Board and an old friend of the Captain's, gave him a series of forty-seven queries to which he was asked to reply in writing.

Jones had been careful to bring with him letters of commendation from Franklin, from the two Ministers of Marine and from Lafayette, as well as the sword presented to him by the King and the royal request to Congress for permission to bestow on him l'Ordre du Mérite Militaire. The cross and ribbon of that order were already in the hands of the Chevalier de la Luzerne, His Most Christian Majesty's minister plenipotentiary to the United States. Jones promptly presented to Congress this evidence of the great esteem in which he was held in France, and Congress was so favorably impressed that on 27 February, without even waiting for Jones's written answers to the queries, it passed a resolve complimentary to him. It entertained "a high sense of the distinguished bravery and military conduct of John Paul Jones, esq. captain in the navy of the United States, particularly in his victory" off Flamborough Head, "which was attended with circumstances so brilliant as to excite general applause and admiration." Dr. Franklin, furthermore, will "communicate to his Most Christian Majesty their high satisfaction" at Captain Jones's having "merited the attention and approbation" of the King, whose "offer of adorning Captain Jones with the cross of military merit, is highly acceptable to Congress."

Paul Jones in his *Mémoire* of 1786 to Louis XVI asserted that Congress deliberately postponed ratification of the Articles of Confederation in order to authorize him to wear the French decoration. It is true that the Articles of Confederation forbade "any person holding any office . . . under the United States" to "accept of any present, emolument, office or title of any kind whatever from any King, prince, or foreign state." But Jones obtained his authorization on 27 February, two days before the Maryland members of Congress ratified the Articles on behalf of their State. Congress then confirmed the ratification and put the Articles of Confederation into force, an event immediately announced by the ringing of bells and the booming of cannon. "*Ariel* frigate, commanded by the gallant Paul Jones," discharged a "feu-de-joye" and dressed ship with flags, pendants and streamers; the President of Congress held a reception, and "the evening was ushered in by an elegant exhibition of fireworks."

A few days later, at a reception to the members of Congress and the principal citizens of Philadelphia, the Chevalier de la Luzerne invested Captain Jones with l'Ordre du Mérite Militaire and himself attached the ribbon and cross to the left lapel of the Captain's uniform coat. Paul Jones was very proud of this distinction, as he had a right to be; he liked to be addressed as the "Chevalier" and even at times signed himself "Chevalier Paul Jones." Military medals and orders were uncommon in that era; Congress created only one, the Purple Heart, and that not until 1782. No other officer in the American armed services except Jones won the Mérite Militaire. General de Kalb had it, but for services in the French Army before the war.

Paul Jones displays this order in the portrait that Charles Willson Peale painted in 1781, and which now belongs to Independence Hall, Philadelphia. The Chevalier is wearing a blue uniform coat with red lapels, a buff waistcoat, a large white braided hat and a cockade with a dash of color in it. The eyes are hazel and such hair as shows under the hat is light brown, turning gray. Richard Dale in 1825 called this an "excellent likeness"; but Thomas Jefferson, who saw much of Jones in his later years, declared it a very bad likeness indeed. The portrait certainly looks like that of a different person from the one depicted by Houdon and Moreau.

On 21 March the Chevalier Jones presented his answers to the forty-seven questions of the Board of Admiralty. Although supported by numerous copies of letters and other documents which impressed the Board, Jones's replies were not altogether candid. The queries were framed in such a way ("When did you sail from Portsmouth . . . What prizes did you take when you commanded *Ranger?*")

as to give him the opportunity, to which he rose with all his art of forceful narration, to write a detailed history of his exploits in British waters. Everything that went wrong was attributed to Chaumont or Landais. A few teasing questions, evidently inspired by the Lee faction, Jones cleverly evaded. He was asked, for instance (Query 34) why *Alliance* did not avail herself of the security of Admiral de Ternay's convoy which departed Brest in May 1780. Jones's absence in Paris was the real reason; but he merely answered that "the reasons already assigned" would explain; and no reasons were earlier assigned except the need to rerig *Alliance* and settle the prize money.

Jones showed himself very cagey in answering Query 35, as to "what induced" Landais to sail contrary to Franklin's orders, what passengers did he take, and what private property? He replied, "Mr. Lee and the rest of his council can best answer why he sailed contrary to *my* orders, as well as the orders of Mr. Franklin." He gave the names of the passengers, starting with "Mr. Lee and his two nephews," but refused to answer as to the private property on board *Alliance*. For he knew that Congress already knew all about it, owing to a complete ventilation in the Landais court-martial. With Query 46, "Did any private property come in the *Ariel?*" Jones had a little fun. His answer was, "Eight or ten small trunks and boxes" containing presents to congressmen, or purchases that he had made at their request.

Most of the munitions did arrive in Philadelphia in time for the Yorktown campaign of 1781. There was some disappointment because *Ariel* brought no clothing, but she did bring 437 barrels of gunpowder, 146 chests of arms and a quantity of shot, sheet-lead and medicine, which was a good lading for a vessel of her burthen. So nobody was now disposed to help Arthur Lee beat the drum of "jobbery" and "corruption."

In the climate of opinion at Philadelphia, then favorable to France and to Franklin, Jones's answers to the forty-seven queries were sufficient not only to exonerate him from his enemies' accusations, but to build up his reputation; they were like the final "despatches" and reports of British and American generals in World War II. The Board of Admiralty on 28 March reported that both Franklin and Jones had "made every application and used every effort" to transport the wanted articles promptly, and that the delay was caused wholly by "the mal conduct of Landais," by weather, and by lack of money to charter merchant vessels. It paid tribute to Jones's "unremitted attention in planning & executing Enterprizes calculated to promote the essential interest of our Glorious Cause." It recommended that Congress give some "distinguishing mark of approbation" to Captain Jones, and Congress on 14 April did so, in a complimentary resolve praising his "zeal, prudence and intrepidity," his "bold and successful enterprizes," and his work on behalf of prisoners, not forgetting "the officers and men who have faithfully served under him." Of this Jones made a graceful acknowledgment.

Still not completely satisfied, Jones sought praise from General Washington, coupled with a plea for his influence to obtain a suitable command. He wished, he wrote, to be "instrumental to put the naval force that remains on a more useful and honorable footing." Washington replied from his headquarters at Windsor, Connecticut, on 19 May, in a cordial letter that filled Jones's breast with honest joy and a proper pride. The General had never suspected him, he said, of having been responsible for the delay in transport; and if he had, Jones's answers to the Board of Admiralty would have satisfied him completely. He alluded delicately to the Battle off Flamborough Head and to the marks of favor from Louis XVI "which can only be obtained by a long and honorable service, or by the performance of some brilliant action."

It was no less true then than it is today that honors beget honors. Paul Jones was adept at managing this; and who can blame him, as a maverick in the Navy? He was careful to bring from France all the testimonials from important people that he could gather to impress the Americans; and now he collected a similar set from America to show in Europe. Those that he considered important were added to the *Mémoire* that he composed for Louis XVI in 1786, and Washington's letter was flourished wherever Jones traveled.

While *Ariel* lay in the harbor of Philadelphia, Jones and the personal steward whom he had engaged in France lodged at the famous Indian Queen Tavern, where their bill for five weeks amounted to $76.87. The Chevalier spent most of his time meeting old friends and cultivating congressmen in the hope of obtaining a new command. On all earlier occasions, Jones had exerted himself to the utmost to have his people paid promptly, had even paid them himself rather than let them wait; but now he neglected *Ariel*. The Admiralty Board observed to him on 19 May that the officers were demanding their pay, which the Board could not give without an official payroll; and over two weeks later the Board peremptorily directed Jones "to exhibit a complete Pay Roll of the *Ariel's* Crew with all possible dispatch."

After this was done, Captain Jones delivered *Ariel* to the Chevalier de la Luzerne, since she was on loan from the French Navy; and she returned to France with a French crew, commanded by the Chevalier de Capellis. The French Marines on board were sent to join the squadron of Admiral de la Touche at Newport.

2. Maneuvers in Congress

Great events that would end the war were in preparation. Washington's Army and Rochambeau's expeditionary force were about to march to Virginia, where Lord Cornwallis had entrenched himself at Yorktown; and the French high seas fleet under Admiral the Comte de Grasse was about to wrest command of American waters from the British Navy. In these events neither Jones nor the United States Navy played any part. Most of our Navy had been captured or destroyed at Charleston in 1780; only a pitiful remnant was left in commission. Frigate *Confederacy* surrendered to two British men-of-war on 15 April 1781 and became H.M.S. *Confederate;* her consort, frigate *Saratoga*, was lost at sea. *Alliance,* now under Captain Barry, was employed as a transport and dispatch boat between America and France. Frigate *Trumbull,* Captain James Nicholson, having finally managed to get out of the Connecticut River, spent the first half of 1781 fitting out at Philadelphia—unfortunately for Jones, as we shall see. Frigate *Deane,* Captain Samuel Nicholson, was making short and ineffectual cruises. Every other United States ship rating as sloop of war or frigate was either bottled up in harbor by the British or on the stocks. In this last category the largest was ship of the line *America,* under construction since 1777. Captain Jones, looking about for a new command, pitched on her.

His worthy ambition was furthered by the virtual dissolution of the Board of Admiralty in June and the assumption of its powers by Robert Morris the Finance Minister, which Congress confirmed on 7 September 1781 by appointing him "Agent of the Marine," corresponding to the British First Lord of the Admiralty or to the American Secretary of the Navy. Morris was not only the ablest administrator in the United States; as an owner of merchant ships and privateers he was conversant with naval matters, and since the death of Joseph Hewes in 1779 he had been Jones's principal supporter in Congress. His coming to power brought an increase of energy to the Navy. Congress on 23 June 1781 ordered him to get *America* launched and equipped for sea, and three days later unanimously elected Jones her commanding officer.

Paul Jones was now captain of the biggest ship in the United States Navy. He might have had flag rank to go with it, but for the malicious intervention of Captain James Nicholson. That gentleman, after being appointed senior captain of the United States Navy, had lost frigate *Virginia* on her maiden cruise, and would shortly lose *Trumbull* too. He got wind of the fact that a committee of Congress had recommended Paul Jones to be promoted Rear Admiral. A congressman tipped off the wife of Captain Thomas Read of Philadelphia, one of those senior to Jones who had never taken his frigate to sea; and Read told Nicholson. The two captains then did some quick lobbying against Jones, the result of which was an order from Congress to the committee to reconsider, and to Nicholson and Read to present their views. That they did, Nicholson protesting that to promote Jones would be a terrible injustice to the captains who were still senior to him, and saying (as he himself admitted in a letter to John Barry) "many things pretty severe of the Chevalier's private as well as Public Carrector too odious to mention." That killed Jones's last chance of promotion. Nicholson even tried to prevent him from getting command of *America* by urging the Agent of Marine, whom he sneeringly calls "Bob Morris the Financier," to offer it in turn to each of the five captains now senior to Jones; but Morris refused. And, when he nominated Jones for that command to Congress, every member present voted for him. Nicholson ended his letter to Barry on a waspish note: "I am convinced he [Jones] will never get her to sea. It will suit his Vanity & only tend to expose himself and his friends to Congress."*

As Lieutenant Mackenzie observed in his 1841 biography, "The same cause which defeated the creation of the grade of Admiral in the service at that time has operated ever since,—namely, jealousy among the older officers as to whom the rank should first be conferred on." The United States Navy was not authorized to have a flag officer until 1861, when Captain David G. Farragut was appointed the first American Rear Admiral.

Captain Jones, who knew perfectly well who had worked against him, consoled himself for the loss of flag rank with the thought that he had command of the only line-of-battle ship in the Navy, which now entitled him to the maximum naval captain's pay of seventy-five dollars per month. If he could only get her to sea, she would make a perfect nucleus for the combined naval and military expedition that he longed to lead against the British Isles. He wished to

---

* Barry, according to his biographer William Bell Clark, took no notice of this letter and remained, as he always had been, a friend of Paul Jones. Nicholson's sole title to fame comes from a tough fight of frigate *Trumbull* against British privateer *Watt* in 1779; he surrendered *Trumbull* to H.M.S. *Iris* (ex-U.S.S. *Hancock*) and *General Monk* (ex-U.S. privateer *General Washington*) in August 1781.

make haste to Portsmouth, where *America* was building, but first he had to draw some of his pay. On the very day of his appointment he submitted his accounts to Congress, which promptly approved them and sent them to the Treasury for payment.

Since Paul Jones had never received a penny of his pay, he put in for the whole of it from his 1775 appointment as lieutenant, and later as captain from 10 May 1776 to 26 June 1781, the entire sum amounting to £1400 5s Pennsylvania currency, equivalent to $3734. Congress was further indebted to him for about $4000 expenditures for *Alfred* and sloop *Providence;* $5900 advance pay, bounties and other expenses on behalf of *Ranger's* crew at Portsmouth; $734.40 paid to the same crew at Nantes; $2891.33 "sundry disbursements incurred on the *Ranger*"; $720.88 spent in Holland and $3802.80 in France, for his later commands. Against this sum of about $17,800 he credits Congress with $4028, advanced by John Langdon at Portsmouth, and $2004 cash received from Jonathan Williams at Nantes. He adds that he feels he has a right to repayment of rations "for my Self and servants" from 7 December 1775, "having been Considered in Europe as an American Flag officer," but leaves that sum blank. One is at a loss to understand how even Paul Jones could claim flag rank privileges when a lieutenant in the Continental Navy.

The United States Treasury was far too impecunious to pay this debt promptly. Jones, with no cash on hand, had to stay at Philadelphia into August, hoping to receive at least his pay, or a part of it; but for that he had to wait eighteen months, and borrow four hundred pounds in Pennsylvania currency from Bob Morris to settle his bills in Philadelphia and the expense of his journey to Portsmouth. On 9 December 1782 he collected in hard cash $20,705.27 in satisfaction of his salary from the beginning of the war, and for his outlays and expenses on public business. Most of this sum he gave to his friend John Ross to invest.

On 8 August, shortly before he left town, Jones received the high compliment of publication in the Philadelphia *Freeman's Journal* of a poem by Philip Freneau "On the Memorable Victory obtained by the Gallant Captain Paul Jones." The twenty-one stanzas of the poem open unhappily with:

> O'er the rough main, with flowing sheet,
> The guardian of a numerous fleet,
> *Serapis* from the Baltic came.

Unhappily, I say, because square-riggers do not let their sheets flow, and it was Jones's squadron, not Pearson's, that sailed before the wind. But some of the lines are memorable, such as:

> 'Twas Jones, brave Jones, to battle led
> As bold a crew as ever bled
> Upon the sky-surrounded main.

3. Building U.S.S. "America"

On 12 August 1781 the Chevalier, having hired a phaeton and three horses for eight dollars a day, departed Philadelphia, with his steward, for Portsmouth. He had to take a circuitous route to avoid British-held New York. As far as White Plains, where he arrived on the 17th, he had the congenial company of Bob Morris and Richard Peters, who were escorted by a troop of dragoons. At White Plains headquarters, where Washington and Rochambeau were anxiously awaiting word from Admiral de Grasse as to his destination on the North American coast, the generals were too busy to make any special effort to entertain a naval hero, but Jones was satisfied with his reception. After resting for a few days, he resumed his journey to Portsmouth. Altogether it consumed nineteen days from Philadelphia and his "cash expenses on road" amounted to $153.00. Someone on Washington's staff, it is said, gave Jones the hint not to wear the cross and ribbon of his French order in New England, where puritan prejudice against crosses had lately been supplemented by republican suspicion of royalty.

Portsmouth, however, was a town of Anglican and royalist traditions, at least among the upper classes, where no prejudice existed against cross or crown; so Captain Jones resumed wearing his Ordre du Mérite Militaire. The town then had less than four thousand inhabitants, some of whom had done very well by selling lumber, building ships, and privateering. When Cornwallis's surrender (18 October 1781) suggested that the war was almost over, they began to spend money liberally. Jones writes on 25 March 1782, "I reached Portsmouth" (after a brief trip to Newburyport or Ipswich) "just when they began to light candles after tea, and the dancing did not end till after two in the morning." The captain of a French squadron which arrived there before Jones departed praised the generous hospitality of the Portsmouth gentry, and wrote in his diary, "I have never seen more affable people, even the country people, including little children who came to greet us." Count Francisco dal Verme, a young Italian nobleman who stayed with Colonel Langdon a year later, attended a horse race and described the dancing school of sixty members which met in a handsome hall where, every winter month, a ball was given. After going to meeting on Sunday he observes, "It is not possible to describe the beauty of the *congregazione* or the elegance of their clothes, made in the fashion of the latest taste in France."

At Portsmouth, where he arrived on 31 August, Jones first put up at the Marquis of Rockingham Tavern, and on 4 October moved to a fashionable boardinghouse kept by the widow of Captain Gregory Purcell.* Into this society, which he had known earlier in the war, Captain Jones fitted easily and happily. His friends Colonel Wendell and General Whipple welcomed him with open arms; Colonel Langdon, disposed to let bygones be bygones, proved to be civil and hospitable; the young girls and widows who had met Jones in 1777 were thrilled by his returning a hero, and charmed by his accounts of life in Paris and Amsterdam. We find him sending to Boston for "a piece

---

* Jones paid ten dollars a week for board and lodging of himself and steward, amounting to $550.00 for 55 weeks. This house, later the property of the Lord family, is now the home of the Portsmouth Historical Society. Jones's name, scratched on a window pane of the best front bedchamber, could still be seen at the close of the last century; and this room is now a Jones museum.

of good linen for shirts, and a piece of cambric for stock," and for a guinea's worth of "good hair powder." Karl Tornquist, a Swedish officer in the French fleet that visited Portsmouth in 1782, met "the famous Pohl Jones" and described him as "of medium height and square built"—his frame had evidently filled out from good living at Paris and Philadelphia. In manners, said Tornquist, he is "far from brutal as report has spread about him," but on the contrary quiet and mild-mannered in society. "He has much knowledge of naval affairs, and speaks, contrary to the custom of Englishmen, tolerably good French." This, incidentally, is the only compliment to Jones's French that has come down to us. And the Swedish gentleman closes with an interesting remark to the effect that Jones "does not seem to have been in as great favor with the Americans as has perhaps been supposed."

That means, probably, that Tornquist picked up some disparaging remarks about Jones from former members of *Ranger's* crew. Elijah Hall, Surgeon Green and Master Cullam were about, and Colonel Langdon may have intimated that Jones was a difficult person to get along with, which was true.

Langdon was responsible for building *America* and had not got very far with her in four years; had even proposed to scrap the partly completed hull to make way for construction of his own. Now Jones appeared and tried to hustle him, and the Colonel was a difficult person to hustle. Although a rich man by the standards of the day, the Colonel's property was mostly tied up in shipping, and unless Congress supplied cash, he had none to pay shipwrights, carpenters and calkers. Robert Morris was so desperate for funds as to make a requisition on the President of New Hampshire for beef to feed the workmen employed on *America*, or else to be sold and the proceeds applied to her construction. Jones found things moving so slowly and the ship so far from ready when he arrived at Portsmouth that he contemplated taking leave of absence to serve on Lafayette's staff in the Yorktown campaign. Lafayette wrote that he would have been charmed to have the Chevalier with him, but Jones's letter did not reach him until after Cornwallis's surrender.

Morris did manage to find just enough money to keep construction going; and Jones, in order to keep men steadily employed while waiting for timber, guns, spars and cordage, designed and oversaw the carving of a figurehead and other devices. At the new ship's prow was the Goddess of Liberty, laurel-crowned, with right arm raised and pointing to Heaven, and on her left arm a shield bearing thirteen silver stars on a blue field. Her feet and legs were wreathed with smoke to indicate that she had been through some tough fights. On the stern, under the windows of the admiral's great cabin, were two figures representing Tyranny and Oppression, in chains and evident discomfort, with a Liberty Cap raised triumphantly over their heads. The starboard quarter gallery was adorned with Neptune and the port quarter gallery with Mars. All this was very fitting for a ship of *America's* size and dignity—182 feet 6 inches long on the upper gundeck, 50 feet 6 inches beam, pierced for 74 guns at least.

The Chevalier felt depressed and gloomy when he reflected on the little good accomplished by the United States Navy, after the high hopes for it in 1776. As he wrote to Captain McNeill: "It has upon the whole done nothing for the Cause and less for the Flag. The Public has been put to a great expense, yet the poor Seamen have, almost in every instance, been *Cheated,* while the public has reaped neither honor nor profit; And the whole result . . . only appears to have augmented the purses of the Agents, besides enabling a few of the Actors, perhaps not the first in merit or abilities, to purchase Farms &c."

Nevertheless, in the prevailing mood and prosperity of Portsmouth, we may be certain that Captain Jones passed a Merry Christmas with plenty of rum punch and plum pudding. And one is glad to find that he took the trouble to write a Christmas love letter to his "Most lovely Delia" in Paris. The concluding paragraph fairly drips with eighteenth-century sentiment; it was just such stuff as Nelson, twenty years later, was writing to Lady Hamilton:

Providence all good and just has given thee a Soul worthy in all respects to animate nature's fairest Work. I rest therefore sure that *absence* will not diminish but *refine* the pure and spotless Friendship that binds our souls together; and will ever impress each to merit the Affection of the other.

It was probably for Delia that Jones wrote a poem in four stanzas, three of which describe Jove returning from a visit to Mount Ida, being greeted by the faithful Juno; but in the fourth stanza we come to the point:

> Thus when thy Warrior, though no God,
>   Brings *Freedom's* standard o'er the main,
> Long absent from thy blest abode,
>   Casts anchor in *dear France* again;
> O! thou more heavenly!—far more kind
>   Than Juno, as thy swain than Jove,
> With what heart's transport, raptur'd mind!
>   Shall *we* approach on wings of Love!

Jones, however, composed a variant for the fourth line—adapting the poem for an American lady love, thus:

> In fair Columbia moors again . . .

—and he does not forget to insert "from" after "standard" in the second line, to make the poem fit a westward passage.

We are not, therefore, surprised to find the gallant Captain writing to his friend John Brown, secretary to Robert Morris, on 25 March 1782: "I say nothing to you at present of my affair of the heart; but wait impatiently to hear *much* on that subject from you. I shall rely on your advice; and . . . treat it with great respect and *attention.*" The two friends met shortly after, so we are ignorant of the advice that Jones received. This lady was evidently a Philadelphian, for Jones writes to Brown at that city on 7 September: "There is one delicate subject *of a private nature* on which you remain silent, though, as I wrote you to Boston, I expected 'to hear much from you on that head.' Your silence, I fear, carries with it a disagreeable meaning."

Owing to Jones's discretion, we have no hint as to the identity of this lady. And no Portsmouth damsel seems to have attracted his attention.

For the present, his main object was to get *America* completed and to sea under his command before the war ended. That proved to be impossible. For a time, Jones and Langdon were not even on speaking terms. If the Captain wanted anything done, he wrote Bob Morris in Philadelphia, or to his secretary John Brown, whom Morris sent to Boston in the hope of getting action.* Morris wrote to Langdon that the coldness subsisting between him and Jones gave him "much concern," and he requested the Colonel to consult the Chevalier "and comply with his wishes more especially when they tend to economy as well as ability." Brown and Jones sometimes conferred at Ipswich, so that Langdon would not know what they were up to. For guns, Jones secured the battery of eighteen-pounders which had been cast for *Bonhomme Richard* and which *Alliance* carried to Boston, and he tried to get more of that caliber from Virginia; but they could not be had, owing to a fairly close blockade that the Royal Navy set up after De Grasse's fleet departed for the West Indies. Jones also obtained, through Brown, some twelve-pounders and swivel guns from a British armed ship which had been brought into Boston as a prize, and from a French vessel condemned at Newport. He desperately needed oil and paint—"send immediately all . . . on hand in Boston," he begs, to preserve the newly-planed green wood from rotting. He even had to accept second-hand cables from a captured British ship. In the matter of boats, to avoid expense (so he wrote to Brown), he was willing "to forego the parade of a barge" (then, as now, a prerogative of flag rank), and "even in the sight of France, to be rowed in an eight-oared pinnace."

As late as 2 April 1782, almost eight months after Jones arrived at Portsmouth, Major Hackett and Colonel Hill, the two master

---

* The Eastern Navy Board at Boston, dominated by James Warren, a crony of Sam Adams and Arthur Lee, was bitterly hostile to Jones. Warren wrote to Robert Morris 20 September 1780 blaming all the troubles of *Alliance* on her homeward passage under Landais as due to the "Caprice & Insolence of Jones," and ascribing the alterations he had made in *Alliance* as "a part of that Jobbing & peculating system which has so long disgraced our affairs there" (in France).

builders, were going up Piscataqua River to bring down newly-cut timber for the quarterdeck and the forecastle deck and beams. Thomas Russell, one of the wealthiest merchants of Boston, wrote to Jones on 1 April that he could not negotiate his bills on Philadelphia, but that, although "greatly distressed" for lack of money himself, he is sending him two hundred Spanish dollars to pay the men. A week later, Langdon threatened to discharge all carpenters working on the warship; he had already taken off a number to fit out his own vessels. At this juncture, when Jones was ready to use all his "art of persuasion" on Langdon, the Colonel received a remittance of ten thousand dollars from Morris. But all that accomplished (so Jones wrote to Brown on 15 April), was to keep at work the few carpenters already employed. By 6 May Jones was becoming desperate. Only eight men were working on *America*. To Brown he wrote a "most confidential" letter, partly in cipher, accusing Langdon of diverting public material to private use, of charging Congress an excessive rent for the "little barren Clod" where his shipyard was located, in the most inconvenient spot on the Piscataqua; that Langdon had mishandled the timber provided for *America* and culled out the best for one of his own ships; that he was paying "honest Hackett" and the workmen in goods at inflated prices, instead of using the cash sent to him by Morris. Since Jones was apt to get excited and to exaggerate difficulties when fitting out, we may discount these charges against Langdon to some extent; but he was right at least about the timber, since *America* lasted only three years.

4. "America" Launched and Given Away

During the spring of 1782 Jones heard rumors that the British Navy was planning to send armed boats into Portsmouth harbor to burn *America* on the stocks. He asked for a guard from the State, but none would New Hampshire give. Jones had to pay the carpenters overtime to do sentry-go at night, to supply them with muskets, powder and ball; and he himself acted as officer of the guard every third night. British frigates were active in the Gulf of Maine in the spring of 1782, and it is possible that one of them did attempt to duplicate Jones's Whitehaven raid in reverse, for mysterious boats rowed by men with muffled oars were reported to have been seen in the Piscataqua River.

Jones also footed the bills for a gala celebration on board the uncompleted *America*. Marie Antoinette in October 1781 gave birth to a son, the unfortunate prince later known as Louis XVII. Congress took cognizance of the happy event by writing to generals and state governors "that there may be universal rejoicing"; and at Portsmouth "the gentlemen of the town, upon the recommendation of the General Assembly, appointed Thursday the 20th of June 1782 for the celebration of the birth of the Dauphin of France as a compliment to his Most Christian Majesty, the great Ally of the United States." Ship *America* was the center of this local celebration.

At sunrise *America* made colors, with the white flag of the Bourbons on a jackstaff (as no mast had been stepped), and fired a 21-gun salute, to which the harbor forts replied. At noon this was repeated as a signal for the official banquet to begin in the town hall. At this dinner thirteen toasts were drunk, and each time the glasses of Madeira wine were raised (since no champagne was available), *America*, warned by a signal from the cupola of the town hall, fired a 21-gun salute. "And all day, up to midnight," wrote the Chevalier, "she kept up a rolling fire of musketry and swivel-guns." At nightfall she was decorated with a quantity of great lanterns, and fireworks were shot off. All the inhabitants gathered on the shore to see the show, which closed at midnight with the sixteenth and last 21-gun salute. That was the sort of thing people enjoyed in the eighteenth century, when America afforded little in the way of spectacles. And it was not long before Jones put on another noisy celebration on the Fourth of July.

Eleven days later, Jones was so desperate about getting *America* completed that he wrote to Gouverneur Morris urging him to get up a subscription for that purpose among the patriotic ladies of Philadelphia. In return he promised to give them a ball on board the first time that *America* sailed into Philadelphia!

Alas, she was destined never to see Philadelphia or any other American port except her birthplace. In July a French fleet of thirteen ships of the line and three frigates, under the command of Lieutenant-Général le Marquis de Vaudreuil, was en route from Cap Haitien to New England. On 9 August the fleet anchored in the King's (now President) Roads, the outer anchorage for Boston. But it suffered a serious mishap in the old ship channel inside Boston Light. The local pilot insisted on entering that day, although there was a head wind, and Vaudreuil did not like it and warned him that his biggest ships drew 25 feet. Upon beating through the narrows between Lovell's and Gallop's Islands, three ships ran aground on a bar off the northwest point of Lovell's, and only two got off. *Le Magnifique* struck a sunken rock near the time of high water, and at the ebb took so heavy a list that, being an old ship, she began to break up. There were no casualties and most of the guns and gear were salvaged, but the ship was a total loss.*

This shipwreck had very unpleasant consequences for Paul Jones. Congress, finding it increasingly difficult to raise money, snapped at this chance of getting rid of *America*. In a grand gesture, it voted on 3 September to present His Most Christian Majesty with our one ship of the line, to replace *Le Magnifique*.

Poor Jones! This was the unkindest cut he had ever had from his own country. He took it manfully, without protest. Robert Morris, communicating the unpleasant news, begged the Chevalier to retain command of *America* until she was launched and in a fit state to hand over to Vaudreuil.

---

* The guilty pilot lost his job, but obtained that of sexton in a Boston church, where small boys used to taunt him with this couplet:

> Don't you run *this* ship ashore,
> Like you done the Seventy-four!

The place where she struck is known as Man-of-War Bar to this day; and there are rumors that gold and silver coins have been recovered from the wreck.

The Marquis now detached three ships of the line and a frigate, under command of his brother, Capitaine de Vaisseau le Comte Rigaud de Vaudreuil, to obtain new spars in Portsmouth. En route they encountered H.M. frigate *Albemarle*, commanded by a twenty-three-year-old captain named Horatio Nelson, whose star was about to rise just as that of Paul Jones was setting. Nelson, who had impressed a Yankee fisherman as pilot, led them a hare-and-hounds race over Georges Bank and shook them off. The French squadron then proceeded to Portsmouth, where *America* was almost ready to be launched.

She was the biggest ship ever to be built in Portsmouth, but the shipyard on Rising Castle (now Badgers) Island was in a difficult spot for a safe launching. From the west side of the ways ran a ledge of rocks, at an acute angle to the ship's keel, and extending almost halfway across the Piscataqua River, which at that point is less than three hundred yards wide. The tidal current continues to run rapidly over this ledge for an hour or more after high water, at which time the ship had to be launched so she would not ground—in that day the river was much less deep than now. Thus, *America* was in grave danger of being swept by the current onto the rocks as soon as she took the water. The river bottom was too hard to permit the driving in of protective piles, so Jones caused the workmen to plant anchors in the river bed, attaching them to cables that led from the ship's stern and quarters, and he stationed plenty of men on board to take up the slack quickly and warp her clear of the ledge.

An unsuccessful attempt was made to launch her on 23 October. She stuck on the ways, and it was necessary to reconstruct the cradle. Jones is discreetly silent about that fiasco, but gives us full details on the second and successful attempt on 5 November, with the help of the French ships' boats and anchors and cables that had belonged to *Le Magnifique*. *America* was nicely dressed, with the ensigns of the United States and France crossed at the stern. When the moment of high water arrived the Chevalier, from his station on a platform near the ship's bow, gave the word; wedges were then driven by a gang of shipwrights to lift her into her cradle, the blocks upon which she

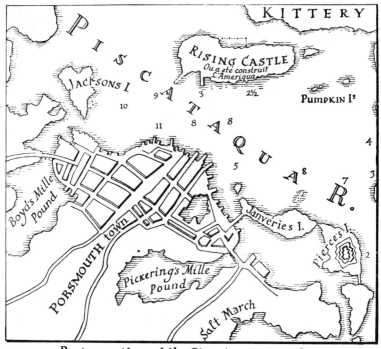

Portsmouth and the Piscataqua in 1782

Where America was launched

was built were split from under her keel, and she started slowly and majestically down the ways. Stout cables, secured to anchors or to bollards on shore, were flaked on deck and stoppered to ring-bolts with lines calculated to break at a given pressure, in order to check her way so she would not crash the rocky shore across the river. Jones directed the entire operation, signaling the gang on board when to snub her to the bow anchors. Everything worked perfectly. And when the ship was safely moored, the Chevalier, with appropriate ceremony, delivered her to Capitaine de Vaisseau de Macarty-Macteigne, former commander of *Le Magnifique*, who was there to induct her into the Royal Navy of France.

"Are we in a condition to make presents?" wrote Jones to Gouverneur Morris when he first got wind of the giveaway. "If we were I should be against offering to give a friend *an empty Egg-shell.*" That remark was not sour grapes, but very much to the point, since *America* had neither masts, spars, sails nor cordage; even the joiner work was not completed, and Colonel Langdon refused to do anything more. Fitted out with gear from *Le Magnifique* and manned by her crew, she finally got to sea eight months after her launching, when the war was over. France appreciated the generosity of Congress in presenting *America* to her, but the ship was not much liked in the French Navy. Broader in the beam and shallower than French ships of the line, she was unable to follow them closely in evolutions. When surveyed at Brest in 1786, she was found to be "entièrement pourri"—riddled with dry rot, almost every plank and timber rotten, although the finish and joiner-work were still good. The Ministry of Marine condemned her to be broken up.

"This examination proves," states the survey, "that the timber of North America can be of no use for ship construction, except perhaps for the highest parts of the superstructure." Dry rot can be caused by green wood or by a construction leaving no air space between a ship's planking and her inner sheathing. In this case, probably, the wood was at fault. Jones in fact confessed that he had to accept green timber supplied by Langdon, and Vaudreuil complained of the quality of spars furnished him at Portsmouth.

America, under Paul Jones's command, would have served well after the war to show the flag in European countries and teach the Barbary pirates respect for the Stars and Stripes. Thus employed, she would have justified her cost many times.

5. Winter Cruise to the West Indies

Although preliminary articles of peace had been signed between France, Great Britain and the United States before Vaudreuil sailed from Boston, neither Paul Jones nor General Washington considered the war to be over. "An honorable Peace is and always was my first wish," wrote Jones to Gouverneur Morris on 2 September. "I can take no delight in the effusion of human Blood; but, if this war should continue, I wish to have the most active part in it."

The Chevalier tarried in Portsmouth only long enough to say farewell to his friends, and on 7 November 1782 set off with his steward in a two-horse phaeton for Philadelphia. The journey took twenty days, and cost him $120 for horse hire and $102 for expenses on the road. He hoped to have a new command, and almost got that of *L'Indien,* his earlier object. As *South Carolina* of that State's navy, under "Commodore" Gillon, she had sailed from Amsterdam to the West Indies and now lay in Philadelphia harbor doing nothing. The Duc de Montmorency-Luxembourg, her owner, never having received a penny of the charter or prize money promised by Gillon, applied to the French minister at Philadelphia to libel her on his behalf. Bob Morris now conceived the idea of wresting this fast and formidable frigate from Gillon's clutches, and placing her and the remnant of the United States Navy under Paul Jones's command, to lift an expeditionary force to Bermuda. But the South Carolina Commodore was too smart for them. He managed to thwart all the legal processes that Luzerne and Morris could bring to bear, and sent her to sea under another South Carolina naval officer. She had scarcely cleared the Delaware Capes when she was pounced upon by three English frigates and captured.

Thus, for the third time, Paul Jones saw *L'Indien* snaked out from under his nose and wasted. The interesting thing about this frigate was her length—144 feet on the keel and 170 feet overall, with a beam of 43 feet, and measuring 1430 tons. This meant that she was almost as long as *America* and much faster than the stubby frigates of 1776. During the six months that she lay idle at Philadelphia, it is probable that her lines were studied by Joshua Humphreys, architect of the first frigates built by the Federal Government; for in design she was the parent of U.S.S. *Constitution* and *Constellation*.

After this second disappointment in two months, the Chevalier conceived the plan of combining pleasure with instruction by embarking as a guest in the fleet of the Marquis de Vaudreuil. He still had a burning desire to study fleet evolutions and battle tactics at first hand. In the interstices of his active commands he had read everything available on these subjects. He expected that an independent United States would build a Navy to make her respected among the nations—an objective not attained until the twentieth century—and he wished to prepare himself for a fleet command.

On Bob Morris's recommendation, Congress on 4 December voted that, "having a high sense of the merit and services of Captain J. P. Jones, and being disposed to favour the zeal manifested by him to acquire improvement in the line of his profession," they recommend him to the favor and countenance of his Excellency the Marquis de Vaudreuil.

Within a few days, Captain Jones departed Philadelphia for Boston in style. He purchased horses and a sleigh, for which he charged Congress $125, and $130 for "expenses on the road, being impeded by the snow." One hopes that he was held up at some town where there was a cozy inn.

M. le Marquis de Vaudreuil, Lieutenant-Général des Armées Navales, received Jones kindly on board his 80-gun flagship *Le Triomphant,* and the Chevalier found a congenial group in the wardroom. Many of them were Army officers who had fought in the Yorktown campaign and would now command the expeditionary force destined for Jamaica. Jones expected to be useful as a pilot, since he was better acquainted with Jamaican waters, owing to his slave-trading voyages, than any of the French on board. Vaudreuil put to sea from Boston on Christmas Eve, and after a rough time beating about the Gulf of Maine, squared away for San Juan. Greatly to Jones's delight, they then spent a week off Puerto Rico, practising naval tactics and evolutions.

Vaudreuil evaded a strong fleet under Rear Admiral Hood that was waiting for him, stood through the Mona Passage and shaped a course for Puerto Cabello. There a rendezvous had been planned with another French fleet under the Comte d'Estaing, and a Spanish fleet under Don Solano. Owing, it seems, to the French navigators taking no account of the westerly current in the Caribbean, Vaudreuil's fleet fetched up on the Spanish Main far to leeward of its destination and wasted three weeks beating up to the rendezvous. In so doing, the seventy-four *La Bourgogne* ran on a rock and was lost with 200 officers and men. In mid-February, when *Le Triomphant* and a few other units of the fleet finally made Puerto Cabello, neither the Don nor D'Estaing was there, nor did anyone have news of them; and at Puerto Cabello they waited, week after week.

My favorite *Sailing Directions for the West Indies,* printed in 1885, warns warships against entering Puerto Cabello, since "the excessive heat in the harbor, the mangroves with which it is surrounded, and the difficulty of keeping the crews from intemperance, occasion almost immediate attacks of putrid fevers and the black vomit." That is what happened to Vaudreuil's fleet. Paul Jones fortunately caught neither the putrid fever nor the black vomit, but what he called an intermittent fever. This may have been a relapsing fever, or common malaria.

Apart from this illness, Paul Jones enjoyed himself thoroughly on board Vaudreuil's flagship. French sailors were well known for their ability to keep comfortable at sea; they carried plenty of wine to help digest the salt beef, grew salad plants in flats, supplying vitamins, and beguiled the time with music, cards, books, and, above all, conversation. Thrown in with over a hundred French officers, many of them the élite of the King's Army and Navy, the Chevalier seized this opportunity to acquire practical knowledge of fleet evolutions, to study books on naval tactics, and to perfect his conversational French. The Marquis treated him with respect and consideration, and he shared a cabin with Lieutenant-Général le Baron de Vioménil, commanding the ground forces. But once more he was to be balked of his dreams of glory, even such glory as falls to a pilot. The peace treaty had been concluded at Paris, and news of it reached Puerto Cabello by a frigate about 1 April 1783. According to one of the articles of the treaty, hostilities in American waters would cease on the 7th.

So, on 8 April 1783, Vaudreuil's fleet sailed for Cap Haitien, where Jones was invited to rest and recuperate at the governor's palace. Remaining there only a few days, he took passage in a merchant ship to Philadelphia, armed with testimonials from Vaudreuil and Vioménil to the wisdom, prudence and courage that he had displayed in the course of this five months' cruise.

By mid-May Jones was in Philadelphia. He was slated to travel to Boston to sit on a court-martial of Captains Nicholson and Manley for having lost their ships during the war. This service would have given Jones great satisfaction, but his health was not up to it; Bob Morris records in his diary for 10 July that "he appeared so unwell that I gave up the expectation of his going." On the advice of friends, the Chevalier spent the rest of the summer at the sanatorium conducted by the Moravians at Bethlehem, Pennsylvania. He took their "cold bath" treatment for the after effects of the fever and left Bethlehem feeling thoroughly cured.

6. À Paris!

Paul Jones now knew that he had to start fresh. What would he do? The debts he had collected from Congress would be enough to buy a farm and settle down, and his biggest packet of prize money, for *Bonhomme Richard's* cruise, was yet to come. From Puerto Cabello on

16 March 1783 he wrote to his friend John Ross (now a merchant at Philadelphia) about turning some of his assets then in hand into a confiscated Tory estate near Newark, New Jersey, only ten miles from New York. He now wished, he said, "if the peace should, as I wish it may, be concluded," to have a place he "could call his own" and to offer his hand "to some fair daughter of liberty." This transaction fell through, like the one for Fox's Ferry in 1777; but not for want of funds.

At this same period Jones wrote to a friend in Paris that he wished to invest three to four thousand pounds sterling in France. That indicates the direction in which his thoughts and longings now lay— *"à Paris!"* Not even Manon Lescaut could have longed more for the glittering *ville lumière* than did Chevalier Jones. Paris was the center of the civilized world, the fountain of military honor, the seat of good literature and of the world's most charming and sophisticated society. Little Manon had never seen Paris, but Jones had; he was a Chevalier de l'Ordre du Mérite Militaire, he had been presented at court, he belonged there. Why vegetate on a Jersey farm and marry some horse-faced Yankee girl when he could enjoy a *petit apparte-ment* in Paris and court a young *comtesse?* Delia was waiting for him; and if Delia had found another lover, there were plenty of others.

But how to get there? He first tried on Bob Morris the idea of "sending a proper person" (himself, naturally) "to Europe in a handsome frigate" to "display our flag" and study the naval organization of different countries. It could even be done without a frigate, "though perhaps not with the same dignity." He further observes that if the United States Navy is to have a proper corps of officers, it must have a "fleet of evolution" for them to learn tactics, and that each ship must have "a little academy on board," and each navy yard a school where junior officers could be taught "the principles of mathematics and mechanics." He does not expect this can be done immediately; but he invites Morris and Congress to reflect on the sad state of Holland, which let her Navy decline. "In time of Peace it is necessary to prepare, and be *always prepared,* for War by Sea."

He remarks justly that the British Navy's system of signaling during the war was very deficient, and that the Chevalier du Pavillon, whom he met at Brest, had invented a system by which 1600 different commands, questions, answers or informations could be communicated through a fleet by flag hoists. (Pavillon, who was killed at the Battle of the Saints, is now considered one of the principal creators of naval communications before the era of radio.*) The major defect that Jones had observed in the French Navy was its paucity of experienced junior officers; the collision between *Zélé* and *Ville de Paris* in April 1782, which led to the French defeat at the Saints, had been caused by an inexperienced ensign's having the deck.

This is one of the most thoughtful and prophetic of Jones's letters on naval subjects. It is interesting how it proceeds from the personal to the general, and from a project immediately interesting to the writer to a plan for naval instruction. Many years would elapse before the Navy had "little academies" on board ship, and more than sixty years before the Naval Academy at Annapolis would be founded. And Jones showed great acumen in pointing out the absolute necessity for clear and quick communications between a flag officer and his fleet. Misreading of signals, as we have seen, was blamed for the inconclusiveness of the Battle of Ushant in 1778. Admiral Graves lost the Battle off the Capes of the Chesapeake, the most decisive naval action of the war, through misunderstood signals; and, in World War II, one reason why Vice Admiral Kurita was defeated off Samar by an inferior force under Rear Admiral Tom Sprague was failure in radio communication.

No frigate was available for Jones to show the flag and study foreign navies. Congress had advertised for sale the uncompleted

---

* Pavillon's system, which is described by Lieut. de Vaisseau Mouchez in *Revue Maritime* Jan. 1929 pp. 641-644, consisted of 10 flags representing numbers zero through 9 and three *flammes* (long pennants) representing 100, 200 and 300. Thus any number through 99 could be made by a two-flag hoist, and any number through 399 by the addition of a *flamme*. By making the hoist on different masts or yards, the possible combinations could be raised to 1600. Each number corresponded to a phrase, and the key was given in a signal book of 100 pp., a copy of which Jones obtained and which he tried to have translated when in the Russian Navy.

frigate *Bourbon* and *The Hague* (ex-*Deane*, name changed owing to Silas's treachery). *Alliance,* in John Barry's capable hands, was mostly doing dispatch-boat work.

But nothing could keep Paul Jones from Paris. He now hatched a trip to France out of the prize-money egg. To Morris he proposed that he be sent to Europe on his Navy pay, plus expenses, to recover prize money due to officers and men of *Bonhomme Richard, Alliance* and *Ranger.* Marvelous to relate, a committee of Congress so resolved on 1 November 1783. Jones was given authority to receive all prize money due in Europe and to take the usual commission allowed to agents; but (a tribute to Lee's fear of "jobbery") he must give bonds to the amount of two hundred thousand dollars for the faithful discharge of his mission. This was done promptly by John Ross and his partner James Wilson the Constitutionalist. Jones also asked for flag rank to enhance his prestige, but that was denied. However, he had the honor of being one of the original members of the Society of the Cincinnati, organized by officers who had served in the United States Army or Navy during the war; and that gave him another decoration to display with the Mérite Militaire.

Still Captain United States Navy, Paul Jones sailed from Philadelphia greatly pleased with his project. Who but he could have converted a packet of unpaid prize money into a free trip to Paris?

XVIII

Autumn
of the
Old
Régime

1783-1788

1. Prize-money Mission

"I embarked at Philadelphia 10 November in the little packet ship
destined for Hâvre de Grace," wrote Paul Jones in his *Mémoire* to
Louis XVI. "And, as this vessel was very old and wet, I did not
care to risk carrying the sword with which His Most Christian Majesty had honored me, and so left it at Philadelphia."

Joshua Barney, destined to be famous in the next war, was master
of this packet, the *General Washington,* which he, when captain of
privateer *Hyder Ally,* had recaptured from the British during the
war. He and Paul Jones had first met in the New Providence expedition, and they got on famously. Every evening, in the first watch,
while the two French passengers stayed below playing trictrac, John
and Joshua walked the quarterdeck or sat on a hencoop, remi-
niscing. Barney found his passenger "reserved, and not entirely free

from moroseness," and he could not make out what was eating him. Frustration was the cause of it; the many, many disappointments Jones had been subjected to since 1776, and the problem of what to do with himself now, at the age of thirty-six. His present mission would not last long, and what then?

At his request, but against Barney's remonstrance, who feared the English would throw him into jail, Jones insisted on being landed at an English fishing village, probably Cawston near Plymouth. This was about 1 December 1783. Jones hastened to London, where he was able to deliver dispatches directly to John Adams, the American minister, instead of forwarding them from Paris. He left London the following day and arrived in Paris five days after disembarking in England.

On this visit to Paris, which lasted more than three years, Paul Jones lodged with a M. la Chapelle, Boulevard Montmartre; at least at first. Benjamin Franklin was still Minister Plenipotentiary, living in the pavilion of the Hôtel Valentinois at Passy. The addresses on some of Jones's letters indicate that he collected mail at Passy, but he evidently never stayed there, since Franklin wrote to him at Paris. The minister did what he could to further Jones's mission, and at least once invited him to dine; but relations between the Doctor and the Chevalier were not as intimate as before. Jones felt that Franklin had let him down in the Landais affair, and Franklin had learned that whenever Jones turned up it meant trouble for him.

This time it did not. Lest there be misunderstanding as to the Chevalier's official position, Franklin on 17 December 1783 supplemented his congressional commission by a personal note granting Jones authority to solicit and receive money due to the officers and men of any American ship formerly under his command. The Chevalier lost no time in presenting himself to the Comte de Vergennes, Minister of Foreign Affairs, and to the Maréchal de Castries, Minister of Marine, who presented him anew to Louis XVI on 20 December. The Maréchal told him later that the King "saw him again with pleasure and would always be ready to promote his interests."

Two years later, Jones inserts this in his *Mémoire* to Louis XVI as a gentle reminder.

Negotiations for the unpaid prize money began immediately, but dragged along for two years. Le Ray de Chaumont, who had collected the proceeds of all condemned prizes taken by the *Bonhomme Richard* squadron, had never paid out a penny of it, on the plea that the Crown was heavily indebted to him for expenses in outfitting these ships. Paul Jones won an initial victory when Castries admitted that, whatever Chaumont might do, the French government was responsible for Jones's people getting paid. Castries then forced Chaumont to disgorge all the documents on the prizes and put them into the hands of M. Chardon, maître des requêtes, the judge of claims under the Duc de Penthièvre, grand admiral of France. Chardon reported on 10 February 1784. Chaumont had sold the prizes for 456,787 livres 2s 9d (about $91,358); but after deducting his expenses, only 283,631 livres 13s (about $56,726) was left to be distributed among all the officers and seamen of the squadron—not merely those of *Richard* and *Alliance* but of *Pallas, La Vengeance* and, to some extent, the two privateers and *Le Cerf*.

Jones objected to this computation on two counts. One of the deductions was 4 deniers per livre—about 1⅔ per cent—for the Hôtel des Invalides. After Jones had observed that no American seaman could conceivably enter this French home for old soldiers and sailors, Castries made the concession.

The other item that Jones took exception to in Chaumont's accounts was his deduction for repairs to *Countess of Scarborough* and *Serapis* at the Texel, and for feeding British prisoners there. Jones declared that had he known what he was in for, he could have made temporary repairs to both ships in two days' time and sailed them to Lorient under jury rig; for it took the British Admiralty a week or more to establish a blockading squadron at the Texel. He felt it grossly unjust to be charged with the English prisoners' board, because they were taken out of his hands and exchanged for Frenchmen, not Americans. Franklin backed Jones in this; and Castries gave in after appealing to Vergennes (who washed his hands of the whole business) and delaying several months. He informed the Commodore in May 1784 that the King agreed to make no deduction for repairs or other expenses at the Texel. After another five months' delay, the Maréchal, on 23 October, signed a document on the liquidation and partition of the prize money which was satisfactory to Paul Jones.

The Chevalier's next problem was to have the money actually paid. Another winter passed before that was effected. He had no objection to spending another spring in Paris, but by June of 1785 he was becoming somewhat impatient. Castries' first excuse for delay was to insist that Ferdinand Grand the banker give security that Jones pay the money to the claimants. Thomas Jefferson, who had succeeded Franklin as American Minister, talked him out of that. Then, since the French treasury was impecunious, Castries gave an order to M. Clonet, Ordonnateur de la Marine at Lorient, to pay Jones the amount due. So, back went the Chevalier to the scene of his frustration at the hands of Landais.

At Lorient he encountered a local character named Puchilberg, a partner of Lee's crony Schweighauser, who flourished a letter of attorney from the officers and men of *Alliance* authorizing payment of their prize money to him; and until this dispute could be cleaned up, M. Clonet refused to pay a sou to Jones. So we find the Chevalier writing to Thomas Jefferson, begging him to obtain an order from Castries to pay the whole amount to him. Castries, apparently pleased by another excuse to stall, favored Puchilberg's claim. Jones remained in Lorient writing countless letters on this subject, and his pertinacity prevailed. The Maréchal consented to order the entire sum to be paid to Jones, in return for a copy of the roll of *Alliance*. On 5 September 1785 the Commissaire de la Marine certified that Clonet had paid the whole amount for the *Alliance* crew to Commodore Jones in addition to *Richard's* shares, which had apparently already been paid in the same manner.

The Chevalier now returned to Paris, and there followed an unexplained delay of ten months before this "lingering and disagreeable business," as he well called it, ended. On 7 July 1786 he submitted his accounts to Thomas Jefferson. He had received from the French government, 181,039 livres 1s 10d, about $36,208 in gold. From that he deducted his "ordinary expenses" since his arrival in Europe in December 1783—47,972 livres 1s (about $9600); advances he had made out of his own pocket to sundry members of *Richard's* crew (about $1300); a pilot's fee that he had paid; and his own share as Commodore of the squadron and Captain of *Bonhomme Richard*, 13,291 livres 5s 6d (about $2660). The balance, 112,172 livres 2s 4d (about $22,435) he paid into Jefferson's hands. On 5 August, Jefferson accepted this as correct, although he disclaimed the authority to make a final settlement. He was supposed to transmit the sum by bills of exchange to Congress; but as his salary had not been paid since he arrived in France, he was very short of cash and gave Congress only his I.O.U.

Jones's naval biographer of 1841 considered his expense account "exorbitant," and pointed out that General Washington charged the public less for his expenses during the entire war than Jones did for the two years spent in France, working on this mission. But the General was living the austere life of bivouac and camp, while the Chevalier had to keep up a proper appearance in the world's most expensive and luxurious capital. A modern auditor, however, might take exception to Jones's deducting his share and his expenses at the same time, which meant that his share escaped paying any proportion of the expenses.

2. Paul Jones, Merchant

In the meantime Paul Jones was considering various projects for investing his money. He sent to Philadelphia a consignment of goods for sale, in care of his friend John Ross, to whom he writes, "Your professions of attachment and friendship for me led me to expect a more delicate attention from you than is commonly to be looked for from one Merchant to another." Jones, at the end of his patience, next orders Ross to hand over the goods to Jonathan Nesbitt.

This business was typical of Jones's brief experience as a merchant.

Fortunately, Robert Morris dissuaded him from making an "adventure" to India; too many Americans were already doing that. But since Morris had undertaken to provide the French tobacco monopoly with all the tobacco it wanted from America, he would give Jones a profitable freight from Virginia to France, if the Chevalier had already purchased a ship.

The Chevalier had not yet purchased a ship but was seriously thinking of it. Since the war, everyone had been talking about trade and exploration in the Pacific. Captain Cook had sailed on his famous voyages; Lapérouse embarked on his latest voyage in the summer of 1785, and at Jefferson's request Jones found information on his preparations. In Paris Jones met John Ledyard, the celebrated rolling stone from Connecticut. Ledyard had sailed around the world with Cook on his third voyage, in the course of which he got wind of immense profits to be made by collecting sea otter pelts on the Northwest Coast of America, selling them in China, and investing the proceeds in Chinese goods wanted in Europe. Ledyard's scheme, which greatly excited Jones, was to fit out a ship of 250 tons, man it with 45 Frenchmen and, with Jones as master, starting about 10 October, to sail around the Horn to Hawaii and Vancouver Island and the coast of Alaska. Jones thought that two ships would be required, and that he could induce Louis XVI to finance them. Somewhere on the Northwest Coast they would set up a "factory" where Ledyard, with one ship and a suitable guard, would spend the summer trading trinkets with the Indians for furs. Jones, with the other ship, would try to market in Japan the first lot collected; and if the Japanese still declined to receive foreigners he would proceed to Macao or Canton and sell the furs there. He would then return to the Northwest Coast for more furs; and both ships, loaded with the valuable sea otter, would dispose of them in the best Oriental market, load tea, silk and porcelain, and return to France around the world. Ledyard calculated on a profit of 1000 per cent in a three- or four-year voyage.

This was not absurdly sanguine, as the profits made by Northwest Coast traders for a number of years prove. Ledyard and Jones might have made a killing, had they started promptly. But several factors stopped them. Dr. Bancroft, who was to be one of the investors, reported that two English merchantmen had got the jump and would cut into the trade. No suitable ship could be had for less than thrice Ledyard's calculated price. The French Navy was not interested. Jones wished to await the approval of Robert Morris, and did not get it. But Spain really killed the plan. Jones wrote to his friend Carmichael, American chargé d'affaires at Madrid, to sound out that government's attitude; and Carmichael's reply was very discouraging. The King of Spain considered the entire west coast of the Americas to be his exclusive domain, and any foreigners attempting to trade there would be treated as poachers. He meant it, too; he almost went to war with England over the "Nootka Sound affair" five years later. The Spanish King's veto ended the Ledyard-Jones plan, because Louis XVI, the King's close ally, would not permit any French ship to break Spanish laws.

Denied this adventure, even the planning of which cost him dear since he had to keep Ledyard for five months in Paris, Paul Jones invested his money mostly in America, in stock of the Bank of North America and in various land companies. He also put eighteen hundred pounds into a scheme of Edward Bancroft's to import quercitron bark from America, and to introduce the yellow dye that it yields among English clothiers. He indulged in an "unfortunate adventure," as he describes it, of shipping American goods to Lorient. A letter to M. Lamoureux of that place ordered him to sell the stuff at public auction and take the loss. Thus, all Jones's schemes for making money were unsuccessful. He was not cut out to be a merchant.

Houdon the sculptor, when making his bust of Jones for the Lodge of the Nine Sisters, retained a terra-cotta mold of it from which the Commodore now ordered copies made for Lafayette and Jefferson; and in 1788 he ordered eight more made for prominent Americans who had been or might be useful to him. Jefferson's bust and at least six others, signed by Houdon and dated 1780, have survived, as well as one in marble made for the Duc d'Orléans, which is now in the Naval Academy Museum.

3. Madame T——

In Paris, Paul Jones renewed many of his former contacts. The Genets again were his principal friends, Masonic lodge meetings one of his chief recreations, and he showed up frequently at the King's levees in order to remind ministers of his existence and of their debt. But he did not reëstablish relations with the Lowendahls. Madame knew that Jones had nothing to offer her husband the Brigadier, and the Chevalier had learned that there was no use making love to her. He sheered off from "Delia," the Comtesse de Nicolson, who was only too ready to *réchauffer* the torrid affair of 1780; for she had become a widow and he did not wish to marry. But before long he was heavily involved with another widow, Madame T——, as he always refers to the lady.

Of this affair we cannot tell when or where it began. Jones probably was attracted to Madame T——, as he had been to the Comtesse Lowendahl, by the supposition that she was of royal blood. She believed that she was—or she pretended to be—a daughter of Louis XV by a "lady of quality" with whom that royal buck had sported before taking on the Du Barry. Her mother, she claimed, had abandoned her at an early age to the Marquise de Marsan, who brought her up and, after the death of her English husband, arranged for her to be presented to her reputed cousin Louis XVI in the hope of receiving a pension; but the presentation never came off.

All this and more was the subject of a letter from Jones to Jefferson, written 4 September 1787 when the Chevalier was in New York. He had received through the diplomatic pouch (by courtesy of William Short, the attaché) a heart-wringing letter from Madame T—— telling of the death of the Marquise, which left her without friends or resources. Jones appears to have been so moved that he told Jefferson, who had never met the lady, about her royal pedigree, and begged him to read and deliver his answer to her, to look her up, and to do something for her, such as presenting her to the King. Quite an order for an American diplomatist! But I dare say Franklin, before leaving Paris, had told Jefferson that one of his duties would be to look out for Paul Jones's mistress of the moment.

In his reply to the pathetic letter from Madame T——, Jones wrote pious platitudes about the death of her friend and protectress; and, referring to a sister-in-law, with whom she lived, added, "I persuade myself she will continue her tender care of her sweet godson, and that you will cover him all over with kisses for me; they come warm to *you both* from my heart!" One can hardly doubt that this sweet child was Madame T——'s by John Paul Jones.

So, who was Madame T——? Many and wild have been the conjectures. She has been wrongly identified as Madame Thilarié, Madame Tessan, Madame Turgot, Madame de la Trémouille, and as the Madame Tellisson to whom Jones wrote a matter-of-fact letter in 1780. Buell invented a pretty name for her, "Aimée Adèle de Telison," which has been widely accepted. The answer, which waited one hundred and seventy years in Thomas Jefferson's papers for Dr. Julian Boyd to discover, is found in the signatures on her letters to the American Minister. Alas for romance, she had the ordinary English name of Townsend! Her first name we do not know, as she signs herself "T. Townsend"; but it was probably Thérèse, since she was a Frenchwoman, and any other woman's name beginning with T is very rare in France. She was the widow of an Englishman of whom nothing whatever is known.

Jefferson gallantly complied with his friend Jones's requests. He received the Chevalier's letter of 4 September, with its amorous enclosure, on 14 October 1787. The very next day he wrote to Madame T——, by a messenger whom she had sent to William Short's office at the American Legation, inviting her to call when she returned to Paris from the country, and enclosing Jones's letter. In her reply, Madame said she wished to make Mr. Jefferson's acquaintance, having a *projet* in which she hopes he will share. Somewhat alarmed, Mr. Jefferson replies that he wishes to be useful to Madame; but if her *projet* is to be presented by him at court he cannot, as he never goes to court. Next day Madame writes that her *projet* is only a trip to London to sell some Bank of England stock that she owns. She has no money; will Mr. J. lend her twenty-five or thirty louis d'or for a month? Mr. J. replies the same day that he is "infinitely distressed" to be unable to help Madame, but he is "incapable" of lending her such a sum; and she in turn gracefully apologizes for having made the request.

Paul Jones, as we shall see in the next chapter, returned to Paris in mid-December 1787, and left for Denmark and Russia about 1 February 1788. During that interval he renewed relations with Mrs. Townsend—the first time he failed to shift mistresses after a voyage. He gave her all the money he could scrape together, and borrowed forty-four hundred livres (eight hundred and eighty dollars) to pay her debts. This we learn from a letter that Jones wrote to Jefferson from Russia on 9 September 1788, in which he asks, "What has become of Mrs. T——?" He has not heard from her in seven months. Will Jefferson kindly look up a certain M. Dubois, rue Neuve des Petits-Champs, who negotiated the loan of forty-four hundred livres, and ascertain whether Mrs. T—— actually received and used it?

The rest is silence. Jefferson did not write to M. Dubois; there is no further mention of the lady or of the baby boy in his or in Jones's correspondence, and the Chevalier did not renew relations with Madame when he returned to Paris in 1790. Probably by that time she and her son and sister-in-law had emigrated to England to escape the French Revolution. Possibly Jones and Jefferson had found out that she was an impostor in claiming royal blood. The Bourbon bastards, all well documented, were well taken care of with titles and pensions. A French historian who has catalogued those of Louis XV reports seven illegitimate daughters, all married into the nobility, and not one who can by any stretch of imagination be identified as Paul Jones's mistress. Obviously, the secretary at the Court of Versailles who kept track of the King's left-handed cousins must have reached the same conclusion, which would explain why Louis XVI broke an engagement to receive Madame T——, of which Jones complained in his first letter on the subject to Jefferson.

We know nothing more about Mrs. Townsend. It may be that she concocted the story of royal blood in order to hook the Chevalier. But her letters to Jefferson are those of a well-educated lady, superior in handwriting to those of the Comtesse de Lowendahl, and in diction to the ungrammatical outpourings of Delia. I prefer to think that the story of royal descent was invented, and told to Thérèse, by her "lady of quality" mother, who abandoned her at an early age to the Marquise. It sounded much better to suppose that Maman had been *la maîtresse du Roi* rather than the victim of some ordinary lover.

However that may be, Mrs. Townsend and her son disappear into the mists of history. Christopher Columbus, in his will, remembered his former mistress and their son. Nelson left his Emma "to the nation"—not that it did her much good. But John Paul Jones said not a word in his will about the woman who had been his mistress for several years, or about that sweet boy whom he once wished to "cover all over with kisses."

Did the little fellow die in infancy? Or did he grow up and fight Napoleon under the English flag, or what? We shall probably never know.

4. Other Paris Friends

Mrs. Townsend moved in a different milieu from Jones's other Paris friends; she knew nought of them, nor they of her. It was at this time that the John Adamses spent a year in Paris and entertained the Chevalier at their residence, the Hôtel de Verrières in Auteuil. He was still intimate with the Genets, and with two charming sisters whom he probably had known in 1780. These were Madame de Bonneuil and Madame Thilarié; the one was wife to Cyrille de Bonneuil, *premier valet de chambre* to the King's younger brother the Comte d'Artois, the other to Jacques Thilarié, a well-known lawyer. The sisters were very close to one another and to Madame Vigée le

Brun the painter, who in her memoirs writes that she often supped at the Thilariés with Paul Jones; and that she "never met a more modest man. It was impossible to make him talk about his great deeds; but on any other subject he conversed freely with great wit and without affectation." She also met Jones at the house of a sculptor named Le Moyne, who entertained him and the two sisters.

There are only two letters in the Jones manuscripts, both undated, connecting the Captain with this circle of friends. The first is a letter from M. de Bonneuil inviting Jones to attend the *Comédie italienne* and take supper with him afterward. The second is a barely literate note signed, *"Angélique, femme de Madame de Bonneuil,"* addressed to *"Monsieur De Paule Jones chez mr franklin a pasy pres pari."* She informs the Commodore that her mistress has charged her to tell him how vexed she is not to have seen him before her departure for Versailles, and begs him to call on her Monday next at 7:00 P.M. Angélique adds that she personally is very much touched with the nice things Jones has said about her, and begs his portrait, a gift which would complete her happiness. One may infer from this letter that the gallant Chevalier, in the manner of eighteenth-century romances, was cultivating the favor of the maid in order to obtain that of the mistress; or that Paul Jones the eternal sailor was having a little fun on the side with Angélique.

The Bonneuil couple managed to survive the French Revolution. After the death of her first husband, Madame Thilarié married Jacques Duval D'Esprémenil, Carlyle's "Crispin-Catiline D'Esprémenil." Both he and his wife were executed during the Terror.

5. The "Mémoire" to Louis XVI

Paul Jones still yearned for active service. Madame Vigée le Brun, on the basis of her frequent conversations with the Chevalier, made the shrewd guess that he was scheming to become an admiral in the French Navy and had even asked it of Louis XVI. Flag rank was the one thing he needed to crown his naval career, and he had about given up hope of getting it from Congress—too many people like Captain Nicholson, Arthur Lee and Sam Adams were interested in thwarting him.

A desire to impress Louis XVI was the obvious motive of the *Mémoire* which Paul Jones drafted during the last months of 1785. He had it translated and copied in neat script by a hack writer named Benoit André. Together with copies of commendatory and other letters that he had received from important people, he had two copies bound in red morocco and emblazoned with the royal arms. One copy was presented to the King early in 1786, the other he kept. The English original, which contained details thought unworthy of the royal notice, has unfortunately disappeared.

The manuscript title page of the King's copy bears this title: *Extrait du Journal des Services principaux de Paul-Jones dans la Révolution des Etats-Unis d'Amérique; écrit par lui-même et presenté avec un profound respect au très illustre Prince Louis XVI*. This is followed by a dedicatory poem, of Jones's composition, which in view of the good King's fate, reads rather sadly:

> Protector of fair Freedom's Rights
>   Louis, thy virtues suit a God!
> The good Man in thy praise delights
>   And Tyrants Trimble at thy nod!
>
> Thy people's Father, lov'd so well,
>   May Time respect!—when thou art gone,
> May each New-Year of Hist'ry tell,
>   Thy Sons, with lustre, fill thy Throne.

This *Mémoire* is not what it purports to be, a series of extracts from Jones's journals, but a fairly detailed story of his life from 1775 to 1784. Toward the end, the author recalls that Louis XVI expressed "the highest confidence" in the Chevalier's employing his presentation sword for the glory of America and the House of Bourbon.

Jones then suggests that the time may soon come when he may prove himself deserving of this compliment.

This hint that he would like a commission in the Royal French Navy could hardly have been more open, at a time when there was talk of another war between England and France. But the war scare passed, a new treaty was signed between France and Britain, and Louis XVI, reducing his naval establishment instead of building it up, had no billet for Paul Jones.

XIX

New York
and
Denmark

1787-1788

1. To America and Back

The only reason for Paul Jones to stay in Paris after 5 August 1786, when Jefferson accepted his account of the prize money, was to negotiate about the prizes which Denmark had delivered to the British consul at Bergen. Jones could accomplish nothing with the Danish minister to France; so, with Jefferson's approval, he set out for Copenhagen in the spring of 1787. But he had only reached Brussels when he made an abrupt decision to return to the United States.

His reasons for this move were somewhat complicated. There was the practical matter of funds for the journey; Jefferson was away when he had set forth, so he could borrow no money from him, and a remittance from Dr. Bancroft in London, a return on Jones's eighteen hundred pounds invested in the dyewood speculation, was not on hand in Brussels as he had ordered and expected. But surely, a journey from Brussels to Le Havre, and thence to New York by sailing packet, was more costly than a trip from Brussels to Copenhagen? To John Jay, Minister of Foreign Affairs in the now expiring Confederation, Jones stated on 18 July 1787, shortly after his arrival in New York, that he had come home owing to unforeseen circumstances in his "private affairs," and that he intended to take the next packet ship to Europe and proceed to Denmark. These New York-Le Havre packets under the French flag made eight round voyages annually; it took them about five weeks going eastward and seven weeks to return to New York.

Jones's uncertainty about congressional approval of his prize money account was probably the main motive for this voyage, and certainly the reason for prolonging into winter his stay in New York, where Congress was sitting.

American eyes and hopes were turned to the Federal Convention then sitting in Philadelphia, and Jones could get nothing out of the Treasury Board of the old Congress in New York. So, there he spent the whole of a hot summer, lodging "in the humble home of a friend of his family, Mr. Robert Hyslop," who kept shop at the foot of Dye (now Dey) Street on the East River, and lived over his shop. The only incident of his stay that has been recorded was an unpleasant encounter with Pierre Landais, who was trying to get money out of Congress. Jones was talking to a friend on a sidewalk when Landais passed behind his back, spat on the ground and remarked, "I spit in your face!" Jones did not even hear him, but Landais circulated the story that he had actually spat in Jones's face, and the Chevalier felt obliged to make a public denial.

The Treasury Board, upon which Arthur Lee now sat, reported to Congress unfavorably to Jones's accounts on 28 September. The report was shown to the Chevalier and he made a lengthy reply on 4 October. He defended the amount of his expenses as necessary to get public business done in France, and asserted that nobody but himself could have got a penny out of that government. He was outraged that the Board's report seemed to be "very zealous" for the interests of Landais, "that broken and disgraced officer," and that it accused him, Chevalier Jones, of leaving undone what he really had done to prevent the deduction from the prize money of the Texel expenses. And the Board's report made some nasty insinuations, obviously inspired by Lee, about Jones's old accounts of 1781, to which he replied sharply and convincingly.

Upon receipt of Jones's reply, a committee of Congress, Edward Carrington of Virginia chairman, reported favorably on his accounts; and Congress, after rejecting an amendment offered by Henry Lee, accepted them on 11 October 1787.

It has been said that first Jefferson and then Congress showed bad faith to the officers and men of *Richard* and *Alliance* in never paying to them the prize money that their Commodore had collected in France. Neither statement is true. Jefferson used the money he received from Jones to pay his own salary and those of other American representatives abroad, but rendered an exact account of it to Congress; and the Treasury Board on 1 May 1787 handed over to William Edgar, its disbursing agent in New York, the entire sum of $20,772.55, together with Jones's rolls of *Richard* and *Alliance* which stated the exact amount due to each officer and man. Edgar paid out to applicants a good part of this, and on 26 February 1789 returned the balance, $5,274.57, to the treasury of the new Federal Government. The United States Treasury in the next four years paid to applicants an additional $1,374.89, leaving an unexpended balance of $3,899.68. In 1848 Congress ordered this to be distributed to the survivors of 1779 and heirs of the defunct. The account was finally closed in 1861, fourscore and two years after the battle.

Paul Jones made another unsuccessful effort in New York to get himself promoted Rear Admiral, yet he did not return to Europe empty-handed. On 16 October 1787 Congress unanimously voted him a gold medal, which Jefferson was instructed to have struck in Paris, and directed that a letter be written to Louis XVI notifying him of this honor. They also begged His Majesty to allow the Chevalier "to embark with one of his fleets of evolution; convinced that he can no where else so well acquire that knowledge which may hereafter render him more extensively useful." This request was doubtless dictated by Jones, always eager to improve his professional knowledge.

It is amusing to find that Paul Jones, anticipating the gold medal, had already caused designs for it to be made by a friend of his, a French medalist named Jean-Martin Renaud. André tells the story that Jones ran up such a bill for these sketches that when he saw the artist approaching on a street, he hid up an alleyway. But Renaud saw him, and upon their meeting next day said, "Can you imagine what happened to me yesterday? I frightened the man to whom all England has never given a moment of fear!" Jefferson took the design out of Renaud's hands and gave it to a more eminent artist, Augustin Dupré, who had already executed medals of Washington and other generals. Fortunately Renaud's designs were preserved by André, who used engravings of them in his printed edition of Jones's *Mémoirs* to Louis XVI. Dupré used the profile of Houdon's bust of Jones, wearing a style of hairdressing that shows off his well-cut features, while Renaud depicted Jones as he appeared in 1786 when he had become a little fleshy from good living in Paris and had dressed his hair in the latest style, with an enormous club behind and two rolls over the ears. The Renaud sketch was also the basis for a wax medallion of Jones made for Mrs. Belches, a Scotswoman, in 1786. Renaud's design for the Battle of Flamborough Head has the merit of showing *Serapis* anchored, the only representation of the battle that does; but Dupré made much the most artistic representation of the battle, with details generally correct. Note especially how the topsides of *Bonhomme Richard* are half shot away, and that *Serapis* has not yet struck her ensign.

The inscriptions on the Dupré medal are:

[*Obverse*]

JOANNI PAVLO JONES CLASSIS PRAEFECTO. COMITIA AMERICANA.
[*To John Paul Jones, Commander of the Fleet. The American
Congress.*]

[*Reverse*]

HOSTIVM NAVIBVS CAPTIS AVT FVGATIS. AD ORAM SCOTIAE XXIII.
SEPT. M.DCCLXXVIIII. DUPRÉ. F.
[*The Enemy's Ships Captured or Put to Flight. At Scotland's
Shore 23 Sept. 1779. Dupré fecit.*]

It was doubtless owing to Jones's absence from Paris (the medal being executed during his Russian sojourn) that Dupré made the mistake of placing the battle off Scotland instead of England, and forgot to anchor *Serapis*.

The original gold medal presented to Jones disappeared after his death, but not before numerous copies had been struck in silver, copper and even Wedgwood porcelain. The matrix of it, however, remained in the Hôtel de la Monnaie, Paris, and was used for a fresh strike in gold which is now in the chapel crypt at Annapolis, near Jones's body.

On 25 October 1787 Congress passed a resolve authorizing Jefferson to settle with King Christian VII of Denmark the claims for prizes handed over by his government to the British, and "to dispatch the Chevalier J. P. Jones or any other Agent" to Copenhagen to negotiate. On the following day Congress ordered its Secretary to communicate this to "the Chevalier John Paul Jones."

At this point occurs one of the things in Paul Jones's career that has mystified his biographers. On 24 October, he wrote to Jefferson that he would have taken passage in the French packet leaving New York the following day but for a rumor "that the English fleet . . . was seen steering to the westward, and that a British squadron is cruising in the North Sea." Consequently he has postponed his passage until he could find one in an American ship. Why should Jones, of all people, have been afraid of a British fleet four years after the war was over? The explanation is simple: there were rumors of impending war between England and France; Jefferson was so alarmed that he wrote to John Jay on 19 September that he had warned American merchants in France against risking property in English or French ships. If war did break out, the French packet would naturally be one of the first to be captured. So Jones waited until he could sail on an American ship, which he did on 11 November 1787. She landed him at Dover, whence he drove to London and conferred with John Adams on the subject of his mission. He then left for Paris and had arrived by 19 December; a remarkably fast journey for that age of horse and sail.

Now, more mystery. On the day of his arrival Jones writes to Jefferson from the Hôtel de Beauvais, rue des Vieux Augustins, that he has both public dispatches and private letters for the Minister; that he has "several *strong reasons* for desiring that no person should know" he is in Paris until he has seen Jefferson and been favored with his "advice on the steps I ought to pursue." He will not budge from the hotel, where he is registered incognito, until he has seen the American Minister; so when Jefferson calls he is "to ask for the Gentleman just arrived, who is lodged in No. 1."

Now, what "strong reasons" could there have been for this secrecy? The ladies, of course! Jones wished to hear all about Thérèse Townsend from Jefferson, and how he stood with her, before he showed his face in the streets of Paris, where he might have been recognized in an embarrassing way by her, or by other women.

Jefferson's visit to the "Gentleman in No. 1" evidently satisfied Jones about Thérèse, with whom he speedily resumed intimate relations. And Jefferson also brought him even more vital news, that the Russian Ambassador at the Court of Versailles wished to know if the Chevalier Jones would be interested in a commission in the Imperial Russian Navy?

The Chevalier was interested, very much so. But before embarking on that risky venture, he had to finish the Danish business.

2. Mission to Copenhagen

The matter of the prizes sent into Bergen, which bedeviled relations between the United States and Denmark for some eighty years, was simple enough. Two of the more valuable prizes taken by Paul Jones's squadron in 1779, letter-of-marque ships *Betsey* of 22 guns and 84 men and *Union* of about the same strength, laden with uniforms and supplies for the British Army in Quebec, were sent from Scots waters into the Norwegian port (then under the crown of Denmark), arriving 12 September. *Charming Polly*, a small prize taken off the English coast, was sent there later and shared the fate of the others. Jones blamed this on Landais; but it was really the fault of Le Ray de Chaumont, who had given orders to that effect, fancying that he had enough influence at Bergen to have the prizes condemned by the French consul there. The Danish government, with the British Navy looking down its throat, naturally did not see eye to eye with M. de Chaumont. Its proper course would have been to order these ships out of Danish waters. Instead, the government leaned over backward to please the British and handed over the prizes to the British consul at Bergen, throwing the American prize crews on the beach to shift for themselves.

Franklin promptly protested, and a tedious diplomatic sparring began. The Doctor, just before leaving the Paris post where he had served so brilliantly, made one of the few mistakes in his diplomatic career in rejecting a settlement of ten thousand pounds which Denmark then offered because she was eager to obtain a commercial treaty with the United States. The French consul at Bergen estimated the value of the three ships and cargoes at fifty thousand pounds and Franklin did not wish to be responsible for settling for less.

There the matter rested when Paul Jones took over. We have already seen that he headed for Copenhagen in the spring of 1787, but went to New York instead. Now he made a fresh start for the Danish capital and got there, but no further in this affair.

Jones arrived at Copenhagen via Hamburg on 4 March, overcome by fatigue and the excessive cold suffered on the journey. He had gone all the way in his own traveling carriage, the least uncomfortable manner for a gentleman to travel in those days. All European governments maintained post roads and post stations, in stages about six English miles apart, where one could hire horses and postilions at a fixed rate to drive one's carriage to the next post where the horses could be changed. It was even possible to drive day and night if you were in a hurry. From the diary of John Quincy Adams we find that between Paris and Brussels there were thirty-three posts, that the French tariff was 1 livre 5s (about 25 cents) per horse per post, with 15s to the postilion who rode the near horse of a pair. In

Belgium the charges were double. It took Adams nine hours to drive fifty-seven miles from Paris to Compiègne, where he spent the first night; the second night was spent at Valenciennes, and at the end of the third day he reached Brussels. The roads were paved with stone blocks, over which the iron-tired wheels rattled abominably.

After keeping his bed for several days in Copenhagen, the Chevalier paid his respects to the French minister plenipotentiary, who in turn presented him to the Danish Minister of Foreign Affairs, Count Bernstorff. Jones (as he wrote to Jefferson) had a favorable reception and discussed the new Federal Constitution with the Count, who thought that it was dangerous to make the President Commander in Chief of the Army and Navy, an opinion which Jones himself shared. A week later the Count presented Jones to King Christian and the royal family, who invited him to "sup" with them at the palace; and that began a round of festivities.

The Chevalier was pleased and flattered by all this, but unable to corner Count Bernstorff and talk business. That astute statesman, observing that Jones had no power to conclude anything, notified him on 4 April that the negotiations would have to be conducted in Paris, where Jefferson possessed full powers. He did so in the most polite manner imaginable, and King Christian further sweetened the pill by offering Jones a pension of 1500 kroner (about $200) per annum, ostensibly to show his esteem in consequence of the respect that Jones had shown to the Danish flag during the war. One suspects that the royal motives may have been different. The Chevalier had the "delicacy," according to his most adoring biographers, to decline the gift. He really had no choice, since the acceptance of such a pension was expressly forbidden, both by the Articles of Confederation and the new Constitution.

Nevertheless, around Christmas 1789, when Jones was feeling very hard up, he proposed to "draw" for the arrears of this pension, presumably by a bill of exchange on the King of Denmark. Fortunately, before taking such a step, he found out that his draft would certainly be dishonored, and did nothing about it. Royal gifts lapsed if not accepted when offered. Yet even at the point of death Jones mentioned in his will "arrears of my pension from the King of Denmark" as an asset.

Although Jones accomplished nothing by his month's mission to Denmark, Jefferson did no more in Paris, nor did anyone else. The United States kept alive this claim for eighty years. Denmark took the attitude that, not having recognized the revolted colonies, she was obliged by her treaty with England to return prizes taken in a British civil war. But lobbyists in Congress were more successful than diplomats in Copenhagen. The Congress, as we have seen, voted four thousand dollars to Captain Landais as compensation for what he might have got if Denmark had paid up. Jones's heirs took the hint. In 1837 his niece Janette Taylor and a son of Captain Matthew Parke USMC revived the subject; and, as a result of persistent pressure by them and others, Congress in 1848 generously assumed that the three prizes of 1779 had been worth fifty thousand pounds as the French consul reported, and voted $165,598.37 to be distributed among the officers and men of *Bonhomme Richard* and *Alliance*, or to their heirs.

Thus, the American taxpayer paid for Chaumont's folly and the Danish breach of international law. The Commodore's share, $24-421.78, distributed among ten of his nephews and nieces, amounted to considerably more than he ever obtained for his share of *Serapis*, *Scarborough* and the prizes sent into France.

The Chevalier was not sorry to be brushed off by Bernstorff; he was eager to proceed to Russia. The Russian minister at Copenhagen had informed him that all had been arranged except the matter of rank, and that the Empress was expecting him. He offered Jones a substantial sum for traveling expenses, which the Chevalier again had the "delicacy" to decline; but later he accepted an even larger sum of expense money from the imperial hand.

Jones's "delicacy" in money matters recalls a quip of the old Federalist Harrison Gray Otis. At a time when the "solid men of Boston" were raising the wind to pay Daniel Webster's debts and keep him in Washington, someone remarked that the proposition was "indelicate," and he wondered how Mr. Webster would take it?

"How will he take it?" snorted Otis. "Why, quarterly, to be sure!"

XX

Kontradmiral Pavel Ivanovich Jones

1788-1789

1. Catherine's Rear Admiral

"The Euxine, the Meotian waters felt thee next, and long-skirted Turks, O Paul; and thy fiery soul has wasted itself in a thousand contradictions:—to no purpose." Thus Thomas Carlyle dismissed Paul Jones's Russian adventure, not unfairly.

Catherine II, Empress of Russia, was one of the ablest rulers of her day, although her personal morals shocked people even then. "With the character of a very great man, she will always be adored as the most amiable and captivating of the fair sex," wrote Jones himself. Born a princess in a petty German state, married at the age of fourteen to the feeble Grand Duke who became Emperor Peter III, she had him quietly strangled and herself proclaimed Empress in 1762. Catherine made Russian interests her own, and adopted the foreign policy, now sadly familiar to the world, of setting up satellites around her borders and annexing them when she was ready. Especially she turned her attention to Russia's southern border, and began a series of intrigues and aggressions against Turkey, with the ultimate object of making the Black Sea a Russian lake and acquiring Constantinople. As a result of her first Turkish war, which ended in 1774, the Porte recognized the independence of the Crimea under a Tartar Khan, from whom she "liberated" it within ten years.

By Catherine, and still more by her lover Grigori Potemkin, the Crimea was regarded as a mere steppingstone. She promoted Potemkin Field Marshal, created him Prince de Tauride, and made him practically vice-emperor for southern Russia. All the world knows the story of her imperial progress down the Dnieper River in 1787 to meet her lover, who built mock-up villages where there were only deserts, dressed up his servants as Khans and Shahs to offer homage, and sent troops of "happy villagers" in fancy dress from one point on the river to another, to sing and dance and flatter the Empress. But it was somewhat humiliating to find the Dnieper estuary (the Liman*) in Turkish hands, with a Turkish fleet blocking its exit to the Black Sea. It was as if some early President had staged a million-dollar pageant down the Mississippi, only to find the Mexicans barring the entrance to New Orleans.

So Russia built up Kherson at the head of the Liman as a naval arsenal, Sevastopol in the Crimea as a naval base, and Ekaterinoslav (now Dniepropetrovsk) as an army supply depot. But the Sultan still held the Bay of Odessa, and with the help of French engineers he constructed a powerful fort at Ochakov, at the mouth of the Liman, which enabled him to block the exit to the Black Sea and prevent the junction of the two Russian fleets that were being built at Kherson and Sevastopol. In the second Russo-Turkish war, which opened in August 1787, it was the object of the Turks to break up these Russian fleets and recapture lost provinces, and of the Russians to clear them out of the Liman and capture Ochakov.

This had to be in part a naval operation, and that is why the

* *Liman in Russian means the submerged mouth of a river.*

Empress wanted the services of John Paul Jones. The Russian Black Sea Fleet was a scratch collection of vessels manned by impressed serfs, Cossacks, Volga boatmen and Levantine pirates, officered in part by adventurers of six or seven nations. Catherine felt that only an outstanding naval officer from another country could weld this horde of scalawags into a real fighting navy.

Jones was first suggested for this job in 1785 by a Paris acquaint-ance known as M. le Comte de Wemyss. This man was David, Lord Elcho, heir to the Fourth Earl of Wemyss, excluded from the title because of an attainder for his part in the 1745 rebellion. Another promoter of Jones was Lewis Littlepage, a roving Virginian who, after serving as an aide to John Jay, and quarreling with him, took part in two campaigns of the War of Independence under French command. After the war he became great friends with the King of Poland, who made him a chamberlain and Chevalier of the Order of Saint Stanislas. Baron Grimm, a faithful correspondent of the Rus-sian Empress, mentioned Jones to her; Jefferson recommended him to M. Simolin, the Russian minister at Versailles; Simolin sounded Jones out on 1 February 1788, and passed the word to the Empress that he was available. Delighted, she cried out, "Jones will get to Constantinople!" Potemkin, though notably less enthusiastic, in-structed Simolin to make the final arrangements, and, at the time Jones was conducting his Danish mission, that was done. The Em-press first created him "Captain of the Fleet with the rank of Major General," which did not suit him; and at his request she ordered Potemkin on 4/15 April* to give him the rank of Rear Admiral in the Imperial Russian Navy. In Russia he was known as Kontradmiral Pavel Ivanovich (Paul the son of John) Jones; or, in the polite lan-guage of the court, Contre-Amiral Paul-Jones.

Flag rank was what Jones had always coveted; it was the principal bait that attracted him to the Russian service. He even hoped thus to impress Congress. He wrote to Jefferson begging him to use his in-fluence to have him promoted Rear Admiral USN, retroactive to the

---

* The first date is that of the Russian (Julian) calendar; the second, of the Gregorian, which was used in the rest of Europe and America.

Battle off Flamborough Head, as a gesture to "gratify the Empress." But as America now had no navy, there was even less chance of Jones's getting flag rank than there had been during the war. He does not appear to have been attracted by the Russian pay—150 roubles (about $145) a month—although that was about twice what he had drawn in the American Navy. And there is no doubt that he craved more action, and hoped that command of a battle fleet, even on an inland sea, would give him more practical experience and qualify him for high command if and when the United States built a navy.

It was not out of the way for a naval officer of one country to enter the service of another when his own was at peace. The British Navy had reduced its personnel from 110,000 to 26,000 after the War of American Independence, which meant that hundreds of officers were without employment. At least twenty of them entered the Russian service, in which the senior admiral was Sir Samuel Greig, a Scot.

As soon as these British officers in the Russian Navy heard of Paul Jones's appointment, they signed a remonstrance, raking up all the old stories about bastardy, piracy, smuggling and Mungo Maxwell, and threatening to throw up their commissions rather than serve under him. Admiral Greig advised them not to present it, as highly offensive to the Empress, nor did they; and since they all were in the Baltic fleet and Jones was especially engaged for the Black Sea fleet, there was no occasion for conflict. As it turned out, British officers were the least of Jones's troubles in Russia.

In mid-April Jones left Copenhagen for Stockholm. After spending but one night there, he proceeded to Grisslehamn, whence he expected to cross the Gulf of Bothnia to Finland in a packet ship. But the Gulf was still full of ice and the road around it closed by snow. So he chartered an undecked boat about 30 feet long, and a smaller one which could be dragged over ice flows if necessary, with the object of getting around the ice to the southward and into the Gulf of Finland. For a day the boat sailed south along the Swedish shore, the oarsmen still ignorant of Jones's intention. At nightfall, when in the latitude of Stockholm, he forced the men at pistol point to steer due east and then northeast. The boat had a small compass and Jones fixed the lamp of his light traveling carriage, which he had brought on board, to serve as binnacle light. Next morning they sighted the south coast of Finland across miles of ice. So up the Gulf they sailed. On the second night the smaller boat sank but the men were saved. Only at the end of the fourth day did the frostbitten crew make land at Reval (now Talinn, Estonia), "which was regarded as a kind of miracle," wrote the organizer of this dangerous passage.

After satisfying the boatmen and procuring them a pilot and provisions for their homeward passage, Jones bought horses and proceeded overland to St. Petersburg (now Leningrad), arriving 23 April by the Russian calendar, which would be 4 May by ours. On that very day the Empress wrote to Baron Grimm in Paris, "Paul Jones has just arrived here; he has entered my service." And, two days later, "I saw him today. I think he will suit our purpose admirably." He presented Her Imperial Majesty with a copy of the new Federal Constitution, which she probably did not read; but she told him "that the American Revolution cannot fail to bring about others and to influence every other government." Smart lady! No other European monarch, not even Frederick the Great, made so accurate an estimate of the American Revolution.

The new Rear Admiral was flattered by and delighted with his reception. "I was entirely captivated," he admitted, "and put myself into her hands without making any stipulation for my personal advantage. I demanded but one favour, 'that she would never condemn without hearing me.'" A Russian diarist in St. Petersburg noted that Jones had "made a good impression on the Empress, has entrée to the Hermitage, is welcomed everywhere, except among the English, who cannot bear him."

At this point the reader doubtless expects Kontradmiral Pavel Ivanovich to fall into the Empress's embrace and a great love affair to begin. For Paul Jones, the American Navy's greatest lover, to encounter Catherine of Russia, the most be-lovered woman on any throne, has been too much for the novelists—even for some of Jones's biographers. He becomes her umpteenth lover, Potemkin is furious and fouls things up so that the Rear Admiral loses his job and is disgraced. Very simple!

Unfortunately for romance, the facts are otherwise. Jones looked to the Empress for confidence and favors, not for love. She was a fat woman in her sixtieth year, with false teeth and swollen legs; she still had the charm that some women exude to their dying day, but her love affairs, if they can be so called, were reduced to a system. When Potemkin found his powers no longer adequate for her demands, he connived at her having a series of youthful lovers, chosen from among the household guards. If her eye fell upon a handsome young guardsman, he was first given a thorough physical examination by the court physician to see if he was "healthy"; then one of the Empress's ladies of honor, known in court circles as *l'épreuveuse* (the prover), tested his capacity in a practical way. If he passed, he became the Empress's lover. This happened no fewer than thirteen times, since none of these young men could stand it very long. The incumbent during Jones's sojourn in Russia was Zubov, a guardsman in his twenties, and he was doing very well. Thus the Empress had no personal need for Jones; and his one thought after seeing her was to get off to the Black Sea and take over his command.

2. Situation in the Black Sea

On 7/18 May 1788, after staying at St. Petersburg only long enough to have some Russian uniforms made (for which the Empress gave him a generous allowance of two thousand ducats, about a thousand dollars),* and after kissing her hand again at the palace of Tsarskoe-Selo, Kontradmiral Pavel Ivanovich set out southward in his now well-broken-in traveling carriage. Pavel Dimitrevski, a secretary and interpreter furnished by the Grand Chamberlain, accompanied him. The American bore a "gracious command" from the

* The Russian naval uniform was cut like the British and the American, but all white, with blue revers or lapels, a blue band on the cuff and gold epaulets.

Empress to Field Marshal the Prince Potemkin, commander in chief of all Russian armed forces and head of the army about to march on Ochakov, that Jones be given the rank of Rear Admiral and employed "in accordance with your best judgment in the Black Sea fleet." The two met at Ekaterinoslav on 19/30 May. Jones appears to have been favorably impressed by the Prince, as he always was by important people who received him with something more than common civility. Potemkin may have thought well of his new flag officer, but he no longer had any great need for him since he already had three rear admirals in the Black Sea. To the Empress he wrote, "Rear Admiral Jones has arrived and I sent him to the fleet. He now has his chance to show his experience and courage. I have given him every chance and facility."

Some chance! Some facility! What Potemkin did was to toss Jones into a pack of sea-wolves, to sink or swim.

It will be observed from the language of the Empress's command to Potemkin that it was left to the Prince where and how to employ his new rear admiral. But Jones somehow got it into his head that he had been promised the over-all naval command in the Black Sea. That misunderstanding spelled trouble.

Potemkin detailed the Chevalier Don José de Ribas, a Spaniard of his staff, as liaison officer between himself and Jones; and with him Jones sailed down the Dnieper to Kherson. There he met Kontradmiral Mordvinov, an English-trained Russian with an English wife, who commanded the naval arsenal. Mordvinov showed his teeth and refused to deliver a command flag to Jones. The new Rear Admiral continued along the north shore of the Liman to the roadstead of Shirokaya, where he found his squadron, and went on board flagship *Vladimir* (which he always spells *Wolodimer*). There he found Brigadier Panaiotti Alexiano, a Greek in the Russian service, who had expected to have Jones's job; and Alexiano also showed his teeth. Jones now discovered that the Flotilla, small craft accompanying his Squadron, was under Kontradmiral the Prince of Nassau-Siegen, who greeted Jones cordially and entertained him for several nights on board his yacht. But it was not long before Nassau-Siegen, too, bared his teeth.

Jones either did not grasp what was going on, or from good policy chose to ignore it. He wrote to Potemkin what a fine fleet of ships and group of officers he had found. In company with Don José de Ribas (the one officer close to him in this campaign who remained loyal), Jones set forth in a small boat to reconnoiter the Liman.

This estuary is about thirty nautical miles in a west-east line from the Black Sea to Shirokaya roadstead, the farthest east that the larger ships could sail. It is nowhere more than eight miles wide, and in some places only two miles wide between mudbanks. The average depth in Jones's day was about 18 feet, and today it is even less, except in a dredged ship channel. The entrance, less than two miles wide, is between Ochakov Point, which the Turks had heavily fortified, and a narrow sandspit called Kinburn Peninsula, held by the Russians. Halfway out on this sandspit was Fort Kinburn where General Suvorov had established his headquarters. Russian strategy aimed to keep this entrance clear, to prevent the Turks from reinforcing Ochakov by sea; Turkish strategy was to close it up. Paul Jones called on Suvorov at Fort Kinburn and was much impressed by him. This shows his good judgment, because that Russian later proved himself to be second only to Wellington as an opponent to Napoleon. And Suvorov promptly adopted Jones's suggestion to build a battery on the tip of the Kinburn sandspit.

Paul Jones and Don José returned to Shirokaya roadstead, where to all appearances the caballing had died down, and the Kontradmiral broke his flag in *Vladimir* on 29 May /9 June. Alexiano reported to Potemkin, "the Squadron has this day been transferred to the command of Rear Admiral and Chevalier Paul Jones."

The chain of command on the Liman was crazy. The only certain point was Potemkin, chief of all armed forces under the Empress. Paul Jones commanded only the "Squadron." This consisted of his flagship, which rated as a ship of the line, eight so-called frigates and four other armed vessels. These were sailing ships of all sizes and rigs, built with shoal draft for navigating the estuary. Flagship *Vladimir* was pierced for 66 guns, but could carry only 24 twenty-four-pounders and two mortars for shooting fire-balls. Independent of Jones, taking orders direct from Potemkin, was the "Flotilla," composed of craft propelled largely by oars. It consisted of 25 galleys, floating batteries, barges and vessels called double-chaloupes, together with a large number of one-gun craft called the "Zaporozhye boats" because they were manned by Cossacks from Zaporozhye at the bend of the Dnieper. The boats carried heavy guns for their size, and a complement of troops who were protected from enemy musket fire by woolsacks piled on the bulwarks. These units corresponded to the LST and other small-craft flotillas in a modern amphibious operation, whilst Jones's Squadron may be compared with the bombardment and covering ships. The Flotilla, a formidable amphibious force, was under Nassau-Siegen.

That so-called prince was the international adventurer whom Jones had met ten years earlier when he failed in his mission to persuade the Dutch government to let *L'Indien* go out. Nassau-Siegen failed in everything he undertook. He went around the world with Bougainville; but, as Jones once remarked, he did not learn enough seamanship to box the compass. The French gave him a small fleet to attack Jersey, whence he was thrown back with heavy loss. At the siege of Gibraltar in 1782, he commanded a gunboat flotilla similar to his Russian one, and was badly beaten by the British. But he was a plausible chap, handsome, self-confident, and noted for gallantry, dueling and personal courage. Arriving in Russia in 1786 on a mission from Poland, Nassau-Siegen struck up a great friendship with Potemkin, who promised him an Army command in the Turkish war. When the Russian officers heard of this they protested so vehemently that Potemkin made him a rear admiral in charge of the Flotilla; and the fellow was pleased, remarking with some sense that his oar-propelled gunboats would be the cavalry to the Squadron's heavy artillery, able to go against the wind and over shoals where the big ships would run aground. For flagship, Nassau-Siegen had what he called a yacht—one of the luxurious barges that had floated the Empress down the Dnieper. But that didn't suit him; he envied Jones his flag barge, which had more giltwork.

Thus Paul Jones had another Landais attached to him, equal in rank, who looked to Potemkin, not to him, for orders; in addition he had a Greek commodore on his flagship, and a shore admiral who disliked him. And Russia had another fleet at Sevastopol under Rear Admiral Voinovitch.

On the other side, watching the Russians from outside the estuary, the Turks had a Black Sea fleet of roughly the same composition and strength as the Russians', under an able admiral named Hassan el Ghazi, who is always referred to as "the Capudan Pasha" (Lord Captain). Jones considered him "a very brave man," and got near enough to him in action to see that he wore a pair of enormous mustaches. The Capudan Pasha had more seagoing ships under him than did Jones, but the Russian Flotilla was more numerous and more heavily armed than the corresponding Turkish fleet of small craft.

3. The Liman Campaign

Potemkin appears to have had no plan for the naval part of the campaign except that the Russian Navy was expected to hold off the Turks, and if possible destroy their fleet, until he was ready to invest Ochakov from the land side. Since Russian intelligence reported the Turkish Squadron to be of deeper draft and more heavily armed than the Russian, while its Flotilla was weaker than Nassau-Siegen's, Jones conceived the sound plan of deploying both Russian Squadron and Flotilla in one line across the Liman, about halfway between its entrance and the mouth of the Bug, and awaiting attack. At the same time the Russian fleet would be covering Kherson and the estuary of the Bug, which the Army, under Potemkin, would have to cross. Jones held a council of war and obtained Nassau's and Alexiano's

The Second Battle of the Liman, 1788.

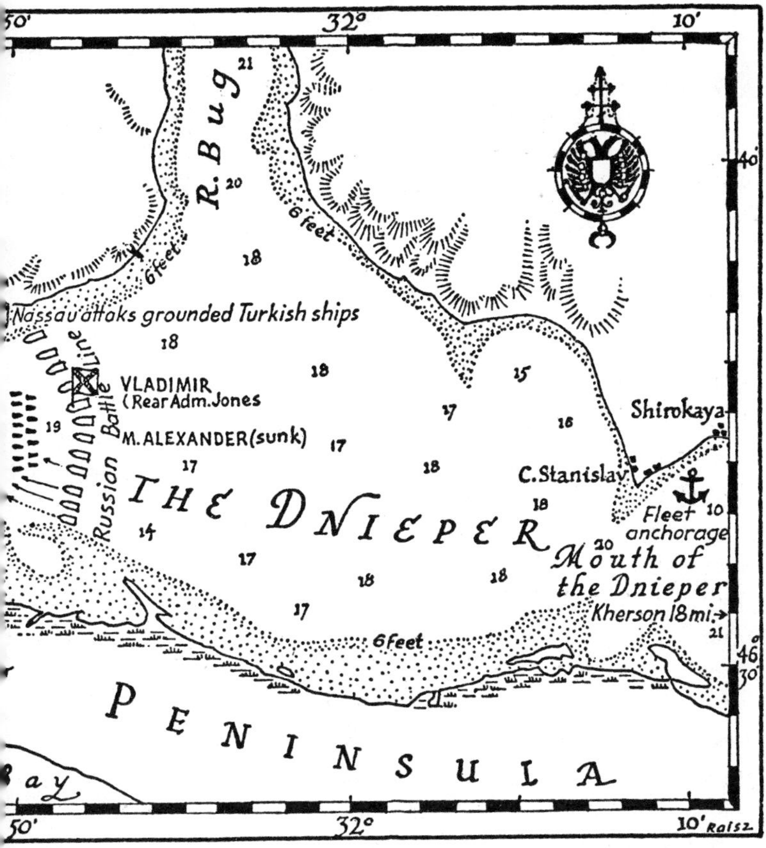

50'
32°
10'
R. Bug
21
20
6 feet
6 feet
18
Nassau attaks grounded Turkish ships
18
18
Russian Battle Line
VLADIMIR
(Rear Adm. Jones
19
M. ALEXANDER (sunk)
17
17
17
18
15
16
Shirokaya
C. Stanislav
THE DNIEPER
14
17
18
18
17
18
20
Fleet anchorage
10
Mouth of the Dnieper
Kherson 18 mi.
21
6 feet
40'
46°
30'
PENINSULA
Bay
50'
32°
10'
Ralsz.

ation at 0400 17/26 June. *Turkish ships are black, Russians outlined.*

consent to this disposition, which was assumed by the night of 5/16 June. The Russian fleet accordingly was drawn up in a NNE-SSW line across the Liman about four miles east of Ochakov.

The Capudan Pasha, in the meantime, had thrust a detachment of his Flotilla inside the entrance. The first Battle of the Liman opened at 2:00 A.M. on the 6/17th with Nassau-Siegen trying to cut off the Turkish retreat; but instead of doing that, he was chased back to the Squadron. Jones, anticipating that this repulse would encourage the Turks, obtained Nassau's and Alexiano's consent to form two reserves; one of 11 craft at the right of the line, one of 6 craft in the center, with 15 Zaporozhye boats in a position to support either reserve in case of need.

The Turks reacted as Jones expected. The Capudan Pasha committed almost his entire small-craft Flotilla and part of his Squadron. During the night he drew up his Flotilla in two divisions close to the north shore, and, favored by a northwesterly breeze, attacked Jones's right flank on the morning of 7/18 June.

Jones had himself rowed all along his front line to issue oral orders to his Squadron (for he had no system of signaling except by voice), and to get the whole Flotilla into action; and he detailed his ships' boats to tow units of the Flotilla which were having difficulty making headway against the wind. The arrival of the Capudan Pasha himself in a *Kirlangitch*—a swift, lateen-rigged galley mounting 14 guns—leading his Flotilla reserve, increased the danger to the Russians, and Nassau-Siegen's reserve at the right of their line began to take punishment. But a lucky change of wind easterly enabled Jones to move the five ships of his left wing out so they made an obtuse angle, with his right center, like a wide-open nutcracker, in order to bring the enemy Flotilla under crossfire. This was the decisive maneuver. The Capudan Pasha, smoking out Jones's intention, retired under sail before falling into the trap, but not before losing two or three vessels as a result of incendiary missiles.

These missiles, which Jones called "brandcougles," were perforated bombs filled with combustibles which spread upon impact.

They were fired from a kind of mortar called a "licorne." Lavishly employed by both sides during the Liman campaign, they created far more destruction than ordinary naval gunfire.

In his later "Narrative" of this campaign, Jones claims all the credit for this First Battle of the Liman, and mentions five or six instances of Nassau-Siegen's stupidity and poltroonery during the day. But in his action report, sent that very day to Potemkin, he goes overboard to praise the Prince's sang-froid and intelligence, and admits that during the fighting he was little more than Nassau's aide-de-camp.

Next day, wrote Jones to Potemkin from on board *Vladimir,* "We sang a *Te Deum* in honor of the victory that the Prince de Nassau won yesterday over the Capudan Pasha's Flotilla." General Suvorov also celebrated at Kinburn. And Potemkin wrote to Jones on 8/19 June praising his "zeal and intrepidity . . . in aiding the Prince de Nassau." But on 11/22 June, Jones wrote to Don José de Ribas at Kherson: "I wish I could tell you that the Prince de Nassau is now as he was before you left; but he has the air of wishing me *au Diable,* for no other reason so far as I know than that I extracted him out of his foul-up and peril in the affair of the 7/18th."

Should one believe the Jones of the action report or the Jones of the letter and "Narrative"? Probably he overdid his praise of Nassau in the report to Potemkin, thinking to please the C. in C., but did less than justice to him in the "Narrative," since by that time the Prince had done him out of his command. Nassau, in turn, begins to complain of Jones in letters to his wife on 14/25 June. He declares that Jones "has changed. Good luck has robbed him of that intrepidity which people said he had."

Jones quickly became conscious that all was not well with his political fences, and even the balmy air of the "Russian Riviera" had not restored his health after the exposure on the boat voyage from Sweden to Reval. To his liaison officer Don José de Ribas, who had now rejoined Potemkin, he wrote on 13/24 June a letter that reveals his state of mind. It is also one of the few partly French documents written in Jones's own hand.

Wolodimer June 13th 1788

My Dear Friend

I am unwell in my turn. Since I wrote you last I have been much indisposed; and, from the within Papers, you will see that I have room enough for vexation. You will doubtless find it necessary to send these Papers to his Altess the Prince de Potemkin, to obtain positive Orders to preventing any too hasty Step. Je vous prie de faire mes excuses à son Altesse, de n'avoir pas ecrit depuis l'Onze. Je n'avais rien de nouveau à lui mander, excepte q'on vient de me dire q'on a vû sortir d'Ochacoff un fort detachement de Troupes, qui parraissait monter au Nord. Je vous envoye ce ci par expres et suis avec un vrai attachement, votre très humble et très Obeissant Serviteur et Ami.

Paul Jones

N.B. be so good as to forward my Letter to Little-Page.

The "too hasty Step" to which Jones refers was the keen desire of Nassau-Siegen, whose Flotilla had been reinforced to 71 units, to thrust outside the Liman and engage the Turkish fleet then hovering off Ochakov and the mouth of the Beresan River. Jones wrote to Nassau a conciliatory letter on the 14/25th, asking what he was annoyed about, and suggesting joint tactics in the next fight. He would dearly have loved to fight a classic line-to-line action with the Capudan Pasha in deep water; but he rightly estimated that to do so would be to sacrifice the superiority of the Russian Flotilla over the Turkish small craft, and risk annihilation of the Russian Squadron by the superior numbers and metal of the enemy's heavy ships. Nassau-Siegen had nothing to lose; if beaten, he could blame it on someone else; but Jones had a professional reputation to sustain, and his mission was to support the Army. If by imprudent action he lost his fleet, the Turks could reinforce Ochakov at will and block the Bug and Dnieper Rivers. So he insisted that the Russian fleet should remain inside the Liman, and invite rather than offer attack. This strategy was correct. The Capudan Pasha had retired to the Black Sea after the battle, but he was impatient for another go at the

Russians, and his impatience led to the Second Battle of the Liman.

The entire Turkish fleet got under way with a fair southwest wind on 16 /27 June and sailed into the estuary, planning to sink the Russian Flotilla by shock tactics and then burn the Squadron with fireships and combustibles. Paul Jones awaited them in approximately the same position as before, his vessels stretched across the Liman, in a NNE-SSW line.

We have the Squadron's line of battle for 17 /28 June with the actual armament of each vessel, in one of Jones's *pièces justificatives* to his "Narrative."

Class	Name	Armament
Battleship	*Vladimir*	24 twenty-four-pounders, 2 licornes (24 lb.)
Frigate	*Aleksandr Nevskii*	Same
Frigate	*Skoryi*	24 twenty-four-pounders, 4 licornes (18 lb.), 12 six-pounders
Frigate	*Kherson*	22 twelve-pounders, 4 six-pounders
Frigate	*Boristen*	18 twelve-pounders, 6 six-pounders
Frigate	*Taganrog*	Same
Frigate	*Ptchela*	16 twelve-pounders, 10 three-lb. falconets
Frigate	*Sv. Nikolai*	4 six-pounders, 4 four-pounders, 12 three-pounders
Frigate	*Malyi Aleksandr*	6 six-pounders
Vessel	*Grigorii Potemkin*	14 three-pounders, 2 one-pounders
Vessel	*Sv. Anna*	6 six-pounders, 10 four-pounders, 6 three-lb. falconets
Vessels	*Mailet* and *Bogomater Turlenu*	each 8 four-pounders, 6 three-pounders

At about noon on the 16 /27th the Turks were seen approaching under full sail, an impressive sight with tall lateeners mixed in among large square-riggers. Kontradmiral Pavel Ivanovich summoned a council of war and made his captains a speech in French, concluding "I see in your eyes the souls of heroes; and we shall all learn together to conquer or die for the country!"

There is something irresistibly comic about this American

commander exhorting his Russian officers to conquer or die; but there was nothing amusing about the situation they were in. The Turks, outnumbering them two to one, were bearing down before the wind, with trumpets braying, cymbals clashing and loud cries to Allah to help them slaughter the unbelievers, drinkers of wine and eaters of swine. But the situation suddenly changed. The Capudan Pasha's flagship, rated as 64 guns, ran aground about 2:00 P.M., two *versts* (a mile and a third) from Jones's flagship *Vladimir*. The rest of the Turkish fleet then anchored in disorder. Nassau-Siegen wished to attack at once, but Jones restrained him—fortunately, because the wind veered to strong northwest, placing the enemy directly to windward so that neither rowing nor sailing vessels of the Russian fleet could make headway.

During the evening Jones made a personal reconnaissance of the Turkish fleet, rowed by a Cossack sailor named Ivak, who many years later told the story to a Russian officer. With an interpreter who told the sailors to call the Admiral "Pavel," Jones boarded the small craft in which Ivak served. He was "dressed like all of us, but his weapons were excellent. He was of brave appearance; his hair was a little gray but he was still strong, fit for work and full of keen understanding of our task." As soon as he came on board the Admiral inspected everything from stem to stern, now rebuking, now praising and now rearranging the equipment himself—Jones all over! He then had a small boat hoisted in, caused a rudder to be fitted, chose a pair of good oars and had them muffled by wrapping the blades with cloth, "and after some further preparations sat down for a rest."

Darkness now descended. Supper was served and the Kontradmiral shared the Cossacks' meal, eating from the same pot. He cracked jokes through his interpreter and after supper served double rations of spirits. This caused the crew to break into song, of such mournful cadence that even Jones, who did not understand the words, shed tears. Ivak sympathized; homesick himself for the steppes, he guessed that the Admiral, too, was thinking of home. Suddenly Jones jumped to his feet saying, "It is time!" After distributing the contents of his

Catherine II Replaces Jones by Fox
in Her Hall of Fame.
English Satirical Print of 1792

Tomb of John Paul Jones
in Naval Academy Chapel

PAUL JONES
D STATES NAVY

House at 19 Rue Tournon
Where John Paul Jones Died. Photo Taken in 1905.
Cross on Wall Indicates the Death Chamber

purse to the crew he patted Ivak on the shoulder and said "Let's go!" The Cossack crossed himself, stepped into the small boat and took the oars. Jones handled the tiller ropes and steered straight for the Turkish fleet. In due course they were challenged by two enemy craft. Fortunately these were manned by Turkish Cossacks, with whom Ivak could converse. Jones had been counting on this to obtain the enemy countersign for the night; and, as had been arranged through the interpreter before they started, Ivak got it by pretending that he was bringing salt to the Turkish flagship, and needed it to get by; and Jones memorized the countersign in Turkish.

"Soon we reached the enemy's fleet," said Ivak. "Like a town it lay at anchor; a whole forest of masts. They gave their countersign and Pavel replied. . . . We darted among the ships like sea-gulls. Some threatened us, some let us through silently; here we crawled, there we swooped." When Ivak thought it was high time to go home, Jones ordered him to approach the stern of one of the biggest ships, and hold onto her. He stood up in the boat while Ivak asked if the captain didn't want some salt; and while the Cossack was palavering with one of his fellows on board, Jones had the audacity to write in French with white chalk over the gilded Turkish insignia on the ship's stern: TO BE BURNED. PAUL JONES. The Turks did not bother to erase this inscription, which the whole Flotilla saw next morning; and this very ship was attacked and burned by the *Vladimir*.

Sheering off from the big Turkish vessel, Ivak rowed Jones to Prince Nassau-Siegen's yacht to deliver the intelligence. "In all my life," said the Cossack, "I have never seen such a person; sweet like a vine when he wished, but when necessary, like a rock. I wonder . . . how I entrusted myself to a man, not a Christian* at that, to be led directly into the hands of the enemy. . . . And how one trusted him! One movement of his hand you obey like a commanding voice. It seems that some people are created to command."

This Cossack came nearer to the heart and soul of Paul Jones

* He meant not a member of the Orthodox Church.

than did most of the Admiral's sophisticated friends. And Jones appreciated stout, simple fellows like Ivak. He gave him a dagger, inscribed "From Pavel Jones to his friend the Zaporozhye Ivak, 1788."

Now that Jones knew accurately the enemy's dispositions, he made his plans to prepare for the attack, which he anticipated would come next morning. He kedged all the vessels on the right (north) flank of his line toward the center so that they made an obtuse angle with the left (south) flank, toward which the Turks were steering—hoping to put a nutcracker on them as he had done in the first battle. This movement was completed by midnight. The Capudan Pasha, whose flagship was now afloat, weighed anchor at 2:00 A.M. 17 / 28 June, and tried to form line of battle. At about 4:00 A.M. his entire fleet advanced to the attack. In the meantime the wind afforded the Russians a lucky break. It veered to northeast, giving them the weather gauge.

An indiscriminate mêlée followed, with no plan or reason; Jones found his fleet less easy to control than the *Bonhomme Richard* task force. Even his flag captain dropped anchor without orders, when Jones was aiming at the Turkish flagship, on the excuse that there was a fifteen-foot shoal ahead, which Jones insists was not true.

First the Turkish deputy commander's ship and then Capudan Pasha's flagship ran aground off the north shore. This was Nassau-Siegen's opportunity. Hitherto he had hung back behind the Squadron, but now he deployed his entire Flotilla to attack the stranded vessels, which were listing so that their guns could not fire. But Nassau did not have the nerve to board, and instead of capturing these ships he destroyed them by brandcougles, to Jones's dismay and disgust.

This concentration of the Flotilla against the two stranded ships left Jones's battle line unprotected from the Turkish small craft facing them. Frigate *Malyi Aleksandr* was sunk by enemy incendiaries, and others were having a tough battle. Jones had himself rowed to Nassau-Siegen's yacht to beg him to lay off and help the Squadron, which the Prince refused to do; but one of his subordinates, a Russian officer named Korsakov, collected as many of the Flotilla as he could persuade to leave off badgering the Turks, and moved over in support. With this reinforcement, Jones drove the entire Turkish fleet back to the mouth of the Liman by 9:30 A.M.

The next move was made by the Russian battery on Kinburn Point, which had been set up as a result of Jones's suggestion to General Suvorov. When, on the night of 17/28 June, the Capudan Pasha tried to withdraw the rest of his ships from the mouth of the Liman, the Kinburn battery opened up and so confused him that no fewer than nine vessels grounded. Early next morning, 18/29 June, Suvorov asked Jones to destroy these ships before they could be salvaged. This gave Nassau-Siegen another chance. He proposed to take the entire Flotilla to do it. Jones said a part only would be sufficient; Nassau-Siegen flew into a passion and said, "I know how to capture ships as well as you!" to which Jones replied, "I have proved my ability to capture ships which are not Turkish." Finally Jones persuaded him to leave five units behind to support the Squadron. Nassau burned seven of the grounded Turkish vessels with brand-cougles and captured the other two ships. "Providence has done much for us," Jones wrote to Potemkin the same day. "We shall chant a Te Deum tomorrow morning. . . . I am delighted with the courage of the Russians, which is the more glorious because it is without showoff *(faste)*." But he made it clear that in his opinion Russia won the battle in spite of Nassau-Siegen.

Such was the Second Battle of the Liman. In two days' fighting, the Turks lost 10 large and 5 small vessels, 1673 prisoners, and an estimated 3000 killed. Russian losses were 1 frigate, 18 killed and 67 wounded. Nassau-Siegen claimed and obtained all the glory. "I am master of the Liman," he wrote to his wife. "Poor Paul Jones! No place for him on this great day!" Potemkin, in his report to the Empress, said, "Prince Nassau was tireless in his efforts. It was all his work," and failed to mention the Squadron commander. But the strategy of awaiting the enemy attack within the Liman was Jones's, and the execution would have been more complete if Nassau-Siegen had obeyed his orders and followed his tactics.

Potemkin, accompanied by several members of his staff, the Chevalier Littlepage (now an observer for the King of Poland) and the Prince de Ligne, a distinguished diplomatist in the Austrian service, dined with Jones on board *Vladimir* a few days later. The visitors interceded with Nassau-Siegen to apologize to Jones for his tantrum on the second day of battle; otherwise there would have been a duel. "I accepted it with sincere pleasure," recorded Jones. "We embraced in the presence of this honorable company, and I believed him as sincere as myself."

But when rewards and distinctions were distributed for the two battles, Jones came off badly. Nassau-Siegen got the Cross of Saint Serge, the highest in Russia; Alexiano was promoted rear admiral; Jones and Mordvinov, the shorebased admiral who had done nothing, were given the Order of Saint Anne. That was really a Holstein grand-ducal, not a Russian imperial order. It was about equivalent to an American Bronze Star or the Royal Victorian Order which Edward VII used to confer on courteous stationmasters. Later there was a distribution of medals and gold-hilted and jeweled swords, and Jones was completely left out.

The alarums and excursions, the altercations between Nassau-Siegen and Jones and Alexiano that followed, are too tedious to repeat. Potemkin now brought his Army across the Bug and ordered an attack on Ochakov by land and by sea on 1/12 July. In this attack, which opened at daylight, the Flotilla again distinguished itself by inflicting severe punishment on the Turkish fleet anchored under the walls of the fortress, and Nassau's stock accordingly rose. Jones properly refused to commit his big ships against shore batteries, but personally he was in the thick of this fight in a *chaloupe,* whence he directed the operations of his ships' boats towing units of the Flotilla that had been carried to leeward by the current. Then, at 6:00 A.M., Jones took his *chaloupe* out ahead of the Flotilla to seize five enemy galleys which lay within case-shot range of the fortress. He boarded the nearest galley himself and had it towed out of danger by a Russian lieutenant. Next he boarded the Capudan Pasha's own galley;

but the business of taking her under tow was bungled by a young officer, and, while cables and anchors were being brought from the flagship, Alexiano, who was in the same boat with Nassau-Siegen and wished to rob Jones of the credit of saving this galley, sent one of his small craft under a fellow Greek to set fire to her. Consumed she was, together with the wretched galley slaves chained to the thwarts, whom the Greek did not trouble to release. The other three galleys were ignited by brandcougles and consumed.

Potemkin's army now sat down to besiege Ochakov. Much to Jones's relief, Nassau-Siegen was sent by Potemkin on an inspection tour to Sevastopol on 10/21 July and was temporarily relieved in command of the Flotilla by Don José de Ribas. Chevalier Littlepage, the roving Virginian, now had a squadron of it under Don José. But for Jones the situation did not improve, and on 1/12 August Nassau-Siegen returned to command the Flotilla, flying a vice admiral's flag, which Rear Admiral Jones refused to salute because he could not believe that the man was entitled to it. But he actually had been so promoted by Potemkin. This was like giving the commander of an LST flotilla in a modern amphibious operation higher rank than that of the admiral of the attack force.

A possible way out for Jones, which he declined to follow, opened for him on 8/19 August. Potemkin, displeased with Kontradmiral Voinovitch of the Sevastopol fleet, who had done nothing but make faces at the Capudan Pasha, dropped the word to his staff that he was considering the relief of this reluctant dragon by Kontradmiral Pavel Ivanovich. Potemkin's secretary on 8/19 August wrote to Jones, asking if he would care for it, "in case His Highness should revert to that idea." Jones replied that he would always obey the orders of the Prince Marshal, but he did not like the idea for several reasons. The Sevastopol fleet was weak and demoralized, without any system of signals, and Jones's signals, which (following Pavillon's system) he had worked out, had not yet been translated into Russian. Obviously you could not maneuver a deep-water fleet, as Jones had maneuvered his Squadron, by being rowed to each individual ship and bellowing your orders through an interpreter. Also, Jones had just received orders from Potemkin to prepare to attack Fort Hassan Pasha on the tip end of Ochakov Peninsula, and wished to carry that out first to prove his competence.

An attack on a fort by warships in those days could succeed only if complete surprise were obtained and the fort overwhelmed with gunfire before the defenders woke up. That is what Jones planned to do, but the operation was bungled because a Greek lieutenant in Littlepage's division opened fire prematurely. Jones then called the attack off, the only sensible thing to do under the circumstances; but Nassau-Siegen claimed that he had been prevented from winning another victory. Littlepage, mortified over this affair and disgusted with service under Nassau, sent in his resignation and returned to Warsaw to enjoy his emoluments as royal chamberlain. His farewell letter to Jones ended, "Adieu, my dear admiral, take care of yourself, and be cautious in whom you trust. Remember you have to sustain here a political as well as military character, and that your part is now rather that of a courtier than a soldier." He could not have been more right; nor could Jones have been more wrong not to jump at the chance to command the Sevastopol fleet, signals or no signals.

September passed with only a few small-craft actions at sea. Jones, in the meantime, had established a fairly effective blockade of Ochakov. On 8 /19 October, when the Capudan Pasha showed up again with a reinforced fleet, Potemkin insisted on withdrawing the Flotilla to save it from possible capture. Jones protested, but obeyed. It turned out as Jones feared; two or three Turkish ships broke through to Ochakov. Next day the Flotilla under Nassau attacked unsuccessfully and lost a galley, for which Jones was blamed. A number of incidents became the subject of an exchange of notes between the Kontradmiral and the Prince Marshal, who was terrified lest the Turks break into the Liman and threaten his headquarters. These headquarters were in a house on the water's edge, and Potemkin had an irritating habit of spotting a Turkish ship or small craft with his telescope and sending Jones an order to "Go get it!" Or, when he saw a small Turkish gun boat aground, "Get out there and throw that gun overboard!" By the time the order reached the Rear Admiral, the ship would be gone or the boat floated, and Jones would be blamed.

The payoff in this ridiculous situation came in the shape of an offensive order from Potemkin to Jones, telling him to receive the enemy "courageously" or he would be accused of "negligence." This brought an emotional protest from Jones, concluding, "If you find me any use to the Imperial Navy, it is for you to keep me in Russia. But, as I did not come here as an adventurer or charlatan or to repair a ruined fortune" (a crack at Nassau-Siegen), "I hope to be subjected to no more humiliation and to find myself soon in the situation that was promised me when I was invited to enter Her Imperial Majesty's Navy." In other words, to command all Russian forces afloat in the Black Sea, which (so far as I can ascertain) he never had been offered.

Blustering got you nowhere with Imperial Russian authorities, and Potemkin was not one to receive backtalk amiably. From the time he wrote this letter, on 18/29 October, Jones was as good as out of the Russian Navy.

*   *   *

It is difficult to make any hard-and-fast estimate of Paul Jones's Russian career. He always functioned best when in undisputed command, which he never had in the Black Sea. He had to deal with characters who were out for themselves and determined to drag him down. He was under a temperamental commander in chief, who seemed to enjoy the dissension created by the fuddled command situation, rather than make any attempt to straighten it out. His position was one from which he could not possibly have derived benefit or glory, however high his merit. Jones's strategy throughout was sound; but Nassau-Siegen's strategy, if it can be called that, of going baldheaded for the enemy whenever he appeared, regardless of circumstances, appealed to Potemkin; and that is what really counted. It is regrettable that Jones had not sufficient serenity to rise above these petty intrigues. But it must be admitted that he showed a patience unusual for him over a period of months and exploded only when Potemkin challenged his honor, and that for months he endured a command situation enough to drive any naval officer mad. "In my whole life," he wrote after it was all over, "I have never suffered so much vexation as in this one Campaign of the Liman, which was nearly the death of me."

The significant fact that stands out from Jones's Russian service is that he won the respect and loyalty of most of the Russian naval officers under him, although they had nothing to gain by it. Many risked getting into Potemkin's black books by writing testimonials or affidavits for Jones to include in his "Narrative of the Liman Campaign." Not one Russian can be counted among those who intrigued against him.

4. On the Beach

Paul Jones now found himself on the beach. On 18/29 October, the very day that he received Jones's emotional letter, Potemkin ordered Rear Admiral Mordvinov to relieve him as commander of both Squadron and Flotilla, and he did so two days later. Jones's face was saved by the assurance that the Empress had need of his services in her Baltic fleet, which was about to fight the Swedes. Before leaving the Squadron he had an interview with Potemkin, who assured him "of his esteem," and gave him a letter to the Empress declaring his satisfaction with the "eagerness and zeal" he had shown in the Liman campaign. But at the same time Potemkin wrote a private letter to the Empress in which he called Jones "sleepy," admitted that he was brave enough as a "corsair," but declared that nobody wished to serve under him.

Rear Admiral Jones left flagship *Vladimir* on 29 October/9 November for Kherson in an open galley. It was very cold and the journey took three night and days. He came down with pneumonia and was unable to leave Kherson until the end of November; he was at Ekaterinoslav when Ochakov was taken by storm on 6/17 December and the Turkish garrison put to the sword. Arriving at St. Petersburg on 17/28 December, the Rear Admiral was promptly received by the Empress at the Hermitage. Jones felt that her attitude was cordial and gracious; but he did not know that Nassau-Siegen, who reached St. Petersburg shortly after, was received by the Empress in such a manner that Princess Nassau-Siegen came on from Warsaw to break up what she judged to be a serious love affair. She need not have worried; in Catherine's system there was no place for casual amours.

The Kontradmiral first stayed at the London Tavern, where he made an unfortunate contact with a young girl who was looking for trouble, and then hired an upstairs apartment in a house called Pokhodyashina in the First Admiralty District, near the great Admiralty building whose slender gold spire still dominates that section of Leningrad. There he set up a small household: his interpreter Pavel Dimitrevski, a German body-servant named Johann Bahl, his Russian seaman orderly from the Black Sea fleet, and a peasant coachman named Ivan Vasiliev, to handle his hired stable of horses, sleighs and carriages. The French ambassador, the Comte de Ségur d'Aguesseau, who had served in America under Rochambeau, and his first secretary Edmond-Charles Genet (the future Citizen Genet), saw to it that the Rear Admiral met prominent courtiers—among others, the Princess Naryshkina. But social calls and supper parties were not enough to occupy a man of Jones's energy.

While awaiting the hoped-for new naval command, he prepared for the Imperial Vice Chancellor a plan for a political and commercial alliance between the United States and Russia. He urged the Empress to put herself at the head of a coalition to suppress the Barbary corsairs. He outlined a reorganization of the Black Sea fleet, which he rightly said was "built on false principles, unable to sustain its enormous artillery, or to maneuver properly." (That was done, under the able Rear Admiral Ushakov, in 1790; and the Turks were then decisively defeated.) Now Jones finished his "Narrative of the Campaign of the Liman." This "Narrative," which, with the aid of his secretary, was written in French, he intended for the eyes of the Empress; but it is doubtful whether she ever looked at it. The tone is that of injured virtue and misunderstood integrity; much like the writings of Columbus toward the end of his life, and with similar self-pity. It is full of statements such as, "So far from being harsh and cruel, nature has given me the mildest disposition"; "I was formed for love and friendship, and not to be a seaman or a soldier"; "since I am found too frank and too sincere to make my way at the court of Russia without creating powerful enemies, I have philosophy enough to withdraw into the peaceful bosom of friendship."

Paul Jones soon needed all the friendship he could muster. He knew no Russian except *da* and *nyet* (as he admitted), and although by this time his conversational French was good, there was nobody to whom he could unburden himself in his own language. America was not yet recognized by Russia, and so not represented in the diplomatic service, and the English representatives would have nothing to do with Jones. The police intercepted his mail, so he was unable to communicate with his friends in Paris or America, and he felt forgotten by the world. He found no mistress to take the place of Madame Townsend.* And he was so lonely as to become imprudent in his personal contacts. The cold winter dragged on, with the snow lying like iron on the earth; before the spring thaws came, Kontradmiral Pavel Ivanovich suffered a worse shock than those inflicted by the brandcougles of his Squadron.

5. Scandal and Departure

During the first week of April 1789, all St. Petersburg was startled, amused, or outraged by a report of the chief of police that Rear Admiral Paul Jones had attempted to rape a ten-year-old girl named Katerina, daughter of a German immigrant named Goltzwart or

---

* In 1926 a woman calling herself the Baroness Weissereich appeared at the American consulate in Riga hoping to obtain an American passport. She claimed to be the descendant of a son of Jones and Princess Anna Kourakina, a lady in waiting to Catherine II. Her story, supported by phony extracts from a nonexistent diary of Catherine II, and by a ring marked "J.P.J.," was investigated and found to be false. There is no evidence or even likelihood that Jones ever had an affair with a lady of the Russian court.

Koltzwarthen, who had a dairy business in a nearby suburb. According to this account, the girl was peddling butter on 30 March when a "lackey" (Jones's German manservant Bahl) told her that his master wanted some, and led her to the Rear Admiral's apartment on the second floor of a house in a well-known street. The master, whom she had never seen before, was dressed in a white uniform, wearing a gold star on a red ribbon. He bought some butter, then locked the door, knocked the girl out with a blow on the chin, dragged her into his bedroom and assaulted her. She ran home and told her mother, who went to the house, identified the rapist as Rear Admiral Jones, and appealed to the police. She was supported by a statement of Bahl, who claimed to have observed some of the goings-on through a keyhole, and affidavits from an Army surgeon and a midwife that she had been raped.

There are three different versions by Jones of what really happened. The one generally known is what the Comte de Ségur announced to the world and printed in his memoirs. The French Ambassador called on Paul Jones a few days after the report came out, and heard from him that this young girl had called to ask if he would give her some linen or lace to mend, but he had none to offer. "She then indulged in some rather lively and indecent gestures," Ségur quotes Jones as saying. "I advised her not to enter upon so vile a career; gave her some money, and dismissed her." As soon as she left his front door the girl tore her sleeves and fichu, started screaming "Rape!" and threw herself into the arms of Mamma Goltzwart, who was conveniently standing by.

This version, the only one on Jones's side known until recently, sounds like another instance of the well-known girl decoy trick for blackmailing middle-aged gentlemen. Ségur may have known of other like cases and confused them with this, or he may have known more about Jones's case than he admitted.

About two weeks after the event, Jones wrote to Potemkin—on whom he had called in his St. Petersburg palace immediately after the alleged rape—a very different version from Ségur's. He says nothing about what happened between himself and Katerina, but complains that his servants were examined by the police and that Bahl was terrorized into signing what they wanted. Jones had placed himself in the hands of a lawyer named Crimpin, who had already been asked by Mamma Goltzwart to take her case and had declined to do so, but who found out some important facts which he used on Jones's behalf. Mamma admitted that *un homme décoré*, a gentleman who wore the star of some order, was behind her; and that her only object was money. She confessed her "innocent" daughter had been seduced by Bahl three months before her alleged encounter with the Admiral. From others, the lawyer learned that immediately after the alleged rape the girl continued to peddle butter instead of rushing home to tell Mamma. A deposition was obtained from Papa Goltzwart stating that Katerina's age was twelve, not ten; that Mamma had left Papa to live with a young lover and had taken the girl with her; and Katerina, after a little pressure, admitted to the police that she had first "sold butter" to Jones at the London Tavern, and had made several such sales since. But, what seemed extraordinary, the Governor of St. Petersburg, an appointee of the Crown, had warned Crimpin to drop the case. Jones concluded to Potemkin, "The charge against me is an unworthy imposture. I love woman, I confess, and the pleasures that one only obtains from that sex; but to get such things by force is horrible to me. I cannot even contemplate gratifying my passions without their consent, and I give you my word as a soldier and an honest man that, if the girl in question has not passed through hands other than mine, she is still a virgin."

Jones wrote this on 13 April. But on 2 April, only three days after the alleged rape, Jones had unburdened himself in French to the chief of police, as follows:

The accusation against me is an imposture invented by the mother of *une fille perdue* [a depraved girl] who came *chez moi plusieurs fois* [several times to my house] and with whom I have often *badiné*, always giving her money, but whose virginity *je n'ai point pris* [I have positively not taken]. . . . I thought her to be several years older than Your Excellency says she is, and each time that she came *chez moi* she lent herself *de la meilleure grace* [very amiably] to do all that a man would want of her. The last time passed off like the rest, and she went out appearing *contente et tranquille,* and having in no way been abused. If one has checked on her having been deflowered, I declare that I am not the author of it, and I shall as easily prove the falseness of this assertion as of several other points included in the deposition which you have sent to me.

I have the honor to be, etc.

PAUL JONES

This letter, written very shortly after the event, is as close to the truth as we are likely to come, and is supported by affidavits from the orderly, the coachman and Dimitrevski that they saw the girl leave Jones's premises quietly, without blood or tears. Jones admits that Katerina was a frequent visitor to his apartment, and the nature of their *badinage* (the word can mean almost anything) may be inferred from his subsequent statement that it comprised "all that a man would want," short of deflowering her.

It may also be counted as certain that Mamma Goltzwart was abetted by somebody of consequence; for affairs of this nature involving someone high in government service are commonly hushed up by the police, as has happened in several notorious cases in our own day. The publicity given to the alleged rape, the efforts to prevent a lawyer from taking the case, clearly point to an important person's using Jones's not-quite-innocent *badinage* with the twelve-year-old to ruin his reputation.

Who could it have been? Both Jones and Ségur were satisfied that the English naval officers in Russian service were incapable of anything so nasty. The Chevalier Littlepage, dashing about as usual, heard from a "gentleman of high rank in the diplomatic service" that the culprit was a courtier who hoped to ingratiate himself with the English government by ruining Jones. That seems rather far-fetched. It seems much more likely that Nassau-Siegen, fearing Jones's competition, was behind it; and that is what Jones came to believe. Whoever the "decorated gentleman" was, he must have employed someone to spy on Jones's habits, and found Mamma Goltzwart a willing instrument of his malice.

When the scandal came out, everyone in St. Petersburg dropped Jones like a hot potato; that is, everyone except the Comte de Ségur. His loyalty to Jones was admirable. He wrote to Potemkin, wrote to the Empress, hinted that his master Louis XVI would take offense at the treatment of the Chevalier, as would he himself as a fellow member of the Cincinnati; he pulled wires and spoke to important people. As the result of his efforts the threatened court-martial of Jones at the Admiralty was dropped. Ségur even wrote a brief statement giving his version of the affair, which he had published in the official *Gazette de France*, whence it was reprinted in the leading journals of Europe. Jones was persuaded to initiate no countersuit against the Goltzwarts, and Katerina went on peddling sex and butter.

The brief Russian spring passed, and the unemployed Rear Admiral continued to wait in St. Petersburg for orders, occasionally bombarding the ministers of state with plans for action against Sweden. By mid-June, he heard the bitter news that the Empress had conferred the command of her Baltic Flotilla on Nassau-Siegen. Before the end of that month he received virtually his dismissal, although he refused to admit it. The Empress granted him two years' leave of absence from her Navy, preserving his rank and emoluments. On 26 June /7 July 1789 he was permitted to kiss her hand at a public audience, and receive a curt *bon voyage*. She had not forgiven him for his indiscretion. Catherine may have been the most dissolute empress since Messalina, but she exacted almost Victorian standards of conduct from those about her. She had undoubtedly been given the police report to read, and was not amused.

It took Jones another two months to get permission to leave the country, with a properly signed commission to prove that he had been a rear admiral, and to draw reimbursement for his traveling expenses. About the end of August he departed in his carriage on the long journey to Warsaw. After his departure, his friend Genet in the French Embassy collected eighteen hundred roubles for him as a year's pay, and sent him a draft for it.

Paul Jones never saw Russia again, but during the few remaining years of his life he could never get Russia out of his thoughts. He was always hoping that the next post would bring an imperial order to return and take over an important naval command. His devastating experiences had been with German and Greek adventurers, but he liked Russian sailors, both officers and enlisted men, and they respected him. He would have appreciated such stout fellows under his command in the American war; and they retained a pleasant memory of their Kontradmiral Pavel Ivanovich Jones.

XXI

The
Empty
Wineskin

1789-1792

1. A Limited Grand Tour

Paul Jones's life after he left Russia is anticlimactic. Never again would he command a ship, much less a fleet. Never, until too late to enjoy it, would he receive a government appointment. Not even the satisfaction of a dignified retirement to the country and writing his memoirs, as retired admirals are wont to do today. Still only forty-two years old, he would have done well to return at once to America, purchase land, marry some "fair daughter of Liberty" as he had often threatened to do, and perhaps play a part in American politics. But he only toyed with the idea. In December 1789 he wrote to Charles Thomson, Secretary of Congress, asking him to look at a "small but convenient estate to be sold in the neighborhood of Lancaster," Pennsylvania, and report whether it would be a good purchase. "I shall probably come to America in the summer if the Empress does not invite me to return to Russia." And to John Ross, the old friend who handled (or mishandled) his investments in Philadelphia, he wrote, "I may perhaps return to America in the latter end of the summer; and in that case I shall wish to purchase a *little farm* where I may live in peace."

Poor Jones!—always reverting to the ideal of "calm contemplation and poetic ease," but unable to bring himself to do anything about it. He never saw America again. Pride, and expectation of something turning up, held him in Europe. He cared not to return with a cloud over his name, to have to explain why he left the Russian service. He asked Baron Grimm and others to intercede for imperial favor. Naïvely, he hoped that if the Empress would only read his account of the Liman campaign, her great heart would melt; she would recall him to active duty; and, since Russia seldom enjoyed more than a year or two of peace, this would afford him fresh opportunity for glory. Up to the year before his death he kept writing letters to her that are almost disgustingly obsequious. He even wrote to Potemkin, reviewing his exploits in the Liman campaign, and demanding that the Cross of Saint Serge be conferred on him for his second victory.

For a time, however, he flirted with the idea of seeking a commission in the Swedish Navy and so getting revenge on Nassau-Siegen. At Warsaw, Chevalier Littlepage saw to it that he was honorably received by King Stanislas, and he became friends with Thaddeus Kosciuszko, the Polish patriot who had fought in the American War of Independence.

Kosciuszko, apparently, was ready to intercede for Jones at the court of Stockholm; but Kontradmiral Pavel Ivanovich felt some "delicacy" at asking for a commission from a king who was then fighting Catherine II. He intimated, however, that if the offer were made without solicitation on his part, he might consider it.

From Warsaw, on 2 November 1789, Paul Jones traveled to Montbéliard in Alsace, where he stayed a few days with the Duke of Württemberg, a friend of his late friend Comte Wemyss. By 23

November he was in Vienna. The purpose of this visit is obscure, for, as a Viennese correspondent of a French paper remarked, "Austria had no navy of sufficient importance to properly occupy the admiral."

On December 9 he was in Amsterdam, and he did not leave Holland until May 1790. We do not know what he was doing there, or whether he renewed acquaintance with M. Dumas and the "Virgin Muse," who was now a wife and mother. But there the Swedish business almost came to a head. Kosciuszko wrote to Jones to see the Swedish minister to Holland and await an offer. Gouverneur Morris, in Amsterdam on American business, talked with Jones about it. But there is no evidence that the offer was ever made. Morris, who had been intimate with Jones when an assistant to Robert Morris, drew out of the Rear Admiral that he "had a plan for going around the Cape of Good Hope and laying under contribution the places subject to the Turk." But this would have been on the side of Russia, not Sweden. Jones later developed the idea in a letter to the Russian minister in Paris. He wanted only a small task force from the Empress, and would fly the American flag if necessary. How he expected to get a big contribution out of *Arabia deserta,* prior to the discovery of oil, does not appear.

At the same time Jones was writing letters to Washington, Franklin and other powerful friends in America, not asking for anything but apparently to remind them of his existence. His extensive journeyings had strapped him for funds. John Ross sent him a bill of exchange to cover his Bank of North America dividends, but the Dutch bankers evidently regarded Ross as a poor risk and refused to cash it. Jones contemplated a visit to Hamburg. He wrote to John Parish, an American merchant there, that he might make him "a visit in the spring, and pay my court to some of your kind, rich old ladies." But he "must stay in Europe till it is seen what changes the present politics will produce."

This, strangely enough, is Jones's first reference in his correspondence to the French Revolution, which was rocking the entire Western world. Gouverneur Morris observed that Jones showed no sympathy with that mighty upheaval. His only interest in it was the possibility that the Revolution might ignite a new European war (which it did), and give him another chance to distinguish himself, which it did not.

Instead of going to Hamburg to court a rich old lady, Jones made a trip to London in May 1790 to try to get something out of his investment in Dr. Bancroft's wildcat scheme. "I escaped being murdered on landing," he wrote. This seems strange, since the English are not a vengeful people; but the *Naval Chronicle,* twenty years later, confirmed the story and gave details from a manuscript journal. Jones was wearing his Russian naval uniform when he landed from the packet at Harwich, but was recognized at the customs house, and in such manner that he "thought proper to retreat to the inn, with the utmost precipitation." The populace "surrounded the inn, and were not sparing in denouncing their intention of exercising vengeance upon him if they laid hold of him; in consequence of which he privately escaped out of town the same day." The probable reason for this belligerent attitude was the story of the alleged rape, a garbled account of which had been sent to Thomas Jefferson by a London correspondent.

We do not know where Jones stopped in London; possibly at the Freemasons' Tavern where room and board was a pound a week. His financial mission was moderately successful; with the very bored assistance of Gouverneur Morris he put Bancroft's debt in a way of settlement. Two years later Bancroft was trying to pay the balance, which still amounted to £1050, with scrip for Mohawk Valley lands.

2. Back to Paris

To Paris Jones returned in May 1790, and Paris he never left again alive. His health was gravely impaired by the winter journey and his disposition saddened by neglect. He had sufficient income to hire an apartment *au premier* (what we should call the third floor) at Number 52 rue de Tournon, a broad and pleasant street which leads up to the Palais du Luxembourg. The house, which still stands, re-numbered 19, belonged to a M. D'Arbergue (whom Jones, knowing his Shakespeare, called "Dogberry"), *huissier* or marshal of an important court of justice. It was new, conveniently situated for attending meetings of the Lodge of the Nine Sisters behind St.-Sulpice and for strolling in the Jardin du Luxembourg.

Paris had changed greatly since the golden era whose brilliant evening Jones had enjoyed in the 1780s. Some of his friends were now *émigrés,* others had retired to country estates where they fearfully awaited the outcome of events in the capital. The King and Queen, forced to leave Versailles by the Paris mob, were practically prisoners in the Tuileries. There were no longer any court ceremonies or levees, and it was not to Jones's taste to attend sessions of the National Assembly or the salons of revolutionary hostesses such as Madame Roland. Thomas Carlyle paints an artist's picture of our hero in these last two years of his life:

> In faded naval uniform, Paul Jones lingers visible here; like a wine-skin from which the wine is drawn. Like the ghost of himself! Low is his once loud bruit; scarcely audible, save with extreme tedium, in ministerial ante-chambers; in this or the other charitable dining-room, mindful of the past. What changes, culminatings and declinings! . . . Poor Paul! hunger and dispiritment track thy sinking footsteps; once or at most twice, in this Revolution-tumult the figure of thee emerges; mute, ghost-like, as "with stars dim-twinkling through."

His stars dim-twinkled through the fog of revolution on 10 July 1790, when he was chosen head of a delegation of the American colony in Paris to congratulate the National Assembly on the new Constitution. But another man acted as spokesman. The same delegation had reserved seats at the Fête de la Fédération, a brilliant ceremony on the Champ de Mars on 14 July 1790, first anniversary of the taking of the Bastille. Jones has not left on record his opinion of these ceremonies; but the indications are that, despite his earlier professions of Liberty, Universal Philanthropy and the like, he regarded the progress of the French Revolution with increasing dismay. He loved kings and queens, lords and ladies, all in their proper place in society like the officers, petty officers and enlisted men of a well-regulated man-of-war. He had tasted democracy on board the *Ranger* and found it disgusting. Like Laurence Sterne and Oliver Goldsmith, he loved the grace, beauty and gaiety of a France not yet torn by revolution, a France which would never return.

His friend Lafayette was now at the height of power and popularity, but too busy to bother with him. The Rear Admiral had brought some "fur linings"—probably sable—from Russia for Lafayette, and a second set that he requested the General to present to the King. In a letter to Lafayette of 7 December 1790, Jones refers to these gifts and makes the strange proposition, "When my health shall be reëstablished M. Simolin will do me the honor to present me to His Majesty as a Russian Admiral; afterwards it will be my duty as an American officer to wait on His Majesty with the letter which I am directed to present to him from the United States." Lafayette did not reply. As Emerson well observed, "Every hero becomes a bore at last."

Jones's notion that it would impress Louis XVI if he were presented to him in a Russian uniform is as grotesque as the proposed expeditionary force to Arabia. It leads one to suspect that he was becoming more than a bore—slightly touched in the head. The letter from the United States that he referred to was John Jay's of 1787, which he had never presented, requesting that the King allow him to embark in a French fleet. Since Jones never again felt well enough to go to sea, he never made the request.

The voluminous diary kept by Gouverneur Morris, American Minister to France, makes it clear that Paul Jones had very little to occupy him. Every week, sometimes oftener, he drops in at the legation, to Morris's annoyance. For instance, on 14 November 1790: "Paul Jones calls on me. He has nothing to say but is so kind as to bestow on me all the Hours which hang heavy in his Hands." On

12 July 1791, after a lapse of time in which Jones did not call, Morris invites him to dine, and again a year later, within a month of his death; but then only because Morris had "sent him away" in the afternoon and was sorry for him. We do, however, obtain from the Morris diary a few rare glimpses of Jones's meager social life. He and Morris are fellow guests, with Dr. Bancroft and mistress, at a dinner given by Willaim Bosville, an eccentric Englishman. And it was at a dinner given by William Short, secretary of the American legation, that Jones met Lord Daer, son of the Earl of Selkirk, and talked about the raid on St. Mary's Isle.

Paul Jones did not acquire another mistress after his return to Paris; the state of his health forbade it. He had a letter of introduction from Genet in St. Petersburg to his sister Madame Campan, lady-in-waiting to Marie Antoinette; but there is no evidence that he ever met her. Madame d'Altigny, whom he had encountered at Warsaw, invited him to visit her at Avignon, but he was no longer inclined to travel. Madame Clément admitted him to her *cercle* in Paris, and he carried on a pleasant correspondence with three of her friends who had retired to Trevoux near Lyons. They, too, urged him to come and share their "frugal meals, freedom, and appreciative hearts," but he was unable to face the journey.

Much of Jones's time and thought was spent in letter-writing, especially to the Empress Catherine, by the intermediary of Baron Grimm. In March 1791, when there were rumors of an Anglo-Russian war, Jones sent her the plan for attacking India, with which he had already bored Morris. Catherine replied to Grimm: "If England does declare war on us, I think that the best plan will be to issue letters of marque to take as much as possible of her shipping, and that will make her end the war quickly. As for India, it is so far that before we got there the peace would be made." And she added that Jones knew very well why he had been given leave of absence—because of the scandal. Undiscouraged, he came up with a plan for a new kind of warship without ballast, which he had obtained from some crank in Paris. The Empress then wrote to Grimm, "I have no more to say to Paul Jones. Tell him to go and mind his business in America. I shall be careful not to be the first to adopt the ship construction that Paul Jones speaks of; let him offer it to England." That ended his attempts to get back in her favor.

The Chevalier also corresponded with his two married sisters in Scotland, who were not on speaking terms, begging them (with quotations from Pope's "Universal Prayer") to make up, and showing an interest in the education of his nephews. Thomas Carlyle imagined that Jones was nostalgic for his native land and regretted the day when, "young fool," he looked "wistful over the Solway brine, by the foot of native Criffel, with blue mountainous Cumberland, into blue Infinitude, environed with thrift, with humble friendliness." Not he! There are no inquiries about Scottish persons or places in his letters; only as a conquering hero would Paul Jones have returned to Galloway. His nostalgia, if he ever indulged in that sentiment, was for the summers with brother William in Virginia, for his first gay cruise in sloop *Providence*, for the joy of combat with H.M.S. *Drake* and *Serapis*, for that glorious spring of 1780 in Paris, for the short week of love with Delia at Hennebont, for his reception at Philadelphia in 1781, for his cruise with Vaudreuil. He regretted nothing that he had done, only what princes and rivals had done to him. If Paul Jones ever read Dryden, he would have found a mirror of his thoughts and feelings in that poet's famous translation of Horace's 29th Ode:

> Be fair, or foul, or rain, or shine
> The joys I have possess'd, in spite of fate, are mine.
> Not Heaven itself upon the past has power,
> But what has been, has been, and I have had my hour.

Even an empty wineskin has to live, and Paul Jones, though never actually hungry, was embarrassed for want of funds; Ross delayed sending him dividends from his bank stock, and his shares in land companies yielded nothing. So he asked William Short to help him obtain a United States consulate in Europe. And he tried to induce the French Minister of Marine to pay arrears of salaries and wages due to the officers and seamen of *Bonhomme Richard*.

As the French Revolution worked up to a crisis in 1792, Paul Jones was in a mental backwater, indifferent to the events about him, forgotten by the world. Not, however, by Thomas Jefferson, Secretary of State under President Washington, who was cognizant of Jones's interest in the American sailors captured by the Barbary powers of North Africa. These pirate princes were not slow to observe that ships under the Stars and Stripes had no navy to protect them. If Paul Jones had been allowed to form a task force under *America* as he had hoped, and to show the flag in the Mediterranean immediately after independence had been achieved, the sordid story of our relations with these squalid powers might have been very different. As it was, they captured American merchant ships at will and enslaved their crews, and in 1785 the Dey of Algiers even had the impudence to declare war on the United States. Jones, notifying John Jay of this, wrote, "This event may, I believe, surprize some of our fellow Citizens; but, for my part, I am rather surprised that it did not take place sooner. It will produce a good effect if it unites the people of America in measures consistent with their national honor and interest, and rouses them from their ill-judged security which the intoxication of success has produced since the Revolution."

Unfortunately the people of America were largely indifferent and Congress, without a Navy, was helpless. It sought the good offices of Portugal, sent a consul with ten thousand dollars (which the Dey of Algiers scornfully rejected) to redeem captive merchant mariners, and concluded a treaty with the least disreputable of the Barbary powers, the Sultan of Morocco. American ships had to shun the Mediterranean.

Paul Jones, always compassionate toward prisoners, had been trying for years to get something done about this. In 1787, during his last visit to New York, he wrote to John Jay suggesting a tax on American seamen of a shilling a month, in order to accumulate a fund like Greenwich hospital money in England, for redeeming captives.

Thomas Jefferson, when American minister at Paris, ascertained to his disgust that every European power paid tribute to the Barbary States rather than fight them, and made ineffectual efforts to form a league to put the pirates down. He and Paul Jones saw eye to eye on the subject. From St. Petersburg in January 1789, when he was hoping for a new Russian naval command, Jones wrote to Jefferson that he had detected Algerians fighting under the Capudan Pasha in the Black Sea. Would it not be a good idea to allow Russia, by treaty, to recruit seamen in America to punish Algiers, in return for granting American vessels free navigation of the Black Sea?

Captain Richard O'Brien, master of one of the American ships captured in 1785, kept writing to American officials about the sad lot of his crew, and in the meantime the Dey's price of redemption had risen to almost three thousand dollars a head. President Washington and Secretary Jefferson communicated these facts to Congress around the turn of the year 1790-1791, leaving to Congress the choice "between war, tribute and ransom, as the means of re-establishing our Mediterranean commerce." The United States Senate piously resolved "that the trade of the United States to the Mediterranean cannot be protected but by a naval force," but did nothing about providing one; and in its next breath the Senate gave its advice and consent to the President's redeeming the captives, provided the expense should not exceed forty thousand dollars. Captain O'Brien wrote to Congress in April 1791 that the only protection to American shipping in the Mediterranean was the Portuguese Navy, then at war with Algiers. Thirteen prisoners, survivors of twenty-one captured seven years earlier, sent to Congress a petition describing their "deplorable situation," threatening that if something were not done for them soon they would have to abandon both Christ and country and turn Moslem.

Faced with this horrid prospect, President Washington at last acted. On 1 June 1792 he signed, and Jefferson countersigned, a handwritten commission appointing "John Paul Jones a citizen of the United States, commissioner with full powers to negotiate with the Dey of Algiers concerning the ransom of American citizens in captivity, and to conclude and sign a Convention thereupon." Next day the President signed a second commission appointing Jones American consul for Algeria. At the same time Jefferson drafted a lengthy set of instructions, giving Jones a history of the unpleasant business, authorizing him to pay twenty-seven thousand dollars to redeem the thirteen captives still alive, twenty-five thousand for a treaty, one thousand to clothe the redemptioners and send them home, and the modest sum of two thousand dollars per annum to cover his own salary and expenses.

3. Death and Funeral

If our hero could only have seen this evidence of Washington's and Jefferson's "special trust and confidence in the integrity, prudence and abilities of John Paul Jones," his last days would have been far happier. But Jefferson, instead of sending the document by the first ship carrying mail to France, entrusted them to Thomas Pinckney, who was going to London as American minister, and Pinckney did not sail until mid-July.

That was too late. Paul Jones departed this life on July 18.

Jones's friends who stood by him stated that he had been suffering from jaundice for two months before he died, and that for about ten days he had been affected by a swelling of the legs, which reached his abdomen. The autopsy performed on Jones's body in 1905 revealed that his kidneys showed signs of glomerulo-nephritis; and that there were indurated masses in his lungs, some having the appearance of broncho-pneumonic lesions. My friend and neighbor Dr. George C. Shattuck, after reading the account of the autopsy, thinks that, on top of jaundice and nephritis, Jones contracted bronchial pneumonia, which finished him off.

He was almost alone, with no mistress or other tender lady to nurse him, and an indifferent physician. His forty-fifth birthday on 6 July had received no notice from anybody. The only friends who stood by were Jean-Baptiste Beaupoil, a former aide-de-camp to Lafayette, and Samuel Blackden, a retired colonel of dragoons from North Carolina. It was fitting that someone from that state, whose delegate Joseph Hewes had obtained Jones his first appointment in the Navy, should be the last to see him alive.

Colonel Blackden and Gouverneur Morris are our authorities on the manner of his death. On the afternoon of 18 July 1792 the American minister received "a message from Paul Jones that he is dying." He hastened to the rue de Tournon with two notaries public. They found Jones in his salon *au premier* "sitting in an easy chair, sick in body but of sound mind, memory, judgment and understanding." He dictated his will to Morris—a simple one, leaving all his property to his sisters Mrs. Janet Taylor and Mary Ann Lowden of Dumfries, and making Robert Morris his executor. And he gave a list of his property to Gouverneur Morris—stock in the Bank of North America to the amount of six thousand dollars, together with accumulated dividends; a loan office certificate for two thousand dollars with ten or twelve years' accumulated interest, in the hands of John Ross of Philadelphia; lands in Vermont; five shares in the Ohio Company; three hundred shares in the Indiana Company; the balance of Dr. Bancroft's debt; claims for the Danish pension; and arrearages of pay from Russia and from the United States.

Morris did not tarry long—he had an important dinner engagement with Lord Gower and Lady Sutherland. But he had Jones on his mind. After dinner, about 8:00 P.M., he collected his mistress Madame Flahaut and an eminent physician, Dr. Vicq d'Azyr, of the Académie Française (who happened to live nearby) and returned to Number 52 rue de Tournon.

John Paul Jones had already died. Colonel Blackden left him sitting in his chair shortly after the will was witnessed, with nobody about but a servant. A few minutes later the Rear Admiral walked into his chamber next the salon and laid himself face down on the bed, with his feet on the floor. There the visitors found his body.

At last this gallant seaman had found in death the calm and ease that he so long had coveted in life.

Gouverneur Morris gave orders to M. d'Arbergue, Jones's landlord, that he should be buried as privately and cheaply as possible, fearing lest the expense fall on himself. Fortunately the matter was taken out of his hands by Colonel Blackden and Pierre-François Simonneau, commissaire of the Paris section in which Jones died. Simonneau reported to the Assemblée Législative, then in session, his indignation that the American minister should wish the body of so distinguished a citizen to be shuffled away in a pauper's burial, and to have it done properly paid the funeral expenses himself. He had the corpse placed in alcohol in a sealed lead coffin, hoping to preserve it against the day when America would wish to translate the remains of her great Captain to her shores.

Owing, perhaps, to a wish to preserve all Jones's effects until his heirs should arrive to claim them, the Admiral was not buried in uniform, nor were any of his decorations placed on the simple winding sheet in which his body was clothed. All his American and Russian uniforms, the gold medal presented by Congress, and other effects were sold at auction on 20 October because, said Gouverneur Morris, of "demands on his estate"—probably bills for rent and provisions. Morris did have the kindness to bid in his cross of the Mérite Militaire and his Cincinnati Eagle, but they too have since disappeared. The gold-hilted sword was reserved by Morris for the family. Apart from that, and his papers, the only objects owned by Paul Jones at the time of his death that have survived are the coat of arms painted in America in 1777, a small pistol, two miniature portraits, his commission as Captain United States Navy and his certificate of membership in the Society of the Cincinnati.

The funeral took place on 20 July 1792, two days after his death. As far as the record goes, Jones had never shown any interest in organized religion or attended church; but since he had been brought up in the Church of Scotland he was considered a Protestant, and the Assemblée Législative appointed the Reverend Paul-Henri Marron, a French clergyman of that faith, to deliver the funeral oration. According to French law, there was only one place where he could be interred, a Protestant cemetery outside the walls of Paris.

The cortège assembled in the rue de Tournon in the late afternoon and moved slowly across the city. At the head of it marched a detachment of grenadiers of the gendarmerie in uniform with loaded muskets, and drums that beat a mournful cadence. Then came the hearse, and, following it, carriages for the committee of the Assemblée Législative. They looked very important in their official black costume with white jabot and ruffled cuffs, silver buckles and tricorne hat with tricolor cockade, and around their necks a broad tricolor ribbon from which hung a gilt sunburst representing the two "Tables de la Loi" (which a few days later were overthrown), one inscribed "Droits de l'Homme" and the other "Constitution." The Paris Protestants were represented by four members of the congregation and their pastor. After the official delegation rode brethren of the Lodge of the Nine Sisters, Colonel Blackden, and a few other friends of Jones who had not left Paris. Gouverneur Morris did not have the decency to attend, on the ground that the funeral conflicted with a dinner party he was giving that evening. He was represented by Major J. C. Mountflorence, an attaché at the American legation, and Thomas Waters Griffith, a traveling American who had met Jones at Morris's and who signed the burial certificate.

Behind the vehicles trudged a score or so of humble folk—Jones's valet and femme de chambre, little business people of the quarter with whom he had dealt or to whom he had spoken pleasantly, lads whom he had tipped, young girls whom he had complimented and kissed, and a few old sailors who wished to pay their last respects to their former commander. It was a hot July evening and the people of Paris were nervous and agitated over the war, which was going very badly for France. A Prussian army had crossed the eastern frontier and, only a week before Jones's death, the Assemblée Législative had proclaimed the country to be in grave danger and ordered a general levy of man power. But Parisians loved a good funeral and they flocked to windows and sidewalks to see the last of "le célèbre capitaine Paul-Jones."

With the aid of old maps of Paris, one can follow the route of the funeral procession today. Most of *vieux Paris* of the old régime is still there, crossed by new boulevards and avenues. The route is about four miles long, and must have taken the people at least an hour and a half to walk. Following the rue de Tournon, the cortège crossed rue St.-Sulpice, catching a glimpse of the famous church, and then by a series of short zigs and zags, reached rue des Fossés St.-Germain, now rue de l'Ancienne Comédie. This leads to the Carrefour de Buci, where five old and narrow streets still meet. One of these, rue Dauphine, leads straight between tall, gray plaster-façaded houses with forged iron balconies to the Quai des Grands Augustins, passing the old monastery of that name. The Seine they crossed by the Pont-Neuf, overlooked by the equestrian statue of Henri VI, which everyone, according to custom, saluted. A great banner, with the legend LA PATRIE EN DANGER, which had been raised on the bridge, must have caused the mourners to wish that France had more men like Paul Jones to defend her.

From the Seine the route is uphill all the way to the cemetery. By a series of short streets—rue des Prouvaires, rue du Roule, and a part of rue St.-Honoré—they passed through the site of Les Halles, obtaining a good view of the great church of St.-Eustache (where a German shell exploded on Good Friday 1918), and then through a maze of tiny streets, such as Rue de la Ferronerie (where Henri IV was assassinated), across rue Quinquampoix to rue St.-Martin, the ancient Roman road that led through Paris to the Channel, the route of the Roman legions. It is still much the same as in 1792. Passing the church of St.-Nicolas-des-Champs and the great Couvent de St.-Martin (now l'Institut des Arts et Métiers), they crossed the Grand Boulevard, then the city boundary, and passed under the Porte St.-Martin, a monumental entrance to Paris built by Louis XIV. Here there would have been a halt for inspection by the customs guards, and perhaps a chance for drivers and mourners to quench their thirst.

Beyond the gate, the rue St.-Martin became a country road, bordered by a few detached houses with gardens and vineyards. Turning right into the rue de Récollets, named after the great buildings there of the Order which sent the first missionaries to Canada, they reached the road later called rue Granges aux Belles alongside the great Hôpital St.-Louis, which is still there, though reconstructed. On the southwest corner made by this road with the one now called rue des Écluses St.-Martin is the little cemetery that had been set aside for the burial of foreign Protestants. Everyone alighted from the carriages and took positions around the open grave. There was no religious service, but M. Marron preached a *discours* in which he begged those present to imitate this "illustrious foreigner" in contempt for danger, devotion to his country, and "his noble heroism, which after having astonished the present age, will continue to be the object of the veneration of future generations."

The coffin was let down into the grave, earth thrown in, and the grenadiers at the command of their officer fired a volley. It was now 8:00 P.M. The important people present signed the burial certificate, and all the mourners straggled back to Paris in the gathering darkness.

A little over three weeks later, on 10 August 1792, a Paris mob assaulted the royal palace of the Tuileries, and the bodies of the Swiss guards murdered while trying to protect the King and Queen were tumbled into a common grave adjoining that of Paul Jones. Shortly after, the cemetery was closed.

Gouverneur Morris thought it very amusing that Paul Jones, who detested the French Revolution and everything connected with it, should be given an official funeral; but Catherine II thought it highly appropriate. To Baron Grimm she wrote a nasty little epitaph for the Rear Admiral who had served her so well and faithfully:

> *Ce Paul Jones était une bien mauvaise tête, et très digne d'être fêté par un ramas de têtes détestables.* [This Paul Jones was a wrongheaded fellow; very worthy to be celebrated by a rabble of detestable creatures.]

Be that as it may, death for Jones was not the adamantine finality that it is for lesser men.

4. America at Last

Long years elapsed before the United States fulfilled the expectations of M. Simonneau that she would reclaim the body of her illustrious naval officer. John H. Sherburne, the earliest biographer of
Jones, tried to do something but got on a wrong scent and gave it
up. After other false starts, General Horace Porter, American Ambassador to France, began a search for the body in 1899. The General spent a great deal of money and time on "researchers," quite
unnecessarily, because the only Protestant cemetery of Paris is clearly marked on maps of 1775 and 1789. A hundred years later the city
had sprawled out over it, and the ancient graveyard was covered by
sheds and buildings of a low order.

One of these "researchers" proved leaky, fabulous sums were demanded for the privilege to excavate the site, and the Ambassador
suspended his project until the excitement had died down. Finally he
obtained the necessary permissions and started excavation early in
the year 1905. Shafts were sunk and gangs of workmen employed
day and night to dig galleries; bones of the unfortunate Swiss were
encountered, piled like cordwood; two lead coffins were opened and
found to contain the remains of civilians. But a third lead coffin,
opened on 7 April, contained a remarkably well-preserved corpse
whose face had an unmistakable resemblance to the portrait of Paul
Jones on the Dupré medal. Within a few hours the body was examined at the Paris École de Médicine by two eminent anthropologists. They made a series of measurements, and recorded character-
istics, such as a peculiar ear lobe, which, compared with the Houdon
bust, proved that this was the corpse of John Paul Jones. It was so
well preserved that physicians were able to perform an autopsy
which laid bare the multiple causes of the Admiral's death.

President Theodore Roosevelt followed these proceedings with
keen interest, recognizing the propaganda value for the United
States Navy, which he was trying to make the strongest in the world
as Paul Jones had predicted it would become. Accordingly, the

President sent four cruisers, U.S.S. *Brooklyn* (flying the flag of Rear Admiral Charles D. Sigsbee), *Tacoma, Chattanooga* and *Galveston*—just such a squadron as Paul Jones had yearned to command—to bring his body home. On 6 July 1905, the 158th anniversary of Jones's birth, an elaborate service was held over the body, replaced in the lead coffin and newly encased in mahogany, in the American Church on l'Avenue de l'Alma. This was followed by a parade in which five hundred American bluejackets, French cavalry and infantry and high officials of the Republic participated. The body was carried by a special train to Cherbourg, where, after another ceremony, a French torpedo boat transferred Jones's coffin to U.S.S. *Brooklyn*. That cruiser—the famous old three-piper of the Spanish War—had the honor to convey across the ocean, which Paul Jones had traversed so many times under sail, the Commodore's mortal remains.

After a leisurely voyage of thirteen days, Rear Admiral Sigsbee's four cruisers were joined off Nantucket Shoals by battleship *Maine* flying the flag of Rear Admiral Robley D. Evans, Commander in Chief North Atlantic Fleet; and, in succession, by battleships *Missouri, Kentucky, Kearsarge* (Rear Admiral Charles H. Davis), *Alabama, Illinois* and *Massachusetts*. Forming one column, these eleven ships passed the Capes into Chesapeake Bay on 22 July. There Admiral Evans's division, the first four battleships, peeled off, each firing a 15-gun salute as she passed *Brooklyn;* while Admiral Sigsbee, with Admiral Davis's second division of battleships, steamed on, to the roadstead off Annapolis. There the body was taken ashore by torpedo boat *Standish* and with due ceremony placed in a temporary brick vault, awaiting the pleasure of Congress as to its final disposition. Commemorative exercises were held on 24 April 1906, with addresses by President Theodore Roosevelt and many others.

What a contrast to the pitiful funeral cortège of 1792!

Fredericksburg in Virginia, Washington, D. C., and other places claimed the right to be the final resting place of Paul Jones; but Congress, guided emphatically by President Roosevelt, decided that the most appropriate spot would be the crypt of the chapel of the Naval Academy, whose establishment Jones had urged and predicted.

In the meantime, irreverent midshipmen were singing a parody on a popular song called "Everybody Works but Father":

> Everybody works but John Paul Jones!
> He lies around all day,
> Body pickled in alcohol
> On a permanent jag, they say.
> Middies stand around him
> Doing honor to his bones;
> Everybody works in "Crabtown"
> But JOHN PAUL JONES!

Congress, with the dilatoriness that its predecessors had observed in most matters relating to the Commodore, finally appropriated money for a permanent resting place, and a marble sarcophagus with surroundings, designed by Sylvain Salières and more or less modeled on the tomb of Napoleon in the Invalides, was erected in the chapel crypt. Here, on 26 January 1913, Paul Jones's body finally came to rest.

It had taken a long time, but at last it was done right.

* * *

There are many ways in which Paul Jones could have been a better man—but he would not then have been Paul Jones. The sea warrior of well-deserved renown, the promoter and prophet of a great United States Navy, was not altogether an amiable character, as the reader has had ample opportunity to learn.

He was a lonely man. All shipmasters who observe the rigid tradition of the sea and live apart from their officers must be lonely on board ship; but Jones was lonely ashore. He was admired, flattered and entertained, especially by women. He could make himself very pleasant in society, as he did in Philadelphia, Portsmouth and Paris;

he was, for aught we know, a good Masonic brother; but that sort of thing was no substitute for the intimate friendship that he craved. Gouverneur Morris, whom he met at Philadelphia during the war, seemed congenial, and Jones wrote him warm letters as "My dear Friend," signing himself, "Yours affectionately"; but when both were living in Paris, Morris did not conceal the fact that he thought Jones a bore. Captains Bell and Hector McNeill were the only two naval officers, John Brown the only naval administrator and Dr. Read the only civilian upon whom Jones could count as thorough-going friends; although there were others, such as John Barry, Joshua Barney and Richard Dale, with whom he always remained on cordial terms, and at least three statesmen, Benjamin Franklin, Robert Morris and Thomas Jefferson, who so highly appreciated Jones's qualities that they were willing to overlook his faults. But these great men were patrons rather than friends. There was nobody, when the war was over, to say to him, "Come and keep bachelors' hall with me until you find something to do"; or "Please stay with my wife and myself as long as you wish."

The reason for Jones's loneliness is clear to anyone who has followed his career. It was his colossal egotism. Paul Jones was never deeply interested in anybody except Paul Jones, or in anything except a navy as a projection of his talents and expectations. His voluminous letters and memorials contain hardly a line on anything not relating to one or the other. One looks in vain for comments on people, places and events. He traversed Russia twice from St. Petersburg to the Black Sea, and during his winter of inactivity at the capital he had plenty of time to write his impressions of that country in a most interesting period of its history. But we have no line from him even on the splendors of the Hermitage and Tsarskoe-Selo. He lived in Paris during two of the most stirring years of the French Revolution, which failed to arouse even his curiosity. His egotism also made Jones bitter over not receiving the credit and the awards to which he believed himself entitled; notably, over his low place on the seniority list of 1776, his receiving no thanks for the capture of H.M.S. *Drake,* and the third-rate decoration for his work in the Liman. Commensurately, he took vast pride in the sword and decoration from Louis XVI, and the vote of thanks and gold medal from Congress for his greatest battle. But he never ceased to resent the failure of Congress to give him flag rank.

Of Jones's patriotism there can be no doubt, despite his claim to be a "citizen of the world" who drew his sword for an abstract principle; he always lived up to his motto, PRO REPUBLICA, which was not incompatible with his love of distinction, or his dislike of democracy. Had he been a mere adventurer, he could easily have quit the service after any one of his many disappointments, such as Commodore Hopkins's denial of the *Alfred* task force, Franklin's failure to get him *L'Indien,* the long delay after he left *Ranger,* the stealing from him of the command of *Alliance* and *America's* being given away. It was only when Congress made it clear that it had no further use for him in any capacity that he sought service under the French flag and accepted it under the Russian.

Since, in the tradition of the United States Navy, Paul Jones has a place similar to that of Nelson in the Royal Navy of Great Britain, it is natural to compare them. Short and slight in stature, both showed the brisk assertiveness that small men often display, and the vanity of the insecure, who fear lest others ignore or forget their worth. Each needed a loving and sympathetic woman friend. Both were avid of glory and of such marks of distinction as rank, orders and medals. Both were courageous in the face of danger to the point of foolhardiness; it was mere fate that Nelson fell in action at Trafalgar, while Jones came through all his campaigns without a scratch. Both were humane and considerate in their dealings with inferiors. Jones's generosity to the impressed Irish fishermen and to pilot Jackson will be remembered; and one of his distinctly amiable traits was his constant concern for the miseries of prisoners and captives, American sailors in English jails, Turkish galley slaves in the Liman, merchant mariners in the dungeons of Algiers. Yet Jones did not, like Nelson, arouse the enthusiastic loyalty of his men, despite the fact that nobody could have been more solicitous than he for their health and welfare. Officers and seamen were offended by his unpredictable outbursts of temper and harassed by his perfectionism in rigging, upkeep and maneuver. Nothing on board ship was ever right enough for Captain Jones, and too few officers and men received the encouraging word, the pat on the back, that build shipboard morale and make a commanding officer beloved.

It was a misfortune for Paul Jones that, unlike Nelson, he never had a proper scope for his talents. His zeal to improve himself as a naval officer, to prepare for a fleet command, makes him stand out from brother officers in the Revolutionary Navy, some of whom may have been his peers in single-ship combat. He despised the commerce-destroying strategy forced on the Navy by its weakness: he believed, correctly, that it could have been more effectively employed in commando raids on the British Isles or British possessions. What could he not have done commanding the *Bonhomme Richard* squadron with captains loyal to him and a landing force under Lafayette embarked! It was his fate never to command a fleet except the Russian squadron in the Liman, and that in a situation to drive any sailor mad.

Thus, although Jones had it in him to be a great naval strategist, he found opportunity to prove himself only on the tactical level. There he was magnificent. Recall how he made prompt and sure decisions in emergencies, perfectly adapting his tactics to suddenly confronted facts, as in those first audacious cruises in *Providence* and *Alfred* and in the battles of *Ranger* vs. *Drake*, *Bonhomme Richard* vs. *Serapis*, and *Ariel* vs. *Triumph*. That sort of thing is the sure mark of a master in warfare. Of the quality of his seamanship, one needs no more evidence than those early escapes from faster and more powerful ships, and the saving of *Ariel* from crashing on the Penmarch rocks. His battle with *Serapis*, as an example of how a man through sheer guts, refusing to admit the possibility of defeat, can emerge victorious from the most desperate circumstances, is an inspiration to every sailor.

To every sailor, I say; not only to Americans. In one of his letters of 1780, Jones wrote, "The English Nation may hate me, but *I will force them to esteem me too."* This prophecy was fulfilled over a century and a half later, when the Right Honourable Albert Alexander, First Lord of the Admiralty, in a broadcast beamed to America, declared that Paul Jones's defiant answer to Pearson expressed exactly what England felt in the dark days of the Battle for Britain. And in the six months of tribulation for the United States that followed the Japanese strike on Pearl Harbor, the one sentiment in the back of every American sailor's mind was that of John Paul Jones:

I HAVE NOT YET BEGUN TO FIGHT

Appendices

1. Illegitimate Birth—Alleged Selkirk Blood

The Third Earl of Selkirk was over eighty years old when he died in 1744, three years before John Paul was born. The Fourth Earl (the one whom Jones tried to kidnap), grandnephew to the third, was living abroad when he succeeded to the title, and did not settle at St. Mary's Isle until after John Paul was born. On unreliable evidence, such as the "Letter of a Fellow Lodger" with Jones in Paris, first printed in an anonymous review of Sherburne's biography in *U.S. Literary Magazine* 15 October 1825, Mrs. De Koven concluded that our John was really born several years earlier, a bastard of the octogenarian Earl, and spent the first years of his life in the family of his uncle George Paul, head gardener at St. Mary's Isle. There was a gardener at Kirkcudbright named George Paul who died before October 1753, but he was no brother to John Paul of Arbigland and he never served the Earl of Selkirk. It is significant that in all the correspondence of the Selkirks about Jones's raid on St. Mary's Isle in 1778, no allusion is made to gardener George Paul. Instead, it is stated over and over again that the subject of this biography was a son of the gardener at Arbigland, and that the Selkirks had never before heard of him.

In answer to an inquiry from Baron Van der Capellen, to whom he sent a copy of his letter to the Countess of Selkirk, "Whether you had any obligations to Lord Selkirk?" Jones replied, 29 November 1779: "I never had any obligation to Lord Selkirk, except for his good opinion nor does he know me or mine, except by *character*." (W. H. de Beaufort *Brieven van en aan J. D. Van der Capellen Van de Poll*, Utrecht 1879, pp. 151-152.) Jones, moreover, was devoted to his parents and his brothers and sisters. But the suggestion that he tried to kidnap his cousin was too spicy for early chapbook writers and gossipmongers to neglect, and there is a type of snobbery which insists that every great man who makes a stir in the world (such as Shakespeare, Columbus and Lincoln) must be either a nobleman in disguise or a man of lefthanded aristocratic lineage.

2. Was Paul Jones Ever in the Royal Navy?

The story that the Duke of Queensberry got John Paul into the Royal Navy is part of the myth that the Duke, seeing little John running about St. Mary's Isle as a Selkirk bastard, patted him on the head and promised to help him in the future. The only authority for it is the anonymous review of 1825 mentioned in Appendix 1. The reasons against believing this tale are as follows:

1. Jones never claimed that he had been in the Royal Navy. He only went so far as to assert, in a letter of 4 September 1776 to Robert Morris, that he had enjoyed "intimacy with many officers of note," which he could have done in the many British and colonial seaports which he frequented as a merchant captain. And Morris wrote to Jones 5 February 1772, "I cannot doubt your being acquainted with these things [naval matters], knowing as I do that

you have been a commander in the West India trade." No mention of the Royal Navy.

2. If Jones had ever served in the Royal Navy, he would certainly have stated it in his many letters to members of the Continental Congress, as a qualification for higher rank; for he knew that Captains Nicholson, Biddle and Manley had so served. And Jones's enemies in the Royal Navy—especially those who protested against his Russian appointment—would certainly have held it against him if he had ever deserted the "Senior Service."

3. With our knowledge of Jones's character and ambition, it is improbable that if he had once got into the British Navy he would have left it. That Navy was then no aristocratic preserve; it was a very "rough" service, compared with what it became in the nineteenth century. There are several instances (such as that of Provo William Wallis, grandson of a Nova Scotia fisherman) of midshipmen of humble origin rising to flag rank. Another Galwegian, Admiral John Campbell, son of a parish minister at Kirkbean, entered the Navy as a volunteer from a small coasting vessel before John Paul was born, rose to flag rank and became Governor of Newfoundland. As C. Northcote Parkinson, biographer of Admiral Edward Pellew, Lord Exmouth, well states, "The eighteenth-century English Navy was a profession open to talent. . . . Influence could assist promotion but the lack of it could not hold back a man of real ability." Lord Nelson, as the son of an English country parson, was born to more privilege than John Paul, but Nelson's sisters married just such middle-class tradespeople as did the Paul girls of Arbigland.

3. Piracy, Smuggling and Play-Acting

Stories of Jones's having been a pirate, smuggler or even a highwayman are inventions of the English chapbook writers, but they die hard. Sir Winston Churchill calls Jones a "Privateer" in *The Age of Revolution* (1957) p. 203, and Kipling calls him an "American Pirate" in the heading to his "Rhyme of the Three Captains" (*Writings*, N. Y.

1897, XI 105-111) although the "Rhyme" really refers to something very different (see New York *Nation* XCIV 130-131). To my astonishment, Mrs. De Koven accepted the piracy yarn related in Thomas Chase *Sketches of the Life, Character and Times of Paul Jones* (Richmond, 1859, 59 pp.). This is simply a belated chapbook, fluffed up from the English ones. It purports to be the reminiscences of the writer's grandfather Thomas Chase, who claimed to have served under Jones in *Bonhomme Richard;* but there was nobody of that name on *Richard's* roll. Chase represents Paul Jones as an orphan bastard brought up at St. Mary's Isle, the raid of 1778 being his revenge. He tells the story of a fictitious cruise by Jones in a Spanish pirate ship *Black Buccaneer,* which called at Martha's Vineyard in September 1773 to bury an officer killed in a fight with a British ship.

The story that John Paul spent a year in Jamaica as an actor in a theatrical company, run by John Moody, is found in a ms. note by the celebrated actor John Philip Kemble in a book in his library (De Koven I 12-13). Kemble probably heard it from Moody, but it cannot be true, because Moody, who was known for lapses of memory, never returned to Jamaica after 1759, and from that date to 1796 was regularly acting with the Drury Lane company in London. No theatrical troupe gave performances in Kingston between 1759 and 1775 (Richardson Wright *Revels in Jamaica,* 1937). An intense search in extant records at the Institute of Jamaica yields no trace of John Paul. He may possibly have left *Two Friends* before her 1767-1768 voyage— Sands states that he did—and engaged in the coasting trade or some other business before he embarked in *John;* but there is no possibility that he filled that, or any other gap in his life, as a professional actor.

4. How Did "John Jones" Reach Virginia from Tobago?

The Willie Jones myth I have discussed in detail in *William and Mary Quarterly* 3d ser. XVI No. 2 (April 1959). This "tradition," now almost an article of faith in North Carolina, is that John Paul somehow got from Tobago to Halifax, North Carolina, where, when wandering disconsolate on the shore, he was rescued and rehabilitated by Willie Jones at "The Grove," and in gratitude adopted the name of Jones. As we have already seen, Paul Jones himself is the authority for saying that he went "incog." because he was a fugitive; and the "Grove" mentioned by Read is not the Jones place at Halifax.

Other reasons why the Willie Jones "tradition" cannot be true are: Paul Jones never wrote to Willie Jones or his brother Allen, or they to him; nor does he ever mention them in his letters to men such as Joseph Hewes who knew them. Although he had made, and sent as gifts to American friends, several replicas of the bust of him by Houdon, he sent none to Willie or Allen Jones. When he adopted arms in 1776 or early 1777, he did not take those used by the North Carolina Joneses, but the stag of the Welsh Joneses, quartered with the arms of a Paul family of Gloucestershire (see my article on Paul Jones's arms and seals in *American Neptune* for October 1958).

In view of Jones's consistent gratitude toward people who helped him in his career, this negative evidence is conclusive that his acquaintance with the North Carolina Joneses, if it existed, was very slight; and his obligations to them, nil.

A possible clue to the way that Jones reached Virginia is in the following article in Purdie & Dixon's *Virginia Gazette*, published at Williamsburg on 17 March 1774:

> Some Time last December a Sloop of about 100 Hogsheads Burthen stood in for Machotick Creek,* on Potowmack, and ran aground on a Mud Bank, a little Way up the Creek. Soon after, a decent well looking Man, dressed in Black, with a Gold laced Hat, came on Shore from the Sloop, and calling at a Gentlewoman's House in the Neighbourhood, told her he was bound for Alexandria, to purchase a Load of Wheat, but that his Hands had left him, and he wanted the Loan of a Horse to carry him to Leeds Town, to engage others. Being

* Now called Machadoc Creek; it is near the Dahlgren Naval Ordnance proving ground.

disappointed in getting a Horse, he went to a Planter's House a few Miles distant, where he lodged all Night, went off in the Morning, and has never been heard of since. On his Way he stopped at a petty Ordinary, where he left three ruffled Shirts, a neat Fowling Piece, and a Great Coat; but carried with him a Pair of Saddle Bags, which the Landlord concluded, from their Weight, contained a considerable Sum of Money. After the Vessel had continued near a Fortnight in the Creek, with her Sails standing, some of the Gentlemen in the Neighbourhood went on Board; and upon searching her, found neither Provisions, Water, Chests, Papers, or any other Effects, then one Feather Bed, a Gold laced Hat, a Sailor's Jacket, a Pair of Trousers, some Cooking Utensils, and two Sea Compasses made in Salem.* She is a long sharp built Vessel, with only a Cabin, containing five Births, and Hold. On her Stern is painted, in white Letters, *Falmouth Packet;* and the same Words, in Letters made of Cloth, are on her Pendant.

That, unfortunately, is all. Neither Purdie & Dixon's *Virginia Gazette* nor their rival of that name make further allusion to "so mysterious an Occurance," as the editor called it. *Falmouth Packet* is not again mentioned; the name of the "decent well looking Man" who commanded her is not given. But one must admit that he sounds like John Paul. The ruffled shirts and gold-laced hats, uncommonly fine garb for a skipper of a little sloop; the fowling piece and the sailors jumping ship; his proceeding to Leedstown on the Rappahannock, a short distance overland from Machadoc Creek, which was the shortest road to Fredericksburg, where his brother William lived.

There are no full records of sailings from the Islands to Virginia at this time. So, let us see if we can find a sloop named *Falmouth Packet.* We can. In six extant *Lloyds' Registers of Shipping* between 1775 and 1783 there is only one vessel of that name. She is of 25 tons' burthen and owned by J. McClure of Cork, where she was built. Unfortunately no Lloyds for 1774 has survived; but the 1775 *Register*

---

* There were no fewer than three compass makers in Salem, Mass., at this time, and they had a wide market for their products.

gives two masters for *Falmouth Packet:* "Js Jones" which is crossed out, and "A. Cosgrave." In the 1779 and 1781-1783 *Registers* "J. Jones" is her master. Her main business was packet service between Falmouth in Cornwall, Portsmouth, the Channel Islands and Cork; but there is no reason why she could not have been sent to the West Indies in 1773; and her burthen, 25 tons, is about right for a sloop of the capacity described in the *Virginia Gazette.*

Here is how I put the puzzle together—let the reader make a better picture if he can! John Paul obtained command of this sloop in Barbados or some nearby West Indian island such as Grenada or St. Vincent, after he fled from Tobago, because her master James Jones had fallen ill of a fever. John now assumed the name Jones, if he had not already done so, because it enabled him to sign entrance and clearance papers as "J. Jones," simulating the name of *Falmouth Packet's* regular master. (Jones had the further merit, from the "incog." point of view, of being a very common name in the merchant marine.) On the passage to Virginia he worked the crew of the sloop so hard, or so exasperated them by outbursts of temper, that they managed to run her aground on Machadoc Creek and jump ship. He decided to go overland to Alexandria, engage another crew, and return in a couple of days. En route to Alexandria he stopped at Fredericksburg to visit his brother, whom he had not seen for nine years, and found him dead or dying. In hope of obtaining some of brother William's property, he decided to remain in Virginia. He obtained, as new master, the A. Cosgrave mentioned in the 1775 Lloyds, who as an Irishman was eager to go home and jumped at the chance to sail *Falmouth Packet* to Cork. Cosgrave with a fresh crew took charge of the sloop and sailed to Ireland in the spring of 1774. In the meantime James Jones, the regular master, had recovered from his fever, sailed in another vessel to Cork, and assumed the command once more, as the 1779 Lloyds records.

Most of this is conjecture, which I shall cheerfully abandon if other evidence on Jones's movements in this mysterious period of his career comes to light.

5. Jones and the American Flag

The controversy as to what ensign Jones raised in *Alfred* was settled by my late friend Commander William D. Miller USNR, an authority on American colors and signals, in his introduction to *The
Correspondence of Esek Hopkins* p. 11. Additional bits of evidence
in favor of its having been the Grand Union flag (the Union Jack
and thirteen red and white stripes) are:

1. Letter of a British Intelligence Officer or spy from Philadelphia, 4 January 1776: "This day about one o'clock sailed the ship
Alfred and the ship *Columbus* with Two Brigs . . . English Colours but more Striped."

2. Captain Howe of H.M.S. *Glasgow* reported that *Alfred* showed
Dutch colors (which was one of Commodore Hopkins's signals),
"the others Strip'd"—*Despatches of Molyneux Shuldham* pp. 120-
186. This points unmistakably to the Grand Union flag. A Rattlesnake Flag (coiled serpent on yellow field with motto, DON'T TREAD
ON ME) was presented by Christopher Gadsden to Commodore
Hopkins, who may have used it; but the Commodore's regular command flag was a broad red pennant. The mezzotint portrait of Esek
Hopkins published in England (reproduced in Allen I 30) is a work
of imagination by someone who never saw Hopkins or his ships;
the Commodore is depicted as a young man of about twenty-five,
and the flags are fantastic.

There is no reason to doubt that Jones flew the Stars and Stripes
in *Ranger;* but were the stripes red and white, or red, white and
blue? Probably the latter. Franklin and John Adams wrote to the
Neapolitan Ambassador 9 October 1778, "It is with pleasure that we
acquaint your excellency that the flag of the United States of America consists of thirteen stripes, *alternately red, white and blue;* a
small square in the upper angle, next the flagstaff, is a blue field,
with thirteen white stars, denoting a new constellation." (Wharton
Revolutionary Diplomatic Correspondence II 759; H. F. Rankin
"The Naval Flag of the American Revolution" *William and Mary
Quarterly* 3rd ser. XI, 1954, 347-353.)

Colored replicas of contemporary Dutch sketches of the flags displayed by Jones's squadron in the Texel are in the Naval Academy Museum at Annapolis. Here the "Noord Americaansche Flag" shows 13 eight-pointed stars, and 13 stripes in this sequence, starting at the top: blue, red, white, red, white, blue, red, white, red, blue, white, blue, red. The two engravings of the Battle off Flamborough Head show *Bonhomme Richard* flying a striped flag with neither union nor canton; so does Robert Dodd's painting of the battle (in the crypt of the Naval Academy chapel), his stripes being red, white and blue. But these were made by English artists ashore and are not a reliable source. George H. Preble *History of the Flag of the U.S.A.* (1894) p. 281 has a sketch of a small Stars and Stripes (12 stars and 13 red and white stripes) which is supposed to have been rescued from the sea, during the engagement, by seaman James B. Stafford, and to have been the flag transferred by Jones to *Serapis*. This yarn is supported by an affidavit, but (1) no Stafford served in the *Richard*, and (2) an examination of the flag, now in the Smithsonian museum, Washington, shows that it is a 15-star, 15-striped flag of the War of 1812 period, from which the topmost 3 stars and 2 stripes have been sheared!

Note also that the two American flags decorating Jones's achievement of arms, painted before he left America, have red, white and blue stripes. It seems clear that this was the "flag of freedom" that he preferred, and that his preference led to its unofficial recognition as the proper American naval ensign, at least in European waters.

For other variants in books or colored sheets showing flags of the world from 1781 on, see John Carter Brown Library *Annual Report* (Providence 1951) pp. 38-47.

6. Buell's Fabrications

Augustus C. Buell is not the "father of lies" about Paul Jones. Nevertheless, his two-volume biography, which first appeared in 1900, tells more of them than all other writers put together; and although it has frequently been exposed,* copies classified as biographies on library shelves continue to mislead the young, as well as writers of articles, books, speeches and moving pictures. Two other biographies, Norman Hapgood *Paul Jones* (1901) and M. MacDermot Crawford *The Sailor Whom England Feared* (1913) are mainly potted Buell; and Valentine Thomson *Knight of the Seas* (1939) is partly that, with several inventions of her own.

The following is an incomplete list of the fictions and forgeries in Buell's two-volume work:

VOL. I, CHAP. i: Anecdotes of John Paul's early life at Arbigland; voyage to India in 1771; early study of French and Spanish; friendship with the élite of colonial society; "quaint old Colonial record" of his inheriting a Virginia plantation in 1773 from brother "William Paul Jones"; Duncan Macbean the overseer; letter to Joseph Hewes, 1774; brawl with British naval officers; conferring with Washington, Jefferson and the Lees on "the situation" in 1775. Here, and in the following chapters, Buell creates a Virginia myth of Jones as a gentleman planter which reappears in the recent "screenplay." Jones never owned any Virginia land, or a slave.

CHAP. ii: Trip to New York in private sloop, 1775, with "his own stalwart young slaves, Cato and Scipio"; letter to Hewes of 27 August 1775; report on ships, meeting Duc de Chartres on a French frigate in Hampton Roads; vote of Naval Committee of Congress 24 June 1775; visit in sloop to Philadelphia; details on *Alfred, Ranger,* and every other ship that Jones commanded; letter on construction and tactics of frigates. The letter of 3 October 1775 to Hewes (I 32-37) is the most famous of Buell's fabrications because, until proved to be false, it was required reading for midshipmen at Annapolis. This is the one describing the qualifications of a naval

---

* C. O. Paullin "When Was Our Navy Founded?" U.S. Naval Inst. *Proceedings* XXXVI (1910) 255-261; A. B. Hart "Imagination in History," *American Historical Review* XV (1910) 231-232; Mrs. Reginald De Koven "A Fictitious Paul Jones Masquerading as the Real" N. Y. *Times,* Sunday 10 June 1906, republished as a pamphlet; Milton W. Hamilton "Augustus C. Buell, Fraudulent Historian" *Penna. Mag. History* LXXX (1956) 478-492.

officer: to speak French and Spanish; to be familiar with international and admiralty law and the usages of diplomacy; to water the "feeble and struggling roots" of the Navy "with his blood"; and "do the best we can with what we have in hand." Admiral Ernest J. King used the last phrase in his General Orders at the beginning of World War II, and the letter is also used in Farrow's "screenplay" of 1959.

CHAP. iii: Debate in Congress on appointments of December 1775; Jones's remarks on "Nick Biddle" and account of the latter's end; account of Jones's flag raising in *Alfred;* letters to Hewes and Morris; British ravaging Jones's mythical Virginia plantation; letter on declining battle with *Milford.*

CHAP. iv: Encounter at Alexandria with Lafayette; Jones insulting John Adams at a reception; Jones threatening to fight a duel with Saltonstall; Washington personally giving Jones command of *Ranger;* Hall's log of *Ranger's* passage to France and chanty sung on board; Jones's remark that the Stars and Stripes and he are "twins."

CHAP. v: Jones's arrival in Paris, relations with Duchesse de Chartres and "John" Austin; Jones's "jet-black hair, swarthy complexion, and Iberian cast of features" (I 103). This personal description, which Buell got from one of the early chapbooks, recurs throughout his volumes and has deceived sundry modern artists who have been given orders to paint portraits of Jones.

CHAP. vi: The account of the descent on Whitehaven and Jones's report; his letter of 22 May 1778 to Hewes on capture of *Drake;* Prof. Laughton's remarks on same; *La Belle Poule;* all documents on Jones's European business, including his letters to Hewes; altercation with Sayre; Franklin's introduction of Jones to the Countess d'Houdetot, and the "frugal dinner."

CHAP. vii: All Jones's letters to Hewes and from the Duc de Chartres; French texts of his letters to Louis XVI and the Duchesse; his interview with her; description of *Bonhomme Richard* from "Pierre Gérard's 'Mémoir de Combat,'" that "exceedingly rare pamphlet" (rare indeed; it doesn't exist), and "profile" of her (redrawn from profile of French 74 *Invincible*, 1747 in John Charnock *Hist. Marine Arch.* III 117); letter to Joseph Hewes on the "Concordat" and "last letter" of 10 October 1779.

CHAP. viii: "English Naval Historian" on cruise of *Bonhomme Richard;* remarks of Cottineau; dialogue between Ricot and Lunt; accounts of the battle by Wright and Bannatyne; log of *Serapis;* Pearson saying "There's work ahead."

CHAP. ix: "Original Sketch by Paul Jones of the Battle," and narrative by Henry Gardner; description from the nonexistent pamphlet by the mythical Gérard; the latter's testimony at a court of inquiry at Lorient which was never held; quotations from Fanning; flag quilting party and Jones's letter to Miss Langdon.

CHAP. x: More fictitious Bannatyne and misquoted Fanning; Landais-Cottineau duel; Lunt's account; letter of Franklin; the Admiral Hood story; Yorke's letters and Jones's reply; Jones's Journals of 1787 and 1791; letter to Bancroft and the rest of the diplomacy; story of middies pursuing Spanish nuns at Corunna.

CHAP. xi: The entire chapter, including "documents" on the love affairs and the description of Jones himself, especially his height of 5 ft. 7 inches, a pure invention.

VOL. II, CHAP. i: Data on Stack and Macarthy; letter to "Adèle"; banquet at Palais Royal, Jones giving Capt. Pearson's sword to the Duchess; his Journal and Louis-Philippe's memoirs; Jones's interview with Louis XVI; rivalry with French officers; Jones on board *Ariel* and British report of fight with *Triumph;* Jones's memorial to Franklin and farewell letter to mistress.

There are six more chapters equally bad. In these, however, I must single out some of the principal "whoppers": Napoleon's praise of Jones, and statement that France should have employed him to oppose Nelson; the account of Jones's death—leaving his sword to Richard Dale and making provision for Madame T——; description of Jones in chap. xi, which is attributed to "Anecdotes of the Court of Louis XVI." This last has been repeatedly quoted because there is an authentic work of that title by P.J.B. Nougaret (6 vols., Paris 1791), but that contains nothing on Jones except chapbook stories and those told by Bachaumont.

Everything here cited is a *complete fabrication* by Buell, not a matter of controversy. He found it easier to write Jones's letters himself than to use the genuine ones in the Library of Congress, which he never visited. How, then, did Buell acquire such a high reputation? He was a clever dog, wrote good salty prose and supported his statements by references to mythical sources and fictitious books, which gave his work an air of scholarly authenticity.

Any librarian who reads this Appendix will do a service to posterity by reclassifying as fiction Buell's book, and the other three mentioned at the head of this Appendix, and so stamping the title pages.

Bibliography

1. General

A comprehensive bibliography of Paul Jones is in Don C. Seitz *Paul Jones, His Exploits in English Seas During 1778-1780* (New York, 1917); and nothing of consequence has appeared since, except the well-documented Lincoln Lorenz *John Paul Jones, Fighter for Freedom and Glory* (846 pp., U.S. Naval Institute, 1943). Don Seitz's extracts from the contemporary English press are not accurate and have important lacunae; my quotations have been collated with the original newspapers in the British Museum by my daughter Catharine. Other newspaper quotations herein are from the collection of clippings in the Naval Academy Museum, or from contemporary newspapers in various libraries.

Jones was a voluminous writer and careful to preserve his correspondence, although it is evident that either he or his heirs did considerable "purification" of his files. The vicissitudes through which Jones's papers passed after his death are described in the foreword of Seitz. Most letters received from October 1775, and drafts of out-letters, were purchased by Peter Force and are now in the Library of Congress Manuscript Division. These I refer to as the Jones Mss. The Library published in 1903 an excellent *Calendar of John Paul Jones Manuscripts in the Library of Congress* by Charles H. Lincoln. Jones's Out-Letter Book for the period 5 March 1778 to 30 July 1779 is in the Naval Academy Museum, Annapolis; the National Archives, Washington, has a negative photostat and typescript copy.

The National Archives also contain several important volumes among the Papers of the Continental Congress: No. 168, "Letters and Papers of the

Chevalier J. P. Jones" in 3 vols.; Nos. 58 and 93, "Correspondence of the Marine Committee"; No. 132, an early (c. 1789) transcript of Jones's official correspondence for 1778-1780; No. 193, Court-Martials; and there are other items in Nos. 37 and 41 (VII and VIII).

Jones's original letters to Franklin, and many other documents on his activities in Europe, are in the Franklin Mss., American Philosophical Society, Philadelphia. These are well indexed in the printed Calendar.

The Filkin Mss. in the British Museum, which have been copied for at least three American libraries, are, in my opinion, worthless.

Since Jones letters and documents have long been "collectors' items," many are in private hands and others have found their way into libraries and museums. The most important collections are in the Naval Academy Museum (Senior); New York Historical Society (Barnes); Library of the Grand Lodge of Masons of Massachusetts in Boston, acquired from Jones's great-grandniece, Mme. Gombault; the J. P. Morgan Library, New York; the Pennsylvania Historical Society (Dreer and Gratz); Harvard College Library (Sparks and Lee); and Clements Library, Ann Arbor, Michigan.

Among foreign archives the "Marine" series in Archives Nationales, Paris, and the Captains' Letters in the British Admiralty Records in the Public Record Office, London, are most important. Many of these have been copied for the Library of Congress.

An important Jones autobiography is in the form of a *Mémoire* to Louis XVI, called "Extrait du Journal des services principaux de Paul-Jones dans la Révolution des Etats-Unis d'Amérique; écrit par lui-même et présenté avec un profond respect, au très illustre Prince Louis XVI," with an appendix of letters and other *pièces justificatives*. This, dated 1 January 1786, is a translation by Benoit André of what Jones himself wrote. There are two almost identical copies, bound in morocco and emblazoned with the royal arms, one in the Archives Nationales (Marine MM 851), the other in the Jones Mss. Library of Congress. André subsequently had it printed as *Mémoires de Paul Jones, . . . écrits par lui-même en anglais et traduits sous ses yeux par le citoyen André* (Paris An VI 1798). The English original has disappeared; but extracts from it, with Jones's annotations, were published in the Sands biography of 1830. A fairly complete re-translation of the *Mémoire* into English is printed in installments in Niles's *Weekly Register* for 1812 (II 230-231, 249-251, 277-278, 296-298, 317-318, 330-331).

Of printed books quoted in the following notes to each chapter, each of the following will be referred to by the author's name:

ALLEN: Gardner Weld Allen *A Naval History of the American Revolution*, 2 vols., Boston, 1913. Best on that subject.

ANDRÉ: The 1798 translation of his *Mémoire* to Louis XVI (See above).

BIXBY: *Letters of John Paul Jones from Mr. W. K. Bixby's Collection*, Boston, Bibliophile Society, 1905. Valuable for correspondence with John Brown.

DE KOVEN: Mrs. Reginald De Koven *The Life and Letters of John Paul Jones*, 2 vols., New York, 1913. Prints many of Jones's letters with fair accuracy, but indiscriminating and unreliable for facts.

LORENZ: See above, first paragraph.

MACKENZIE: Alexander Slidell Mackenzie *The Life of John Paul Jones*, 2 vols., Boston, 1841; New York, 1845 (the edition I used), and later editions. An excellent work by a professional naval officer, a lieutenant at the time. He was the C.O. of U.S.S. *Somers,* and is chiefly remembered for hanging the nephew of the Secretary of War from a yardarm for mutiny.

Memoirs (Edin. 1830): *Memoirs of Rear Admiral Paul Jones, . . . now first compiled from his Original Journals and Correspondence*, 2 vols., Edinburgh, 1830; also 1 vol., London, 1843. This, probably by Sir John Malcolm, is one of the two biographies supervised by Janette Taylor and containing data directly from her; the other is the next item.

SANDS: [Robert C. Sands] *Life and Correspondence of John Paul Jones* including his *Narrative of the Campaign of the Liman*, New York, 1830. Has original material not found elsewhere.

SEITZ: See above, first paragraph.

SHERBURNE: John Henry Sherburne *Life and Character of the Chevalier John Paul Jones*, Washington, 1825. The first serious attempt at a biography of Jones, compiled by printing letters with little order or sense; but Sherburne thus preserved a number that have since been lost.

2. Principal Authorities Used for Each Chapter

Abbreviations

AN—Archives Nationales, Paris
APS—American Philosophical Society, Philadelphia
HCL—Harvard College Library

LC—Library of Congress, Washington
NA—National Archives, Washington
NAM—Naval Academy Museum, Annapolis
PCC—Papers of the Continental Congress
PRO—Public Record Office, London

Chapter *I*   **Barefoot Boy**

Mackenzie, Lorenz, and my own investigations in Scotland.

Chapter *II*   **Apprentice Seaman to Naval Lieutenant**

Lloyd's Register of Shipping for 1764 and following years. Naval Office lists of sailings, PRO; records of Masonic Lodge at Kirkcudbright; R. H. Kinvig *History of the Isle of Man* (1950); "Hotel Keepers of Bridgetown" in *The Bajan* (Barbados), VI, No. 2, Oct. 1958; Jones's letter to Leacock of 1773, NAM; letter on Tobago mutiny in APS Franklin Mss., XIII 176, printed in A. H. Smyth ed. *Writings* of Franklin, VII 248-253; "John Paul Jones as a Citizen of Virginia" *Virginia Magazine of History*, VII (1900) 286-293, William Paul's will in XV (1908) 215. It is not true, as this article states, that records of the county court show that John Paul administered the estate. He is nowhere mentioned in any of the documents on the estate of William Paul, which have been examined by Miss Philibert. For Dr. Read, W. B. Blanton *Medicine in Virginia in the Eighteenth Century* (Richmond, 1931), and researches of Miss Philibert in Register of Marriages in Goochland Co. Papers, Va. State Library; W.P.A. ms. Survey of Hanover Co., Nov. 1937, in same. The records of Hanover Co. were destroyed in the Civil War.

Chapter *III*   **Earliest Service**

Here the Jones Mss., LC, begin to be useful, as well as NA, PCC No. 58. John Adams, *Works,* and Adams Mss., Mass. Hist. Society. Robert Beatson *Naval and Military Memoirs of Great Britain,* VI for disposition of R.N.; earliest U.S.N. Regulations, reprinted by Naval Historical Foundation. Howard I. Chapelle *History of the American Sailing Navy* (1949), Marion Brewington on ordnance in *American Neptune,* III (1943) 11-13. For the New Providence expedition and the fight with H.M.S. *Glasgow,* the principal logs are reprinted in Allen, chap. iv; other materials are in the R.I. Hist. Society's publications, *The Letter Book* and *The Correspond-*

ence of Esek Hopkins (Providence, 1932, 1933), and Edward Field *Esek Hopkins* (Providence, 1898). R. W. Neeser ed. *The Despatches of Moly-neux Shuldham Jan.-July 1776* (Naval History Society, 1913) include the captured log of *Andrew Doria*. E. E. Rogers ed. *Connecticut's Naval Office at New London* (New London Co. Hist. Soc., 1933) includes some local data from Nassau. The Letters of Nicholas Biddle in *Penna. Mag. of History*, LXXIV (1950) 348-405 are most valuable, as are those of Lt. Gov. Brown of New Providence in same, XLIX (1925) pp. 352-357.

Chapter IV First Independent Commands

André, Bixby, Sands and Sherburne. Same references as for III, plus Jones's letter of 19 May 1776 to Hewes in Hayes Papers, Edenton, N.C., with permission of the owners, Mr. and Mrs. John G. Wood. Orders of 6 Aug. in NA, PCC No. 58 161-162. Letter of 31 Oct. 1776 in NAM. Letter of 4 Sept. 1776 to Hopkins in John S. Barnes (ed.) *Log of Serapis*, etc. (Naval Hist. Soc. 1911), p. 129. Letters from Napier and Admiral Howe in Admiralty 1-487 and 1-1221, PRO; logs of *Solebay*, *Milford* and *Flora* also in PRO. S. B. Luce *Naval Songs* (1902) for the ballad. For prize distribution, Jones to Castries 1 Feb. 1784, Bibl. de la Serv. Hist. de la Marine, Paris, and AN Marine F² 82. Comparative pay table in LC Jones Mss. I 6517; uniforms in Sherburne p. 128, and Calendar p. 20. Jones's station bill for *Alliance* in Mss. VI 7543. For *Alfred's* cruise, Jones's "Texel Memorial" 7 Dec. 1779, in his Mss. at LC, VI 7469-7476. Barnes ed. *Letters of Continental Marine Committee;* Boston *Independent Chronicle* 17 Oct. 1776.

Chapter V Promotion and the New Navy

W. C. Ford ed. *Journals of Continental Congress;* Chapelle and Brewington (see Chapter III); William Bell Clark, biographies of John Barry, Nicholas Biddle and Lambert Wickes. Letter of 21 Jan. to Morris in Jones Mss. I 6539; Franklin's rebuke in De Koven, II 131; Hancock's letter on "Little Jones" in Stan V. Henkels *Catalog no. 1183* (1907); Morris's orders of 1777 in Paullin ed. *Out-Letters of Continental Marine Committee* I 65-71; Hector McNeill's letters in Mass. Hist. Soc. *Proceedings*, LV (1923) 46-152.

Chapter VI "Ranger" and Her Maiden Voyage

Jones to Roche 12 July 1777, *N.E. Hist. and Genealogical Register*, XLVIII (1894) 461; Whipple's letter on the privateers, July 1778, in *Historical*

Magazine, VI (1867) 75; dimensions of *Ranger* from Ms. Register of R.N. at Admiralty, London; Captain Gurley's letter in PRO Admiralty 1-3972. *Ranger's* logbook, typescript in NA of now destroyed original, begins 26 Nov. 1777; Ezra Green's *Diary* (reprinted from *N.E. Hist. Gen. Register,* Boston, 1875) covers whole voyage; Jones to Whipple on the voyage 11 Dec. 1777 in *Penna. Mag.,* XI (1887) 338-340. The letter to John Wendell is owned by William G. Wendell of Portsmouth. Petitions against Jones which give names of crew are in APS Franklin Mss., VI 24 and LXI 96-97; and Jones's letters to Franklin in same, V 2 and VI 45. Letters of Jones to Langdon in A. L. Elwyn (ed.) *Letters by Washington . . . to John Langdon* (Philadelphia, 1880); Jones to John Brown on Langdon in Morgan Library, N.Y.; Dr. Read to Jones in Jones Mss. II 6703. His expense account for fitting out *Ranger* is in Library of Grand Lodge of Masons of Mass., Boston. For Portsmouth, N.H., L. S. Mayo *John Langdon* (1937); C. W. Brewster *Rambles About Portsmouth,* 1st ser. 1859, 2nd ed. 1873.

Chapter *VII* **From the Loire to the Solway**
Sections 1-3. *Ranger's* logbook and Green's *Diary* (see Chap. VI). In NA PCC No. 58 and Jones's Letter-Book for 1778. For Jones's plan, De Koven I 256-257 and AN Marine B⁷ 459. On the salute: Allen I 340-341, D'Orvilliers' letter in LC, Jones Mss. II 6694, Jones's report to Silas Deane in Doniol *Hist. de la Participation de la France* III 3. *Penna. Gazette,* 23 May 1778. Wharton *Revolutionary Diplomatic Corresp.* II; Wm. Bell Clark *The First Saratoga.* Franklin Mss., VII 129, VIII 103, IX 11.

Sections 4 and 5. André and Jones's "Texel Memorial" (see Chap. IV); Report to Commissioners of 27 May 1778, Sands pp. 79-81. Newspapers of British Isles (some reprinted inaccurately in Seitz pp. 1-20), esp. Dublin *Saunder's News-Letter* 28 April 1778. AN Marine B⁷ 459; Capt. Gurley's report in PRO Admiralty 1-3972. Meijer's deposition, 14 April 1780, in NA, PCC No. 168, II 71 (trans. with wrong date in De Koven, I 287-288); Lt. Gov. Dawson mss. in Manx Museum Library.

Chapter *VIII* **Raid on St. Mary's Isle**
The original Jones-Selkirk correspondence in possession of the late Sir Charles Dunbar Hope-Dunbar of St. Mary's Isle, descendant of the Fourth Earl of Selkirk. It was first copied, 1895, by Mrs. John Hope, and her copies have frequently been recopied; all these versions are inaccurate. The house

whence Jones took the plate was taken down in 1894, and a larger one built, which was burned in 1940, but most of the documents and plate returned by Jones were saved and are now kept in Park House on the road to Dundrennan, where Lady Hope-Dunbar lives. The original logbooks in the collection perished in the fire. The "Extract from letter from Holland" is in Jones scrapbook, NAM; the estimate of the plate's value is in Schweighauser to Arthur Lee, 30 Dec. 1779, in Lee Mss., HCL, VI 136. This was almost twice its price in silver bullion, assuming that the reported weight, 250 ounces, was correct.

Chapter IX **"Drake" Captured**
André, Seitz and Sherburne; Franklin Mss. APS, LXI 95, LXVII 110, for altercations. Jones's Letter Book for 1778. PRO Admiralty 1-3972; British newspapers as in Chap. VII plus *Saunder's News-Letter* for 1, 5 and 6 May; Islay story from letter of 28 May 1957 of Charles D. MacTaggart Esq., who was born in Lochindael and heard the story from descendants of the fishermen. Neither *Ranger's* log of 1778 nor *Bonhomme Richard's* of 1779 mention calling at Lochindael.

Chapter X **In Irons**
Materials from now on are voluminous, because Jones in 1778 began keeping all letters that he received and drafts of all that he sent; both are in the Jones Mss., LC, and well calendared by Lincoln. Several letters that have since disappeared are printed by Sands and Sherburne. The important diplomatic correspondence about Jones's activities is printed in Francis Wharton *Revolutionary Diplomatic Correspondence*.

On the prisoner question, Allen chap. xviii and Wm. Bell Clark *Ben Franklin's Privateers* (1956); Admiralty's "Orders to the Commissioners for Taking Care of Sick and Hurt Seamen," National Maritime Museum, Greenwich; J. L. Banks *David Sproat and Naval Prisoners* (1909; this was Jones's former host in Philadelphia, a noted Tory). On Fanning, Barnes ed. of his *Narrative* and *Logs of Serapis-Alliance-Ariel*. Jones's letter on Gain in Mss. III 6772. *Ranger's* log for 24 Aug. 1778—2 March 1779, owned by the Maritime Museum of Newport News, is printed in *Granite Monthly* V (1882) and in part in U.S. Naval Inst. *Proceedings*, LXII (1936) 201-211. *Granite Monthly*, LIX 58 (Feb. 1927) has an article on *Ranger's* subsequent history. The complaints against Jones are in APS Franklin Mss., LXI

95-99, XLVII 102-111, 124-129, X 10-24, and Jones's letters to the Plenipotentiaries in same, XI and XII. For Green's remarks, Jared Sparks Journal for 27 June 1845 in Sparks Mss. HCL. McNeill's letter, Mass. Hist.
Soc. *Proceedings* LV 127.

Definition of a naval battle in Ch. de la Roncière *Hist. de la marine
française* (1934) p. 157; Jones's letter of 18 June 1778 in Alderman Library
U. of Va.; his refusal of Sartine's offer in AN Marine B⁷ 459. For relations with John Adams see *Calendar* of Jones Mss. pp. 138, 165-166, 182
and Adams's Autobiography (reel no. 180 microfilmed Adams Mss.); the
letter to Dumas was printed in *The Port Folio,* XI 43 (11 Feb. 1804). Bell's
letter and Jones's answer in Jones Mss. III 6879, 6903.

Chapter XI   **The "Bonhomme Richard" Squadron**

Allen, André, Sands and Sherburne. Jones Mss. IV 7014; and A. H. Smyth
ed. *Writings of Franklin,* VII 253-255 for the chambermaid's prank. Jones's
Letter-Books of 1778 and 1779 in NA. On *Bonhomme Richard,* AN
Marine B¹ 89 B³ 665 (the task organization), B⁴ 158; Nicodème "Notice
historique sur le *Bonhomme Richard*" *Revue Maritime* CLXXIII (1907)
545-554; Franklin Mss. APS X 2, XV 15; Minutes of court-martial in
Jones Mss. LC V 7225-7246. Dossier on Landais in Bibl. de la Serv. Hist.
de la Marine, Paris. John Adams Ms. Diary for 12 and 15 May 1779.

Chapter XII   **A Mad Cruise**

Jones Letter-Book for 1779, NA; John Adams ms. Diary, Mass. Hist. Soc.;
Middlebrook ed. *Log of the Bon Homme Richard* (Mystic, Conn. 1936)
from the now lost original. Her roll is in Sherburne, p. 141. Thévenard's
Reports in AN Marine B⁴, 138 f.158 and Jones Mss. at LC V 7255. Docu-
ments on the alarm in the Firth of Forth and extracts from Scots papers by
F. C. Inglis in Soc. of Antiquaries of Scotland *Proceedings* 4th ser., IV
(1906) 89-125; others in Seitz. Jones's accounts of it are in his Mss. V 7286,
7289, 7289C. Napier's letters in PRO Admiralty 1-2221, Captains' letters
"N." References to British depredations on American coasts in Douglas S.
Freeman *George Washington* V 111-112, and B. J. Lossing *Pictorial Field-
Book of the Revolution* I 96-99, 422-426; the Collier and Tryon mani-
festo to the people of Conn. is in Sparks Mss., HCL LII 314. John Kilby's
ms. narrative in NAM, printed in *Scribner's Mag.,* XXXVIII (1905) 24-41.
Marquis of Rockingham's letter in *Amer. Hist. Rev.,* XV 567-571.

Chapter XIII **Battle off Flamborough Head**

Most of the references under Chapter XII. Jones's action reports are in his Mss. at LC, VI 7209, 7300-7302. The one of 3 Oct. 1779 to Franklin is printed in *Old South Leaflets*, No. 152; original of the one of 13 Oct. to Morris is in Hist. Soc. Penna. Dale's account written for Sherburne is in the latter's biography of Jones, 1825 ed. pp. 126-129; Fanning's is in the Barnes ed. of his *Narrative*. Thomas Berry's deposition is quoted in Graham's letter of 23 Sept. to Philip Stevens, PRO Admiralty 1-1838 G; the letter of the "respectable inhabitant" in same 1-3973. Capt. Pearson's letter on the Battle in same, 1-2305. The depositions that Jones took about Landais' conduct are in Sherburne pp. 162-177; originals in PCC No. 168 II.

There are two logs of the battle; the deck log of *Richard* printed by Middlebrook (see Chap. XII) and Lieut. Henry Lunt's "Remarks," entered in logbook of *Serapis* after her capture, and they generally agree. The latter is printed in Barnes ed. *Logs of Serapis-Alliance-Ariel*. Capt. Cottineau's letter of 4 Oct. 1779 in Arthur Lee Mss., VIII 43 and VI 117, HCL. Franklin's orders to Landais and his observations on the conduct of Landais in the battle are in same, VI 15. The best secondary account of the battle is by Capt. Alfred T. Mahan in *Scribner's*, XXIV (1898) 206-215.

The times given by Dale and Fanning, written from memory many years later, differ widely; those in Capt. Pearson's report are an hour or more later than Jones's. I have used the times in Middlebrook ed. *Log of the Bon Homme Richard* pp. 45-46, and in Jones's first draft of his Action Report, 25 Sept., in Mss. V 7289 B. There were no standard time zones in 1779; each commodore or captain set noon every few days for his squadron or ship by a meridional observation of the sun. Pearson may have been using the time that he had set in Norway, about an hour later than Greenwich. Jones probably set his time by pocket watch in the Firth of Forth and corrected it from one of the Humber pilots. Nobody in the task force had a chronometer.

Chapter XIV **Aftermath of Battle**

Extracts from contemporary newspapers in Seitz, and London *Gazetteer and New General Advertiser* 19 Oct. 1779. Copies of Sir Joseph Yorke correspondence in Sparks Mss. HCL; originals in PRO S.P.Y. 84 Holland. Wharton *Revolutionary Diplomatic Correspondence*, Vols. I-III. John Adams's comment in Autobiography (reel no. 180 of Adams Mss. microfilm).

Jones's letter to Carmichael in Hist. Soc. Penna. Frederich Edler *The Dutch Republic and the American Revolution* (1911); W. H. de Beaufort *Brieven van en aan Joan Derck Van der Capellen Van de Poll* (Utrecht 1879), pp. 158, 163. For Sayres, Julian P. Boyd in Princeton Univ. Libr. *Chronicle,* II (1941) 51. Poem "Virgin Muse" from *Memoirs* (Edin. 1830). Sandwich's impatient letter in Mass. Hist. Soc. *Proceedings,* VIII 77. Information on prisoners and prize money in NA PCC No. 168 II 272-280, and AN Marine B³ 683, 684, 705, B⁴ 198, and 30th Cong. 1st Sess. Ho. Report No. 9 p. 53. Neufville correspondence about Jones in "Diplomatic and other Letters, Holland, 1779-1781," NA PCC Box No. 4; Gillon's letter to Chaumont in Sparks Mss. HCL XI 231.

The Paul Jones Ballad, 1st ed. Pocklington 1779, is in the British Museum. A later version, *Paul Jones's Victory,* printed about 1805 (Am. Antiq. Soc., Worcester, reproduced by Old Sturbridge Village), has 13 stanzas, extends the "four glasses so hot" to eight, and the casualties from 95 to 160. Even here, the "Lieutenant Grub" incident does not appear. Another version which assigns the *Richard* to Baltimore is in *Forget Me Not Songster* (N.Y. c. 1820) p. 24. Other Paul Jones ballads are in J. Woodfall Ebsworth *The Roxburghe Ballads* VIII pt. 1 (Hertford 1895) and James Maidment *A North Countrie Garland* (Edin. 1824) p. 47. For the curious history of Kipling's "Rhyme of the Three Captains" see the N.Y. *Nation,* XCIV 130 (8 Feb. 1912). The Dutch ballad is in *Nederlandsch Volksliederenboek* (Leiden, Sijthoff, 1940); with additional stanzas recorded in F. D. Roosevelt Library, Hyde Park. *Elegiac Epistles* in NAM, which also has best collection of chapbooks. The log of *Alliance* does not support John Kilby's thrilling yarn of her escaping a British blockading fleet of 52 ships of the line under Admiral Hardy by logging 14 knots (!) close-hauled.

Chapter XV **Pinnacle of Fame**
Station bill in Jones Mss., VI 7543. Fanning's *Narrative;* Wharton *Rev. Dipl. Corresp.* V 513; Barnes ed. *Logs of Serapis* etc.; Julian Boyd ed. *Papers of Thomas Jefferson* XII, XIII; *Letters of Mrs. Adams* (Boston 1848) p. 208; anecdotes of Jones in Paris in *Correspondance littéraire de Diderot,* etc. Mai 1780 (1880 ed. XII 394), Bachaumont *Mémoires secrètes* (London 1781) VI 181-182. Jones's correspondence with Mlle. de Hunolstein in Louis Gottschalk *Lady-in-Waiting* (1939). Lowendahl's letters are in Jones Mss., as are those of Delia except that of 1783, known only through the

trans. in *Memoirs* (Edin. 1830) II 278. Miss Edes's chitchat in same, 249-250. Description and history of the sword in *Proceedings* U.S. Nav. Inst. XXXIII (1907) 710-715.

Chapter XVI **"Alliance" and "Ariel"**
Mackenzie and refs. under Chap. XV; E. E. Hale *Franklin in France* (1888) I ch. xvii. St. Helena project in Archives des Affaires Étrangères, Paris, "Docs. Angleterre 1527-1794" ff. 255-259. Record of Landais court-martial in NA PCC No. 193 ff. 451-589, printed in part in De Koven II 467-473; story of Landais bonus in *Annals of Congress*, 11th Cong., 2d sess. 893, 1427; 3d sess. 462. Jones to Robert Morris 27 June 1780 in NAM; Franklin's reproof in De Koven II 130-131. Landais *Memorial to Justify Conduct during the Late War* (Boston 1784). S. Adams to R. H. Lee 17 Dec. 1785, Cushing ed. *Writings of S. Adams* IV 318. Franklin to Francis Lewis 17 March 1781, NA PCC No. 168 II. Other details in Thévenard's letters, AN Marine B³ 363, 682, 683. His *"Détail des Dispositions"* at Port-Louis to stop Landais, and Jones to Deane 1 Nov. 1780, in F. D. Roosevelt Library, Hyde Park. For Arthur Lee's side, letter to James Warren 30 Oct. 1780 in *Warren-Adams' Letters* (Mass. Hist. Soc. *Collections* LXXIII) II 143-144, and to the President of Congress 11 Aug. 1781 in NA PCC XIV 453-464; also Lee Mss. HCL VII and mss. in Alderman Library, U. of Va. Schweighauser claim in *Docs. accompanying Bill . . . to settle the account of. . . Schweighauser Feb. 27 1809* (Washington, 1809).

Chapter XVII **"America" Gained and Lost**
Allen, André, De Koven, Mackenzie, Sherburne, Sands and Bixby (for letters to John Brown). Chapelle *American Sailing Ships*. Ford ed. *Journals of Cont. Congress. Ariel's* celebration in Phila., *Penna. Packet*, 3 March, and *Penna. Gazette*, 7 March, 1781. Queries to Jones, his answers, and Board of Admiralty recommendations in NA PCC No. 37, copy in Sparks Mss. HCL; answers only in Sherburne, pp. 222-234. French data on *America* in AN Marine B⁷ 459, B¹ 101 f. 93, C⁶ 802, and in "Notes de Campagne de Comte Rigaud de Vaudreuil," *Neptunia*, Nos. 49 and 50 (Musée de la Marine, Paris), 1958. Nicholson's disparaging letter, in N. Y. Hist. Soc., is printed in Barnes ed. *Logs of Serapis* etc. pp. 125-127; Warren's ditto in NA, Letter Book of Navy Board of Eastern Dept. Jones's expense accounts in 24th Cong. 2nd session Ho. Doc. No. 19, contemporary copies of parts

are in Mr. Joseph M. Roebling's private collection, and Jones Mss. LC, IX 7960; his receipt for back pay to 26 June 1781 in NAM. Fake letter of 7 Mar. 1781 in Franklin's fake Boston *Chronicle.*

For Portsmouth, N. H.: authorities mentioned under Chapter VI; ms. diary of Francisco dal Verme, in private hands at Milan; Karl G. Tornquist *The Naval Campaigns of Count de Grasse* (Amandus Johnson trans.), Swedish Colonial Soc., 1942; Gershom Bradford "Nelson in Boston Bay" *American Neptune,* XI 239 (Oct. 1951). Jones to Gouverneur Morris of 15 July 1782 in Lloyd W. Smith collection, Morristown, N.J.; of 2 Sept. 1782, in NAM; to Robert Morris 10 Oct. 1783, in Jones Mss., IX 7963-7974; Morris's ms. Diary, LC.

For Pavillon and signals, Lt. de V. Mouchez "Les signaux dans la marine française" *Rev. Maritime* Jan. 1929, pp. 629-58. For membership in the Cincinnati, E. E. Hume *Washington's Correspondence concerning the Society* (1941), pp. 140, 222, 426. Jones originally joined the General Society at Philadelphia and was assigned to the Virginia Society in 1785; his certificate of membership is in NAM.

Chapter XVIII **Autumn of the Old Régime**
André, Sands, Lorenz and Jones Mss. Mary Barney *Joshua Barney a Biographical Memoir* (1832); dossier on Jones's claims in Bibl. de la Service Hist. de la Marine, Paris; correspondence on same in Julian Boyd ed. *Papers of Thomas Jefferson,* VIII, IX and X. Morris's letter of 1 Dec. 1783 is in interleaved Cooper's *Naval History* at N. Y. Hist. Soc. Jared Sparks *Life of John Ledyard* (1864); Sparks Mss. HCL, vol. 132. For Madame T——, Boyd ed. *Jefferson,* XII, XIII; Henri Vrignault *Les Enfants de Louis XV* (1954). Madame Vigée le Brun *Souvenirs* (1882), II 305.

For the Houdon bust: Charles H. Hart and Edward Biddle *Memoirs of the Life and Works of Jean Antoine Houdon* (Philadelphia, 1911), 125-142, and Georges Giacometti *La vie et l'oeuvre de Houdon* (Paris, n.d.), I 125-135; partial list of recipients in Boyd ed. *Jefferson* IX 305-307, XIII 587. But Hart and Biddle, p. 134, state that 16 in all were made. Of these, the Naval Academy Museum has two (that of the Duc d'Orléans and a second in plaster); the Boston Museum of Fine Arts has Jefferson's; the National Academy of Design New York City has two; and the Pennsylvania Academy of Fine Arts has General Irvine's, all signed by Houdon and dated 1780. Judging from accounts printed in Giacometti, p. 133, these replicas cost Jones only 60 to 100 livres each. The original at the Lodge of the Nine Sisters, which was of plaster colored like terra-cotta, and the terra-cotta mold, have disappeared.

Chapter XIX **New York and Denmark**

Journals Cont. Cong., Sands and Jones Mss. C. O. Paullin *Diplomatic Negotiations of American Naval Officers* (1912); Boyd ed. *Jefferson*, IX, X, XII, esp. letter of Carrington in XII 336-337. 24th Cong. 2nd Sess. Ho. Docs., Nos. 19 and 115; 30th Cong. 1st Sess. Ho. Report, No. 9; 37th Cong. 2nd Sess. Senate Exec. Doc., No. 11. For the Renaud medal see André; for the Dupré medal, Carl Zignosser "The Medallic Sketches of Augustin Dupré" *Proceedings* Am. Philosophical Soc. CI (Dec. 1957), 535-550.

Chapter XX **Kontradmiral Pavel Ivanovich Jones**

Jones's original "Narrative of the Campaign of the Liman," in French, has disappeared, but Sands translated the text into English for his 1830 *Life* of Jones, and a complete ms. copy of the *pièces justificatives,* in French, is in the Library of the Grand Lodge of Masons of Massachusetts, Boston. F. A. Golder *John Paul Jones in Russia* (1927) prints Jones's letters in the Russian archives, and has a good introduction. Lincoln Lorenz, in addition to the chapters in his 1943 biography, wrote *The Admiral and the Empress* (1954) using transcripts from the Russian archives in Senior Collection NAM. The only attempt in English by a scholar who knows Russian to write an account of the Liman campaign is by Roger C. Anderson, in *Naval Wars in the Levant 1559-1853* (Liverpool 1952), chap. xii. He remarks justly that, in view of the lack of Turkish sources and the Russian rivalries, it is difficult to get at even the approximate truth. *Istoriia russkoi armii i flota* (Moscow 1912) from which our charts are derived, and Beskrovnyi *Russkaia armiia i flot XVIII veke* (Moscow 1958) have short accounts of the campaign. Nassau-Siegen's letters to his wife are in Marquis d'Aragon *Un paladin au xviii* siècle* (Paris 1893). Comte de Ségur *Mémoires, souvenirs et anecdotes* (Paris 1842), III, tells about Jones's indiscretion, on which there is a sheaf of documents in the Senior Collection, NAM. For the Anna Kourakina story, Valentine Thomson in *N. Y. Times Magazine*, 23 and 30 Sept. 1934. Ivak's story, told to a Russian officer when he was 100 years old, is in *Biblioteka dlia Chteniia* LXV (1844), Section 3 pp. 1-46; my translation is by Mr. P. H. Bonnell.

Chapter XXI **The Empty Wineskin**

No letters for this period in Jones Mss. LC, but several were printed by Sherburne and Sands. For Algiers, *Naval Documents Relating to the United States Wars with the Barbary Powers* (Dudley W. Knox ed.), Vol. I, Washington 1939. For death, burial and translation, De Koven, Gen. Horace Porter "Recovery of the Body of John Paul Jones" in Bixby 59-123 and also in *John Paul Jones, Commemoration at Annapolis Apr. 24, 1906* (59th Cong. 1st Sess. Ho. Doc., No. 804, Washington 1907). The original report by the anthropologists Capitan and Papillault appeared in *Bulletins et Mémoires de la Société d'Anthropologie de Paris* series 5, vol. VI (1905), and is translated in Philip M. Dale *Medical Biographies* (1952), pp. 127-135.

General Porter, who also wrote an article on the subject in *Century Magazine* Oct. 1905 pp. 927-955, let himself in for criticism because he first identified the corpse from the fictitious biography by Buell and the "Anecdotes of the Court of Louis XVI" which Buell made up; see Seitz p. 316 for bibliography of the controversy. I am satisfied by the striking correspondence of measurements between the head of the corpse and those of the Houdon bust that no mistake was made.

Index

A note about
the production
of this book

The typeface for the text of this special edition of *John Paul Jones* is Garamond, named for the 16th Century French designer Claude Garamond. The text was photocomposed at Time Inc. under the direction of Albert J. Dunn and Arthur J. Dunn.

The book was printed and bound by J. W. Clement Co. of Buffalo, New York. The cover was printed by Livermore and Knight Co., a division of Printing Corporation of America, in Providence, Rhode Island.

x

The paper, TIME Reading Text, is from The Mead Corporation, Dayton, Ohio. The cover stock is from The Plastic Coating Corporation, Holyoke, Massachusetts.